10

COTOJI

D0053082

AnneHappy♪
unhappy
go lucky!

CONTENTS
ANNE HAPPY
VOLUME TEN
COTOJI

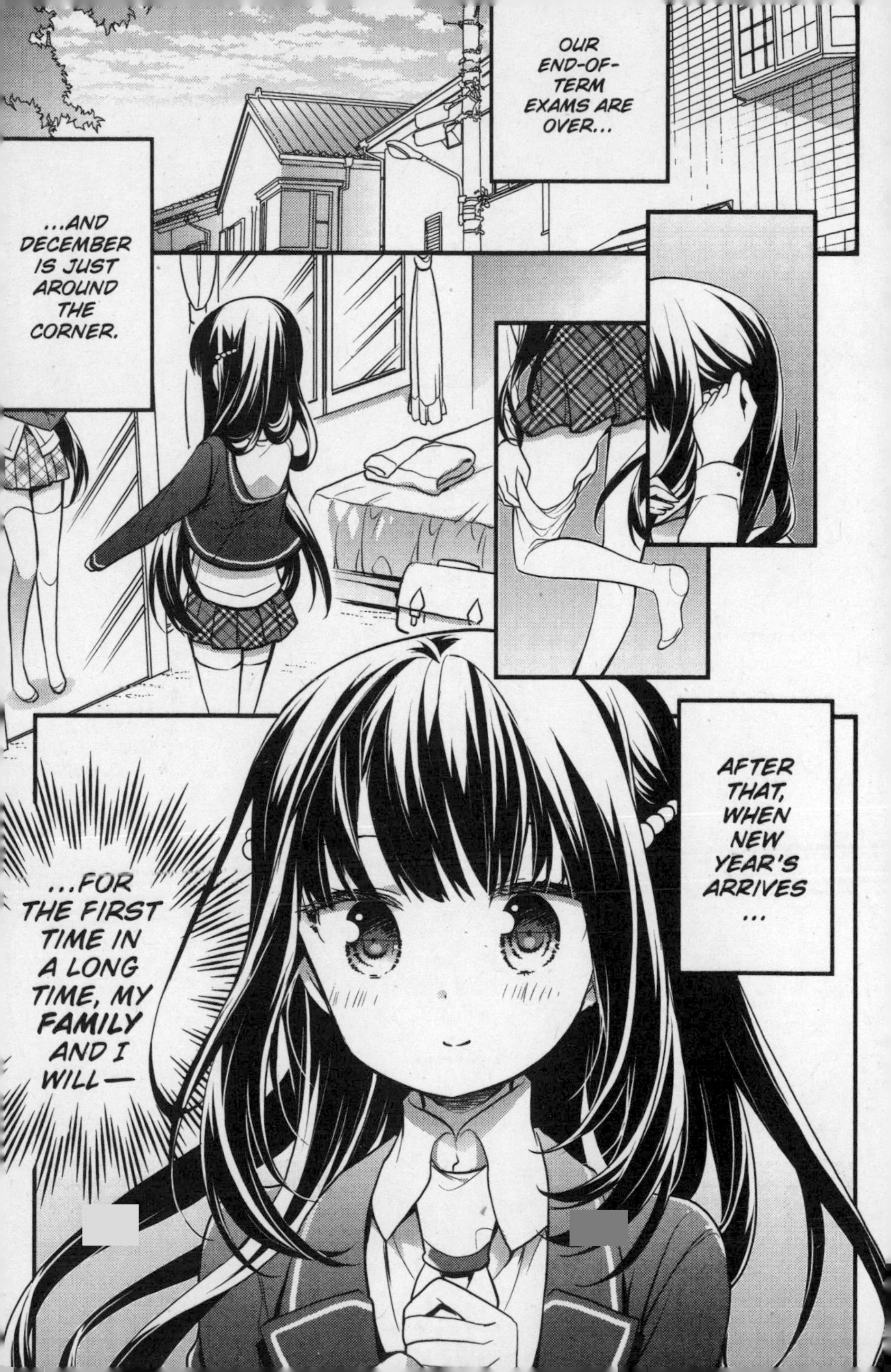
OUR END-OF-TERM EXAMS ARE OVER...
...AND DECEMBER IS JUST AROUND THE CORNER.
AFTER THAT, WHEN NEW YEAR'S ARRIVES...
...FOR THE FIRST TIME IN A LONG TIME, MY FAMILY AND I WILL—

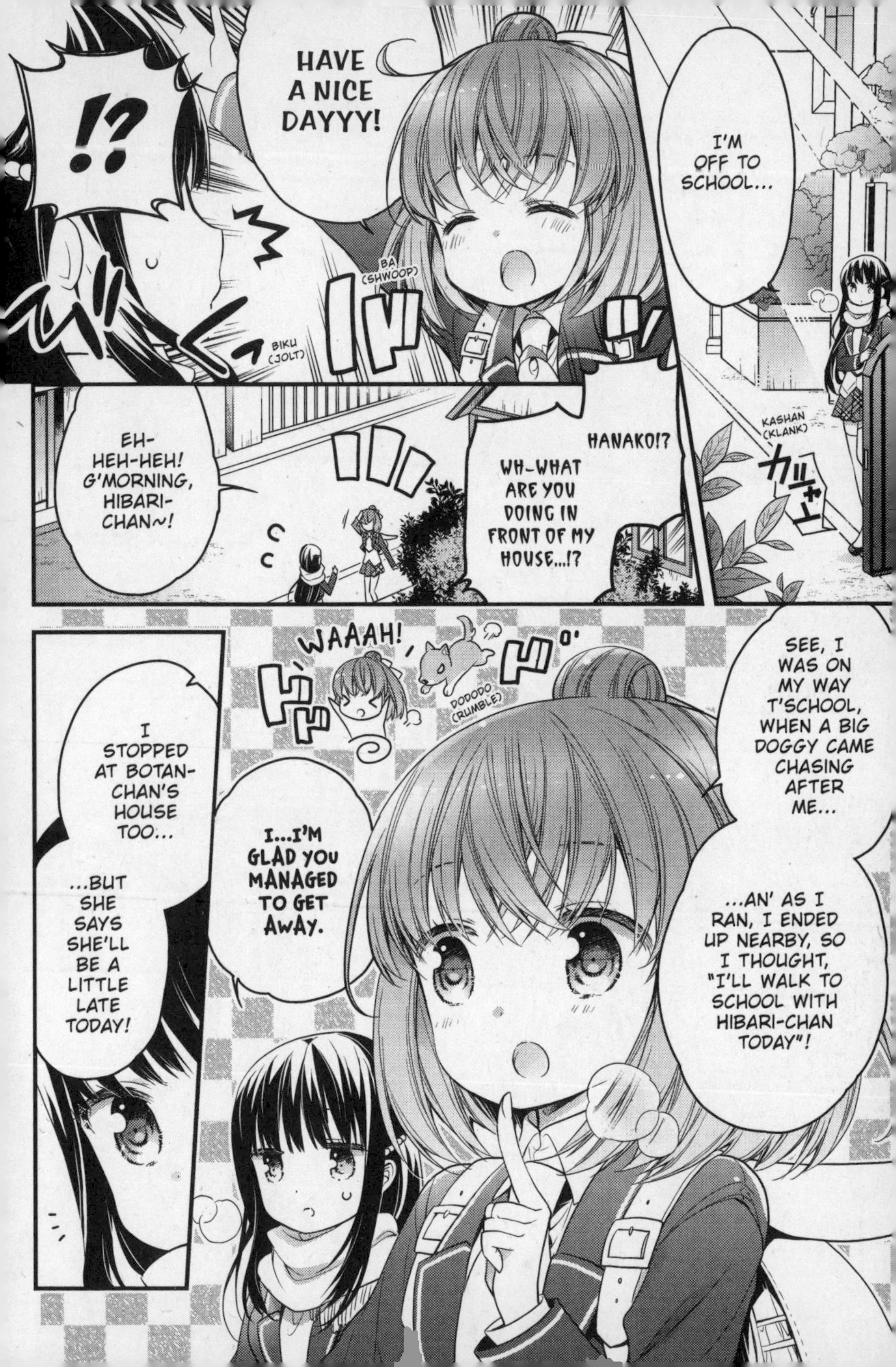

I'M OFF TO SCHOOL...
KASHAN (KLANK)
HAVE A NICE DAYYY!
!?
BA (SHWOOP)
BIKU (JOLT)
HANAKO!?
WH-WHAT ARE YOU DOING IN FRONT OF MY HOUSE...!?
EH-HEH-HEH! G'MORNING, HIBARI-CHAN~!
SEE, I WAS ON MY WAY T'SCHOOL, WHEN A BIG DOGGY CAME CHASING AFTER ME...
...AN' AS I RAN, I ENDED UP NEARBY, SO I THOUGHT, "I'LL WALK TO SCHOOL WITH HIBARI-CHAN TODAY"!
WAAAH!
DODODO (RUMBLE)
I...I'M GLAD YOU MANAGED TO GET AWAY.
I STOPPED AT BOTAN-CHAN'S HOUSE TOO...
...BUT SHE SAYS SHE'LL BE A LITTLE LATE TODAY!

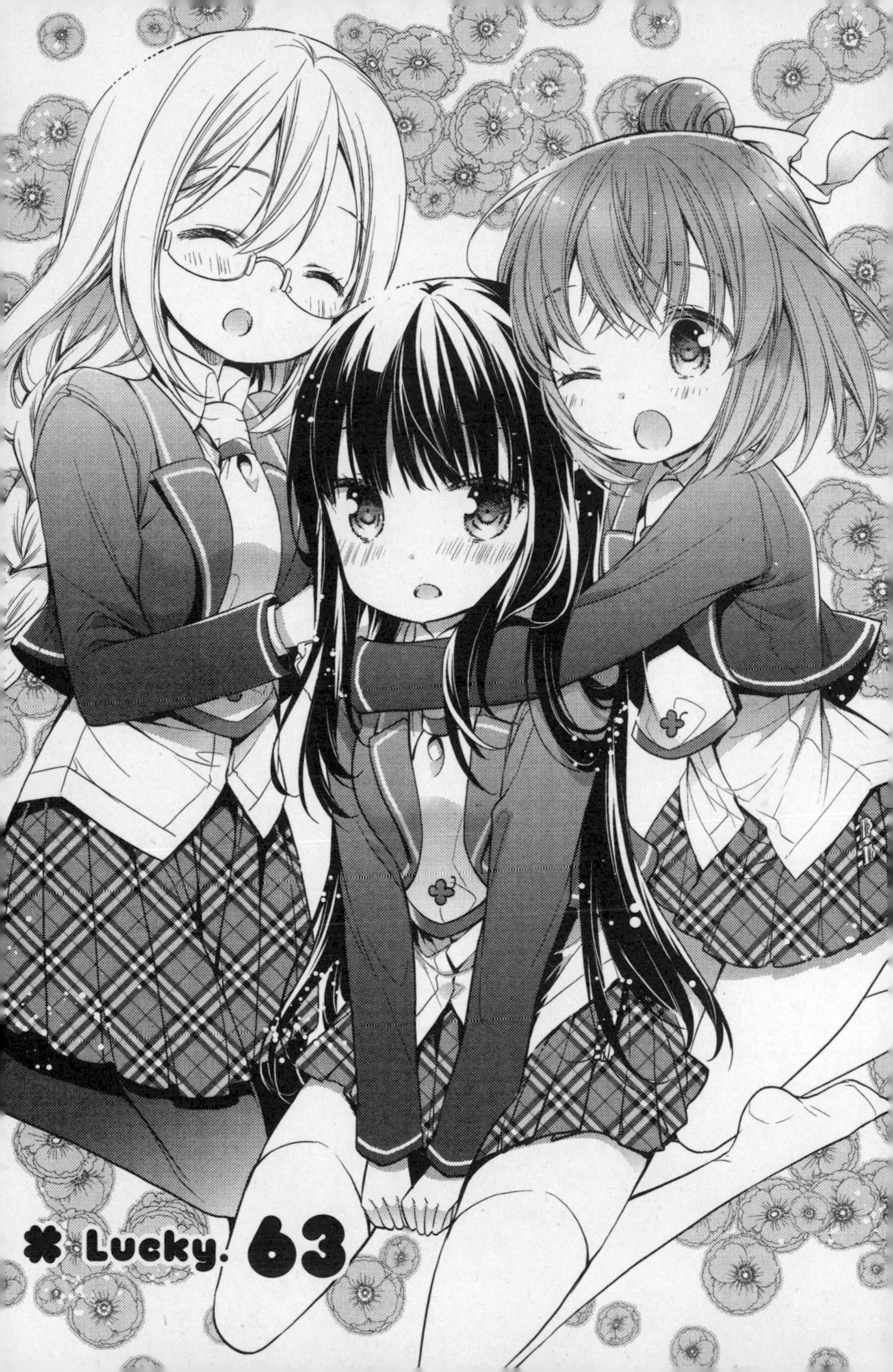
* Lucky. 63

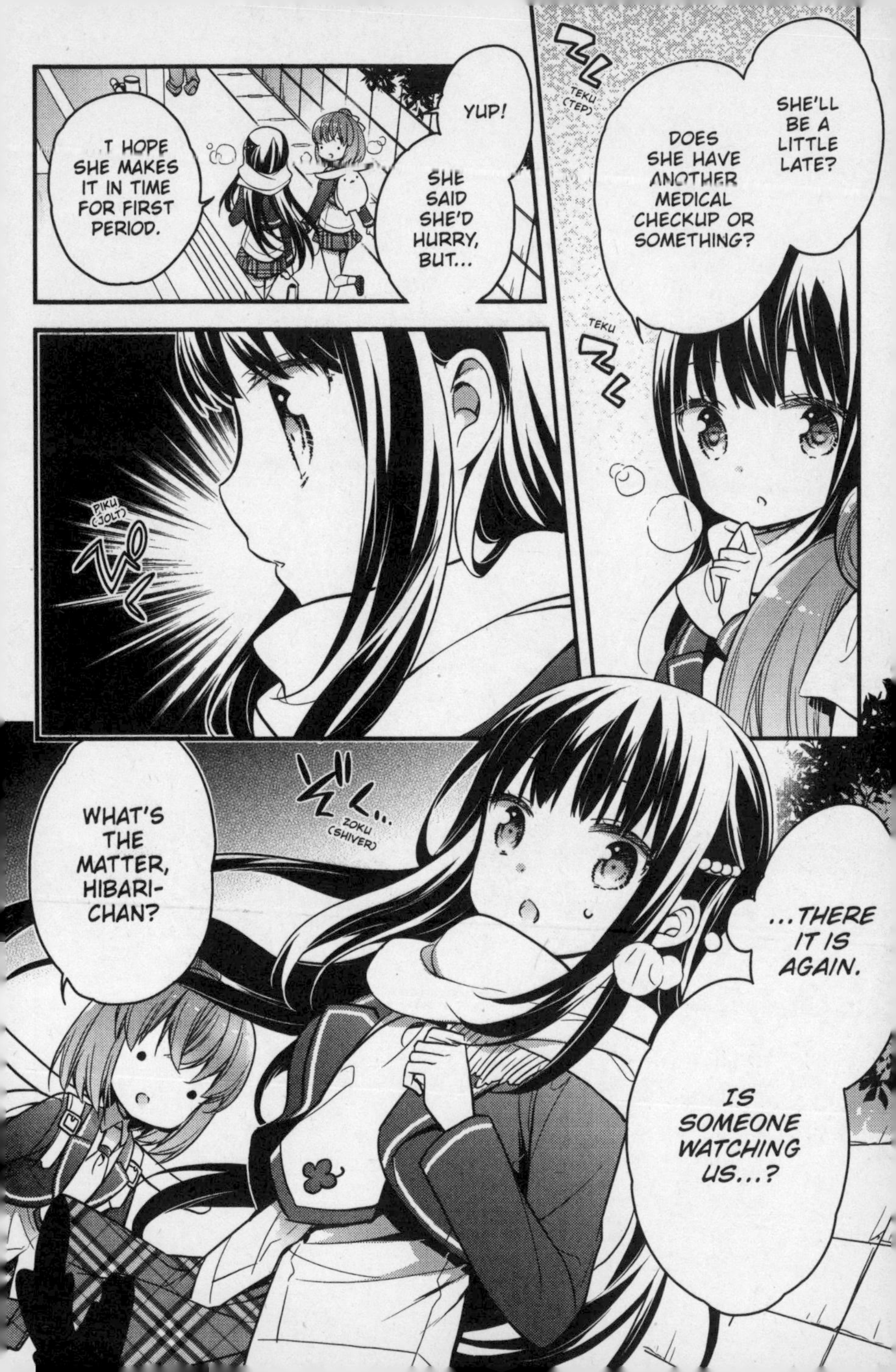
TEKU (TEP)
SHE'LL BE A LITTLE LATE?
DOES SHE HAVE ANOTHER MEDICAL CHECKUP OR SOMETHING?
TEKU
YUP!
SHE SAID SHE'D HURRY, BUT...
I HOPE SHE MAKES IT IN TIME FOR FIRST PERIOD.
PIKU (JOLT)
...THERE IT IS AGAIN.
IS SOMEONE WATCHING US...?
ZOKU (SHIVER)
WHAT'S THE MATTER, HIBARI-CHAN?

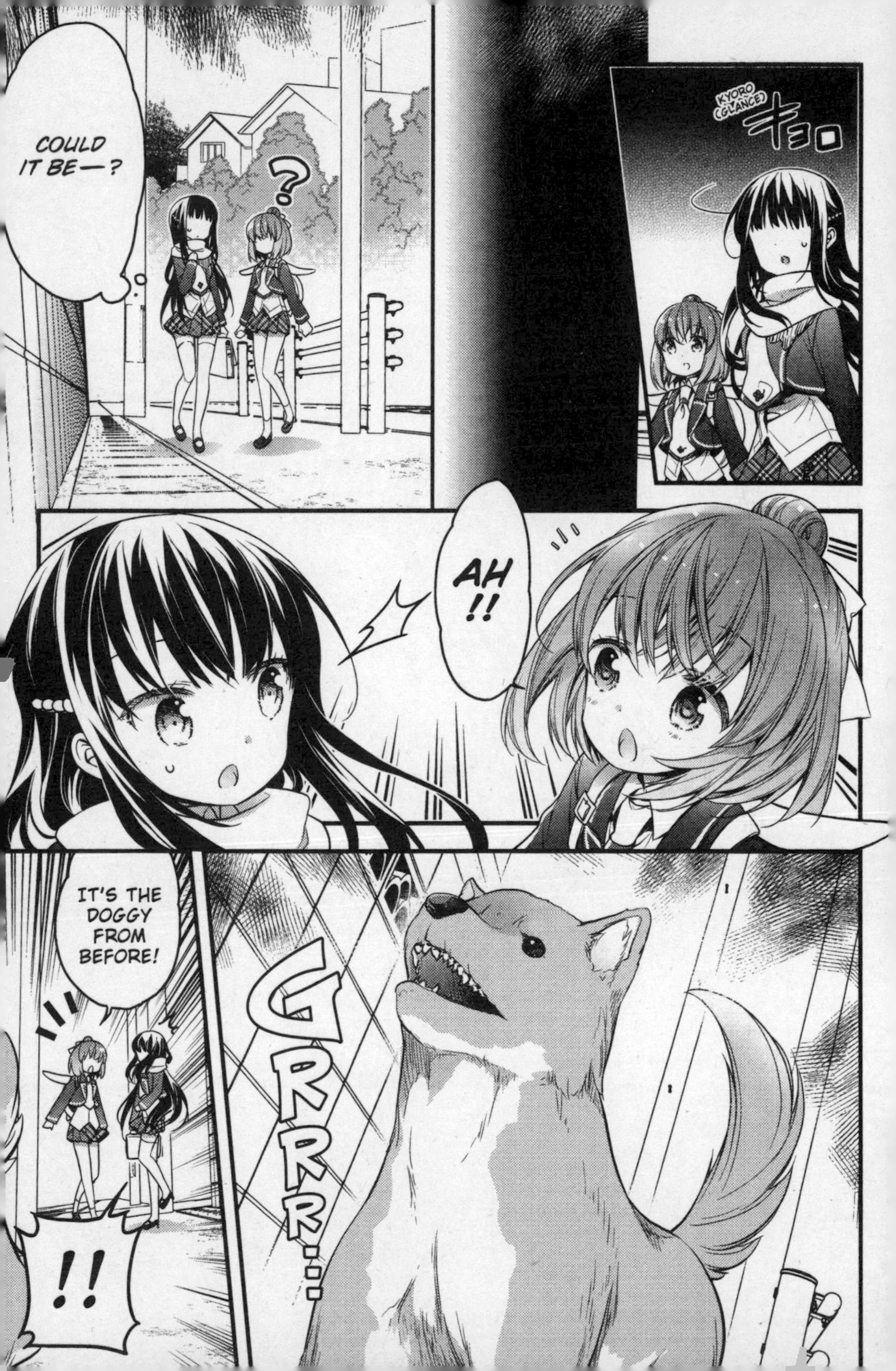
KYORO (GLANCE)
キョロ
COULD IT BE—?
?
AH!!
GRRR...
IT'S THE DOGGY FROM BEFORE!
!!

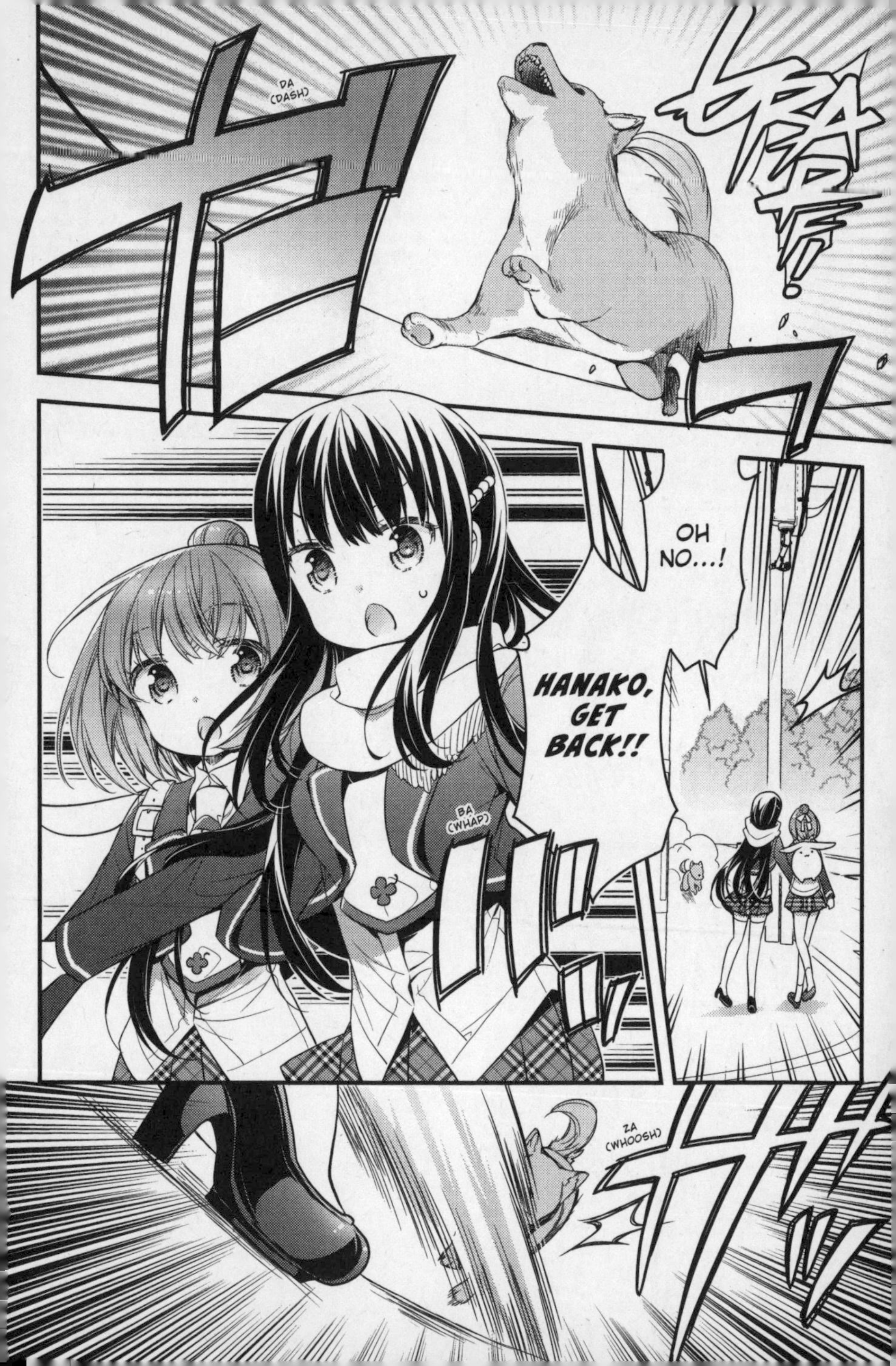
DA (DASH)
OH NO...!
HANAKO, GET BACK!!
BA (WHAP)
ZA (WHOOSH)

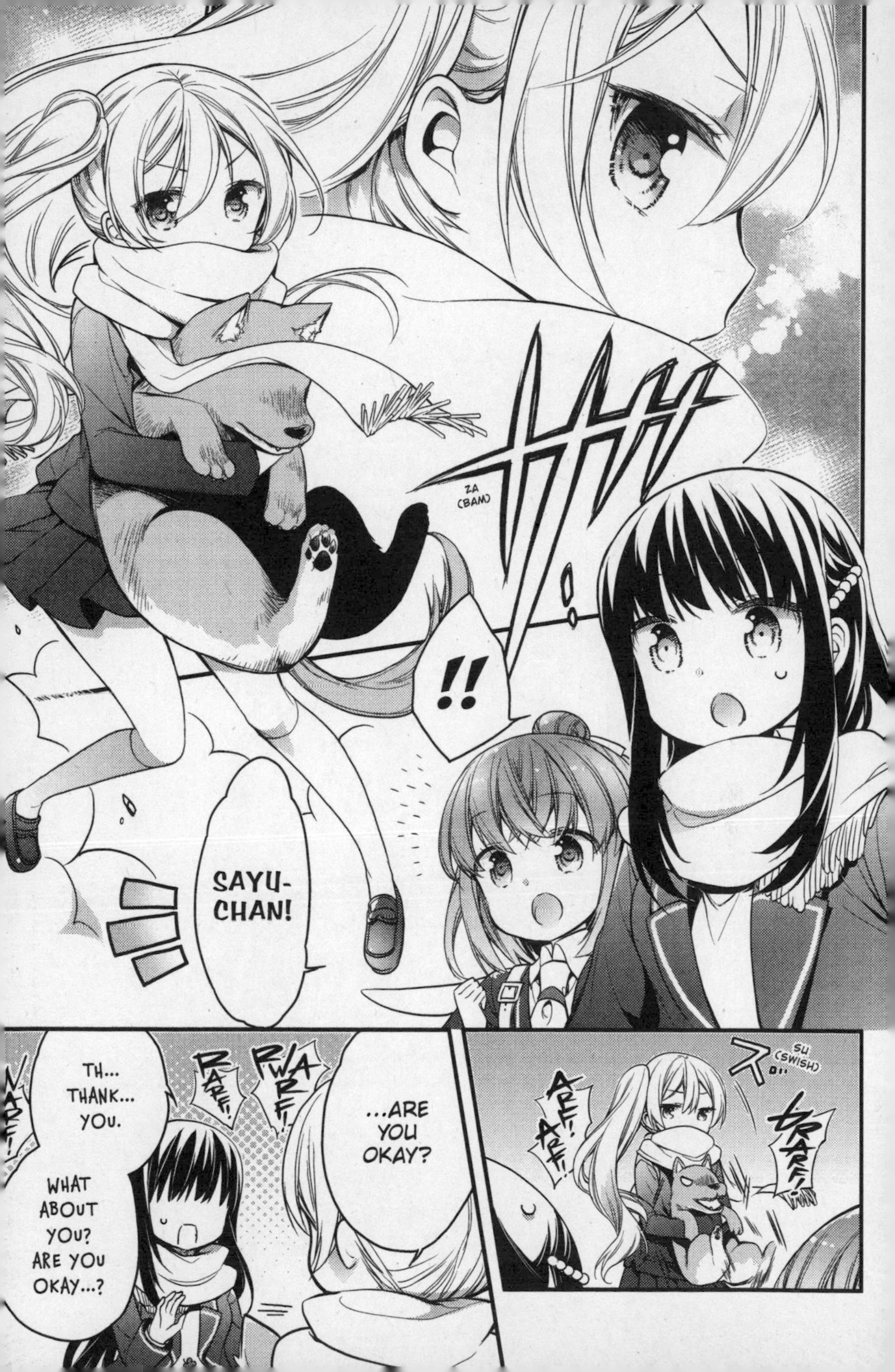
ZA
(BAM)
!!
SAYU-
CHAN!
SU
(SWISH)
ARF! ARF!
GRARF!
...ARE YOU OKAY?
RWARF!
RARF!
TH... THANK... YOU.
WHAT ABOUT YOU? ARE YOU OKAY...?
WARF!

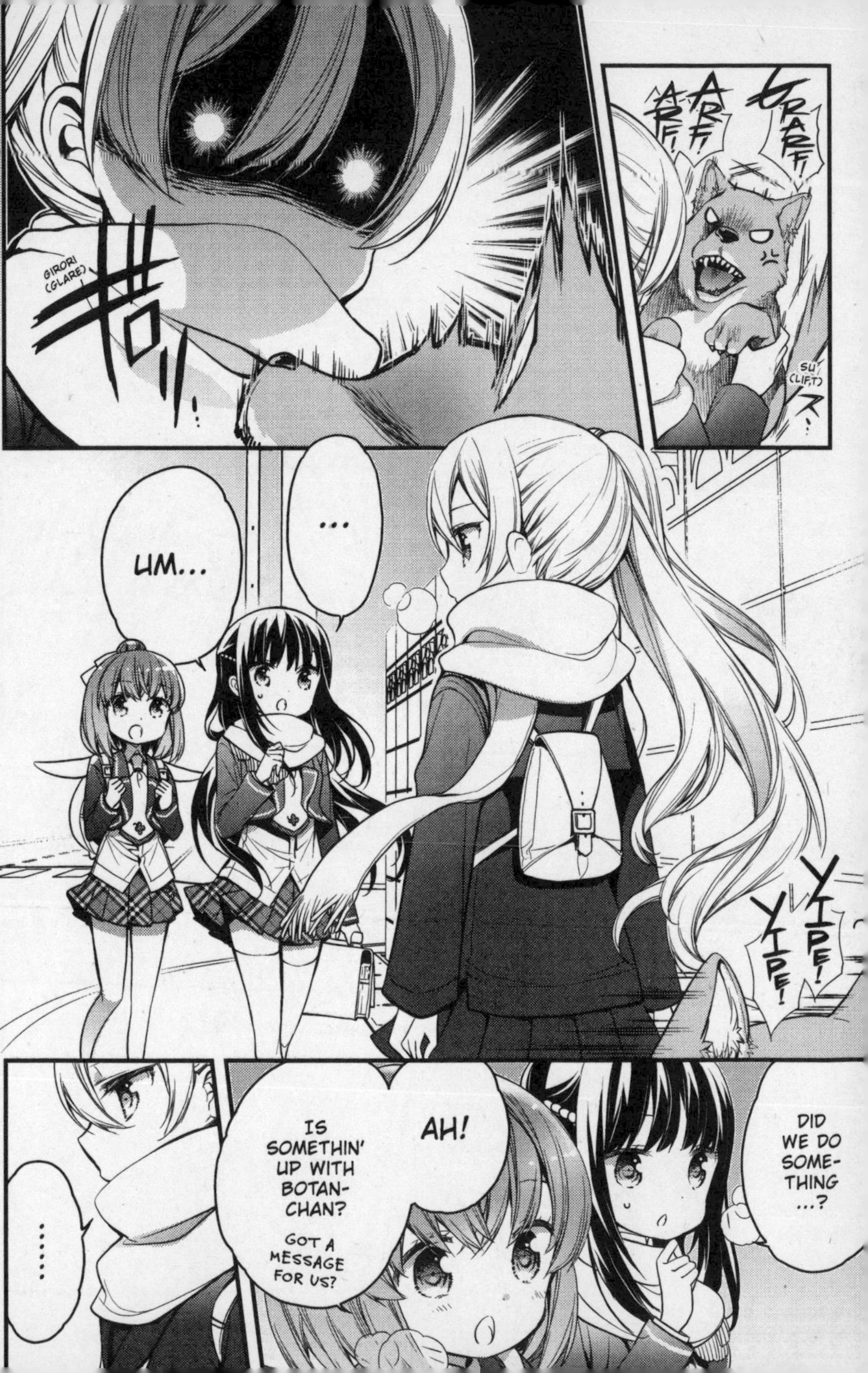
GRARF!
ARF! ARF!
SU (LIFT)
GIRORI (GLARE)
YIPE! YIPE!
...
UM...
DID WE DO SOMETHING ...?
AH!
IS SOMETHIN' UP WITH BOTAN-CHAN?
GOT A MESSAGE FOR US?
......

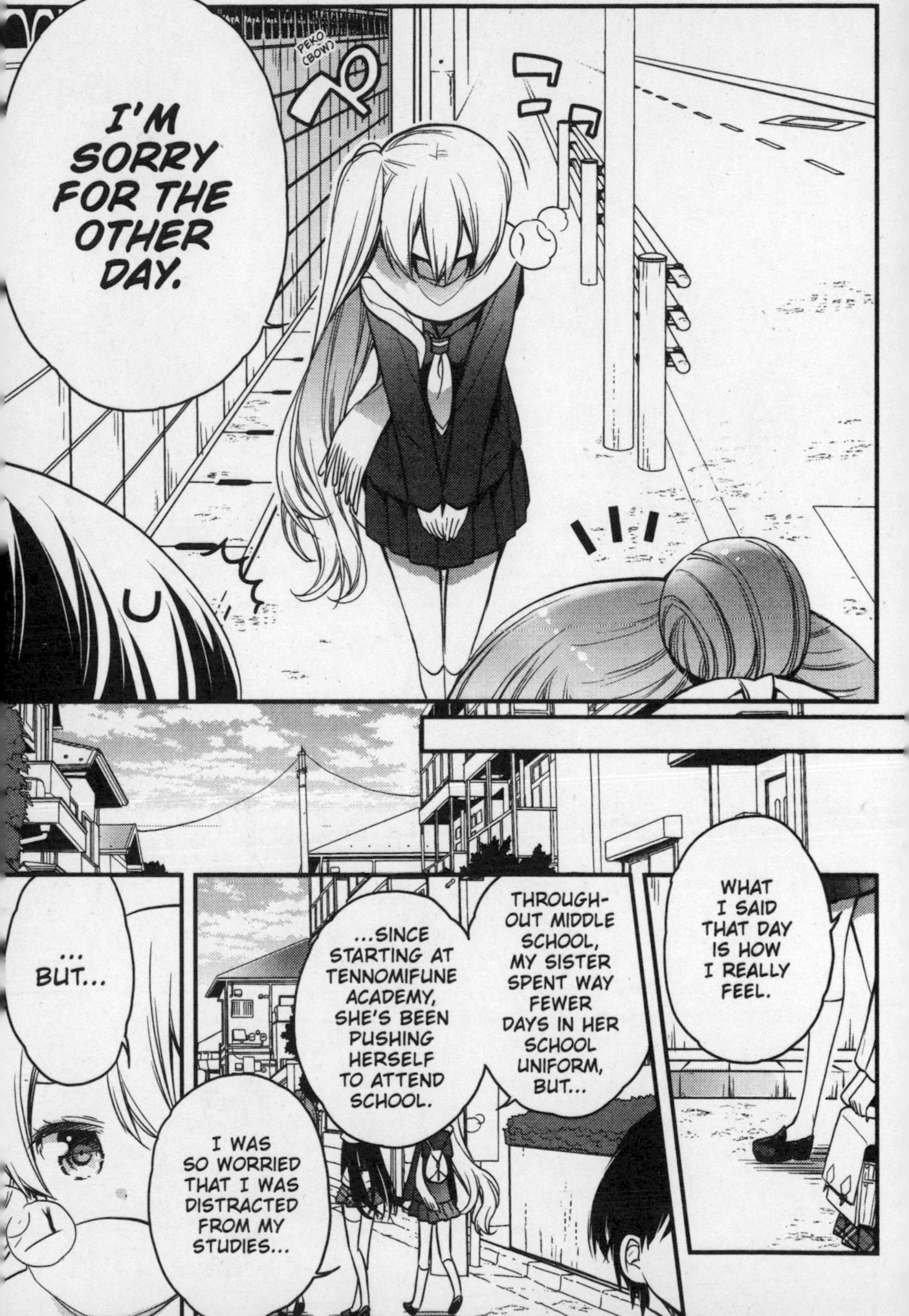
PEKO (BOW)
I'M SORRY FOR THE OTHER DAY.
WHAT I SAID THAT DAY IS HOW I REALLY FEEL.
THROUGH-OUT MIDDLE SCHOOL, MY SISTER SPENT WAY FEWER DAYS IN HER SCHOOL UNIFORM, BUT...
...SINCE STARTING AT TENNOMIFUNE ACADEMY, SHE'S BEEN PUSHING HERSELF TO ATTEND SCHOOL.
I WAS SO WORRIED THAT I WAS DISTRACTED FROM MY STUDIES...
... BUT...

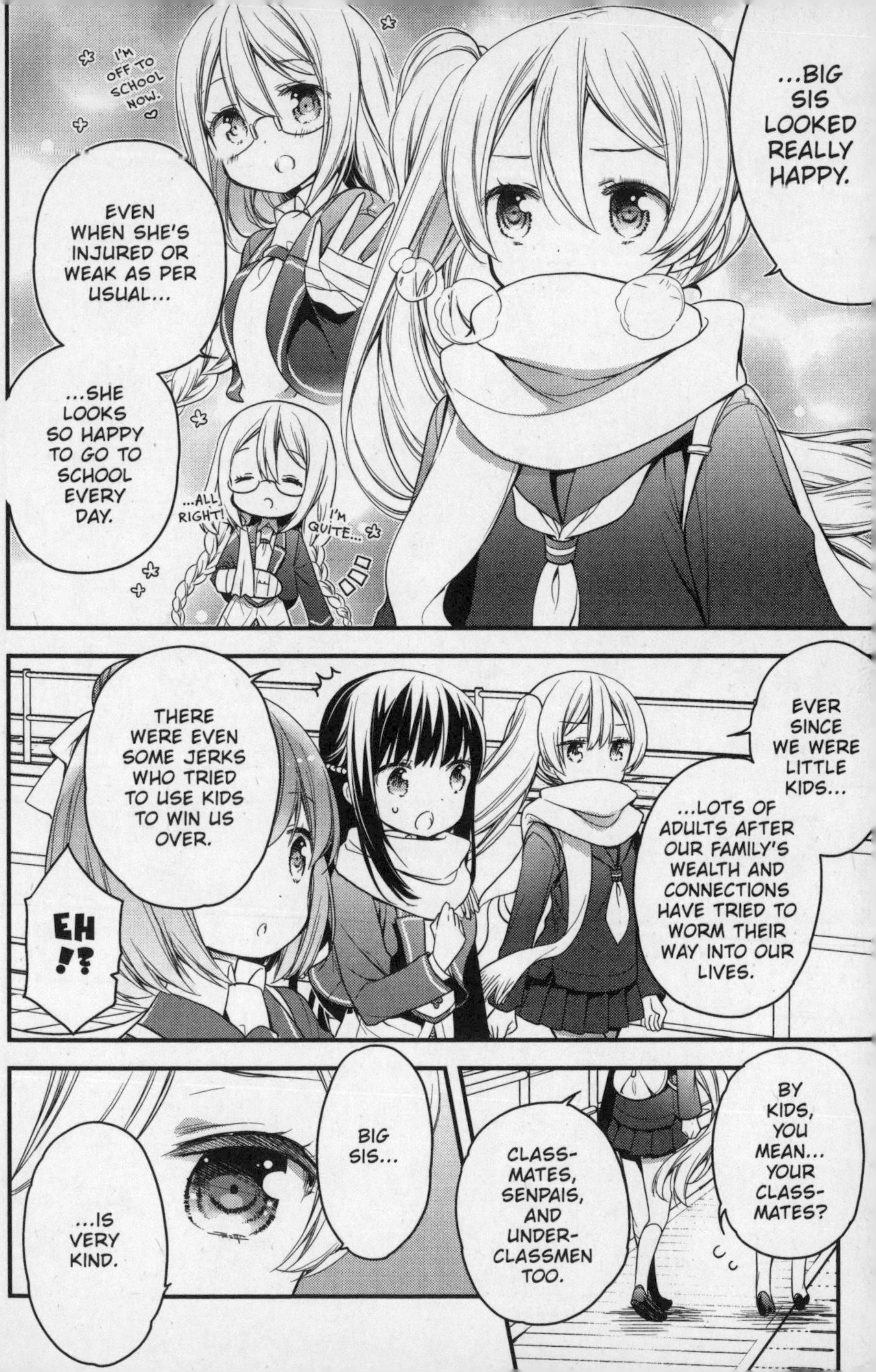
...BIG SIS LOOKED REALLY HAPPY.
I'M OFF TO SCHOOL NOW.
EVEN WHEN SHE'S INJURED OR WEAK AS PER USUAL...
...SHE LOOKS SO HAPPY TO GO TO SCHOOL EVERY DAY.
I'M QUITE...
...ALL RIGHT!
EVER SINCE WE WERE LITTLE KIDS...
...LOTS OF ADULTS AFTER OUR FAMILY'S WEALTH AND CONNECTIONS HAVE TRIED TO WORM THEIR WAY INTO OUR LIVES.
THERE WERE EVEN SOME JERKS WHO TRIED TO USE KIDS TO WIN US OVER.
EH!?
BY KIDS, YOU MEAN... YOUR CLASSMATES?
CLASSMATES, SENPAIS, AND UNDERCLASSMEN TOO.
BIG SIS...
...IS VERY KIND.

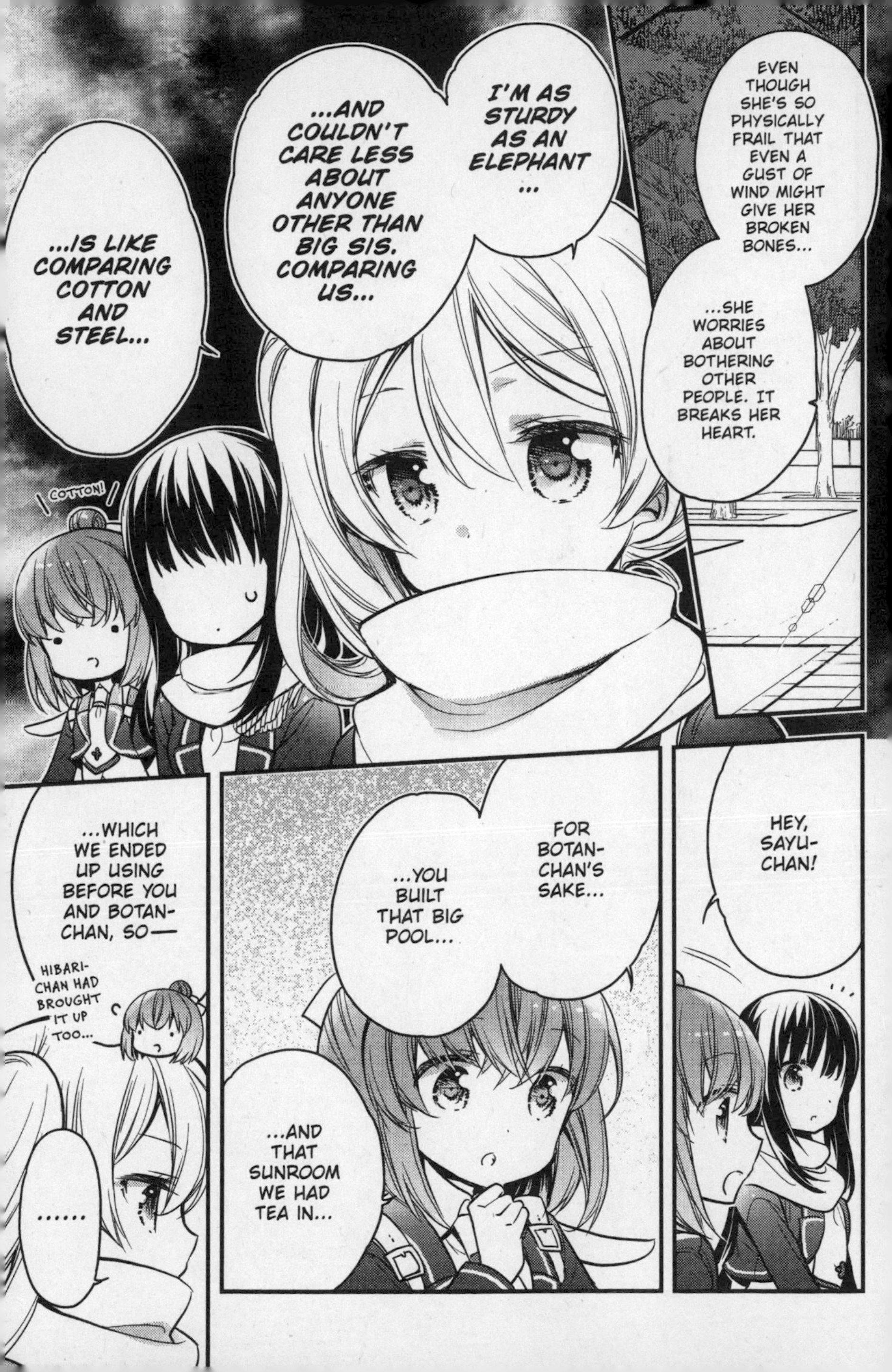
EVEN THOUGH SHE'S SO PHYSICALLY FRAIL THAT EVEN A GUST OF WIND MIGHT GIVE HER BROKEN BONES...
...SHE WORRIES ABOUT BOTHERING OTHER PEOPLE. IT BREAKS HER HEART.
I'M AS STURDY AS AN ELEPHANT ...
...AND COULDN'T CARE LESS ABOUT ANYONE OTHER THAN BIG SIS. COMPARING US...
...IS LIKE COMPARING COTTON AND STEEL...
COTTON!
HEY, SAYU-CHAN!
...
FOR BOTAN-CHAN'S SAKE...
...YOU BUILT THAT BIG POOL...
...AND THAT SUNROOM WE HAD TEA IN...
...WHICH WE ENDED UP USING BEFORE YOU AND BOTAN-CHAN, SO—
HIBARI-CHAN HAD BROUGHT IT UP TOO...
......

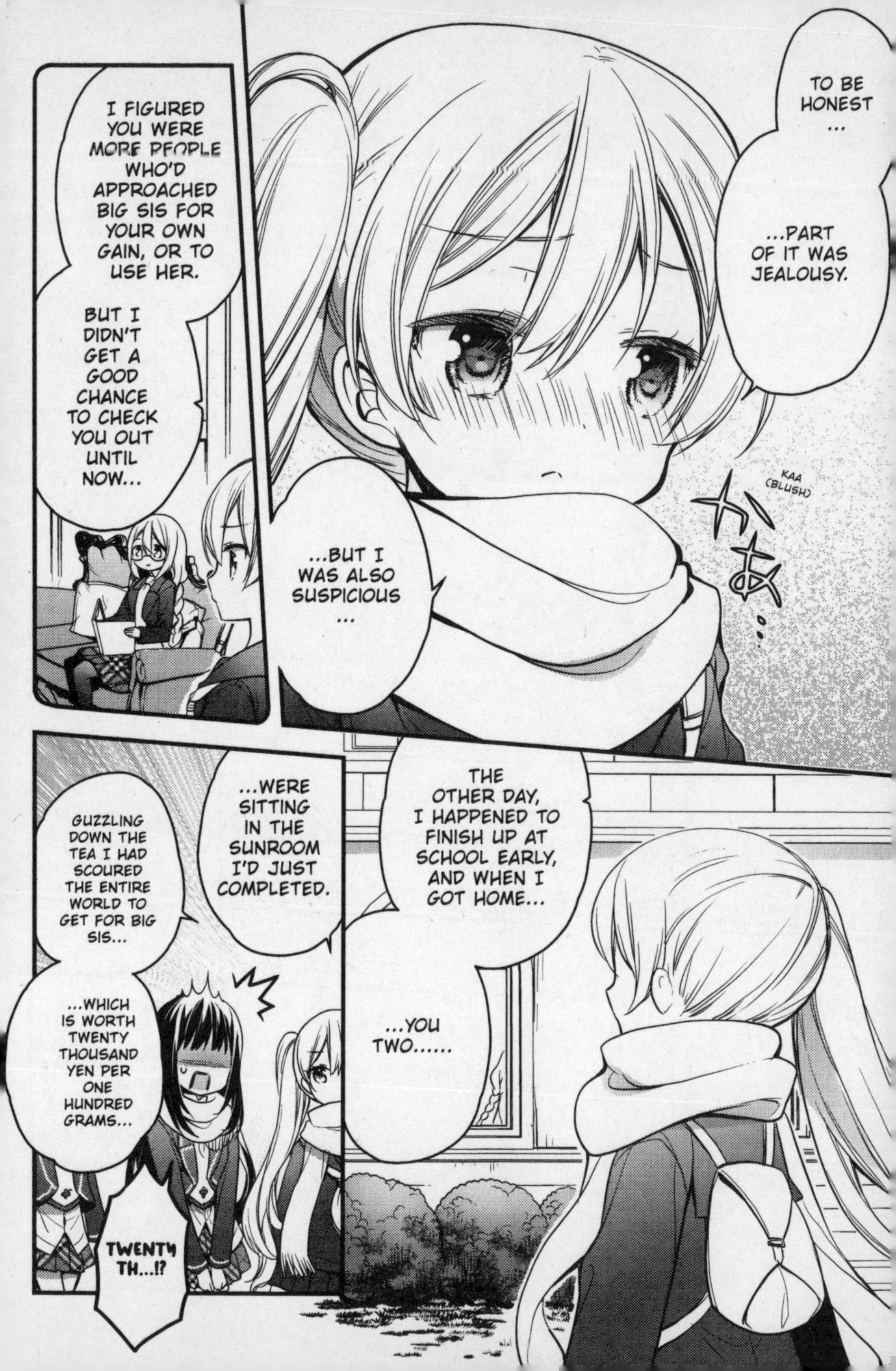
TO BE HONEST ...
...PART OF IT WAS JEALOUSY.
KAA (BLUSH)
...BUT I WAS ALSO SUSPICIOUS ...
I FIGURED YOU WERE MORE PEOPLE WHO'D APPROACHED BIG SIS FOR YOUR OWN GAIN, OR TO USE HER.
BUT I DIDN'T GET A GOOD CHANCE TO CHECK YOU OUT UNTIL NOW...
THE OTHER DAY, I HAPPENED TO FINISH UP AT SCHOOL EARLY, AND WHEN I GOT HOME...
...YOU TWO......
...WERE SITTING IN THE SUNROOM I'D JUST COMPLETED.
GUZZLING DOWN THE TEA I HAD SCOURED THE ENTIRE WORLD TO GET FOR BIG SIS...
...WHICH IS WORTH TWENTY THOUSAND YEN PER ONE HUNDRED GRAMS...
TWENTY TH...!?

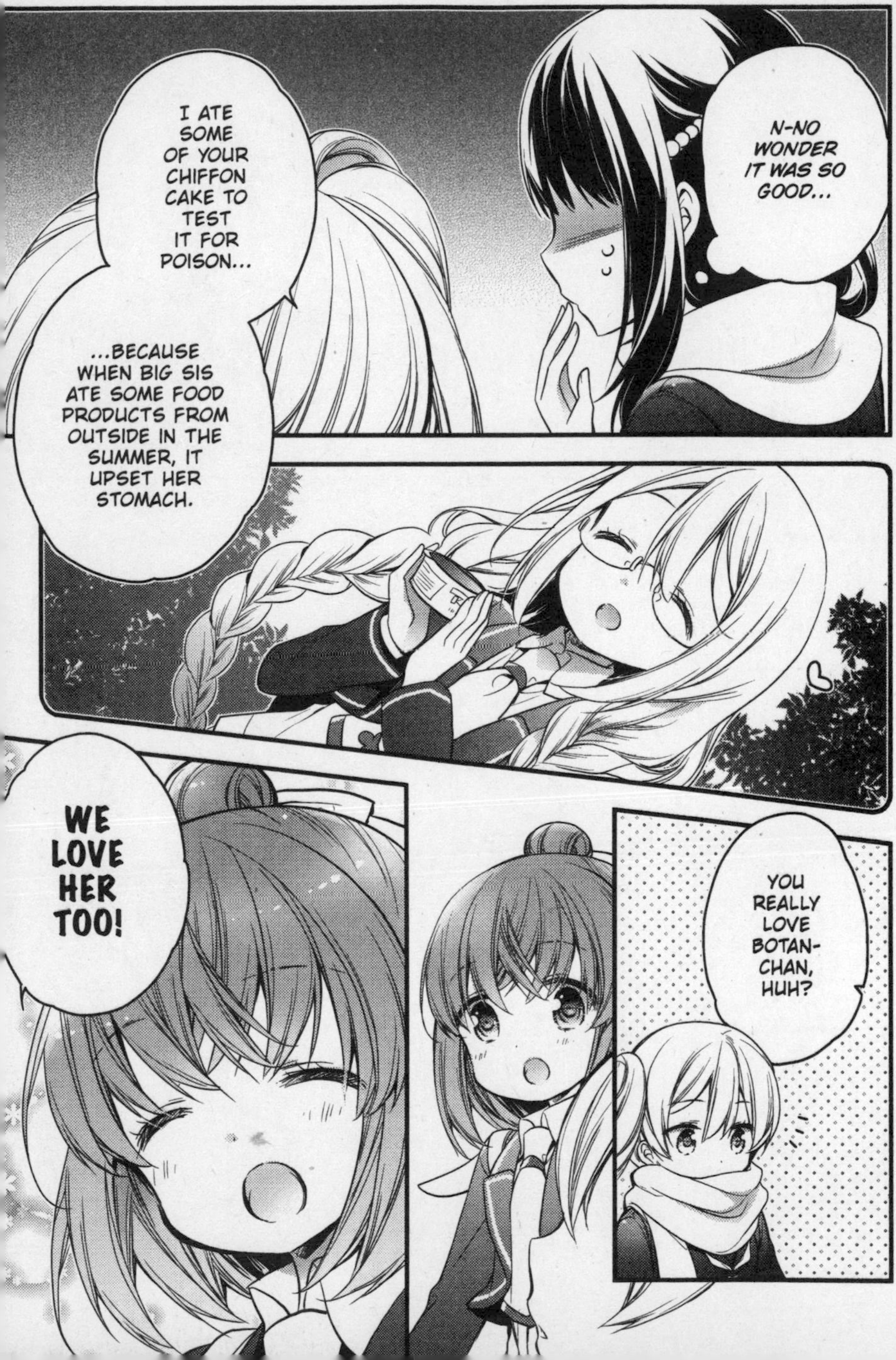
N-NO WONDER IT WAS SO GOOD...
I ATE SOME OF YOUR CHIFFON CAKE TO TEST IT FOR POISON...
...BECAUSE WHEN BIG SIS ATE SOME FOOD PRODUCTS FROM OUTSIDE IN THE SUMMER, IT UPSET HER STOMACH.
YOU REALLY LOVE BOTAN-CHAN, HUH?
WE LOVE HER TOO!

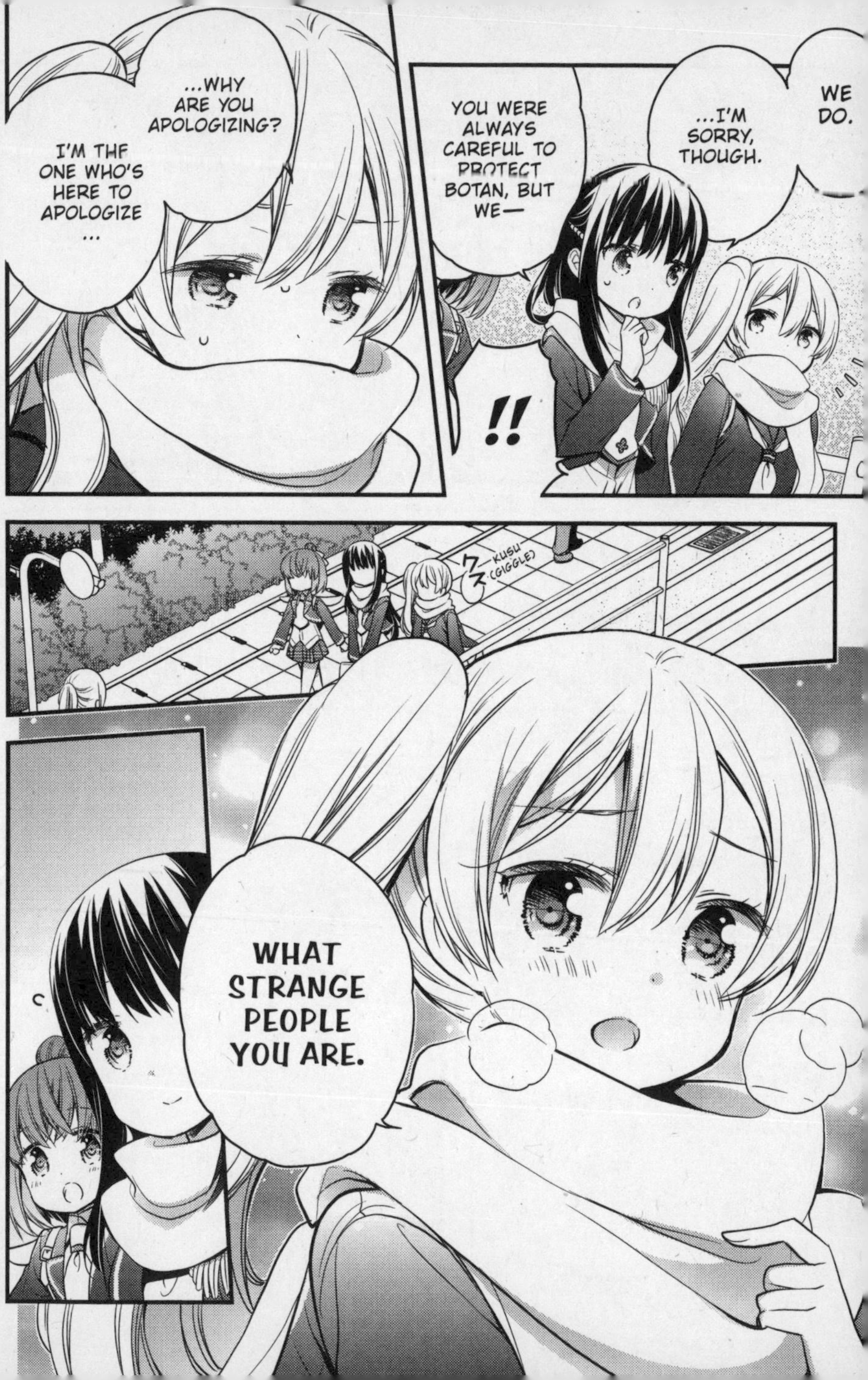
WE DO.
...I'M SORRY, THOUGH.
YOU WERE ALWAYS CAREFUL TO PROTECT BOTAN, BUT WE—
!!
...WHY ARE YOU APOLOGIZING?
I'M THE ONE WHO'S HERE TO APOLOGIZE ...
KUSU (GIGGLE)
WHAT STRANGE PEOPLE YOU ARE.

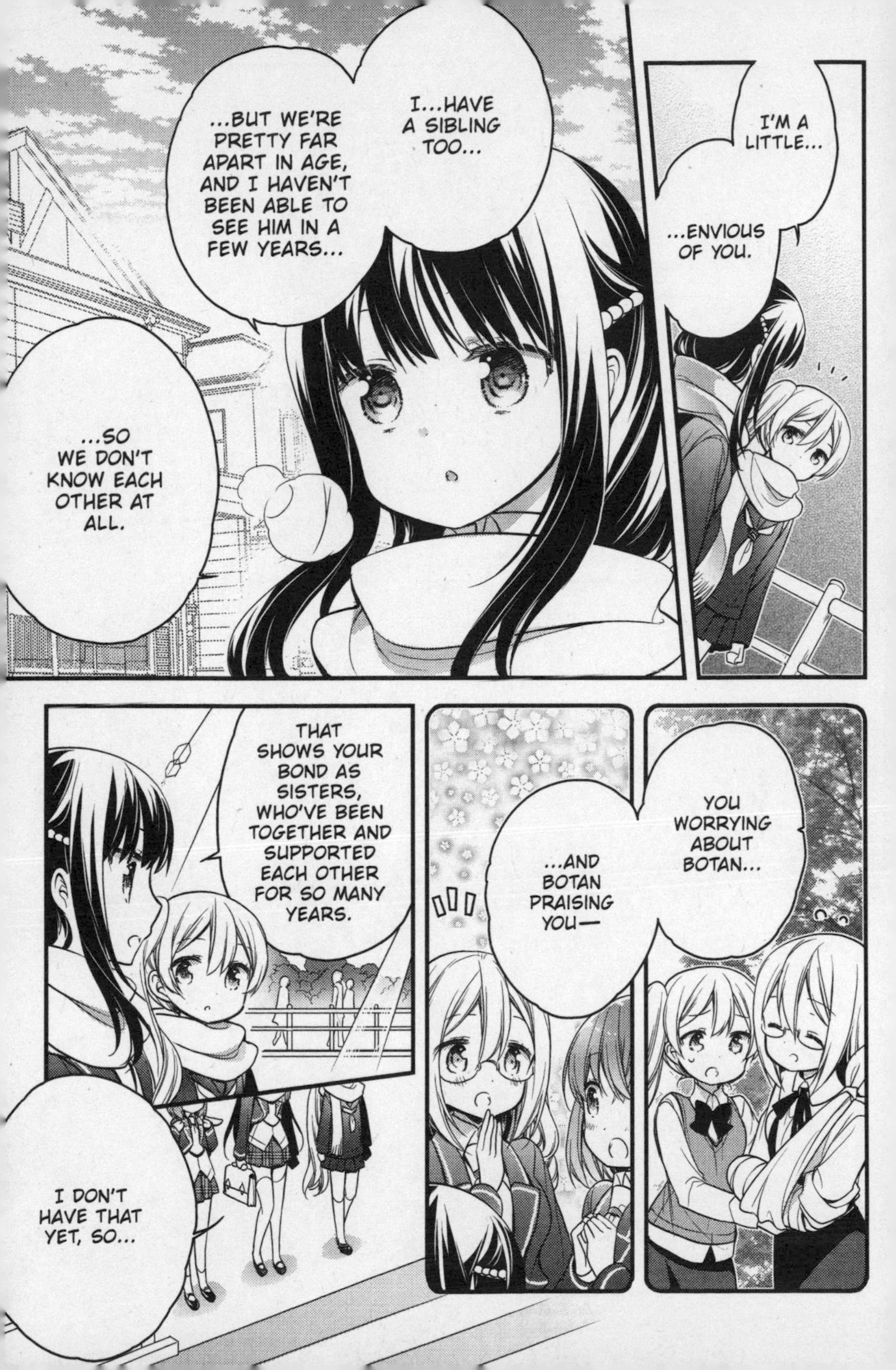
I'M A LITTLE...
...ENVIOUS OF YOU.
I...HAVE A SIBLING TOO...
...BUT WE'RE PRETTY FAR APART IN AGE, AND I HAVEN'T BEEN ABLE TO SEE HIM IN A FEW YEARS...
...SO WE DON'T KNOW EACH OTHER AT ALL.
YOU WORRYING ABOUT BOTAN...
...AND BOTAN PRAISING YOU—
THAT SHOWS YOUR BOND AS SISTERS, WHO'VE BEEN TOGETHER AND SUPPORTED EACH OTHER FOR SO MANY YEARS.
I DON'T HAVE THAT YET, SO...

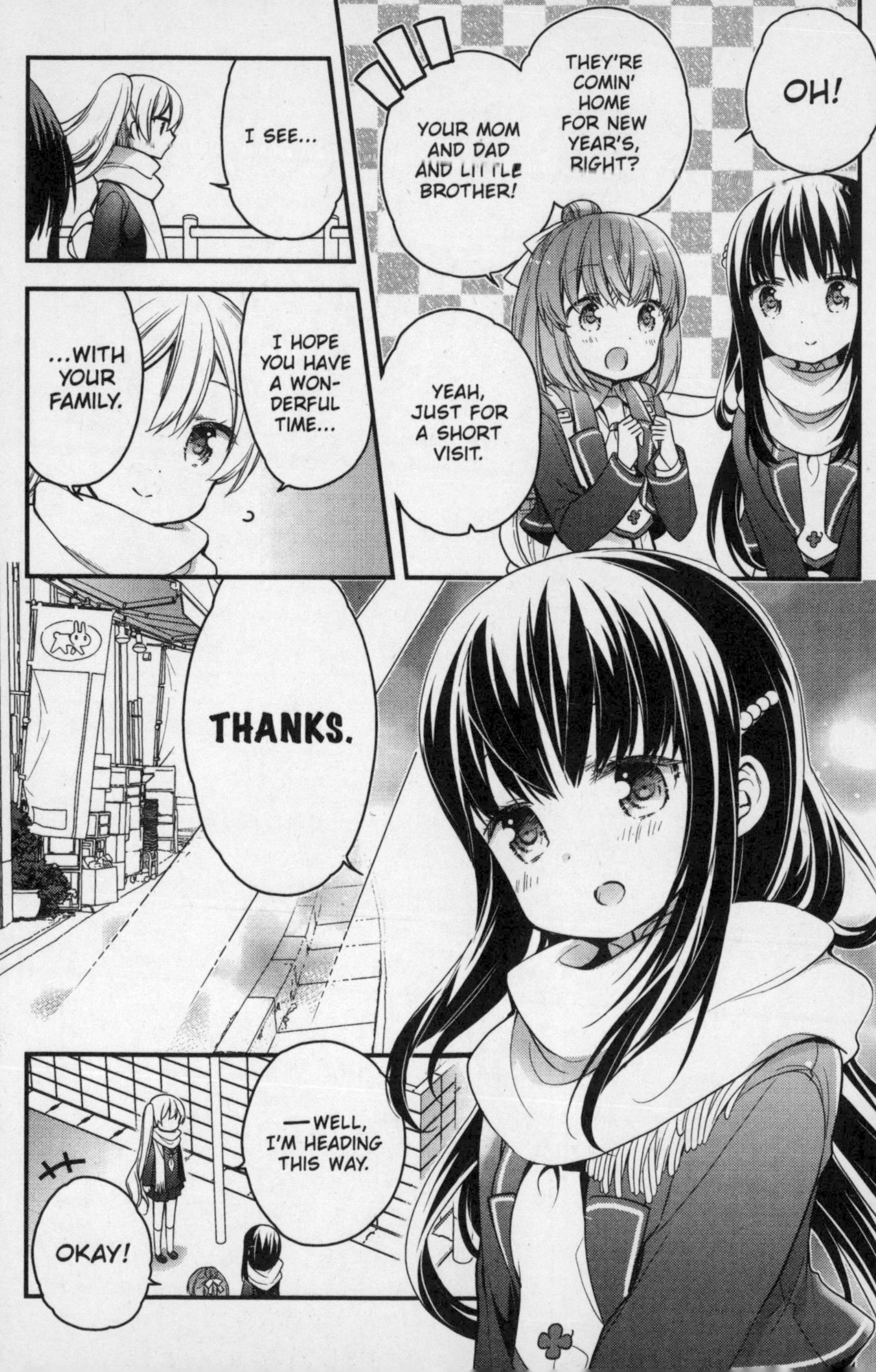
OH!
THEY'RE COMIN' HOME FOR NEW YEAR'S, RIGHT?
YOUR MOM AND DAD AND LITTLE BROTHER!
YEAH, JUST FOR A SHORT VISIT.
I SEE...
I HOPE YOU HAVE A WON-DERFUL TIME...
...WITH YOUR FAMILY.
THANKS.
—WELL, I'M HEADING THIS WAY.
OKAY!

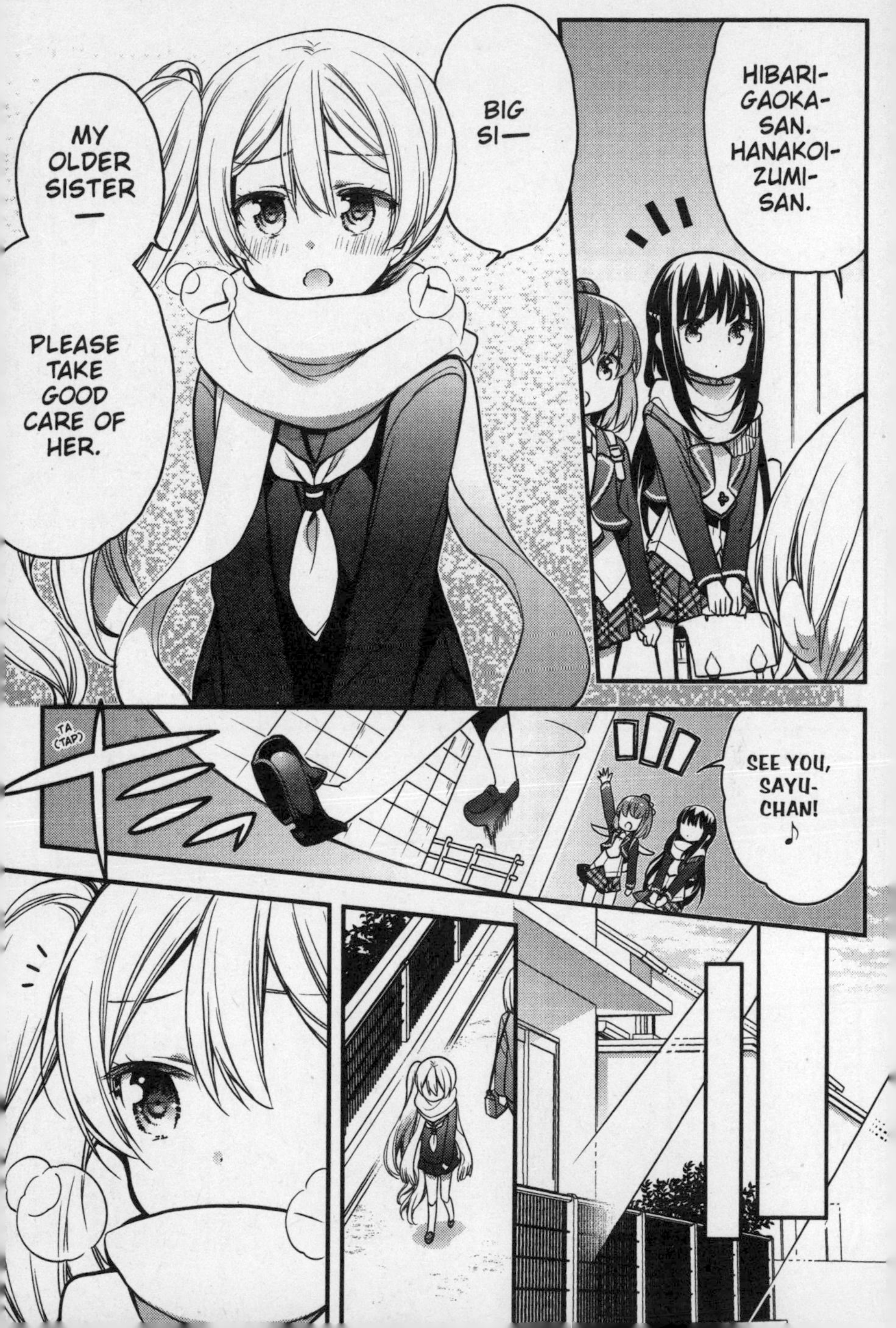
HIBARI-GAOKA-SAN. HANAKOI-ZUMI-SAN.
BIG SI—
MY OLDER SISTER—
PLEASE TAKE GOOD CARE OF HER.
SEE YOU, SAYU-CHAN! ♪
TA (TAP)

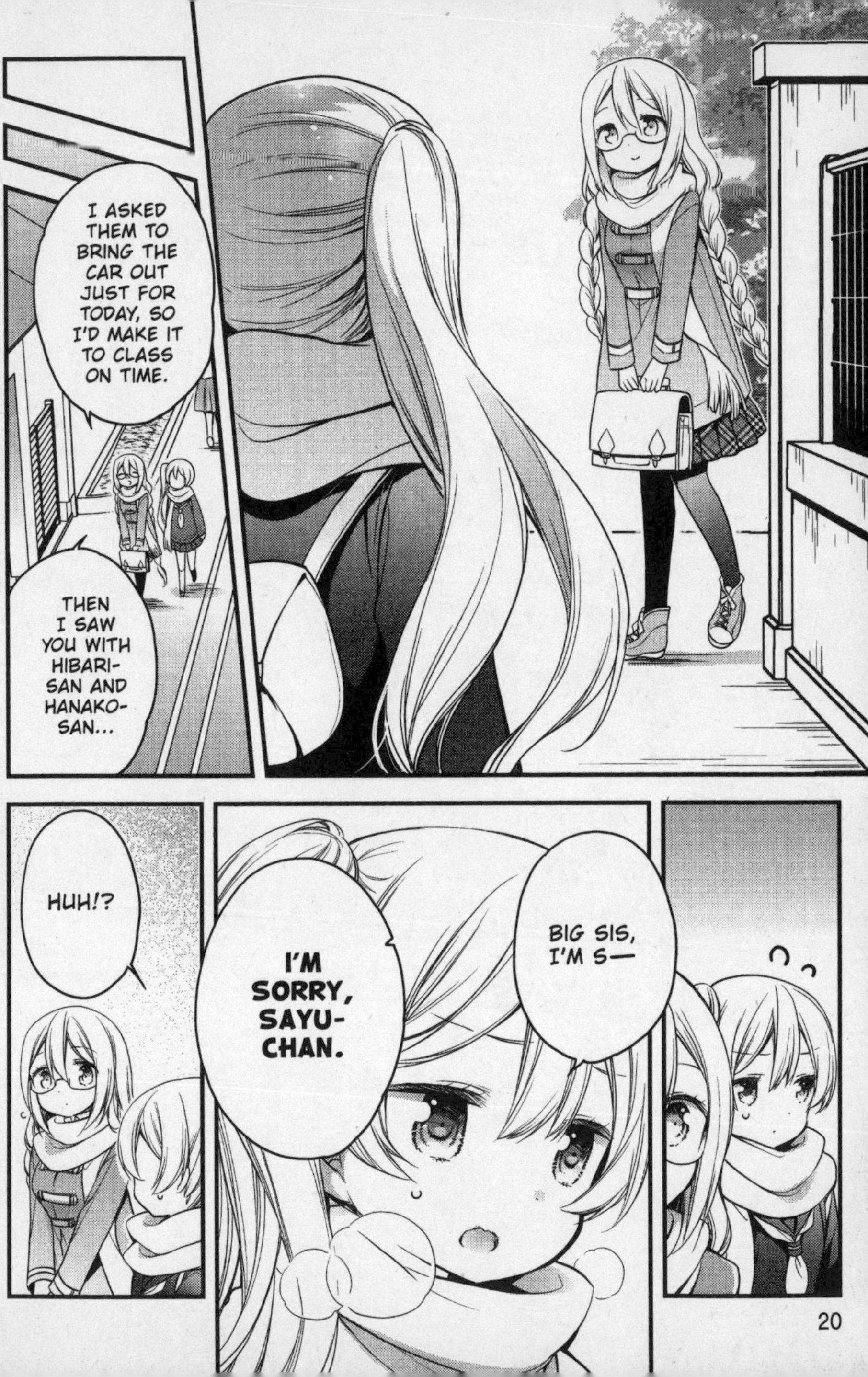
I ASKED THEM TO BRING THE CAR OUT JUST FOR TODAY, SO I'D MAKE IT TO CLASS ON TIME.
THEN I SAW YOU WITH HIBARI-SAN AND HANAKO-SAN...
BIG SIS, I'M S—
I'M SORRY, SAYU-CHAN.
HUH!?

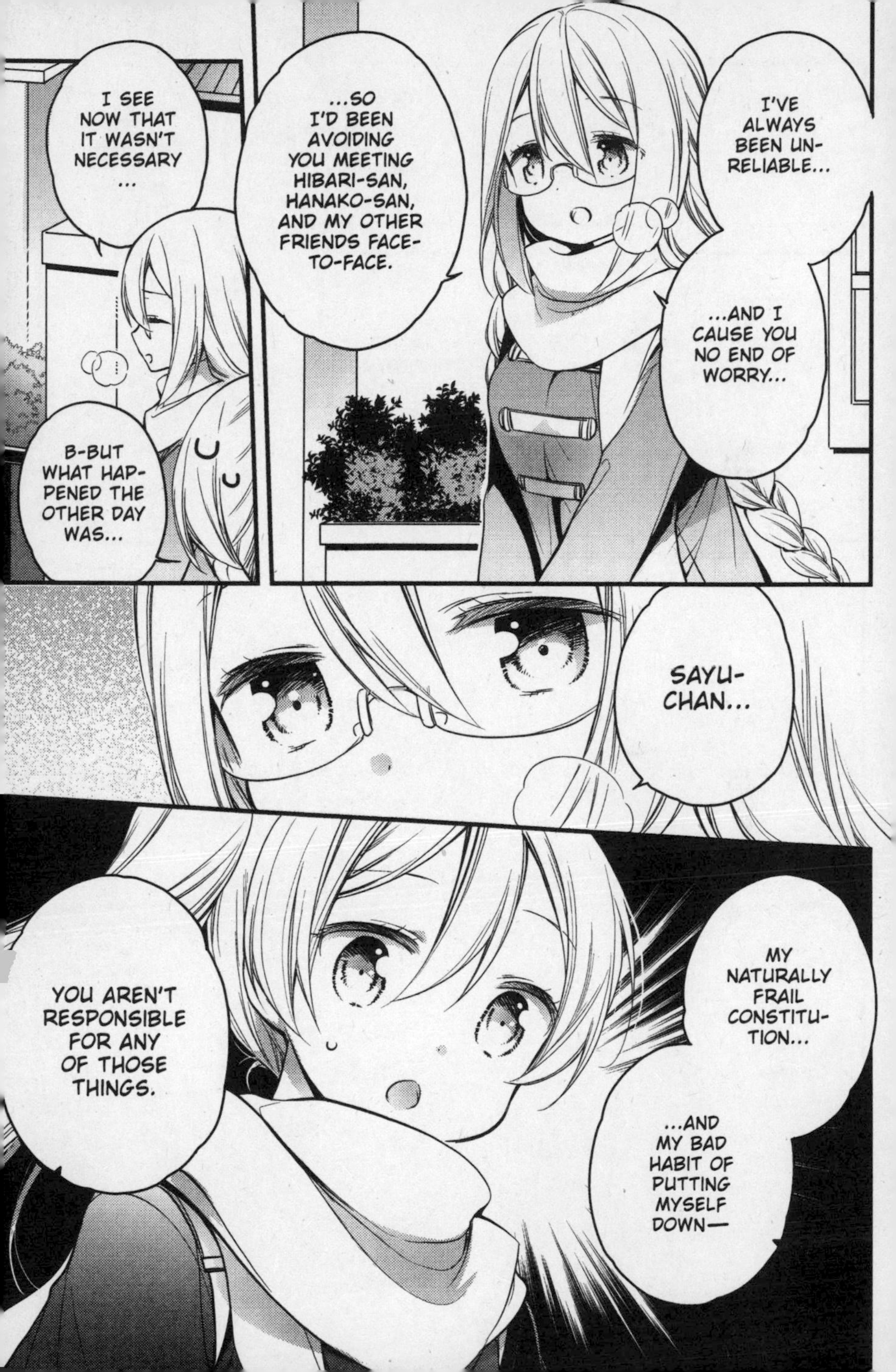
I'VE ALWAYS BEEN UN-RELIABLE...
...AND I CAUSE YOU NO END OF WORRY...
...SO I'D BEEN AVOIDING YOU MEETING HIBARI-SAN, HANAKO-SAN, AND MY OTHER FRIENDS FACE-TO-FACE.
I SEE NOW THAT IT WASN'T NECESSARY...
B-BUT WHAT HAP-PENED THE OTHER DAY WAS...
SAYU-CHAN...
MY NATURALLY FRAIL CONSTITU-TION...
...AND MY BAD HABIT OF PUTTING MYSELF DOWN—
YOU AREN'T RESPONSIBLE FOR ANY OF THOSE THINGS.

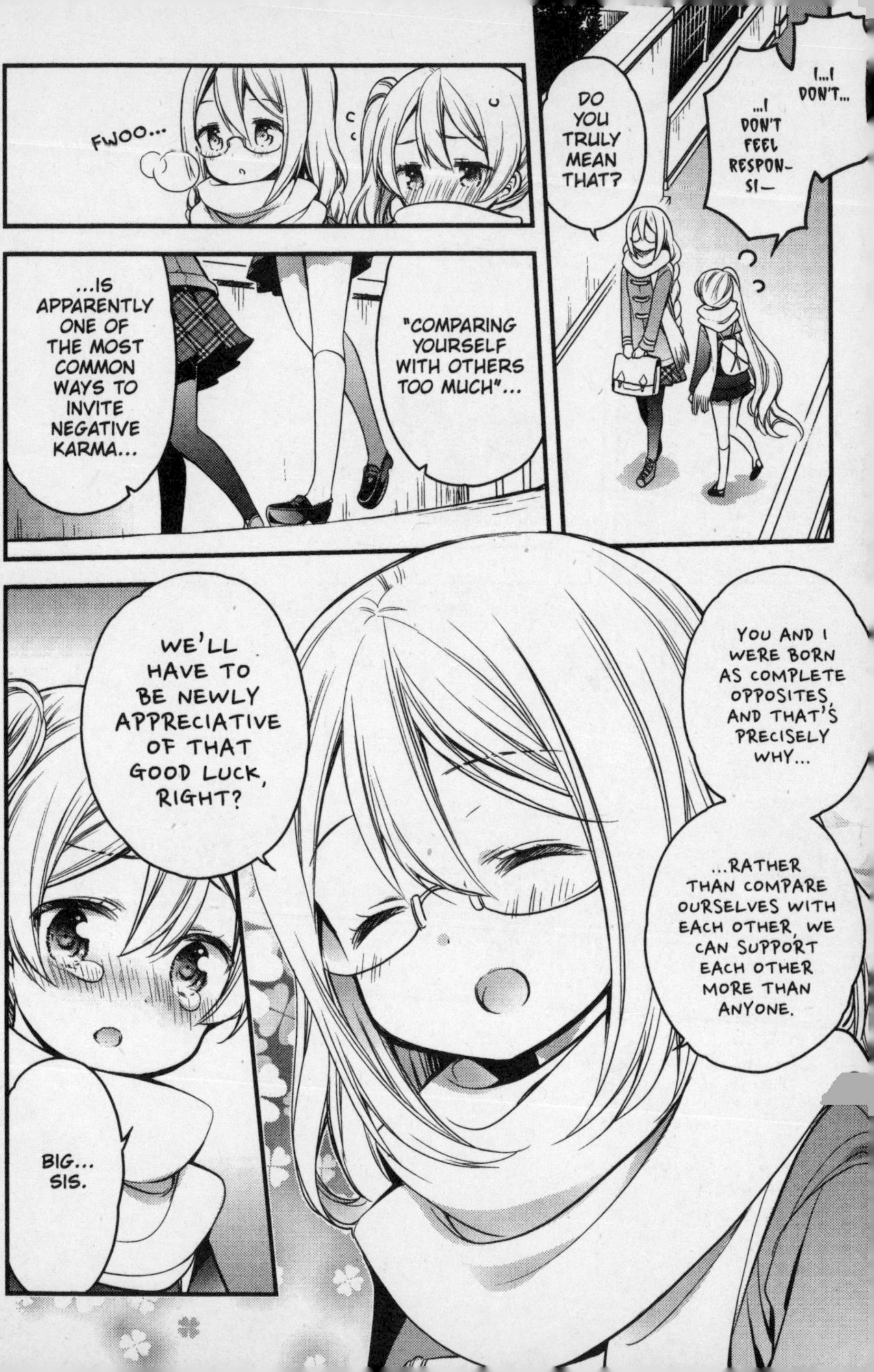
I...I DON'T...
...I DON'T FEEL RESPONSI—
DO YOU TRULY MEAN THAT?
FWOO...
"COMPARING YOURSELF WITH OTHERS TOO MUCH"...
...IS APPARENTLY ONE OF THE MOST COMMON WAYS TO INVITE NEGATIVE KARMA...
YOU AND I WERE BORN AS COMPLETE OPPOSITES, AND THAT'S PRECISELY WHY...
...RATHER THAN COMPARE OURSELVES WITH EACH OTHER, WE CAN SUPPORT EACH OTHER MORE THAN ANYONE.
WE'LL HAVE TO BE NEWLY APPRECIATIVE OF THAT GOOD LUCK, RIGHT?
BIG... SIS.

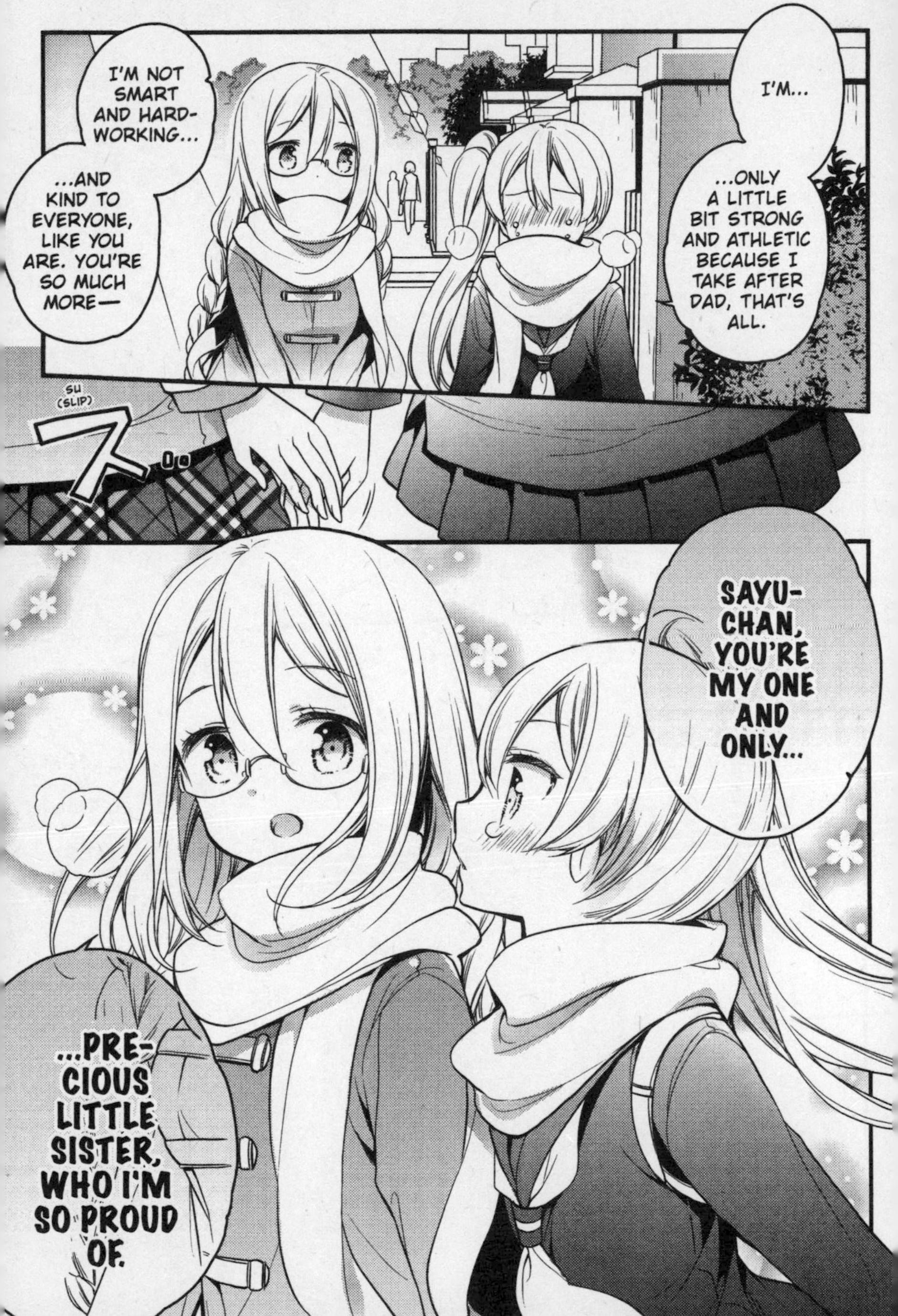
I'M...
...ONLY A LITTLE BIT STRONG AND ATHLETIC BECAUSE I TAKE AFTER DAD, THAT'S ALL.
I'M NOT SMART AND HARD-WORKING...
...AND KIND TO EVERYONE, LIKE YOU ARE. YOU'RE SO MUCH MORE—
SU (SLIP)
SAYU-CHAN, YOU'RE MY ONE AND ONLY...
...PRECIOUS LITTLE SISTER, WHO I'M SO PROUD OF.

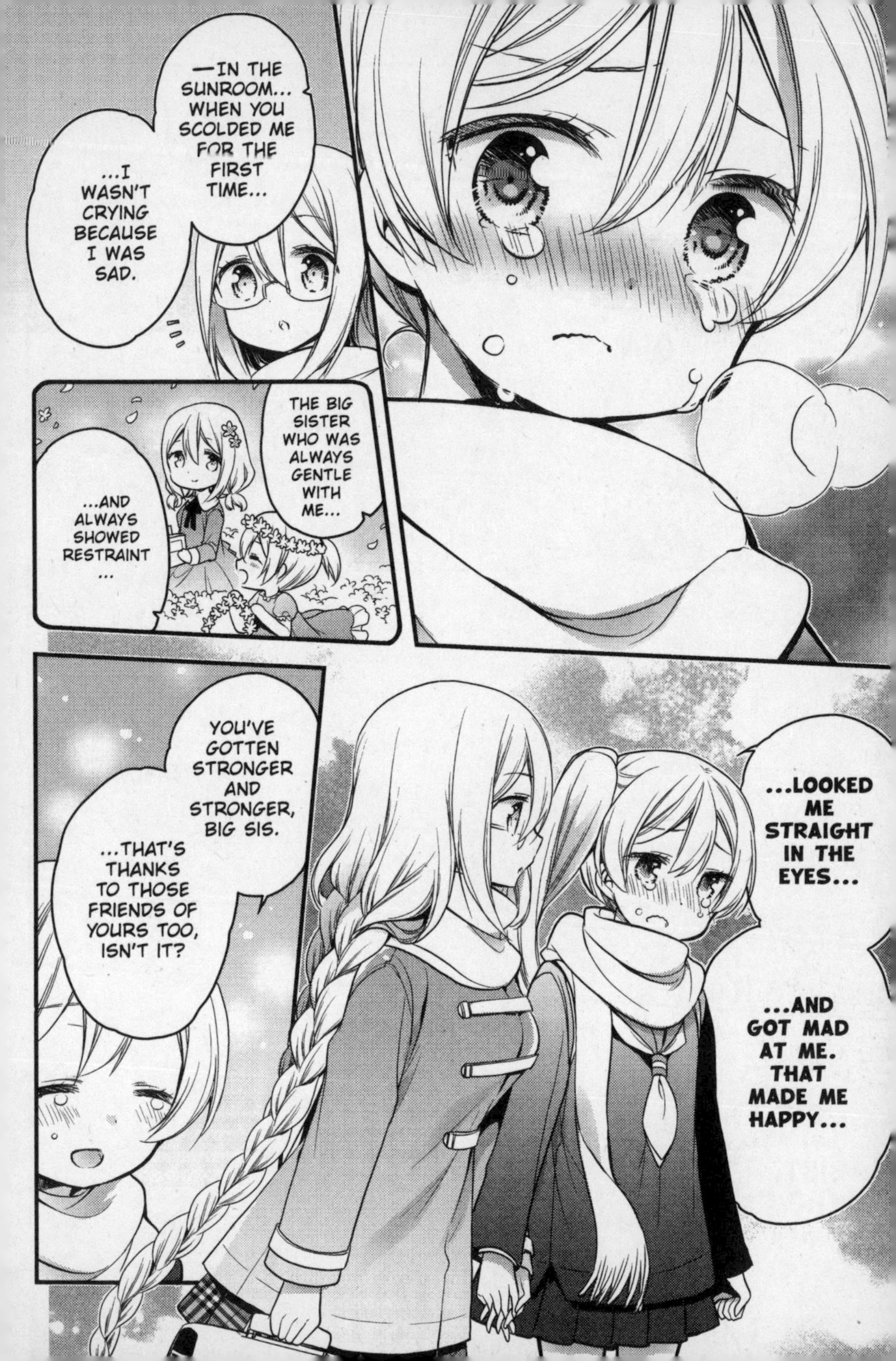
—IN THE SUNROOM... WHEN YOU SCOLDED ME FOR THE FIRST TIME...
...I WASN'T CRYING BECAUSE I WAS SAD.
THE BIG SISTER WHO WAS ALWAYS GENTLE WITH ME...
...AND ALWAYS SHOWED RESTRAINT...
...LOOKED ME STRAIGHT IN THE EYES...
...AND GOT MAD AT ME. THAT MADE ME HAPPY...
YOU'VE GOTTEN STRONGER AND STRONGER, BIG SIS.
...THAT'S THANKS TO THOSE FRIENDS OF YOURS TOO, ISN'T IT?

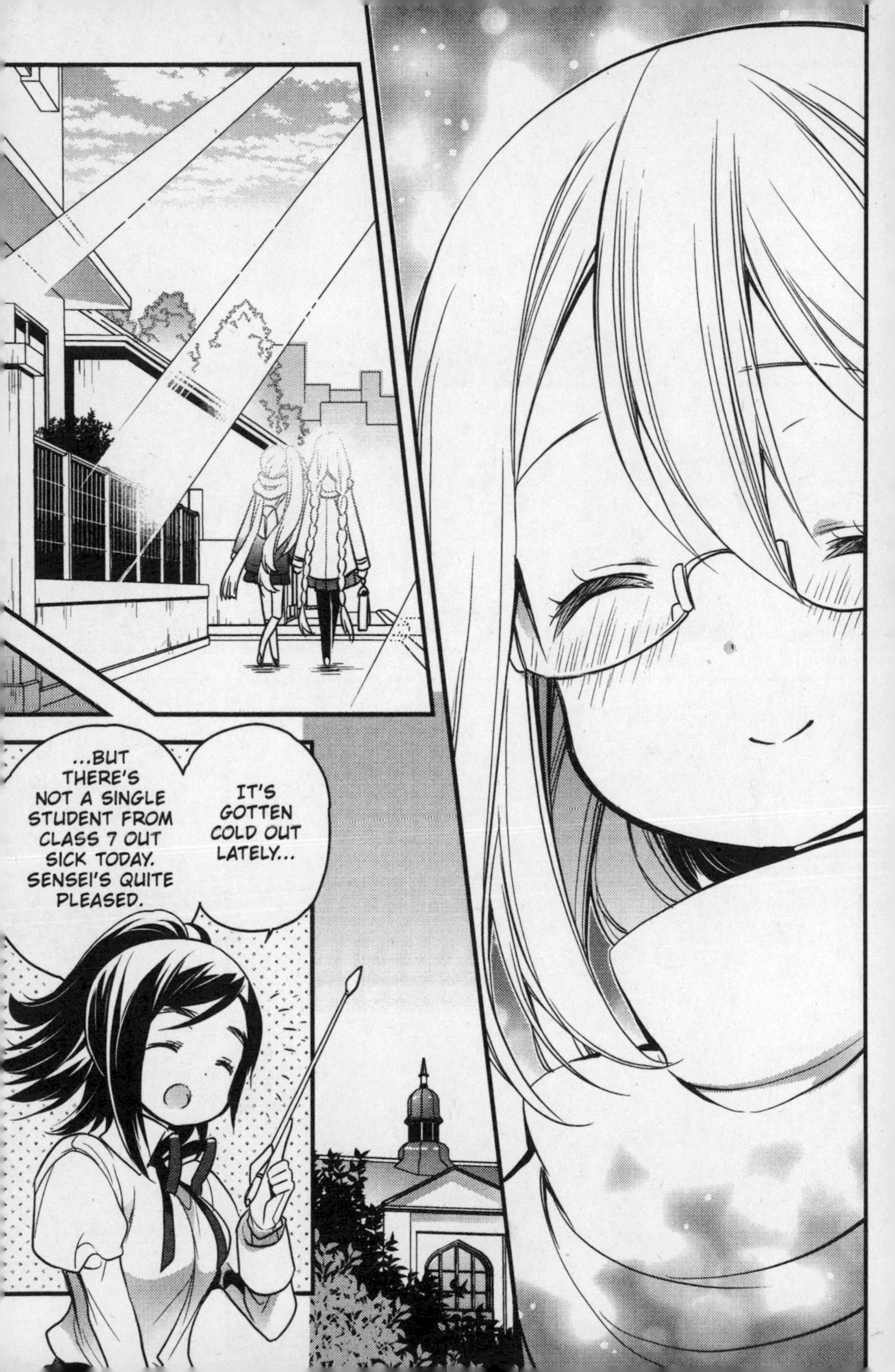
IT'S GOTTEN COLD OUT LATELY...
...BUT THERE'S NOT A SINGLE STUDENT FROM CLASS 7 OUT SICK TODAY. SENSEI'S QUITE PLEASED.

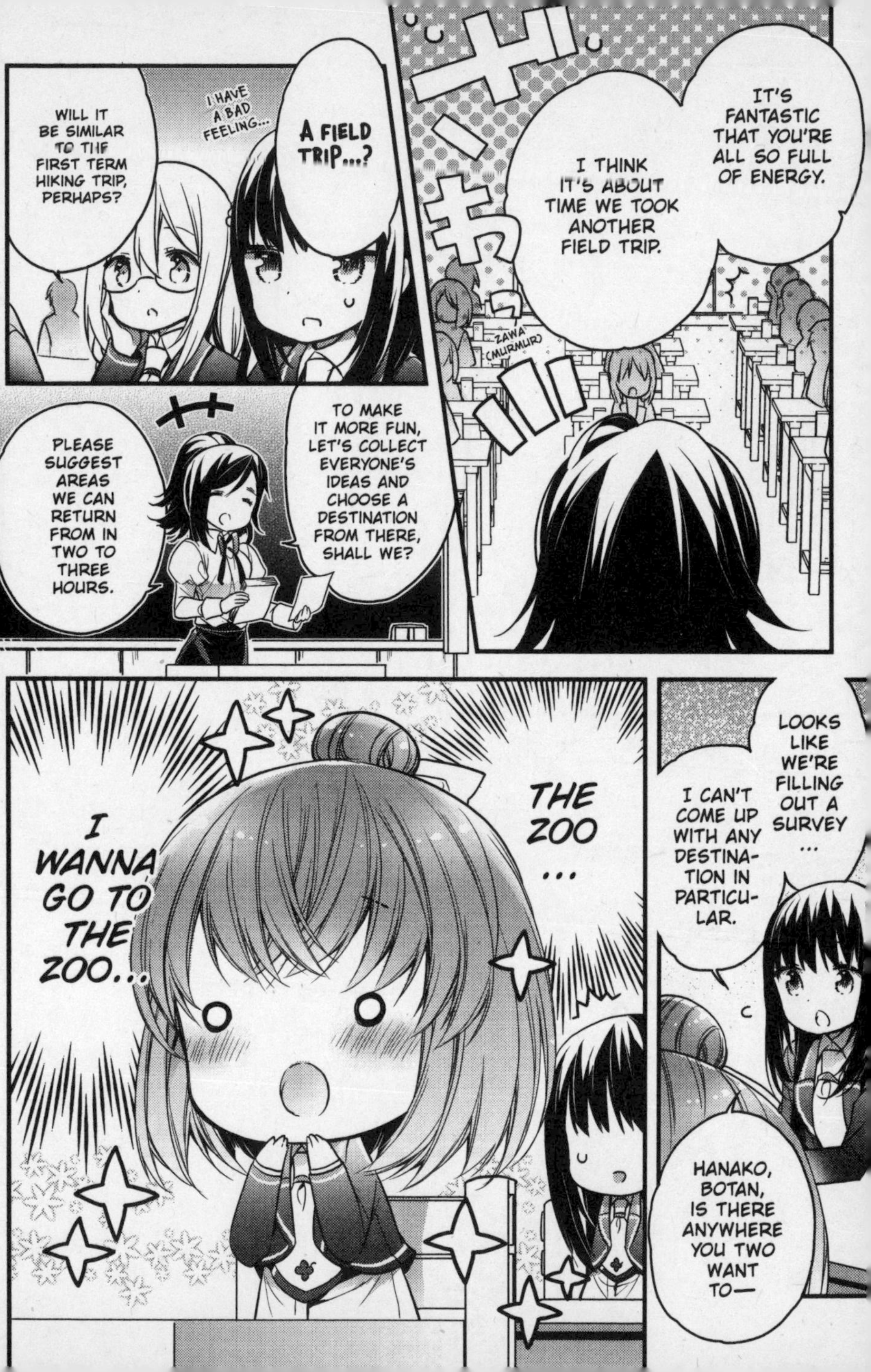

IT'S FANTASTIC THAT YOU'RE ALL SO FULL OF ENERGY.
I THINK IT'S ABOUT TIME WE TOOK ANOTHER FIELD TRIP.
ZAWA (MURMUR)
A FIELD TRIP...?
I HAVE A BAD FEELING...
WILL IT BE SIMILAR TO THE FIRST TERM HIKING TRIP, PERHAPS?
TO MAKE IT MORE FUN, LET'S COLLECT EVERYONE'S IDEAS AND CHOOSE A DESTINATION FROM THERE, SHALL WE?
PLEASE SUGGEST AREAS WE CAN RETURN FROM IN TWO TO THREE HOURS.
LOOKS LIKE WE'RE FILLING OUT A SURVEY...
I CAN'T COME UP WITH ANY DESTINATION IN PARTICULAR.
HANAKO, BOTAN, IS THERE ANYWHERE YOU TWO WANT TO—
THE ZOO...
I WANNA GO TO THE ZOO...

Anne Happy

unhappy go lucky!

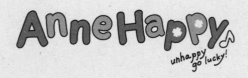

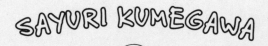

SAYURI KUMEGAWA

BOTAN CALLS HER "SAYU-CHAN."
BOTAN'S LITTLE SISTER IS THE COMPLETE OPPOSITE OF HER BIG SIS, WHO INHERITED THEIR MOTHER'S FRAIL HEALTH. SAYURI TOOK AFTER THEIR FATHER—SHE'S STRONG AND ATHLETIC.
PRETTY OVERPROTECTIVE OF HER KIND, FRAIL BIG SISTER, OUT OF WORRY. SHE'LL ELIMINATE ANYTHING AND ANYONE THAT HARMS BOTAN!!
ONE YEAR YOUNGER THAN BOTAN. A THIRD-YEAR IN MIDDLE SCHOOL.
SHE SECRETLY ADMIRES HER BIG SISTER AND IS GROWING HER HAIR OUT TO BE MORE LIKE HER.

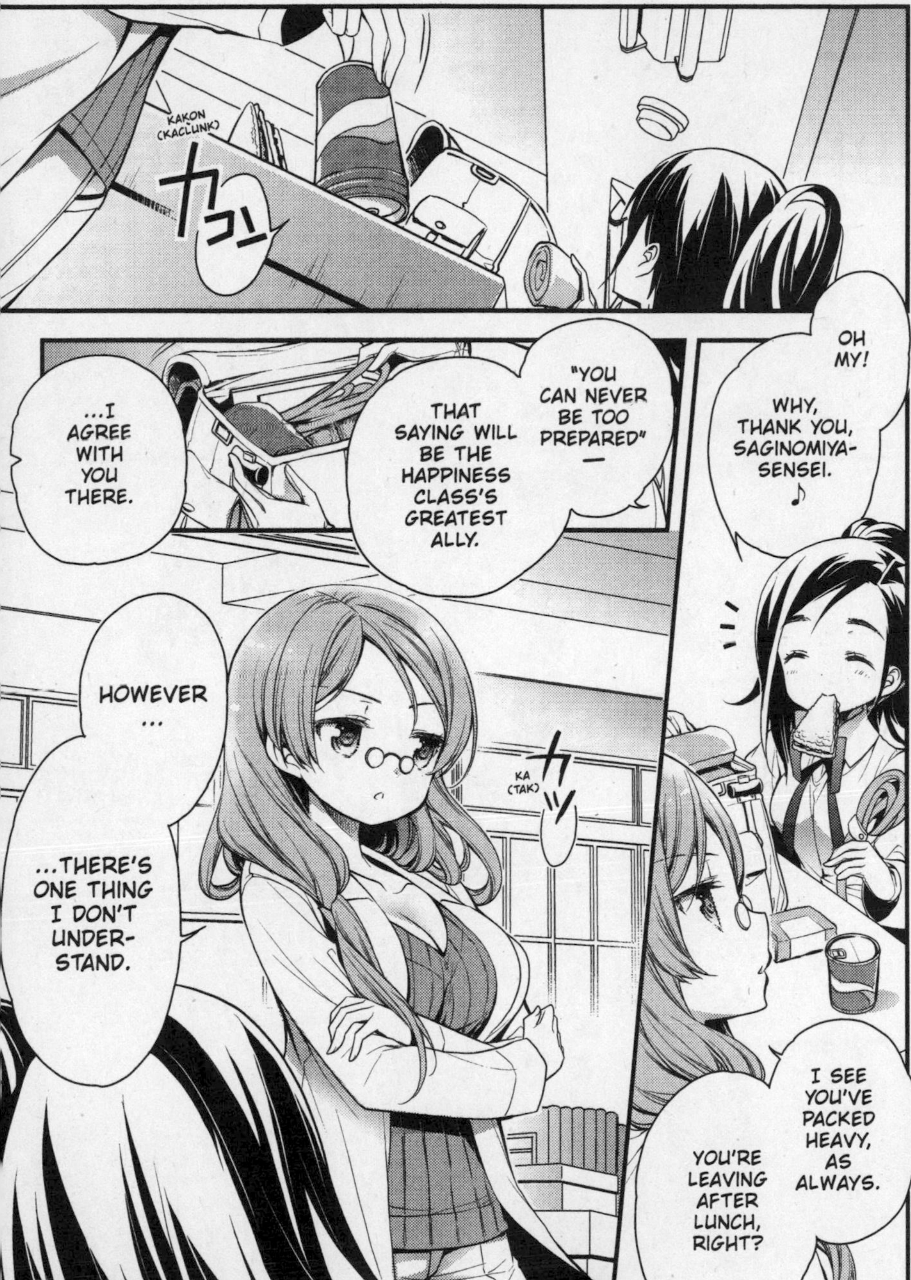
KAKON (KACLUNK)
カコン
OH MY!
WHY, THANK YOU, SAGINOMIYA-SENSEI. ♪
I SEE YOU'VE PACKED HEAVY, AS ALWAYS.
YOU'RE LEAVING AFTER LUNCH, RIGHT?
"YOU CAN NEVER BE TOO PREPARED"—
THAT SAYING WILL BE THE HAPPINESS CLASS'S GREATEST ALLY.
...I AGREE WITH YOU THERE.
KA (TAK)
カッ
HOWEVER...
...THERE'S ONE THING I DON'T UNDER-STAND.

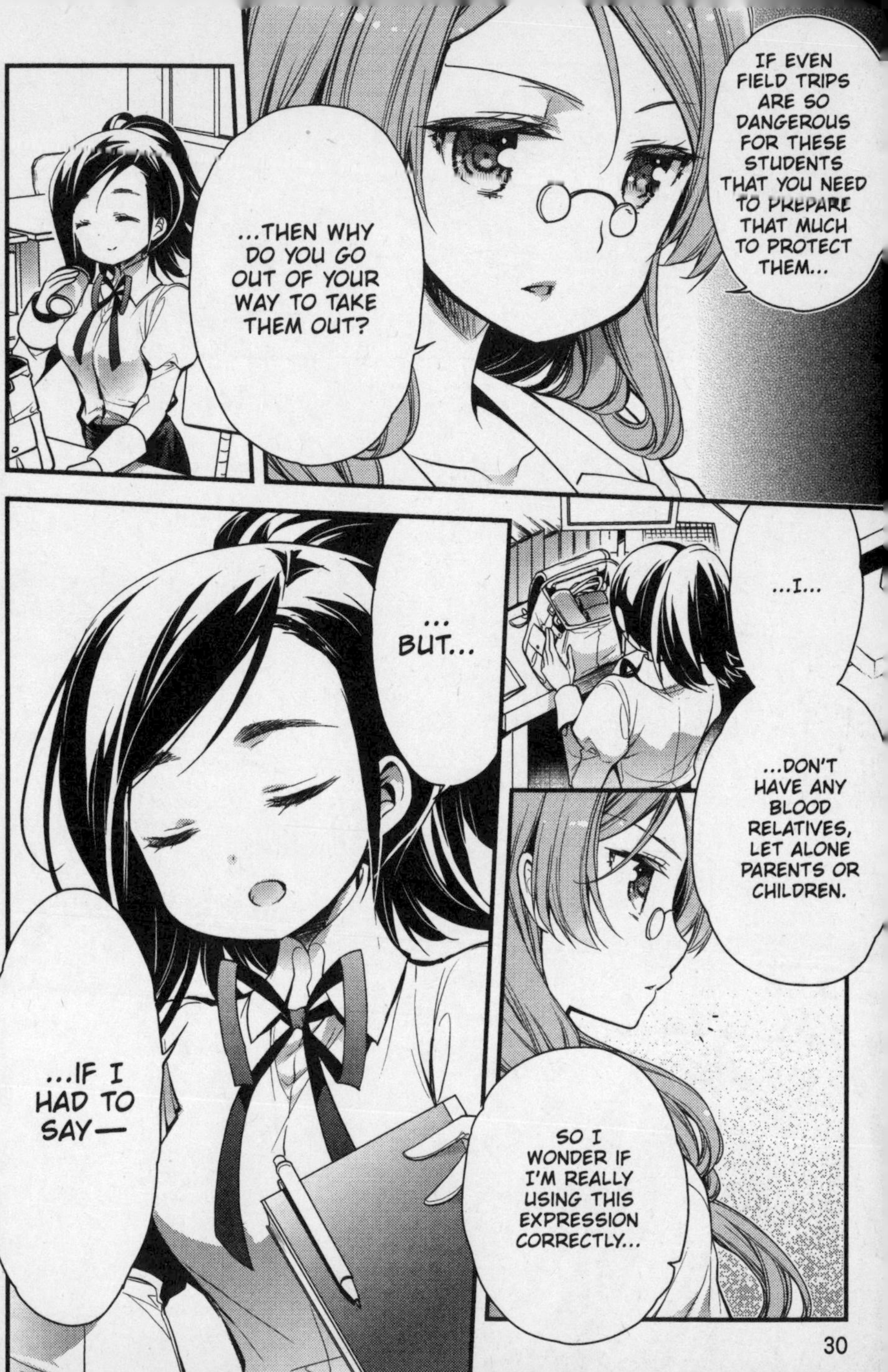
IF EVEN FIELD TRIPS ARE SO DANGEROUS FOR THESE STUDENTS THAT YOU NEED TO PREPARE THAT MUCH TO PROTECT THEM...
...THEN WHY DO YOU GO OUT OF YOUR WAY TO TAKE THEM OUT?
...I...
...DON'T HAVE ANY BLOOD RELATIVES, LET ALONE PARENTS OR CHILDREN.
SO I WONDER IF I'M REALLY USING THIS EXPRESSION CORRECTLY...
... BUT...
...IF I HAD TO SAY—

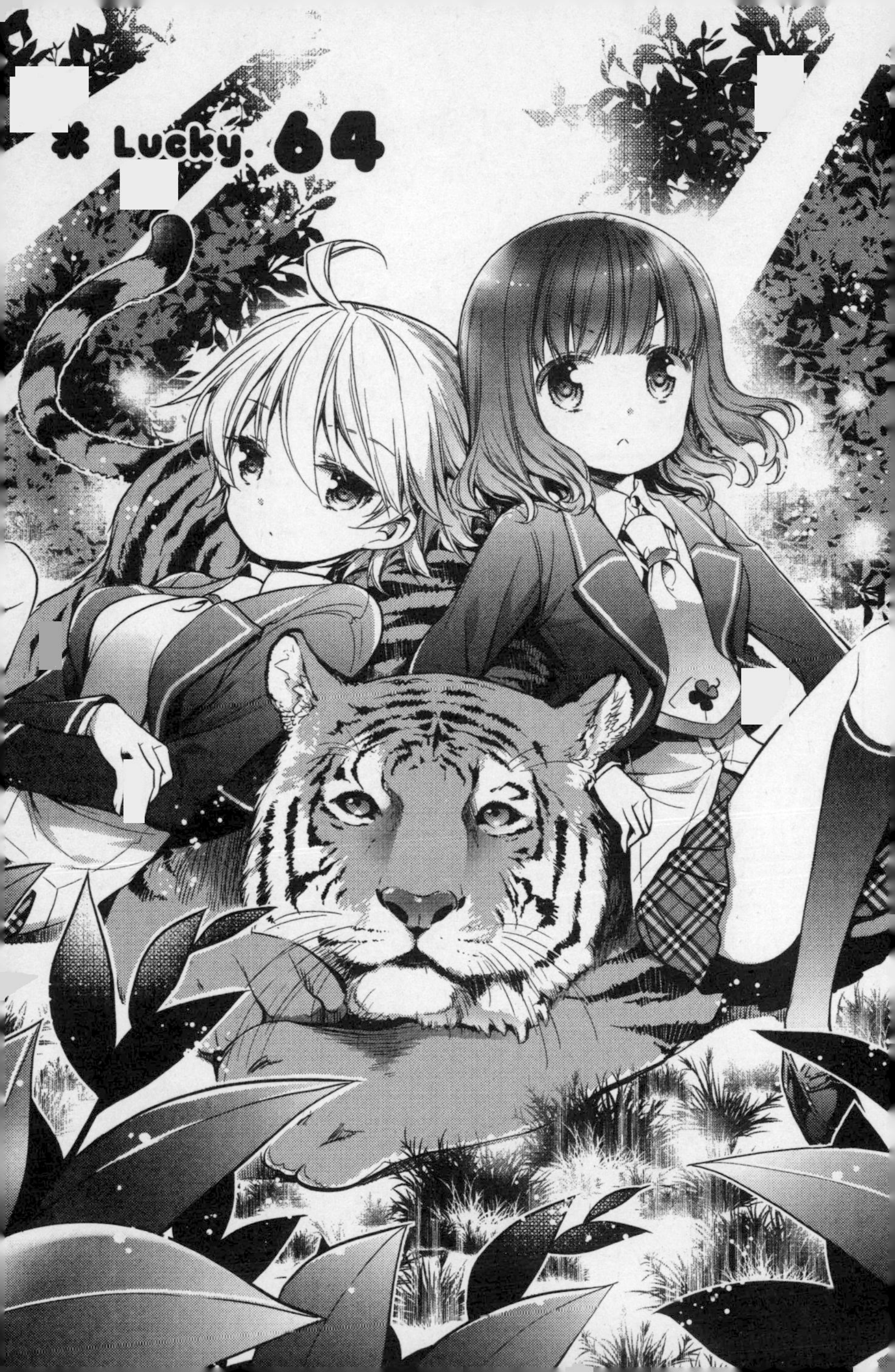
Lucky. 64

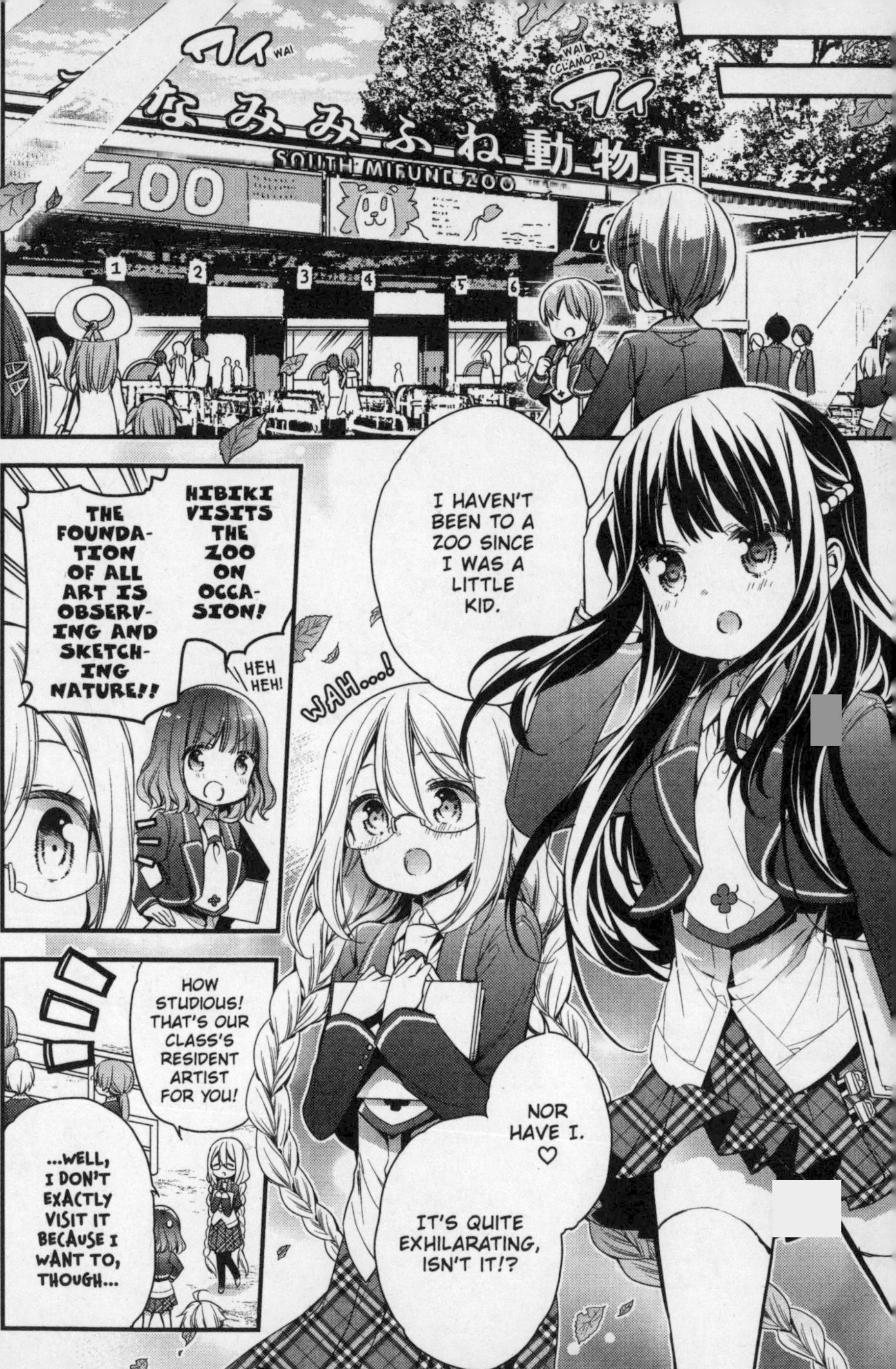
WAI
WAI (CLAMOR)
SOUTH MIFUNE ZOO
ZOO
I HAVEN'T BEEN TO A ZOO SINCE I WAS A LITTLE KID.
WAHooo!
NOR HAVE I. ♡
IT'S QUITE EXHILARATING, ISN'T IT!?
HIBIKI VISITS THE ZOO ON OCCASION!
THE FOUNDATION OF ALL ART IS OBSERVING AND SKETCHING NATURE!!
HEH HEH!
HOW STUDIOUS! THAT'S OUR CLASS'S RESIDENT ARTIST FOR YOU!
...WELL, I DON'T EXACTLY VISIT IT BECAUSE I WANT TO, THOUGH...

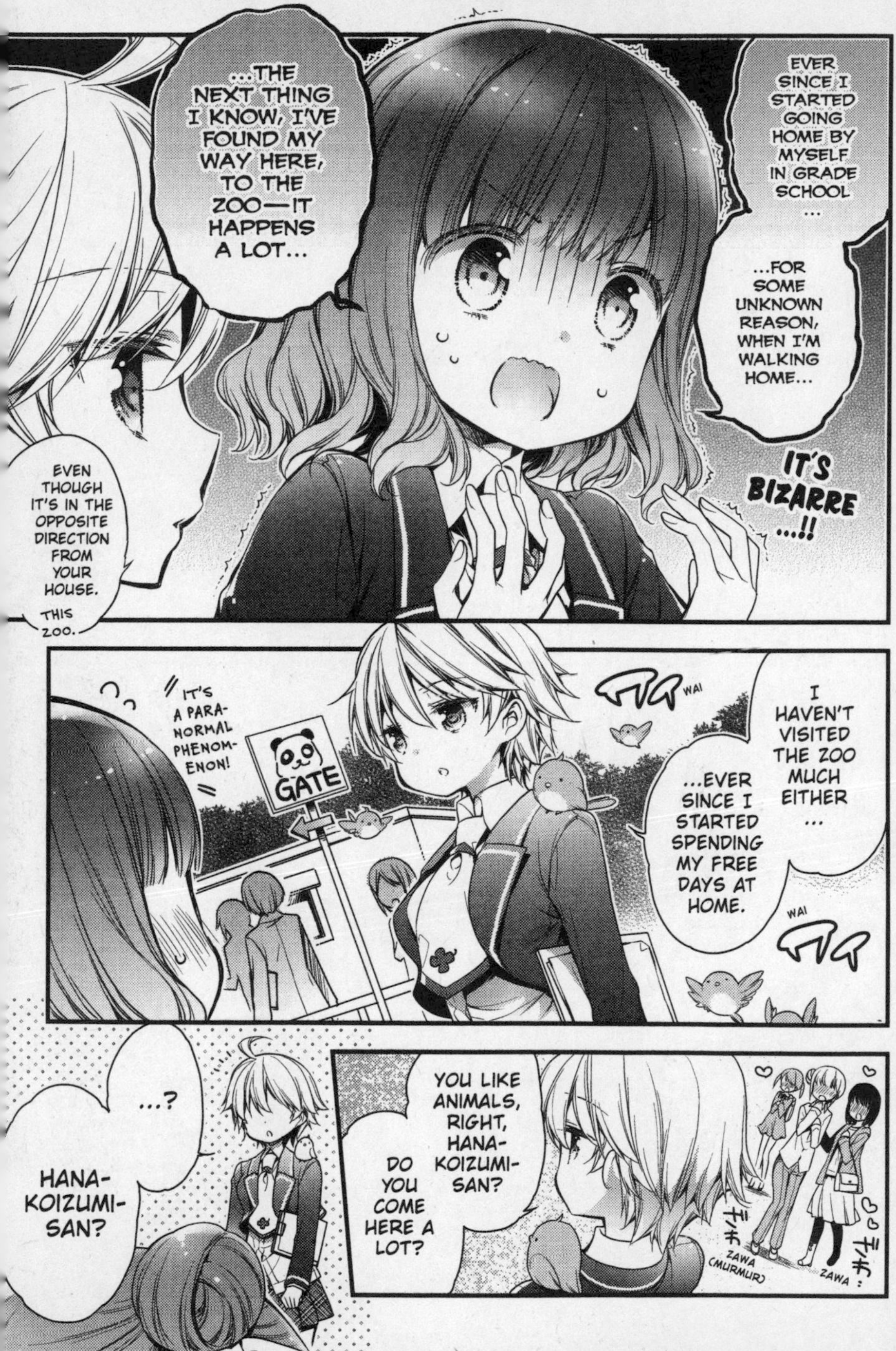
EVER SINCE I STARTED GOING HOME BY MYSELF IN GRADE SCHOOL...
...FOR SOME UNKNOWN REASON, WHEN I'M WALKING HOME...
IT'S BIZARRE...!!
...THE NEXT THING I KNOW, I'VE FOUND MY WAY HERE, TO THE ZOO—IT HAPPENS A LOT...
EVEN THOUGH IT'S IN THE OPPOSITE DIRECTION FROM YOUR HOUSE.
THIS ZOO.
WAI
I HAVEN'T VISITED THE ZOO MUCH EITHER...
...EVER SINCE I STARTED SPENDING MY FREE DAYS AT HOME.
WAI
IT'S A PARANORMAL PHENOMENON!
GATE
YOU LIKE ANIMALS, RIGHT, HANAKOIZUMI-SAN?
DO YOU COME HERE A LOT?
ZAWA
ZAWA (MURMUR)
...?
HANAKOIZUMI-SAN?

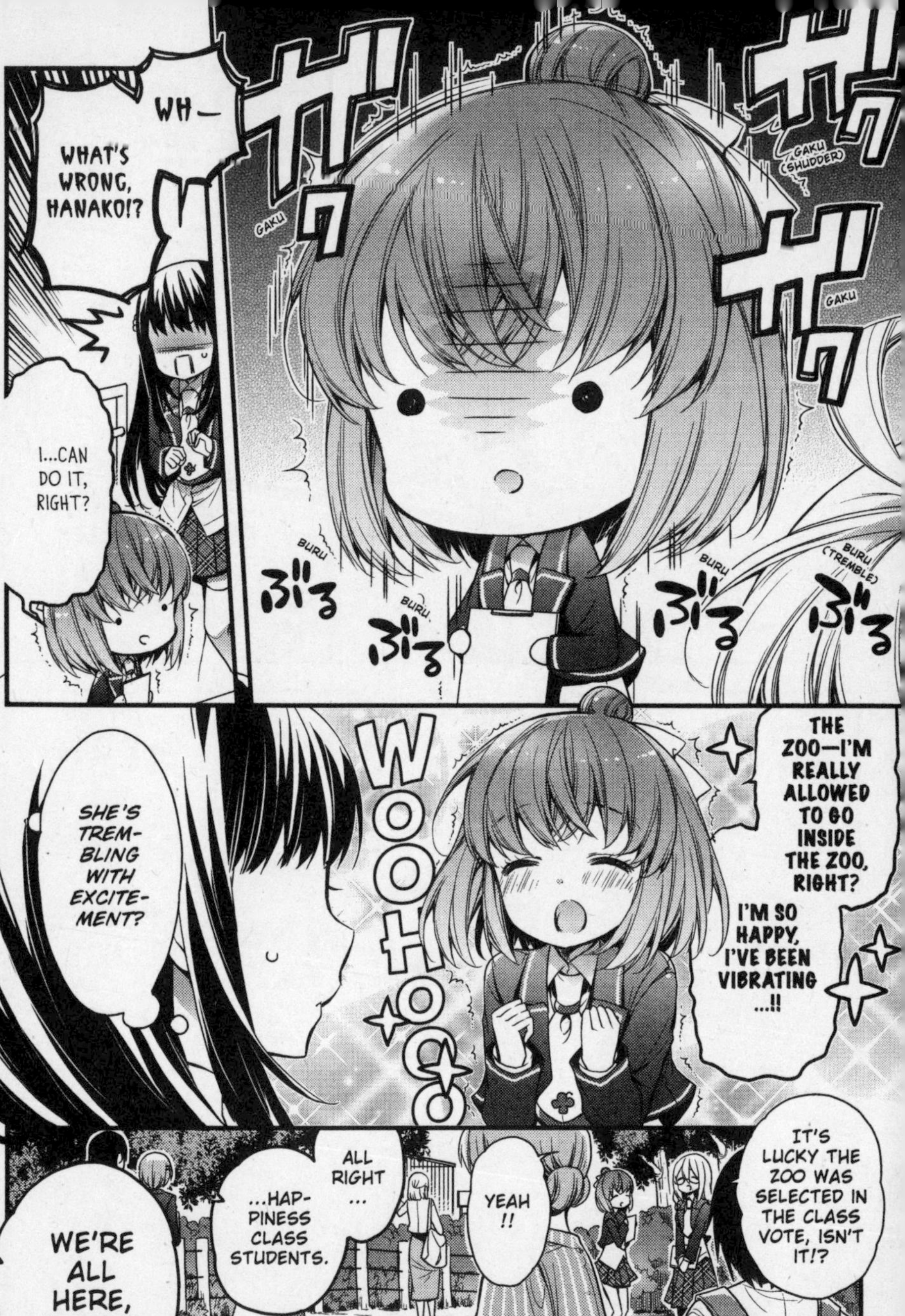
GAKU
GAKU (SHUDDER)
GAKU
BURU
BURU
BURU
BURU (TREMBLE)
WH—
WHAT'S WRONG, HANAKO!?
I...CAN DO IT, RIGHT?
THE ZOO—I'M REALLY ALLOWED TO GO INSIDE THE ZOO, RIGHT?
I'M SO HAPPY, I'VE BEEN VIBRATING ...!!
WOOHOO
SHE'S TREM-BLING WITH EXCITE-MENT?
IT'S LUCKY THE ZOO WAS SELECTED IN THE CLASS VOTE, ISN'T IT!?
YEAH !!
ALL RIGHT ...
...HAP-PINESS CLASS STUDENTS.
WE'RE ALL HERE, RIGHT?

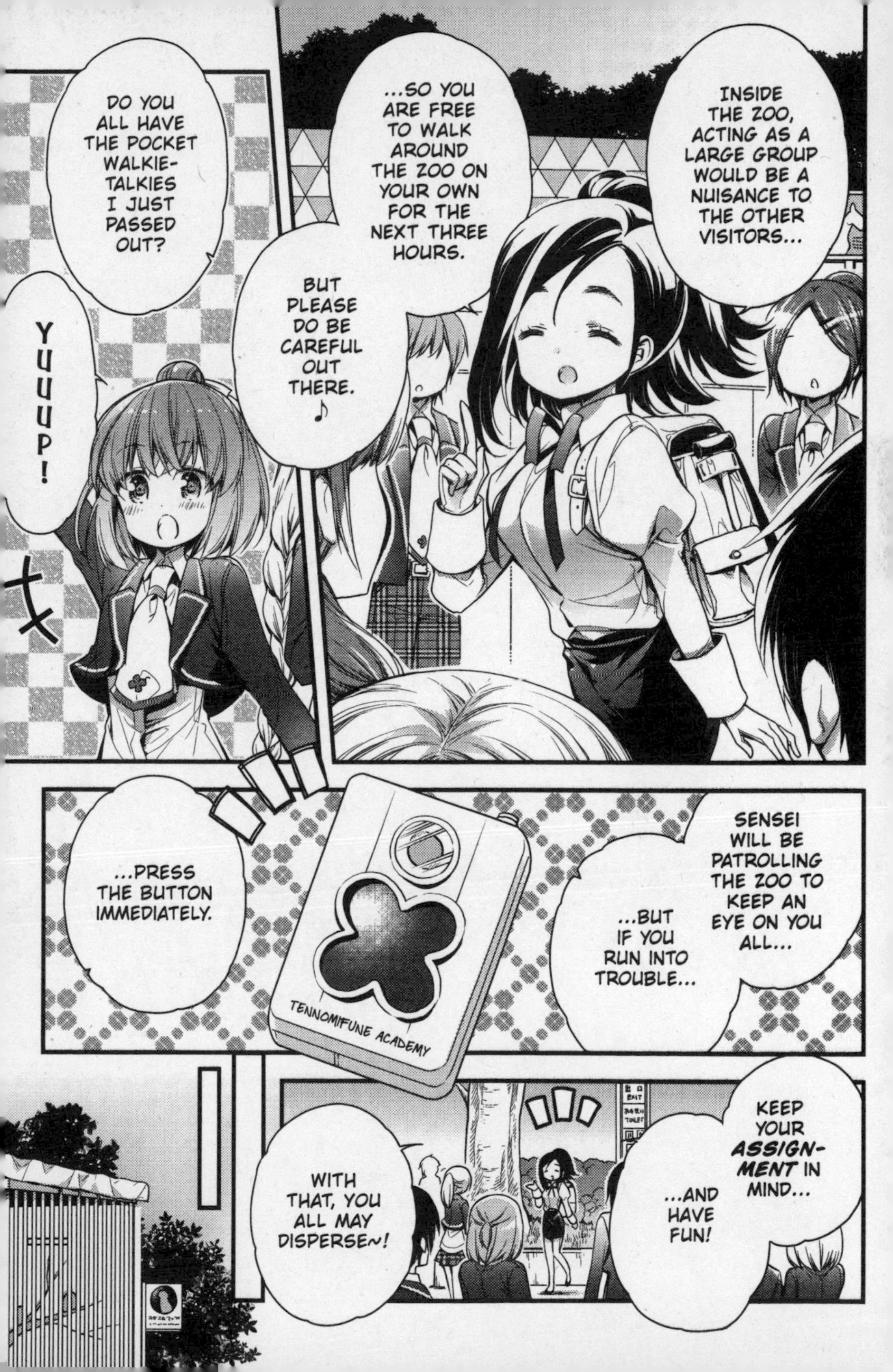
INSIDE THE ZOO, ACTING AS A LARGE GROUP WOULD BE A NUISANCE TO THE OTHER VISITORS...
...SO YOU ARE FREE TO WALK AROUND THE ZOO ON YOUR OWN FOR THE NEXT THREE HOURS.
BUT PLEASE DO BE CAREFUL OUT THERE. ♪
DO YOU ALL HAVE THE POCKET WALKIE-TALKIES I JUST PASSED OUT?
YUUUP!
SENSEI WILL BE PATROLLING THE ZOO TO KEEP AN EYE ON YOU ALL...
...BUT IF YOU RUN INTO TROUBLE...
...PRESS THE BUTTON IMMEDIATELY.
TENNOMIFUNE ACADEMY
KEEP YOUR ***ASSIGNMENT*** IN MIND...
...AND HAVE FUN!
WITH THAT, YOU ALL MAY DISPERSE~!

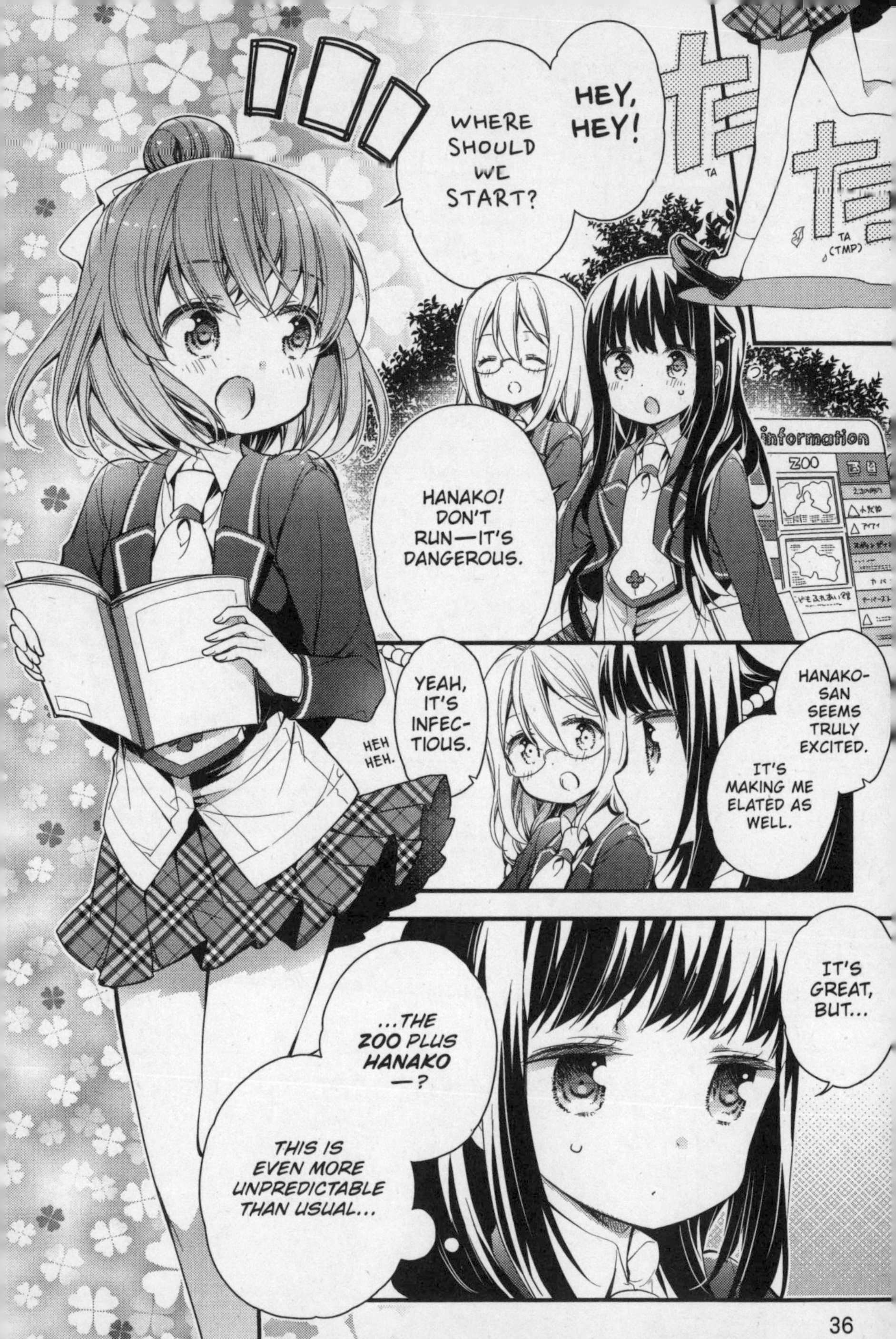
TA
TA (TMP)
HEY, HEY!
WHERE SHOULD WE START?
information
ZOO
HANAKO! DON'T RUN—IT'S DANGEROUS.
HANAKO-SAN SEEMS TRULY EXCITED.
IT'S MAKING ME ELATED AS WELL.
YEAH, IT'S INFECTIOUS.
HEH HEH.
IT'S GREAT, BUT...
...THE ZOO PLUS HANAKO—?
THIS IS EVEN MORE UNPREDICTABLE THAN USUAL...

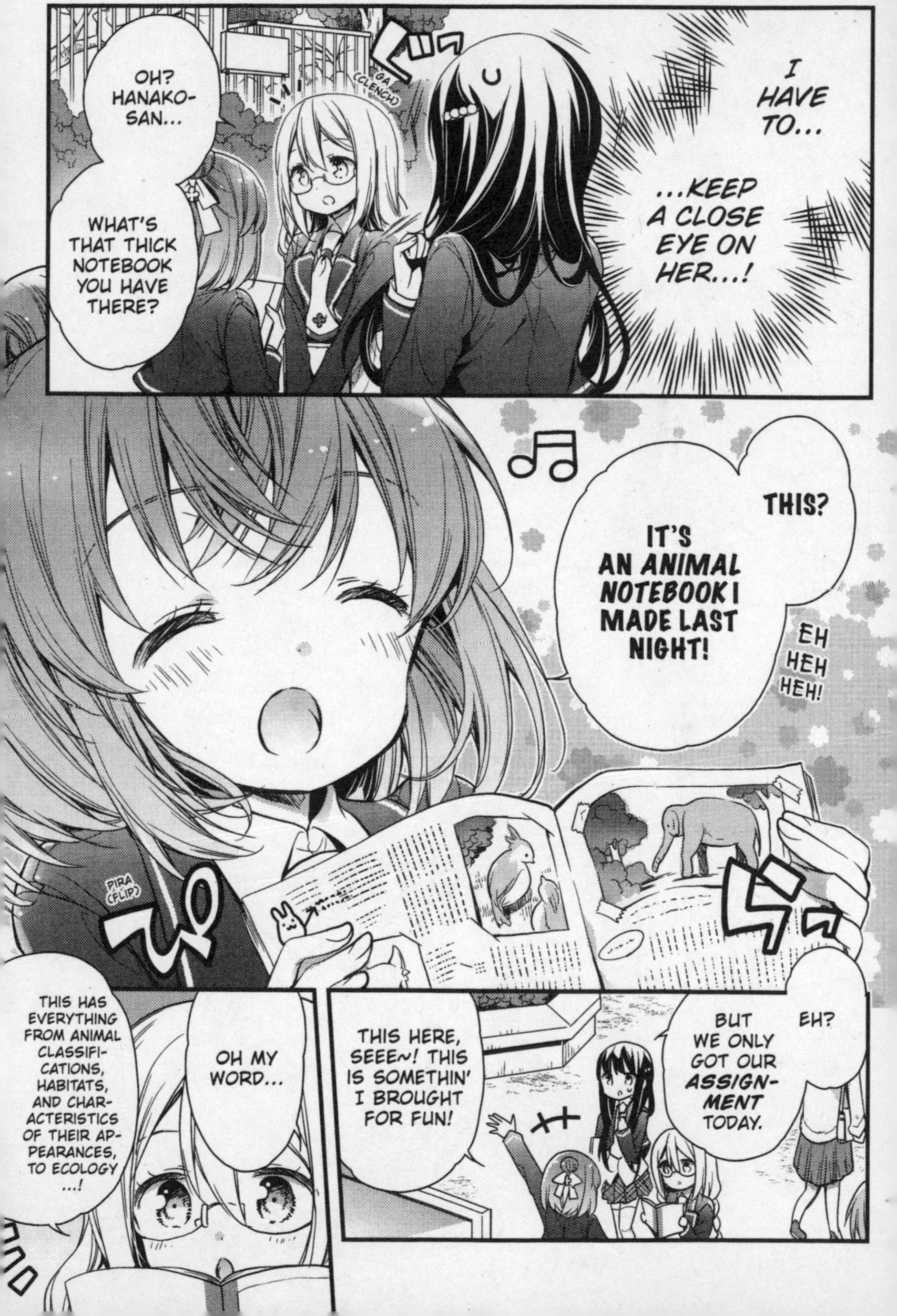
I HAVE TO...
...KEEP A CLOSE EYE ON HER...!
GA (CLENCH)
OH? HANAKO-SAN...
WHAT'S THAT THICK NOTEBOOK YOU HAVE THERE?
THIS?
IT'S AN ANIMAL NOTEBOOK I MADE LAST NIGHT!
EH HEH HEH!
PIRA (FLIP)
EH?
BUT WE ONLY GOT OUR ASSIGNMENT TODAY.
THIS HERE, SEEE~! THIS IS SOMETHIN' I BROUGHT FOR FUN!
OH MY WORD...
THIS HAS EVERYTHING FROM ANIMAL CLASSIFICATIONS, HABITATS, AND CHARACTERISTICS OF THEIR APPEARANCES, TO ECOLOGY ...!

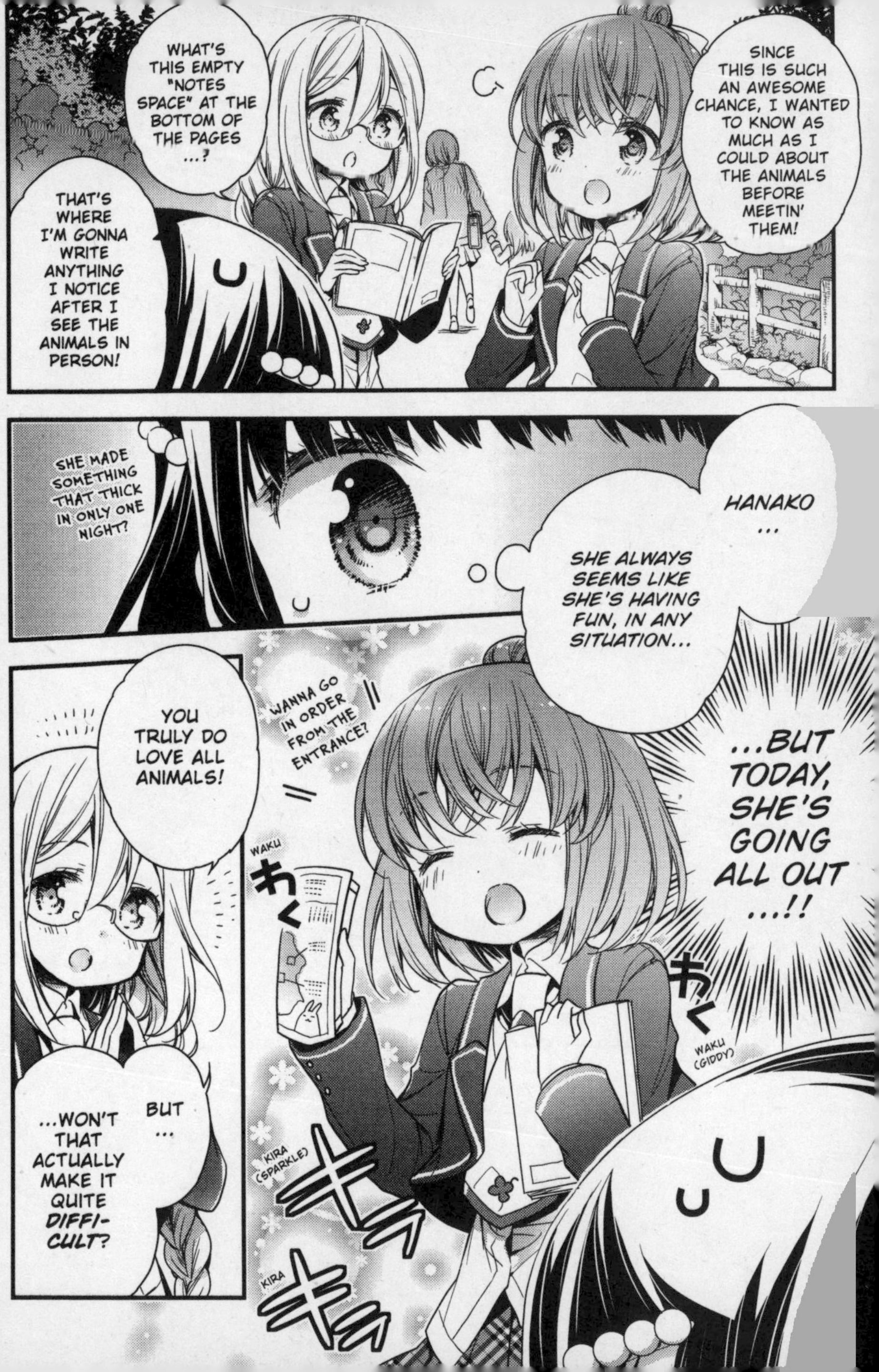
SINCE THIS IS SUCH AN AWESOME CHANCE, I WANTED TO KNOW AS MUCH AS I COULD ABOUT THE ANIMALS BEFORE MEETIN' THEM!
WHAT'S THIS EMPTY "NOTES SPACE" AT THE BOTTOM OF THE PAGES ...?
THAT'S WHERE I'M GONNA WRITE ANYTHING I NOTICE AFTER I SEE THE ANIMALS IN PERSON!
HANAKO ...
SHE ALWAYS SEEMS LIKE SHE'S HAVING FUN, IN ANY SITUATION...
SHE MADE SOMETHING THAT THICK IN ONLY ONE NIGHT?
...BUT TODAY, SHE'S GOING ALL OUT ...!!
WAKU (GIDDY)
WANNA GO IN ORDER FROM THE ENTRANCE?
WAKU
KIRA (SPARKLE)
KIRA
YOU TRULY DO LOVE ALL ANIMALS!
BUT ...
...WON'T THAT ACTUALLY MAKE IT QUITE DIFFI-CULT?

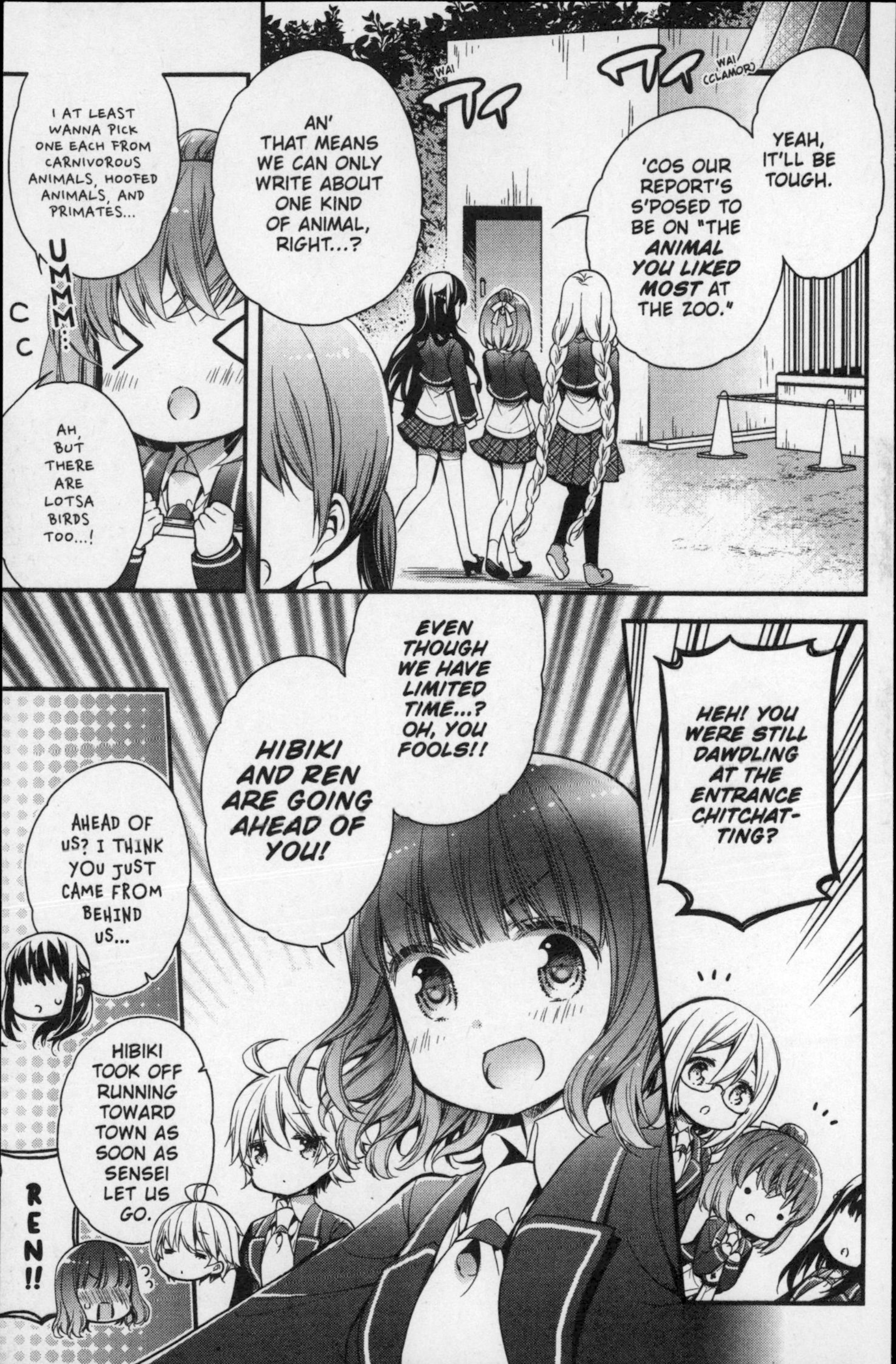
WAI WAI (CLAMOR)
YEAH, IT'LL BE TOUGH.
'COS OUR REPORT'S S'POSED TO BE ON "THE *ANIMAL YOU LIKED MOST* AT THE ZOO."
AN' THAT MEANS WE CAN ONLY WRITE ABOUT ONE KIND OF ANIMAL, RIGHT...?
I AT LEAST WANNA PICK ONE EACH FROM CARNIVOROUS ANIMALS, HOOFED ANIMALS, AND PRIMATES...
UMMM...
AH, BUT THERE ARE LOTSA BIRDS TOO...!
HEH! YOU WERE STILL DAWDLING AT THE ENTRANCE CHITCHAT-TING?
EVEN THOUGH WE HAVE LIMITED TIME...? OH, YOU FOOLS!!
HIBIKI AND REN ARE GOING AHEAD OF YOU!
AHEAD OF US? I THINK YOU JUST CAME FROM BEHIND US...
HIBIKI TOOK OFF RUNNING TOWARD TOWN AS SOON AS SENSEI LET US GO.
REN!!

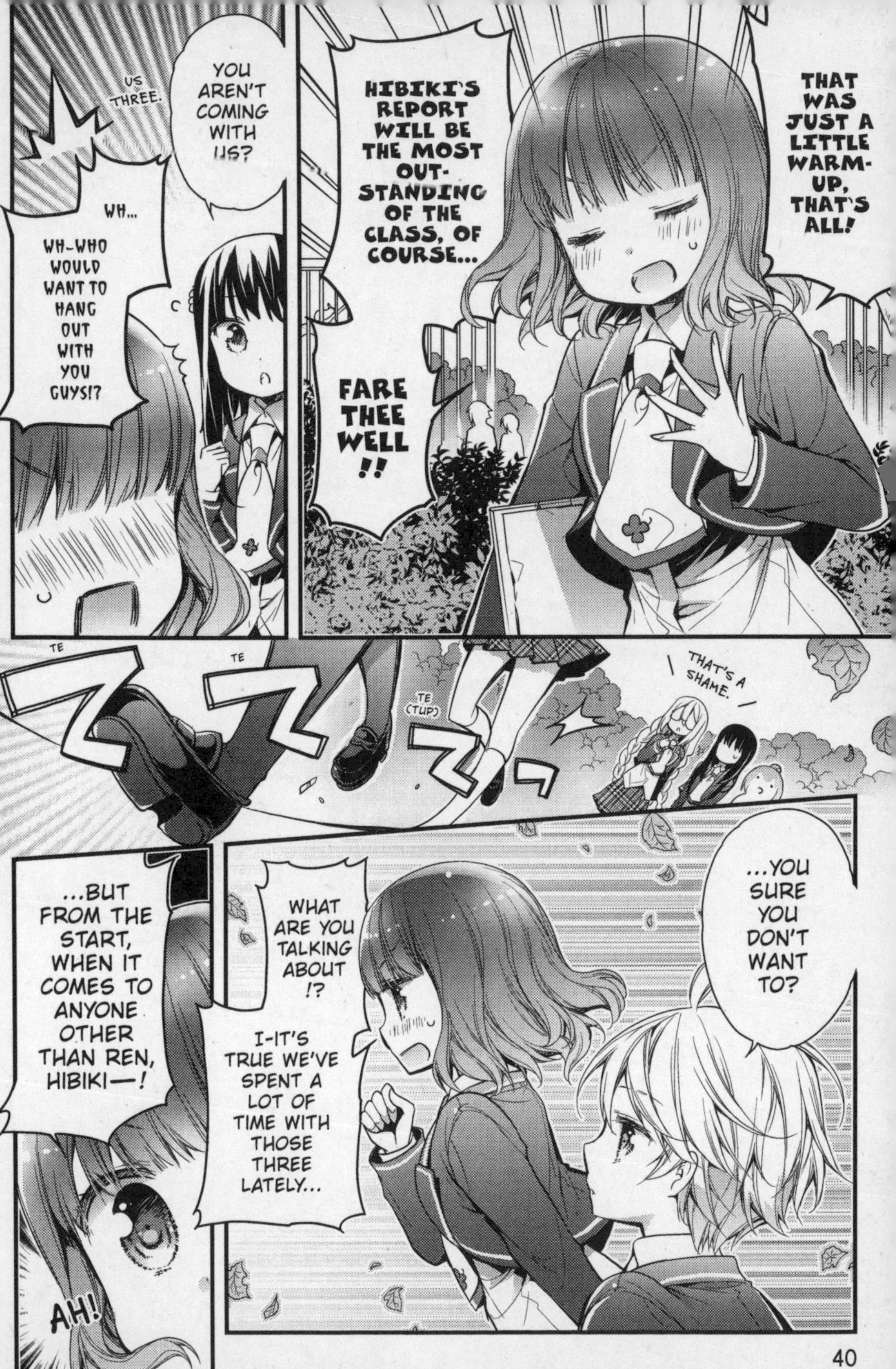
THAT WAS JUST A LITTLE WARM-UP, THAT'S ALL!
HIBIKI'S REPORT WILL BE THE MOST OUT-STANDING OF THE CLASS, OF COURSE...
FARE THEE WELL!!
YOU AREN'T COMING WITH US?
US THREE.
WH...
WH-WHO WOULD WANT TO HANG OUT WITH YOU GUYS!?
THAT'S A SHAME.
TE (TUP)
TE
TE
...YOU SURE YOU DON'T WANT TO?
WHAT ARE YOU TALKING ABOUT!?
I-IT'S TRUE WE'VE SPENT A LOT OF TIME WITH THOSE THREE LATELY...
...BUT FROM THE START, WHEN IT COMES TO ANYONE OTHER THAN REN, HIBIKI—!
AH!

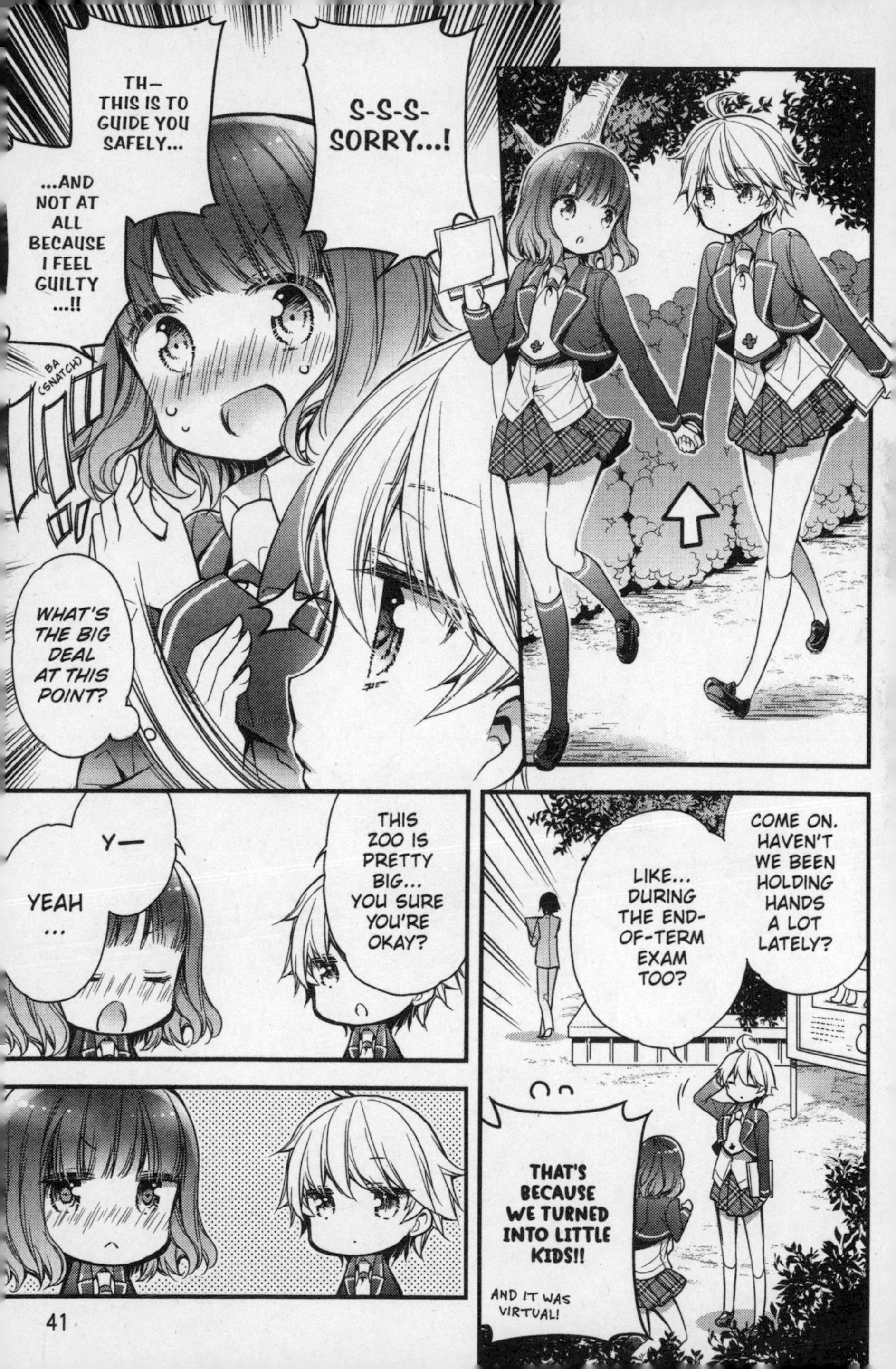
S-S-S-SORRY...!
TH— THIS IS TO GUIDE YOU SAFELY...
...AND NOT AT ALL BECAUSE I FEEL GUILTY ...!!
BA (SNATCH)
WHAT'S THE BIG DEAL AT THIS POINT?
COME ON. HAVEN'T WE BEEN HOLDING HANDS A LOT LATELY?
LIKE... DURING THE END-OF-TERM EXAM TOO?
THAT'S BECAUSE WE TURNED INTO LITTLE KIDS!!
AND IT WAS VIRTUAL!
THIS ZOO IS PRETTY BIG... YOU SURE YOU'RE OKAY?
Y— YEAH ...

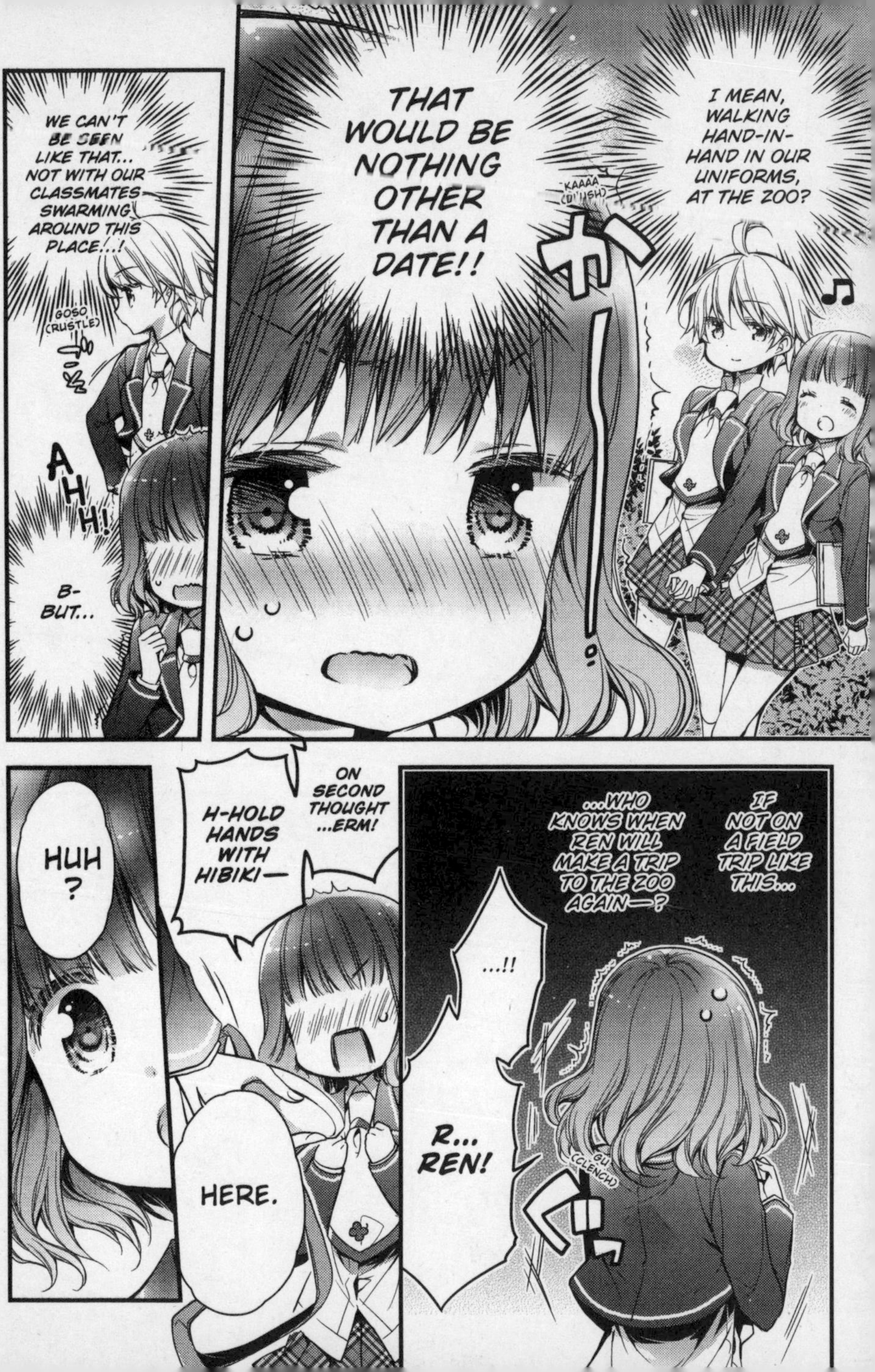
I MEAN, WALKING HAND-IN-HAND IN OUR UNIFORMS, AT THE ZOO?
KAAAA
THAT WOULD BE NOTHING OTHER THAN A DATE!!
WE CAN'T BE SEEN LIKE THAT... NOT WITH OUR CLASSMATES SWARMING AROUND THIS PLACE...!
GOSO (RUSTLE)
AHH!
B-BUT...
IF NOT ON A FIELD TRIP LIKE THIS...
...WHO KNOWS WHEN REN WILL MAKE A TRIP TO THE ZOO AGAIN—?
...!!
GU (CLENCH)
R... REN!
ON SECOND THOUGHT ...ERM!
H-HOLD HANDS WITH HIBIKI—
HUH?
HERE.

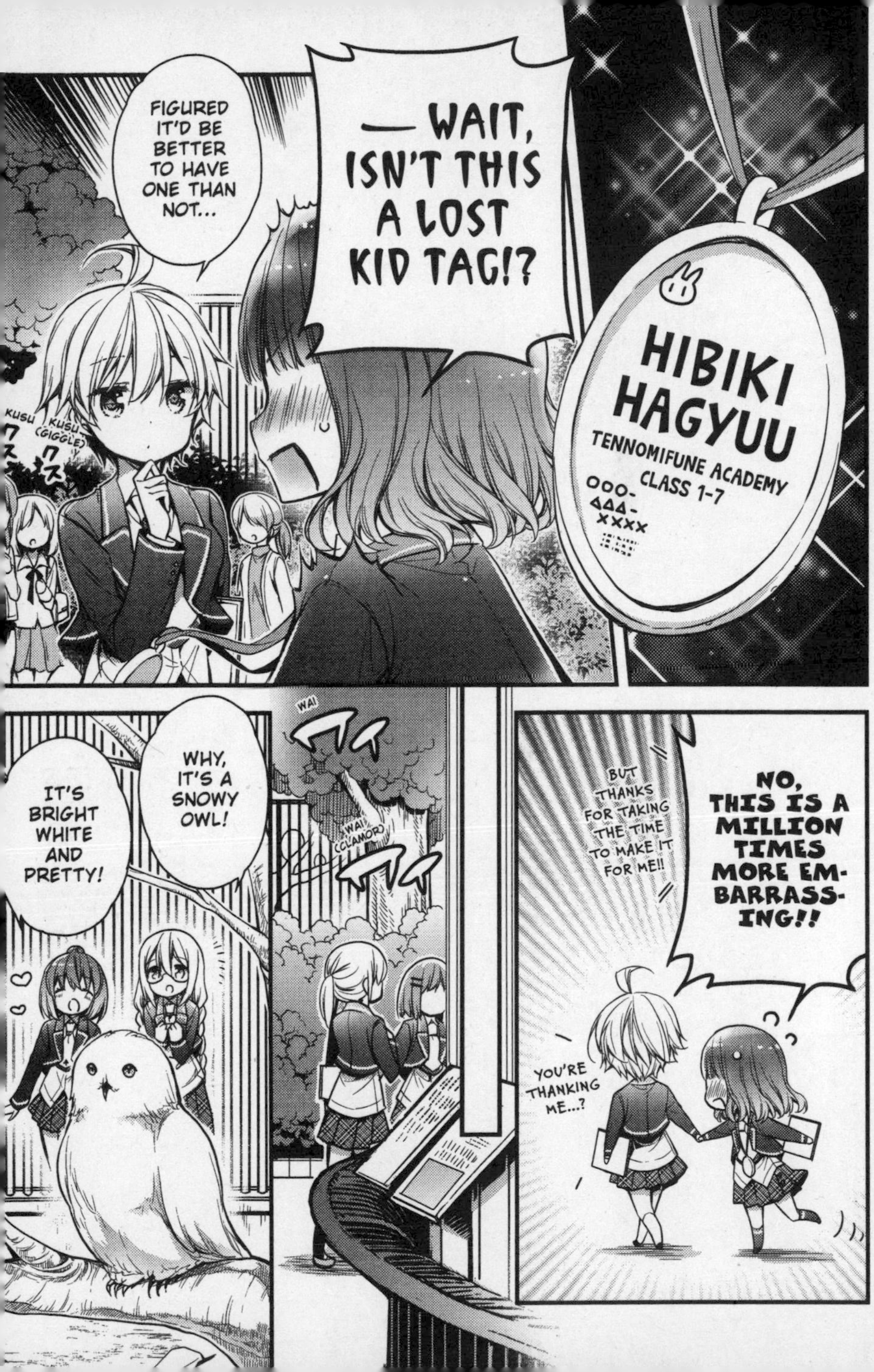
HIBIKI HAGYUU
TENNOMIFUNE ACADEMY CLASS 1-7
○○○-△△△-XXXX
— WAIT, ISN'T THIS A LOST KID TAG!?
FIGURED IT'D BE BETTER TO HAVE ONE THAN NOT...
KUSU KUSU (GIGGLE)
クスクス
NO, THIS IS A MILLION TIMES MORE EM-BARRASS-ING!!
BUT THANKS FOR TAKING THE TIME TO MAKE IT FOR ME!!
YOU'RE THANKING ME...?
WAI
WAI (CLAMOR)
WHY, IT'S A SNOWY OWL!
IT'S BRIGHT WHITE AND PRETTY!

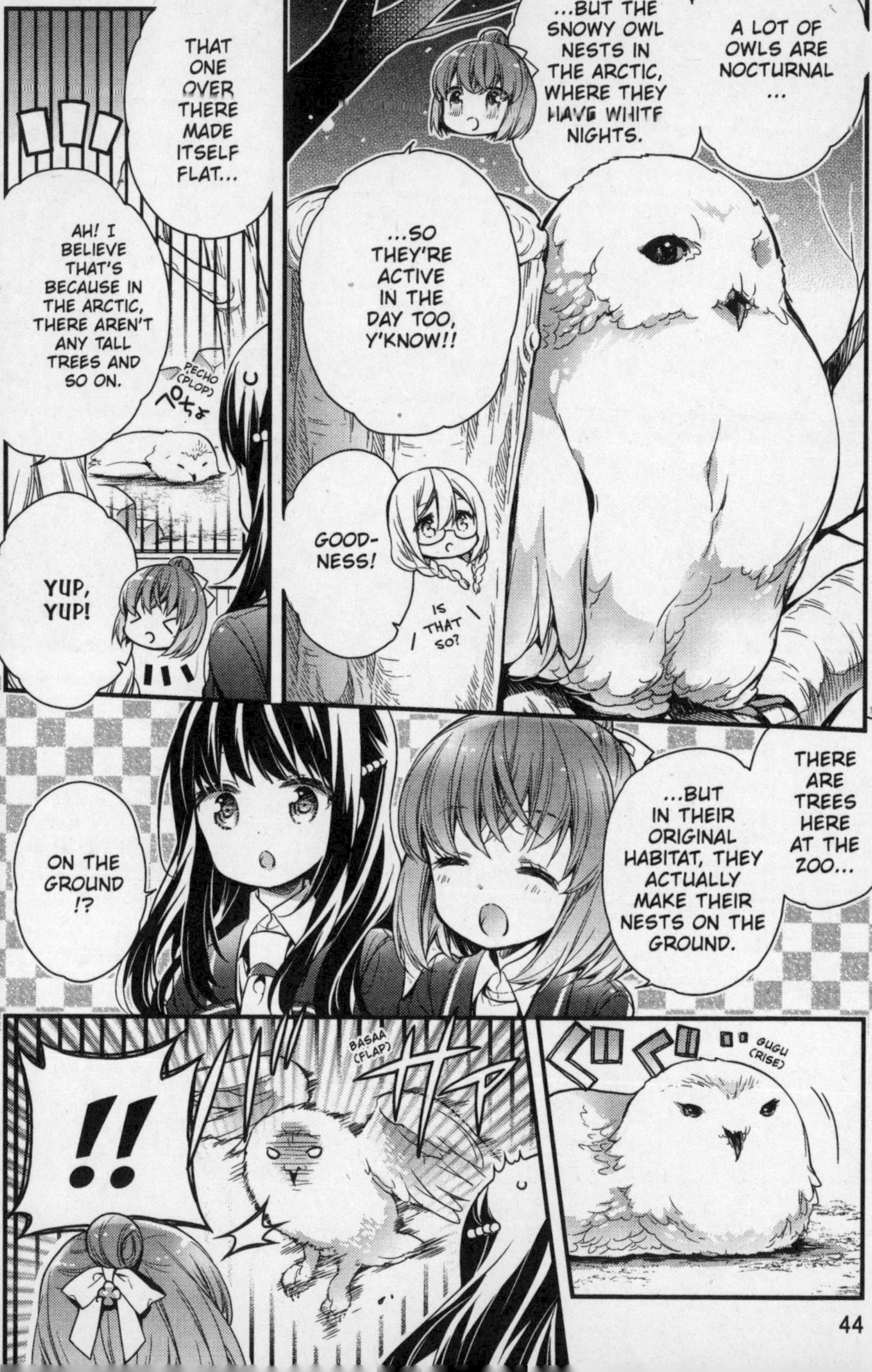
A LOT OF OWLS ARE NOCTURNAL...
...BUT THE SNOWY OWL NESTS IN THE ARCTIC, WHERE THEY HAVE WHITE NIGHTS.
...SO THEY'RE ACTIVE IN THE DAY TOO, Y'KNOW!!
GOOD-NESS!
IS THAT SO?
THAT ONE OVER THERE MADE ITSELF FLAT...
AH! I BELIEVE THAT'S BECAUSE IN THE ARCTIC, THERE AREN'T ANY TALL TREES AND SO ON.
PECHO (PLOP)
YUP, YUP!
THERE ARE TREES HERE AT THE ZOO...
...BUT IN THEIR ORIGINAL HABITAT, THEY ACTUALLY MAKE THEIR NESTS ON THE GROUND.
ON THE GROUND!?
GUGU (RISE)
BASAA (FLAP)
!!

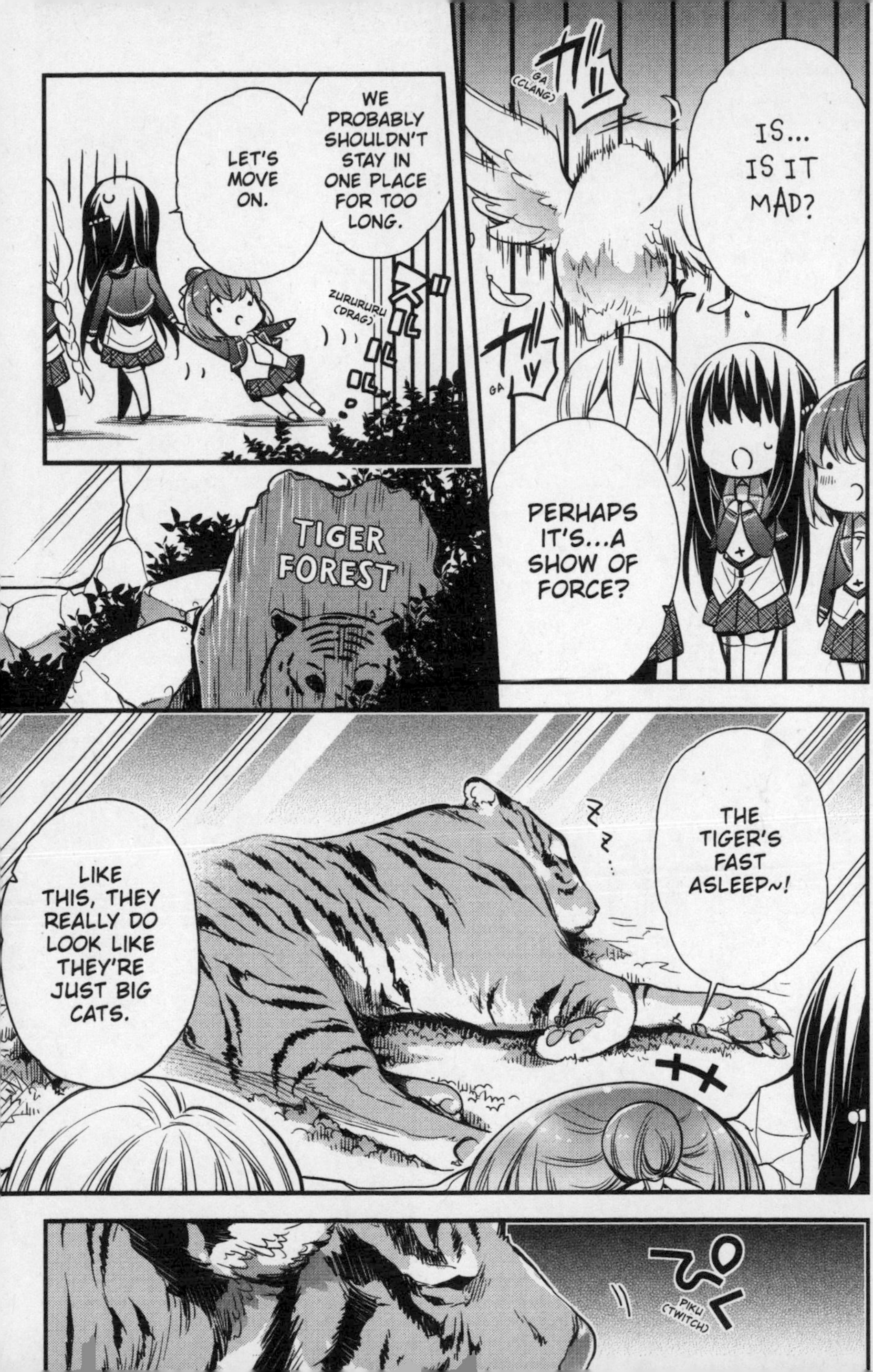
GA (CLANG)
IS... IS IT MAD?
GA
PERHAPS IT'S...A SHOW OF FORCE?
WE PROBABLY SHOULDN'T STAY IN ONE PLACE FOR TOO LONG.
LET'S MOVE ON.
ZURURURU (DRAG)
TIGER FOREST
THE TIGER'S FAST ASLEEP~!
Z Z...
LIKE THIS, THEY REALLY DO LOOK LIKE THEY'RE JUST BIG CATS.
PIKU (TWITCH)

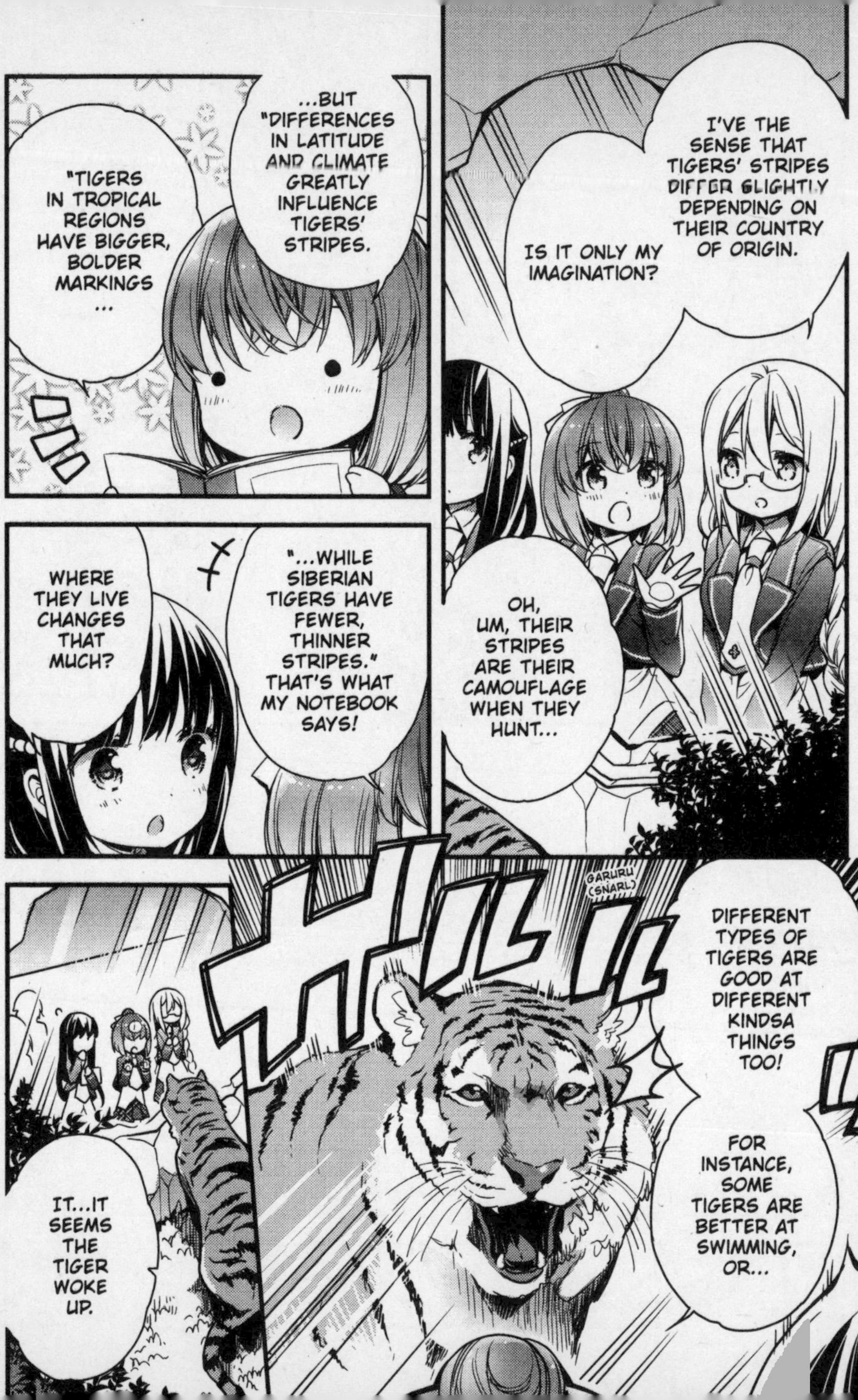
I'VE THE SENSE THAT TIGERS' STRIPES DIFFER SLIGHTLY DEPENDING ON THEIR COUNTRY OF ORIGIN.
IS IT ONLY MY IMAGINATION?
OH, UM, THEIR STRIPES ARE THEIR CAMOUFLAGE WHEN THEY HUNT...
...BUT "DIFFERENCES IN LATITUDE AND CLIMATE GREATLY INFLUENCE TIGERS' STRIPES.
"TIGERS IN TROPICAL REGIONS HAVE BIGGER, BOLDER MARKINGS...
"...WHILE SIBERIAN TIGERS HAVE FEWER, THINNER STRIPES." THAT'S WHAT MY NOTEBOOK SAYS!
WHERE THEY LIVE CHANGES THAT MUCH?
GARURU (SNARL)
DIFFERENT TYPES OF TIGERS ARE GOOD AT DIFFERENT KINDSA THINGS TOO!
FOR INSTANCE, SOME TIGERS ARE BETTER AT SWIMMING, OR...
IT...IT SEEMS THE TIGER WOKE UP.

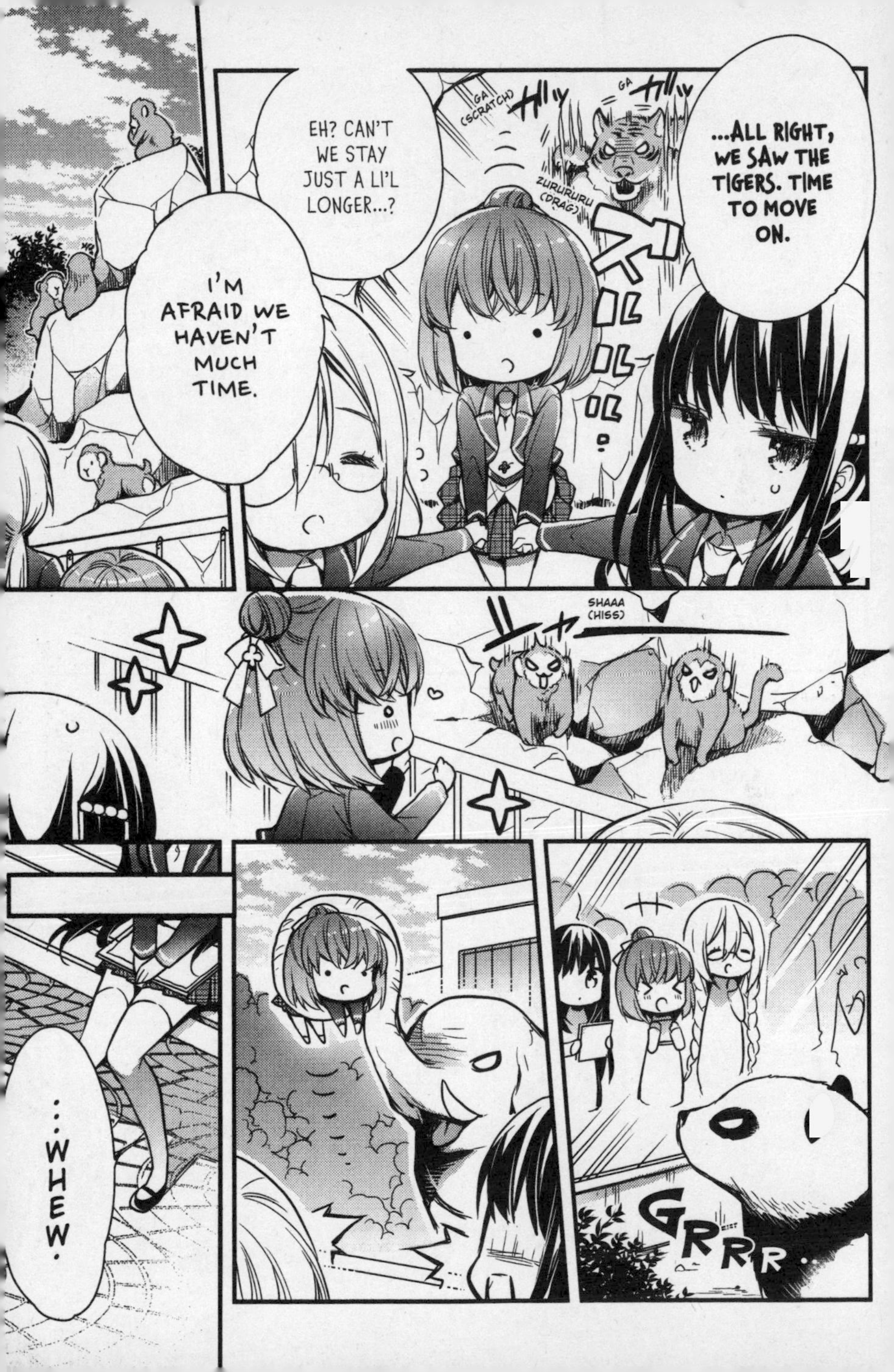
...ALL RIGHT, WE SAW THE TIGERS. TIME TO MOVE ON.
GA
GA (SCRATCH)
ZURURURU (DRAG)
EH? CAN'T WE STAY JUST A LI'L LONGER...?
I'M AFRAID WE HAVEN'T MUCH TIME.
SHAAA (HISS)
GRRRR
...WHEW.

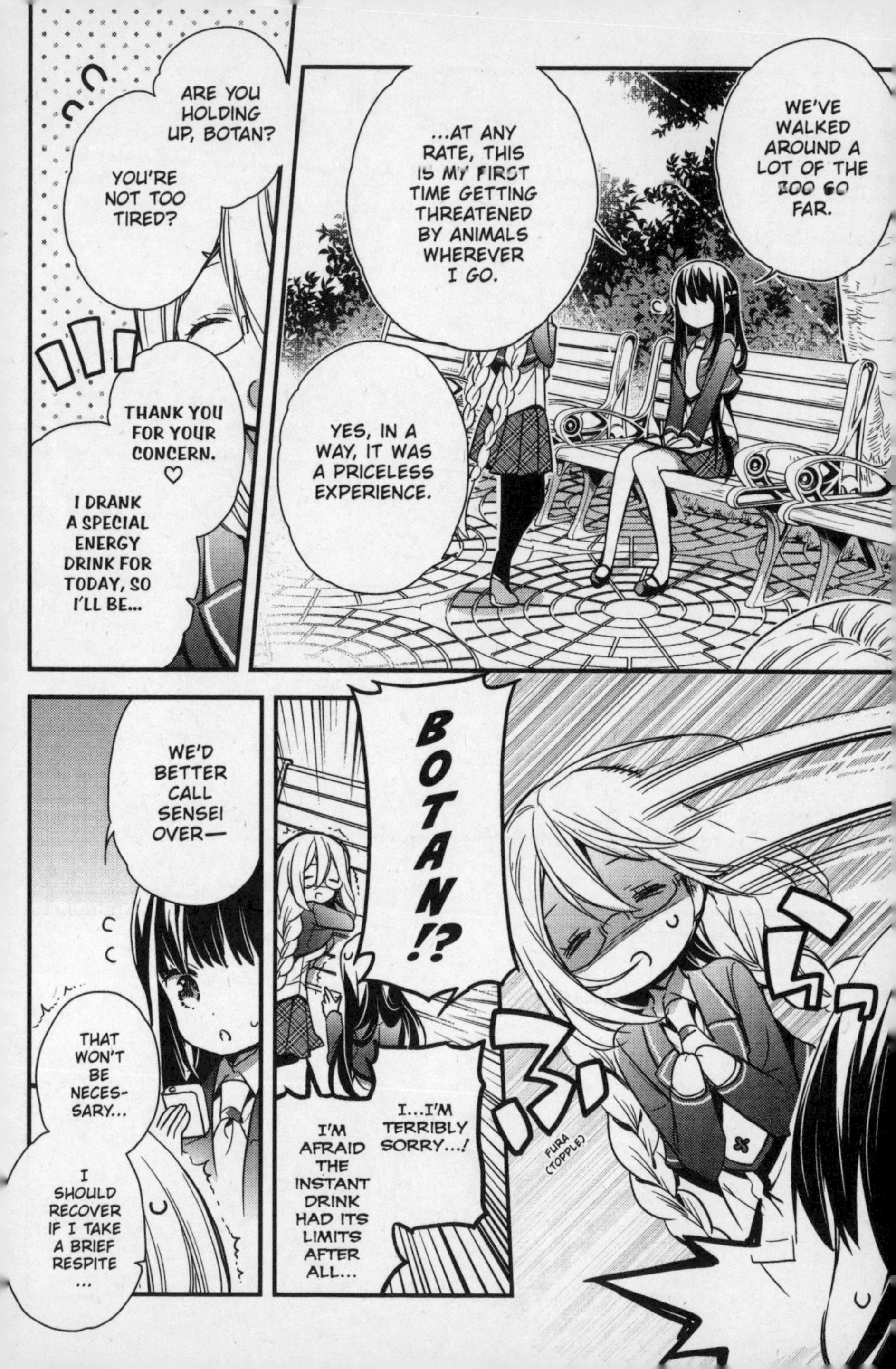
WE'VE WALKED AROUND A LOT OF THE ZOO SO FAR.
...AT ANY RATE, THIS IS MY FIRST TIME GETTING THREATENED BY ANIMALS WHEREVER I GO.
YES, IN A WAY, IT WAS A PRICELESS EXPERIENCE.
ARE YOU HOLDING UP, BOTAN?
YOU'RE NOT TOO TIRED?
THANK YOU FOR YOUR CONCERN. ♡
I DRANK A SPECIAL ENERGY DRINK FOR TODAY, SO I'LL BE...
FURA (TOPPLE)
BOTAN!?
I...I'M TERRIBLY SORRY...!
I'M AFRAID THE INSTANT DRINK HAD ITS LIMITS AFTER ALL...
WE'D BETTER CALL SENSEI OVER—
THAT WON'T BE NECES-SARY...
I SHOULD RECOVER IF I TAKE A BRIEF RESPITE ...

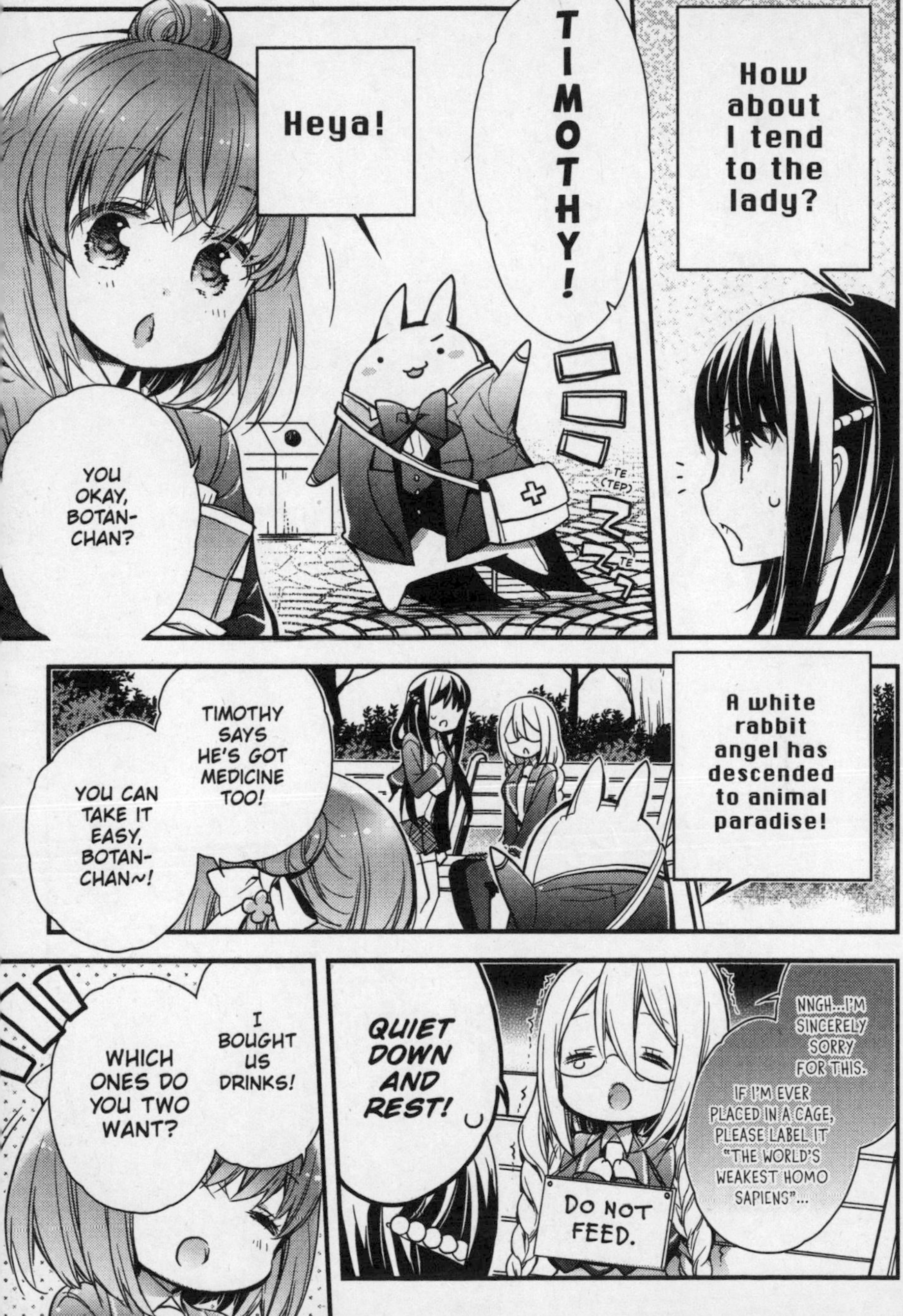
How about I tend to the lady?
TIMOTHY!
Heya!
TE (TEP)
TE
YOU OKAY, BOTAN-CHAN?
A white rabbit angel has descended to animal paradise!
TIMOTHY SAYS HE'S GOT MEDICINE TOO!
YOU CAN TAKE IT EASY, BOTAN-CHAN~!
NNGH...I'M SINCERELY SORRY FOR THIS.
IF I'M EVER PLACED IN A CAGE, PLEASE LABEL IT "THE WORLD'S WEAKEST HOMO SAPIENS"...
QUIET DOWN AND REST!
DO NOT FEED.
I BOUGHT US DRINKS!
WHICH ONES DO YOU TWO WANT?

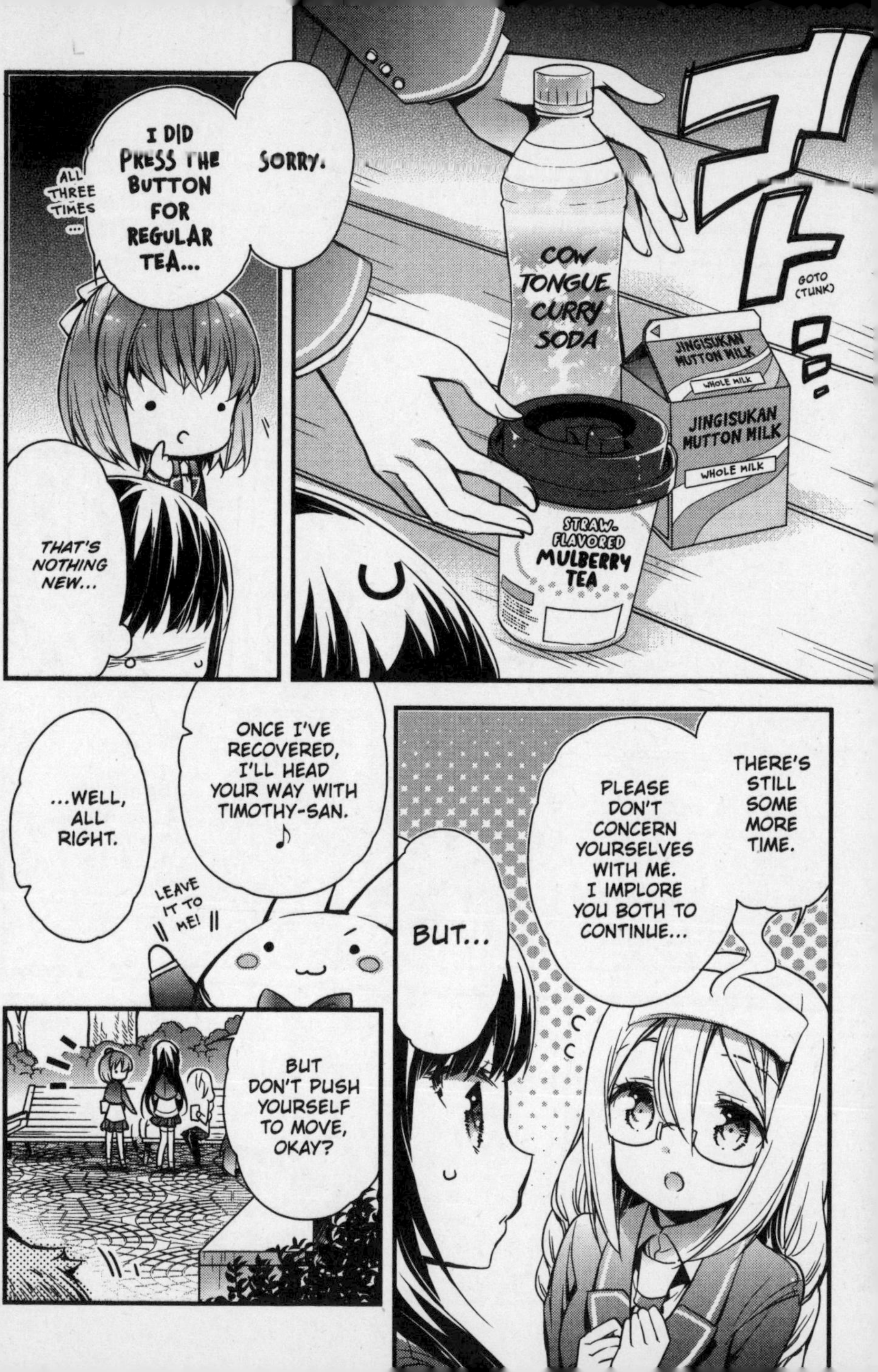
GOTO (TUNK)
COW TONGUE CURRY SODA
JINGISUKAN MUTTON MILK
WHOLE MILK
JINGISUKAN MUTTON MILK
WHOLE MILK
STRAW-FLAVORED MULBERRY TEA
SORRY.
I DID PRESS THE BUTTON FOR REGULAR TEA...
ALL THREE TIMES...
THAT'S NOTHING NEW...
THERE'S STILL SOME MORE TIME.
PLEASE DON'T CONCERN YOURSELVES WITH ME. I IMPLORE YOU BOTH TO CONTINUE...
BUT...
ONCE I'VE RECOVERED, I'LL HEAD YOUR WAY WITH TIMOTHY-SAN. ♪
LEAVE IT TO ME!
...WELL, ALL RIGHT.
BUT DON'T PUSH YOURSELF TO MOVE, OKAY?

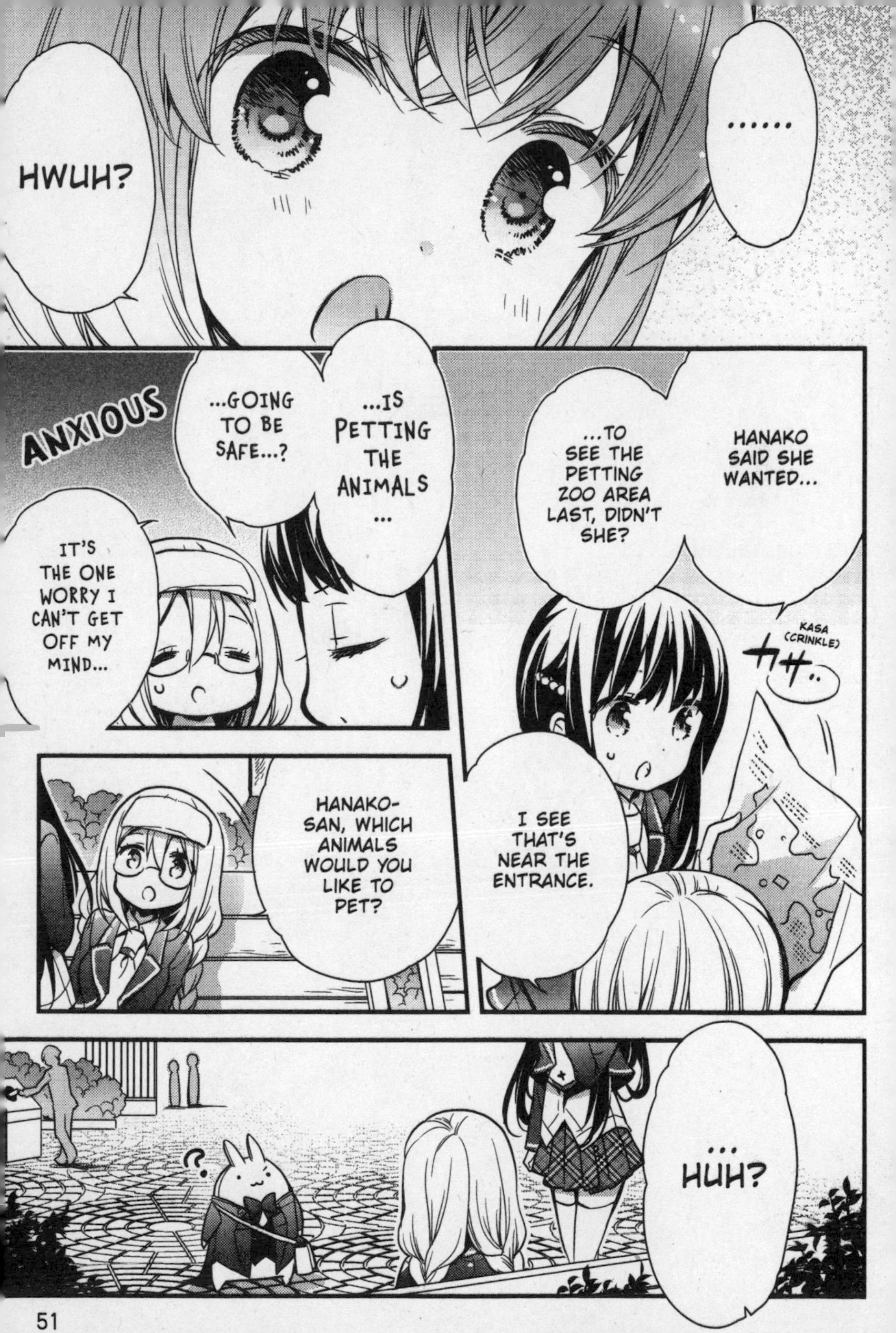
......
HWUH?
HANAKO SAID SHE WANTED...
...TO SEE THE PETTING ZOO AREA LAST, DIDN'T SHE?
KASA (CRINKLE)
...IS PETTING THE ANIMALS ...
...GOING TO BE SAFE...?
ANXIOUS
IT'S THE ONE WORRY I CAN'T GET OFF MY MIND...
I SEE THAT'S NEAR THE ENTRANCE.
HANAKO-SAN, WHICH ANIMALS WOULD YOU LIKE TO PET?
... HUH?

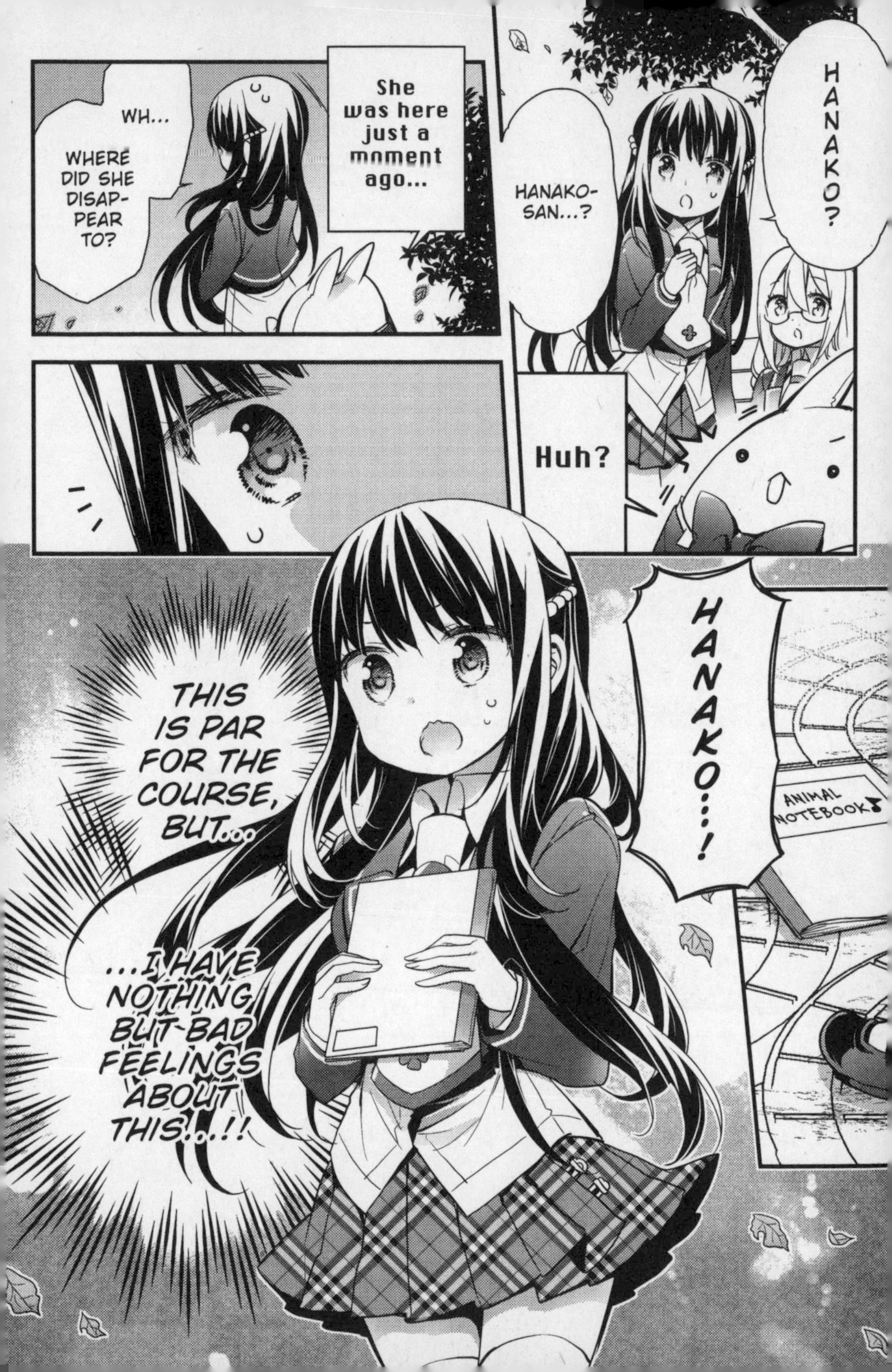
HANAKO?
HANAKO-SAN...?
Huh?
She was here just a moment ago...
WH...
WHERE DID SHE DISAP-PEAR TO?
HANAKO...!
ANIMAL NOTEBOOK
THIS IS PAR FOR THE COURSE, BUT...
...I HAVE NOTHING BUT BAD FEELINGS ABOUT THIS...!!

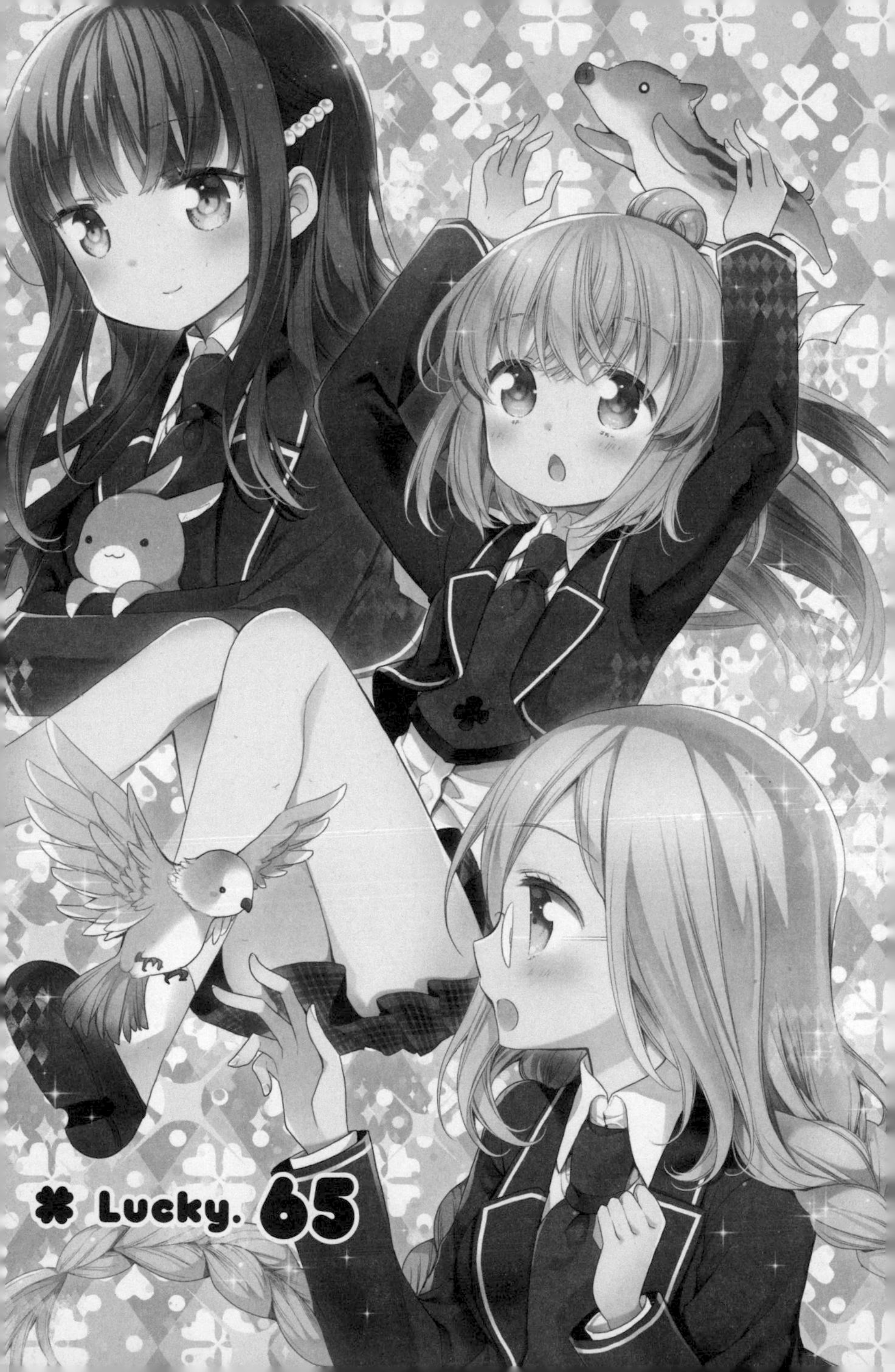
Lucky. 65

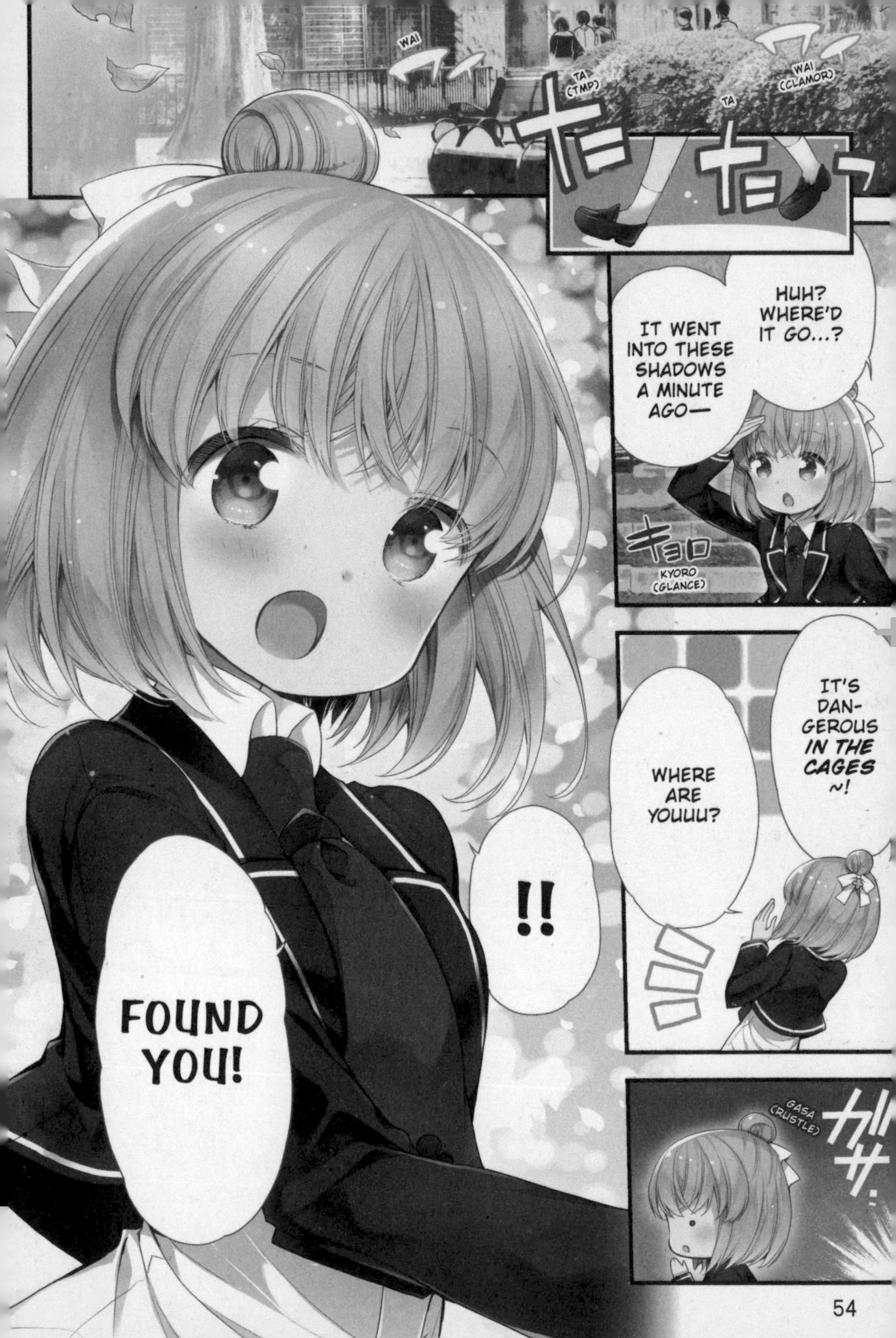
WAI (CLAMOR)
TA
TA (TMP)
WAI
HUH? WHERE'D IT GO...?
IT WENT INTO THESE SHADOWS A MINUTE AGO—
KYORO (GLANCE)
IT'S DAN-GEROUS IN THE CAGES ~!
WHERE ARE YOUUU?
GASA (RUSTLE)
!!
FOUND YOU!

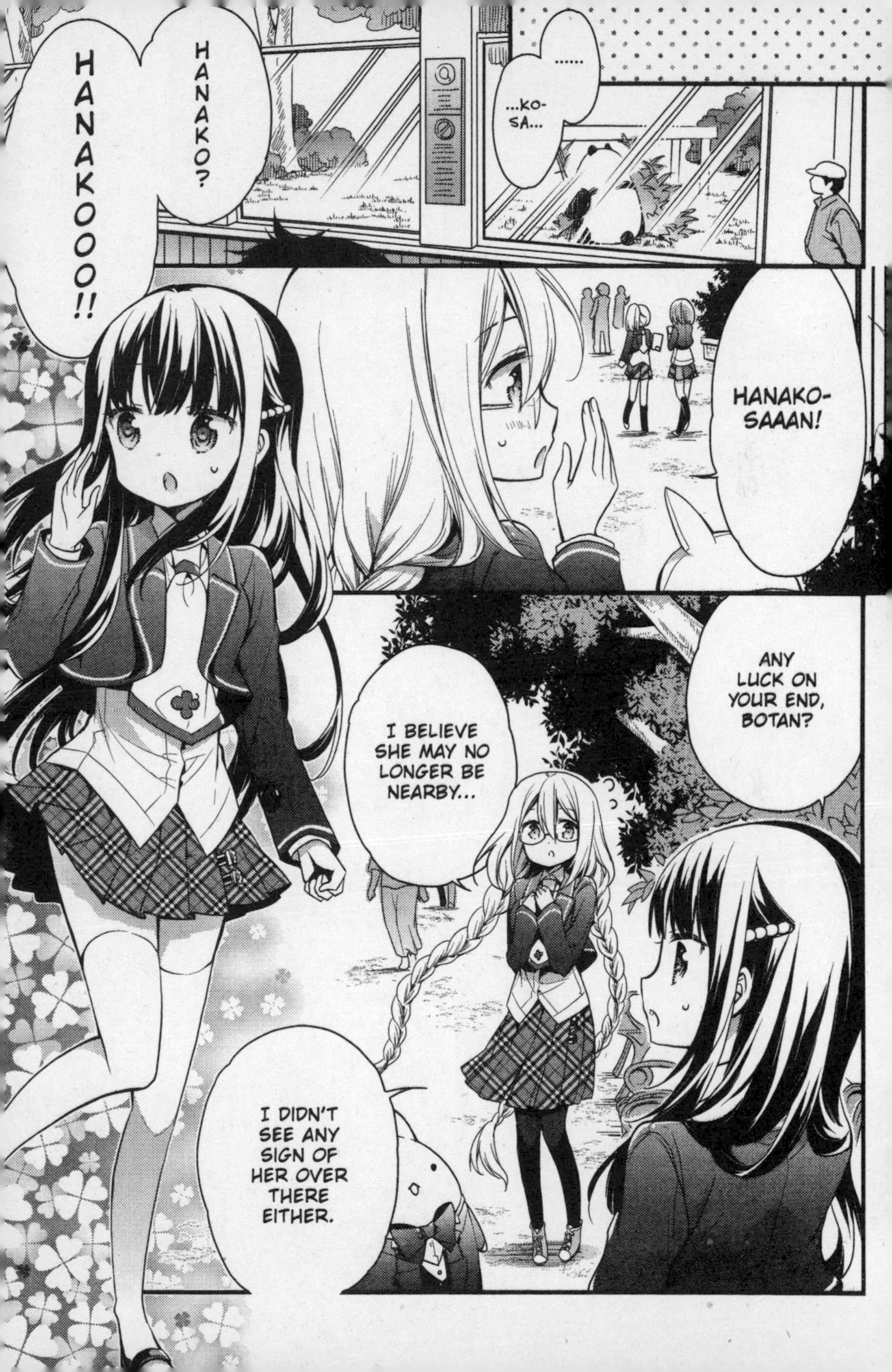
......
...KO-SA...
HANAKO?
HANAKOOOO!!
HANAKO-SAAAN!
ANY LUCK ON YOUR END, BOTAN?
I BELIEVE SHE MAY NO LONGER BE NEARBY...
I DIDN'T SEE ANY SIGN OF HER OVER THERE EITHER.

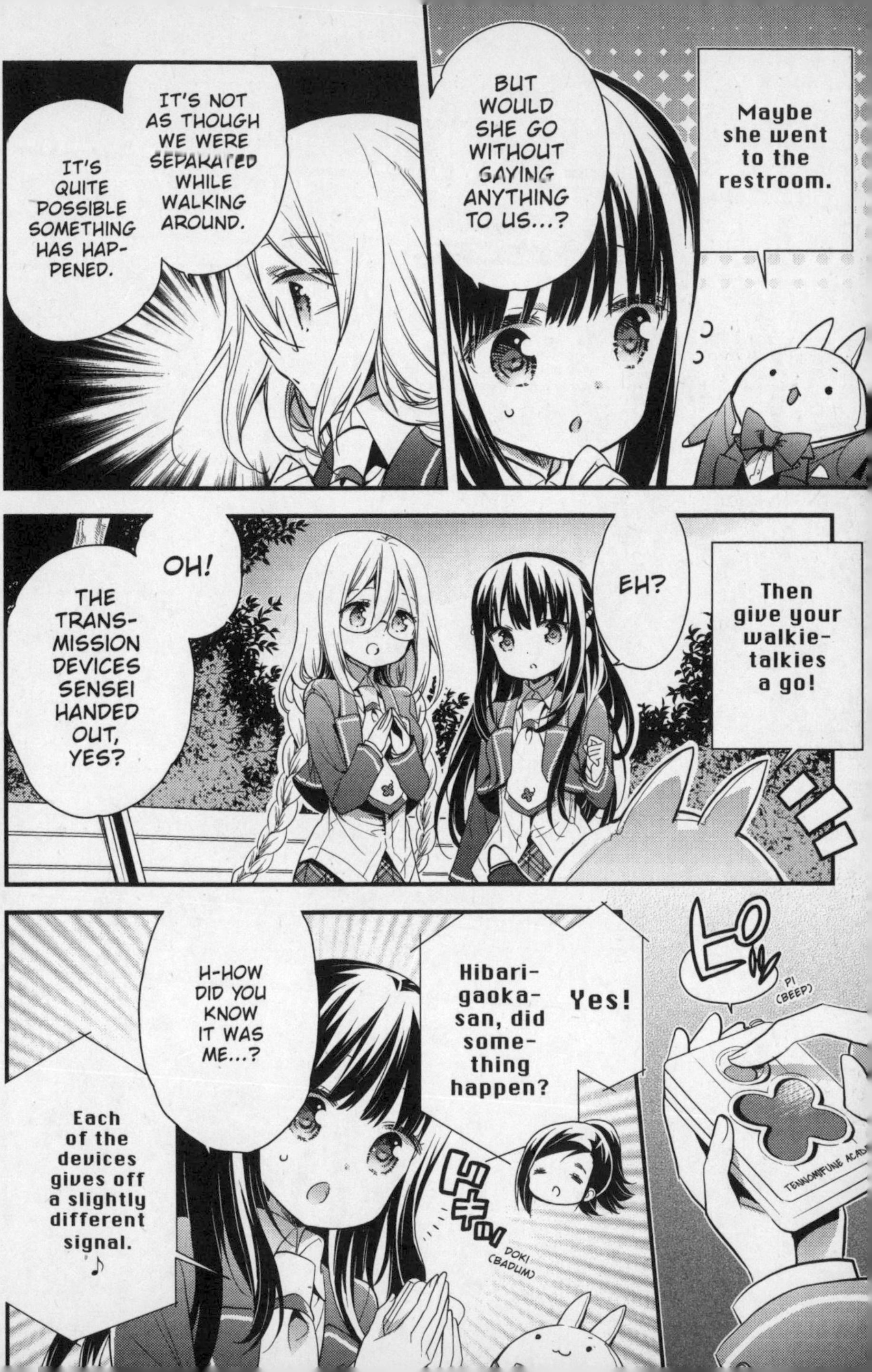
Maybe she went to the restroom.
BUT WOULD SHE GO WITHOUT SAYING ANYTHING TO US...?
IT'S NOT AS THOUGH WE WERE SEPARATED WHILE WALKING AROUND.
IT'S QUITE POSSIBLE SOMETHING HAS HAP-PENED.
Then give your walkie-talkies a go!
EH?
OH!
THE TRANS-MISSION DEVICES SENSEI HANDED OUT, YES?
PI (BEEP)
Yes!
Hibari-gaoka-san, did some-thing happen?
DOKI (BADUM)
H-HOW DID YOU KNOW IT WAS ME...?
Each of the devices gives off a slightly different signal. ♪

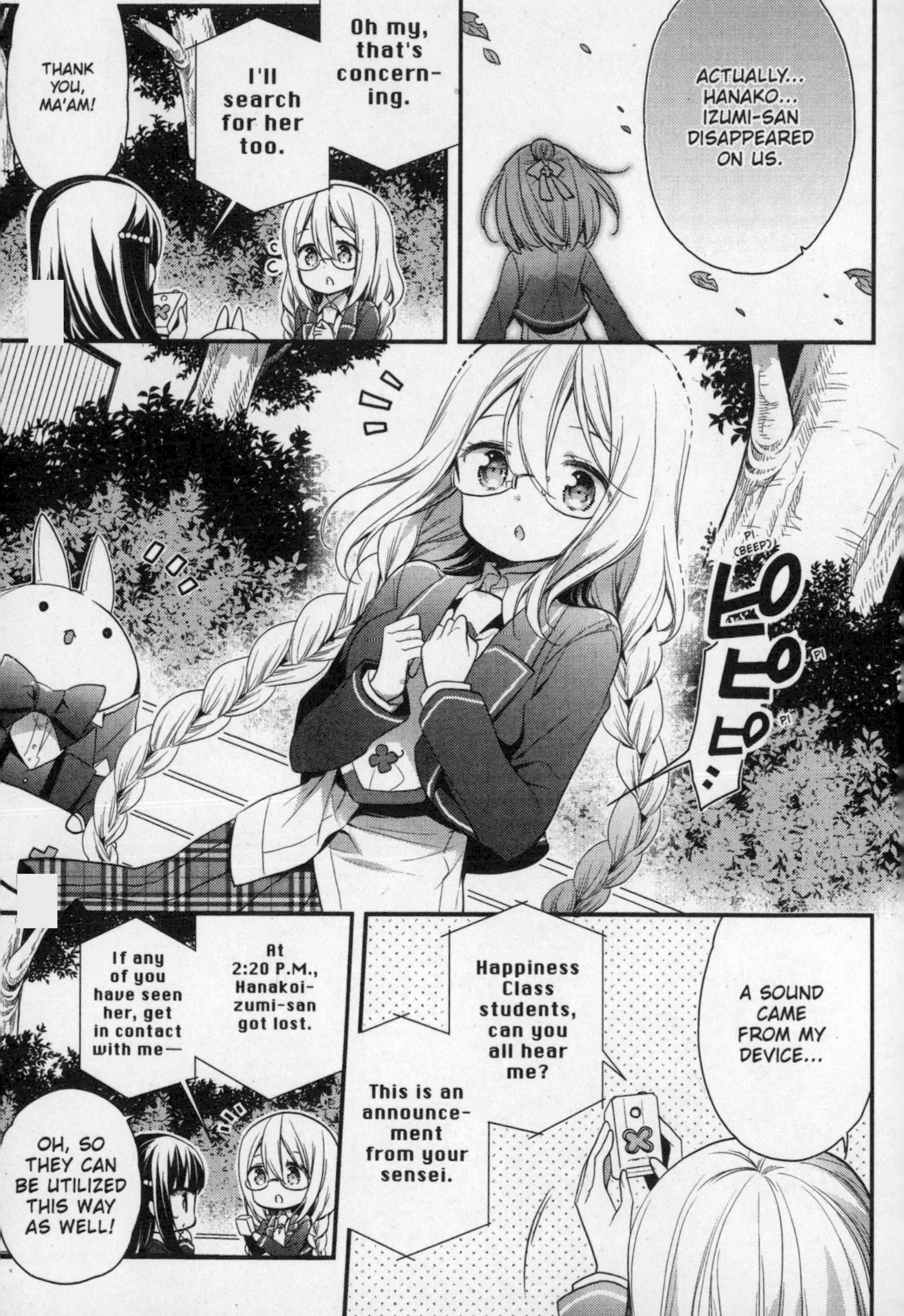
ACTUALLY... HANAKO... IZUMI-SAN DISAPPEARED ON US.
Oh my, that's concern-ing.
I'll search for her too.
THANK YOU, MA'AM!
PI (BEEP)
PI
PI
A SOUND CAME FROM MY DEVICE...
Happiness Class students, can you all hear me?
This is an announce-ment from your sensei.
At 2:20 P.M., Hanakoi-zumi-san got lost.
If any of you have seen her, get in contact with me—
OH, SO THEY CAN BE UTILIZED THIS WAY AS WELL!

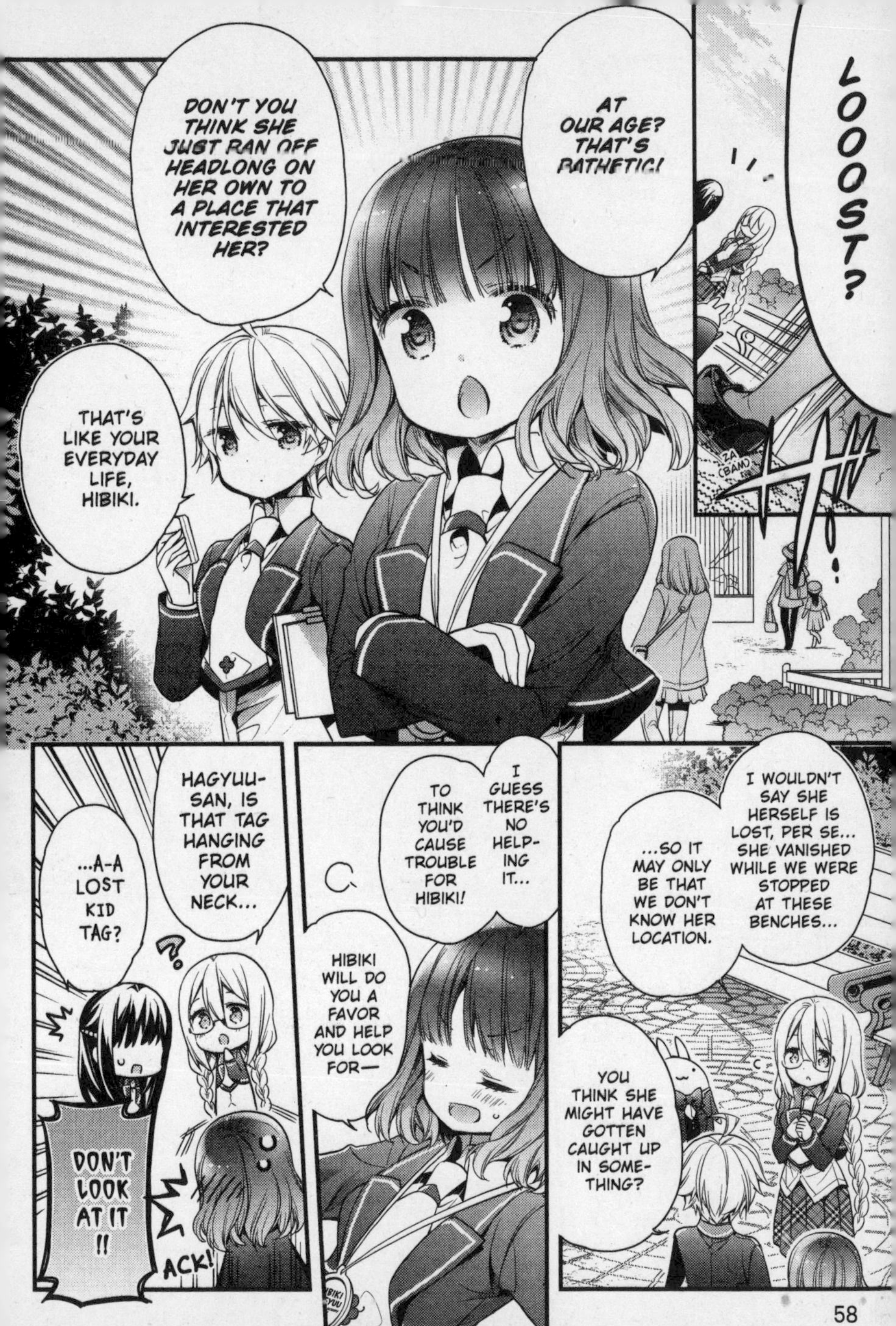
LOOOOST?
ZA (BAM)
AT OUR AGE? THAT'S PATHETIC!
DON'T YOU THINK SHE JUST RAN OFF HEADLONG ON HER OWN TO A PLACE THAT INTERESTED HER?
THAT'S LIKE YOUR EVERYDAY LIFE, HIBIKI.
I WOULDN'T SAY SHE HERSELF IS LOST, PER SE... SHE VANISHED WHILE WE WERE STOPPED AT THESE BENCHES...
...SO IT MAY ONLY BE THAT WE DON'T KNOW HER LOCATION.
YOU THINK SHE MIGHT HAVE GOTTEN CAUGHT UP IN SOMETHING?
I GUESS THERE'S NO HELPING IT...
TO THINK YOU'D CAUSE TROUBLE FOR HIBIKI!
HIBIKI WILL DO YOU A FAVOR AND HELP YOU LOOK FOR—
HAGYUU-SAN, IS THAT TAG HANGING FROM YOUR NECK...
...A-A LOST KID TAG?
DON'T LOOK AT IT !!
ACK!

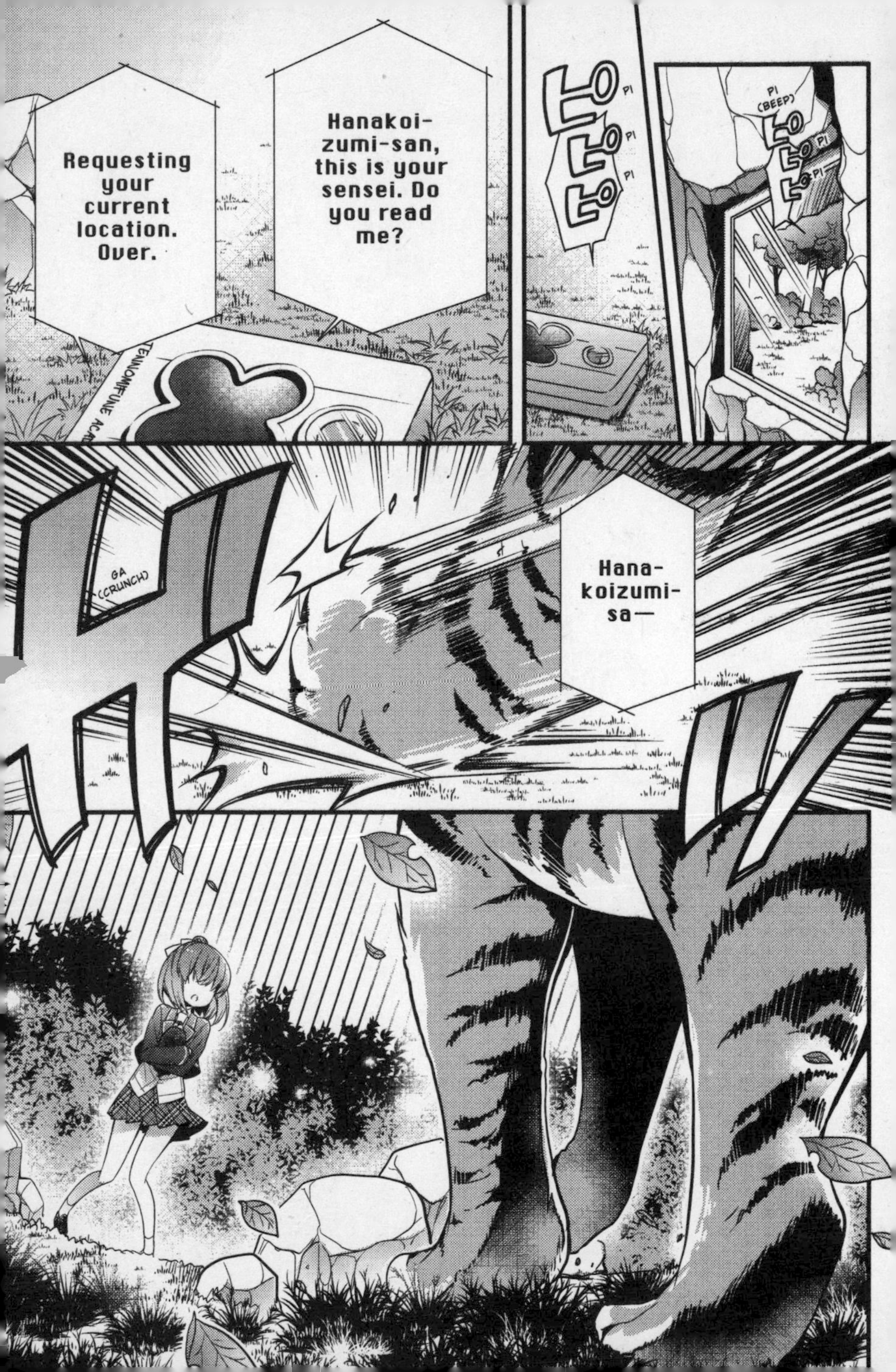
PI (BEEP)
PI
PI
PI
PI
PI
Hanakoi-zumi-san, this is your sensei. Do you read me?
Requesting your current location. Over.
Hana-koizumi-sa—
GA (CRUNCH)

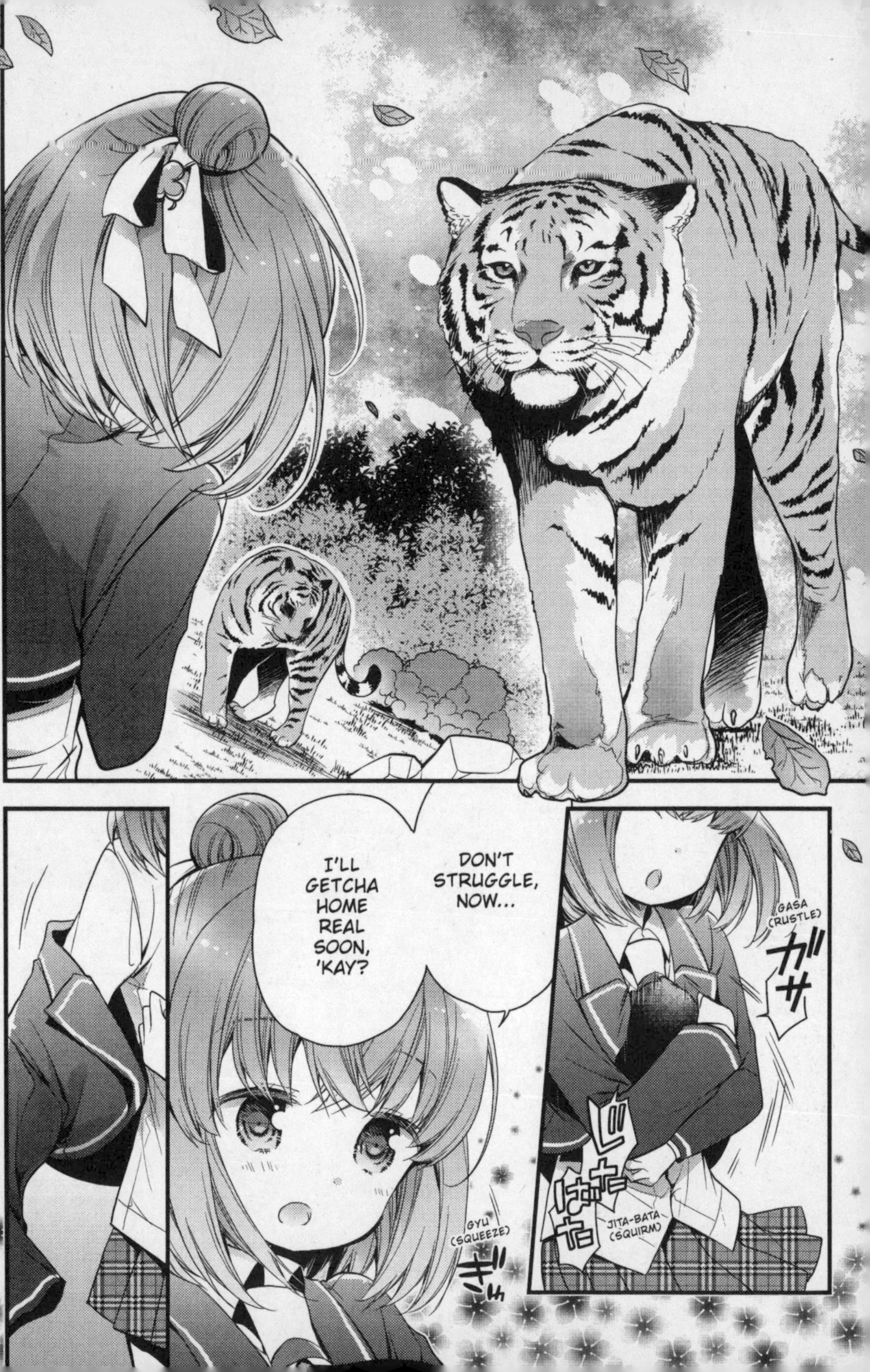
GASA (RUSTLE)
ガサ
JITA-BATA (SQUIRM)
じたばた
DON'T STRUGGLE, NOW...
I'LL GETCHA HOME REAL SOON, 'KAY?
GYU (SQUEEZE)
ぎゅ

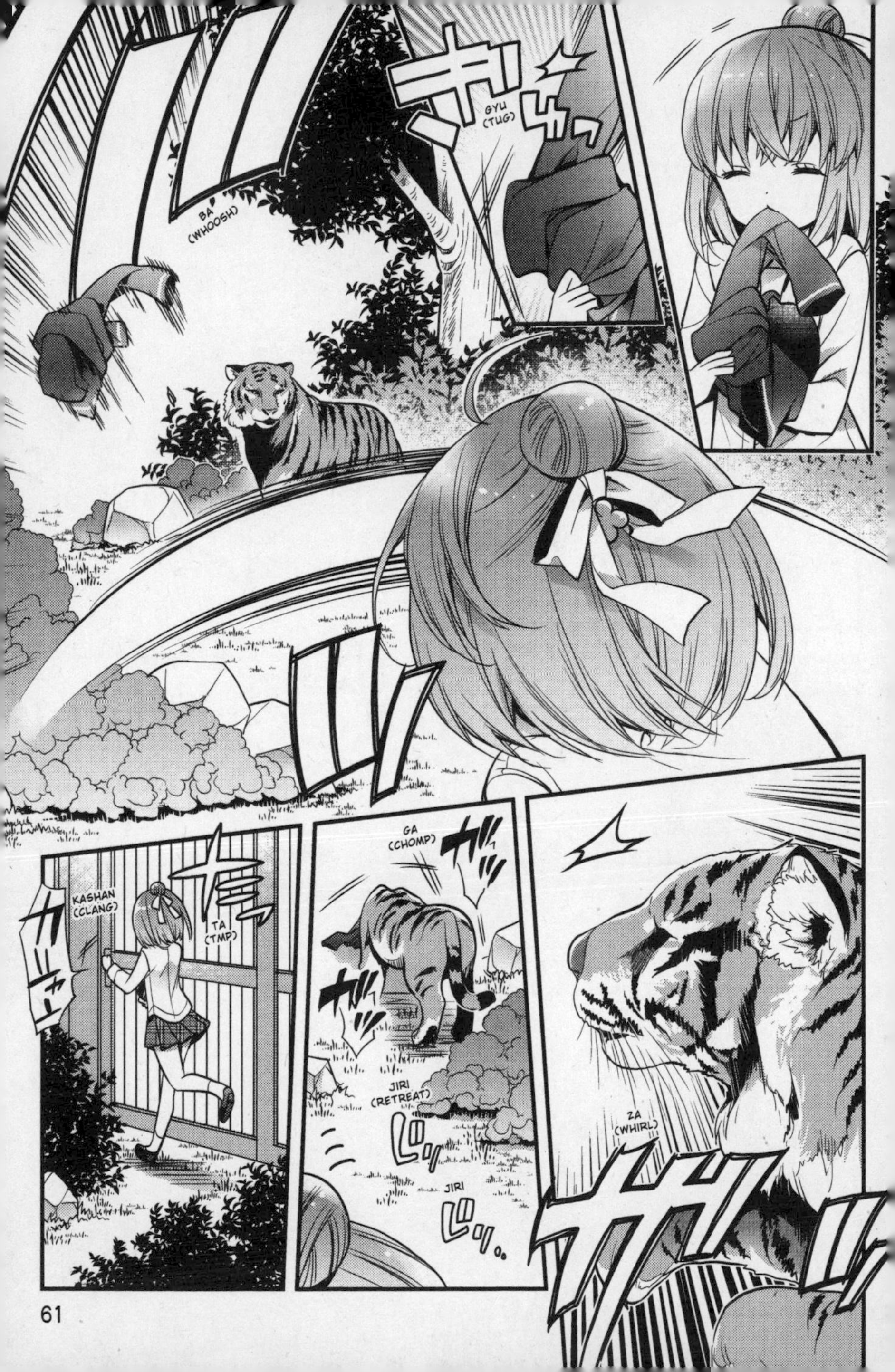

GYU
(TUG)
BA
(WHOOSH)
ZA
(WHIRL)
GA
(CHOMP)
JIRI
(RETREAT)
JIRI
KASHAN
(CLANG)
TA
(TMP)

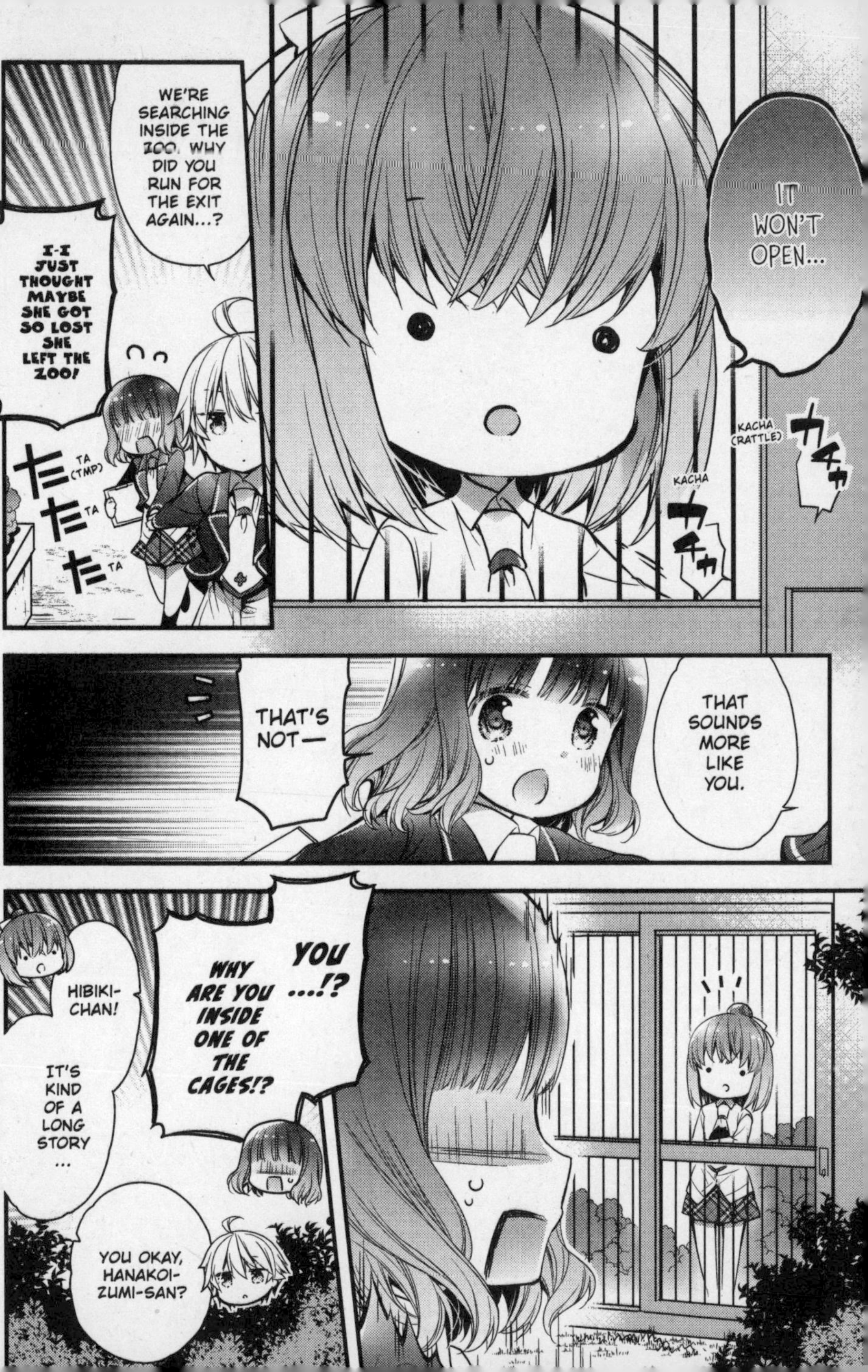
IT WON'T OPEN...
KACHA (RATTLE)
カチャ
KACHA
カチャ
WE'RE SEARCHING INSIDE THE ZOO. WHY DID YOU RUN FOR THE EXIT AGAIN...?
I-I JUST THOUGHT MAYBE SHE GOT SO LOST SHE LEFT THE ZOO!
たた
TA (TMP)
TA
TA
THAT SOUNDS MORE LIKE YOU.
THAT'S NOT—
YOU ...!?
WHY ARE YOU INSIDE ONE OF THE CAGES!?
HIBIKI-CHAN!
IT'S KIND OF A LONG STORY ...
YOU OKAY, HANAKOIZUMI-SAN?

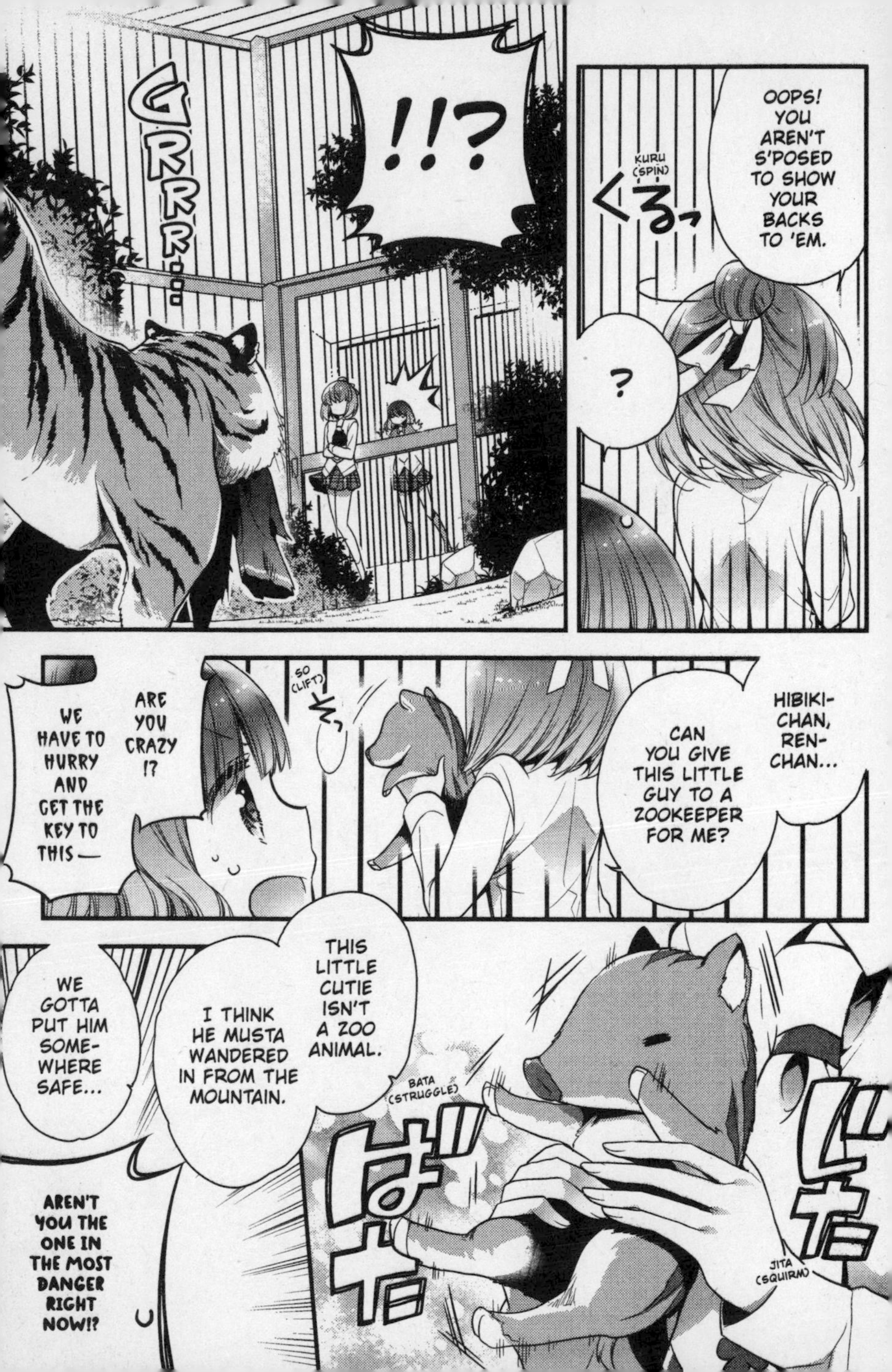
KURU (SPIN)
くる
OOPS! YOU AREN'T S'POSED TO SHOW YOUR BACKS TO 'EM.
?
!!?
GRRR...
HIBIKI-CHAN, REN-CHAN...
CAN YOU GIVE THIS LITTLE GUY TO A ZOOKEEPER FOR ME?
SO (LIFT)
ARE YOU CRAZY !?
WE HAVE TO HURRY AND GET THE KEY TO THIS—
JITA (SQUIRM)
THIS LITTLE CUTIE ISN'T A ZOO ANIMAL.
I THINK HE MUSTA WANDERED IN FROM THE MOUNTAIN.
BATA (STRUGGLE)
WE GOTTA PUT HIM SOME-WHERE SAFE...
AREN'T YOU THE ONE IN THE MOST DANGER RIGHT NOW!?

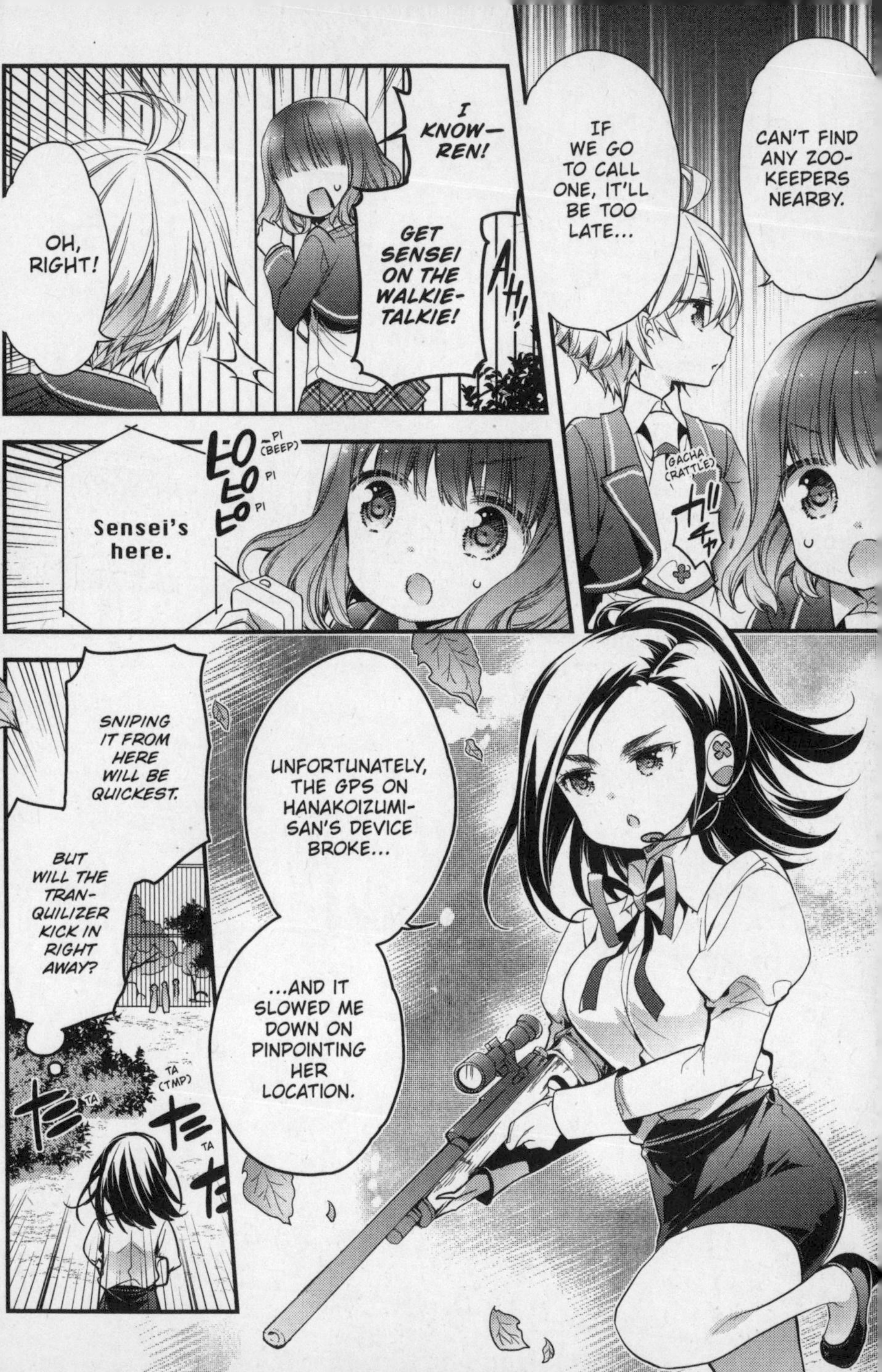
CAN'T FIND ANY ZOO-KEEPERS NEARBY.
IF WE GO TO CALL ONE, IT'LL BE TOO LATE...
GACHA (RATTLE)
I KNOW— REN!
GET SENSEI ON THE WALKIE-TALKIE!
AH!
OH, RIGHT!
PI (BEEP) PI PI
Sensei's here.
UNFORTUNATELY, THE GPS ON HANAKOIZUMI-SAN'S DEVICE BROKE...
...AND IT SLOWED ME DOWN ON PINPOINTING HER LOCATION.
SNIPING IT FROM HERE WILL BE QUICKEST.
BUT WILL THE TRAN-QUILIZER KICK IN RIGHT AWAY?
TA (TMP) TA TA

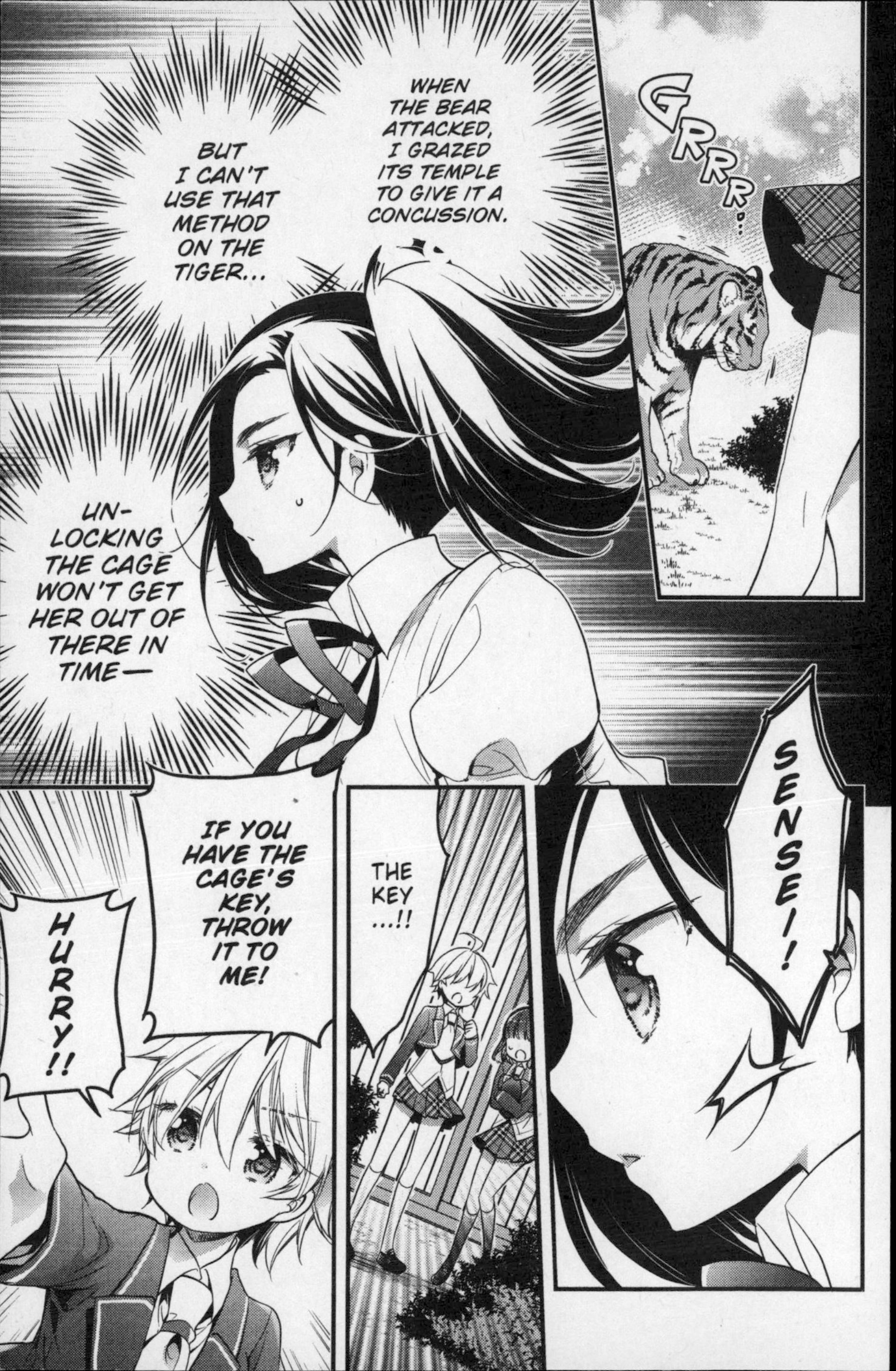
GRRR...
WHEN THE BEAR ATTACKED, I GRAZED ITS TEMPLE TO GIVE IT A CONCUSSION.
BUT I CAN'T USE THAT METHOD ON THE TIGER...
UN-LOCKING THE CAGE WON'T GET HER OUT OF THERE IN TIME—
SENSEI!!
THE KEY ...!!
IF YOU HAVE THE CAGE'S KEY, THROW IT TO ME!
HURRY!!

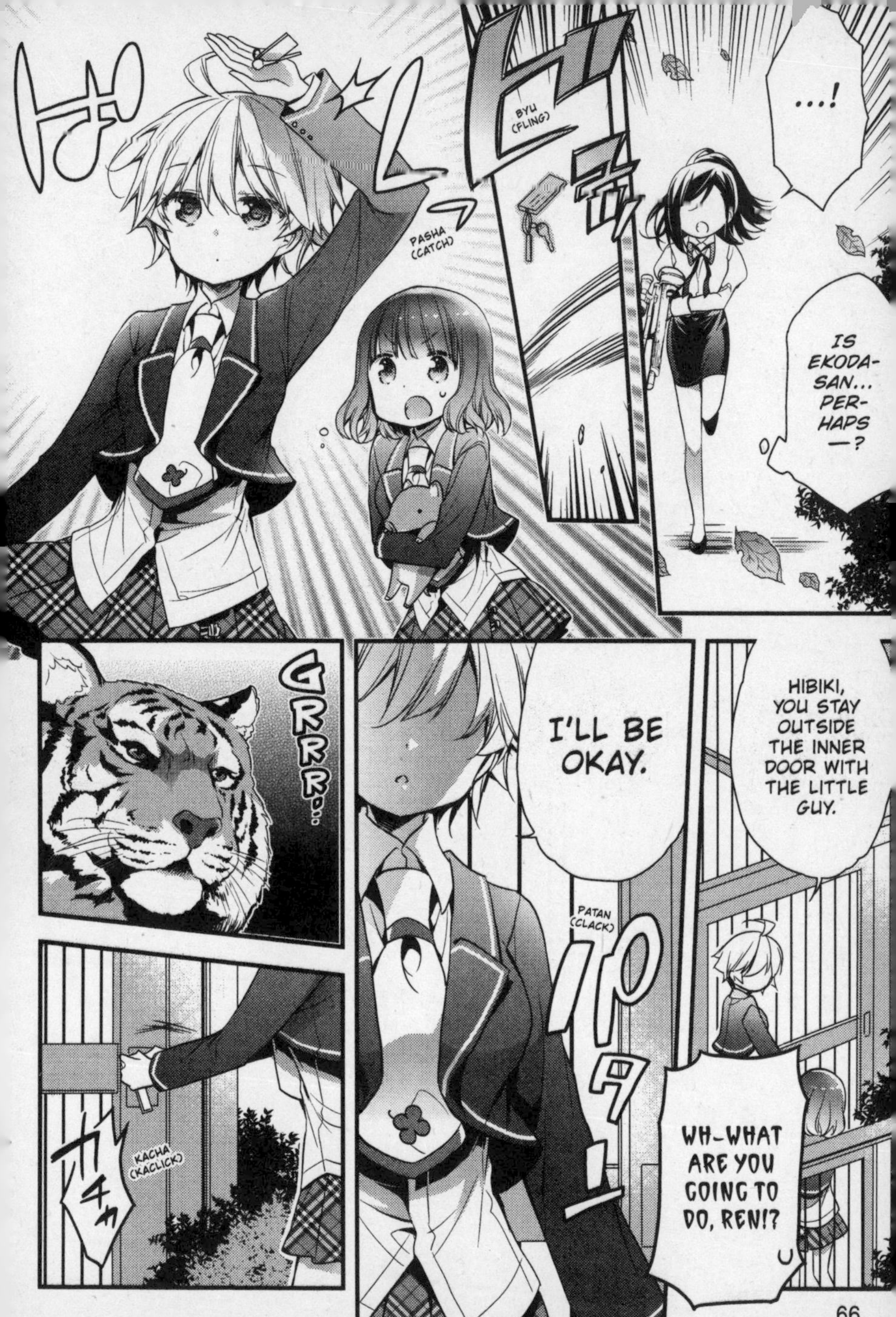
...!
IS EKODA-SAN... PER-HAPS—?
BYU (FLING)
PASHA (CATCH)
HIBIKI, YOU STAY OUTSIDE THE INNER DOOR WITH THE LITTLE GUY.
WH-WHAT ARE YOU GOING TO DO, REN!?
I'LL BE OKAY.
PATAN (CLACK)
GRRR..
KACHA (KACLICK)

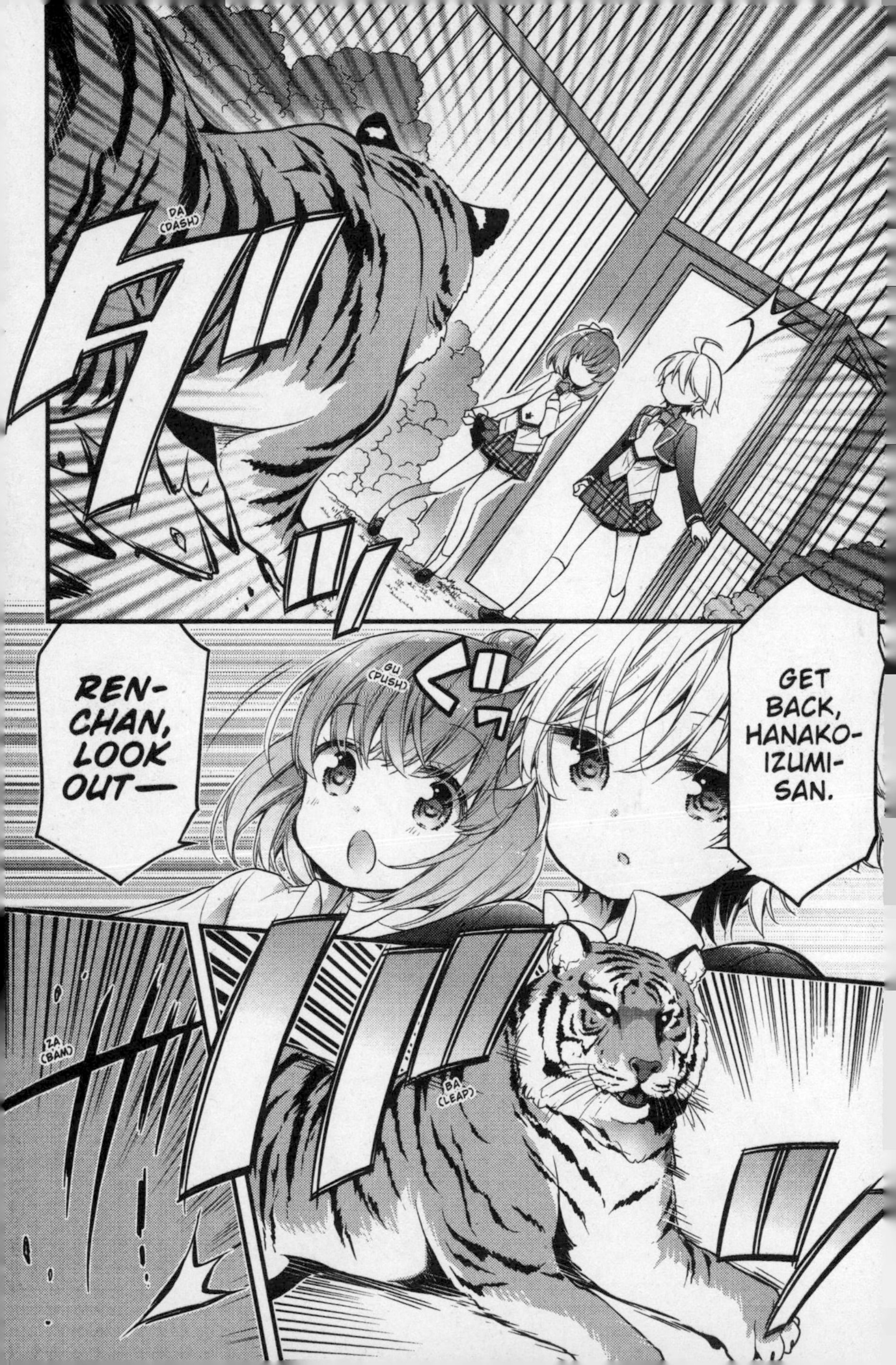
DA (DASH)
GET BACK, HANAKO-IZUMI-SAN.
GU (PUSH)
REN-CHAN, LOOK OUT—
BA (LEAP)
ZA (BAM)

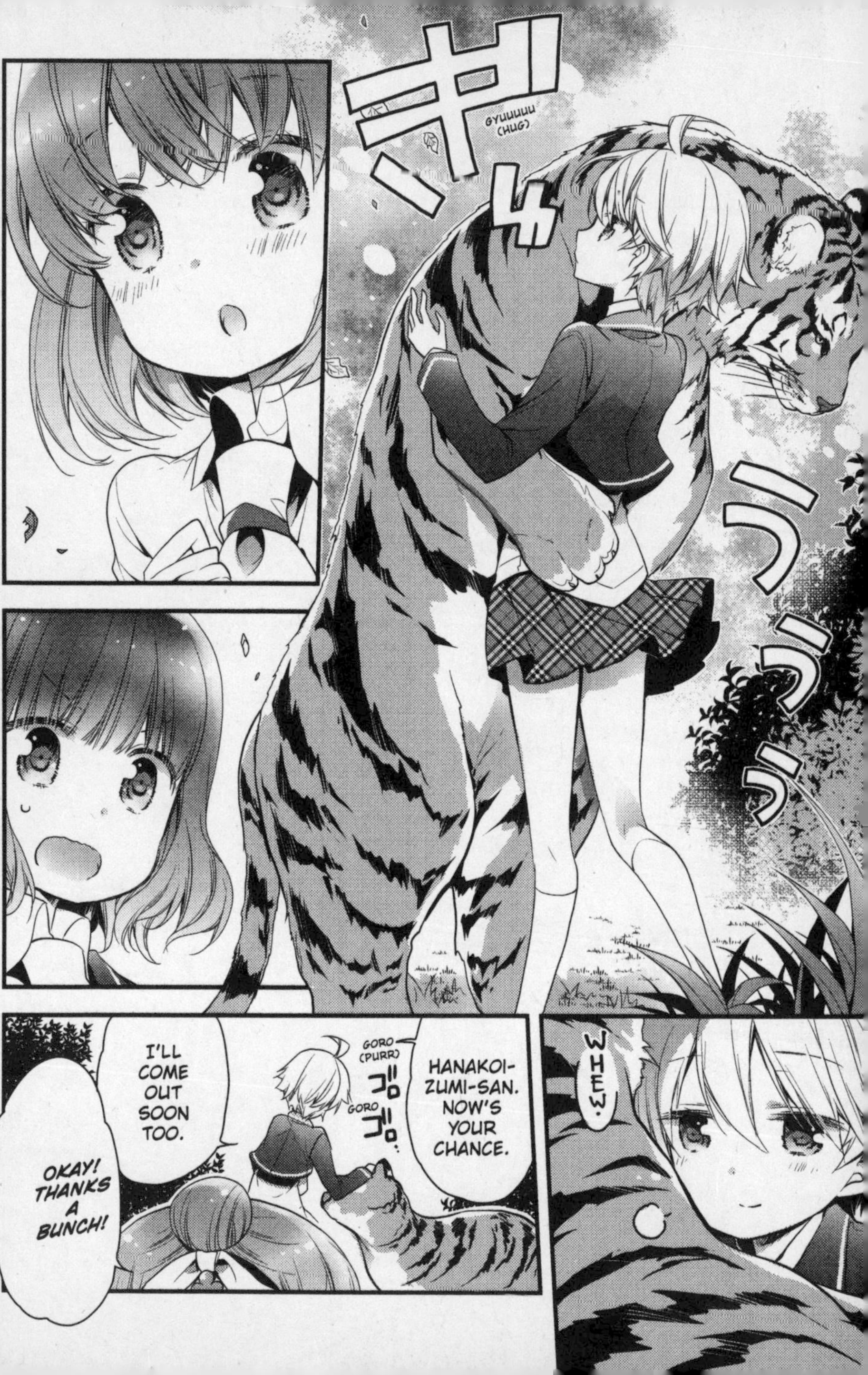
GYUUUUU (HUG)
WHEW.
HANAKOIZUMI-SAN. NOW'S YOUR CHANCE.
GORO (PURR)
GORO
I'LL COME OUT SOON TOO.
OKAY! THANKS A BUNCH!

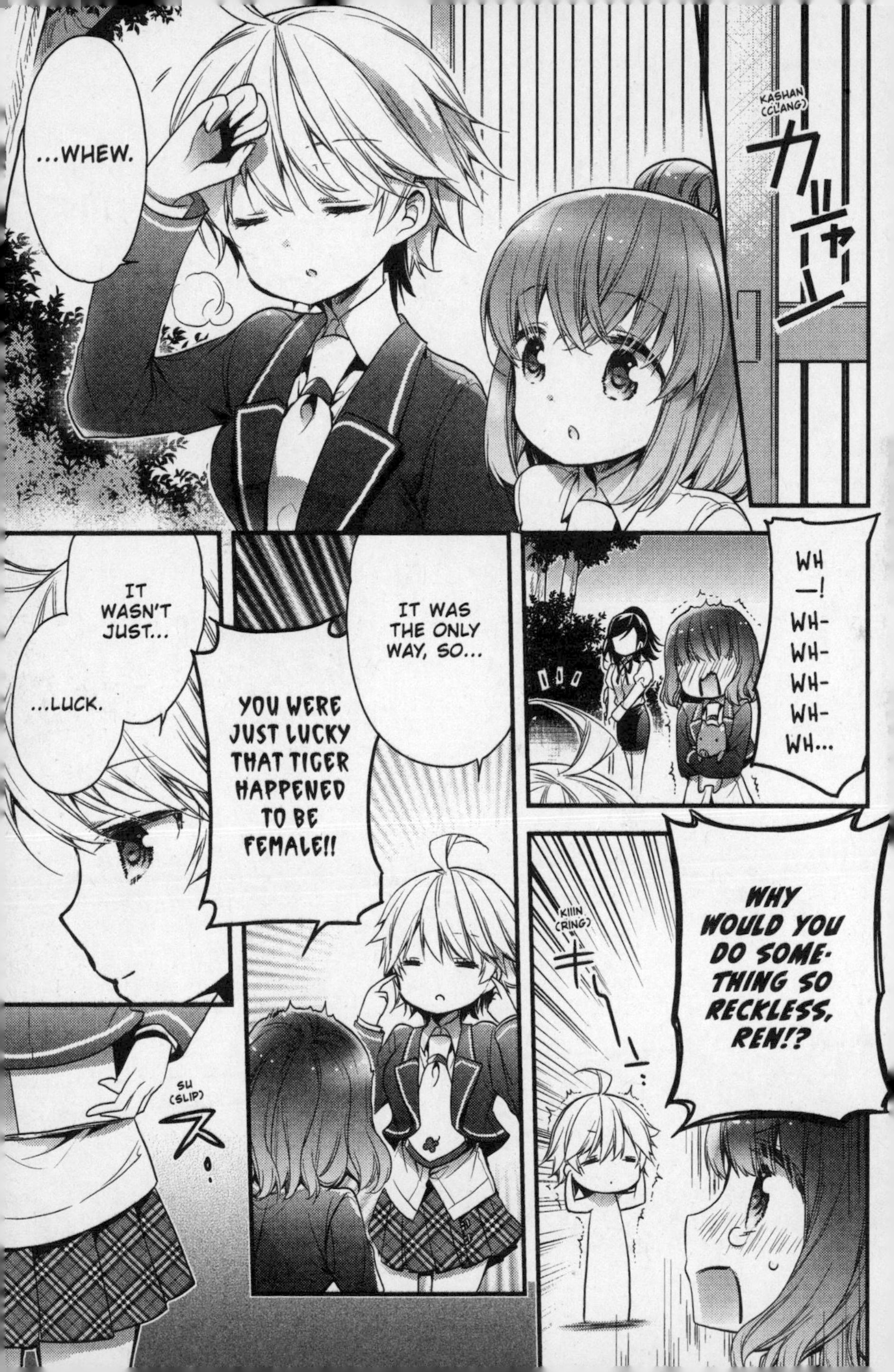
KASHAN (CLANG)
...WHEW.
WH—! WH-WH-WH-WH-WH...
WHY WOULD YOU DO SOME-THING SO RECKLESS, REN!?
KIIIN (CRING)
IT WAS THE ONLY WAY, SO...
YOU WERE JUST LUCKY THAT TIGER HAPPENED TO BE FEMALE!!
IT WASN'T JUST...
...LUCK.
SU (SLIP)

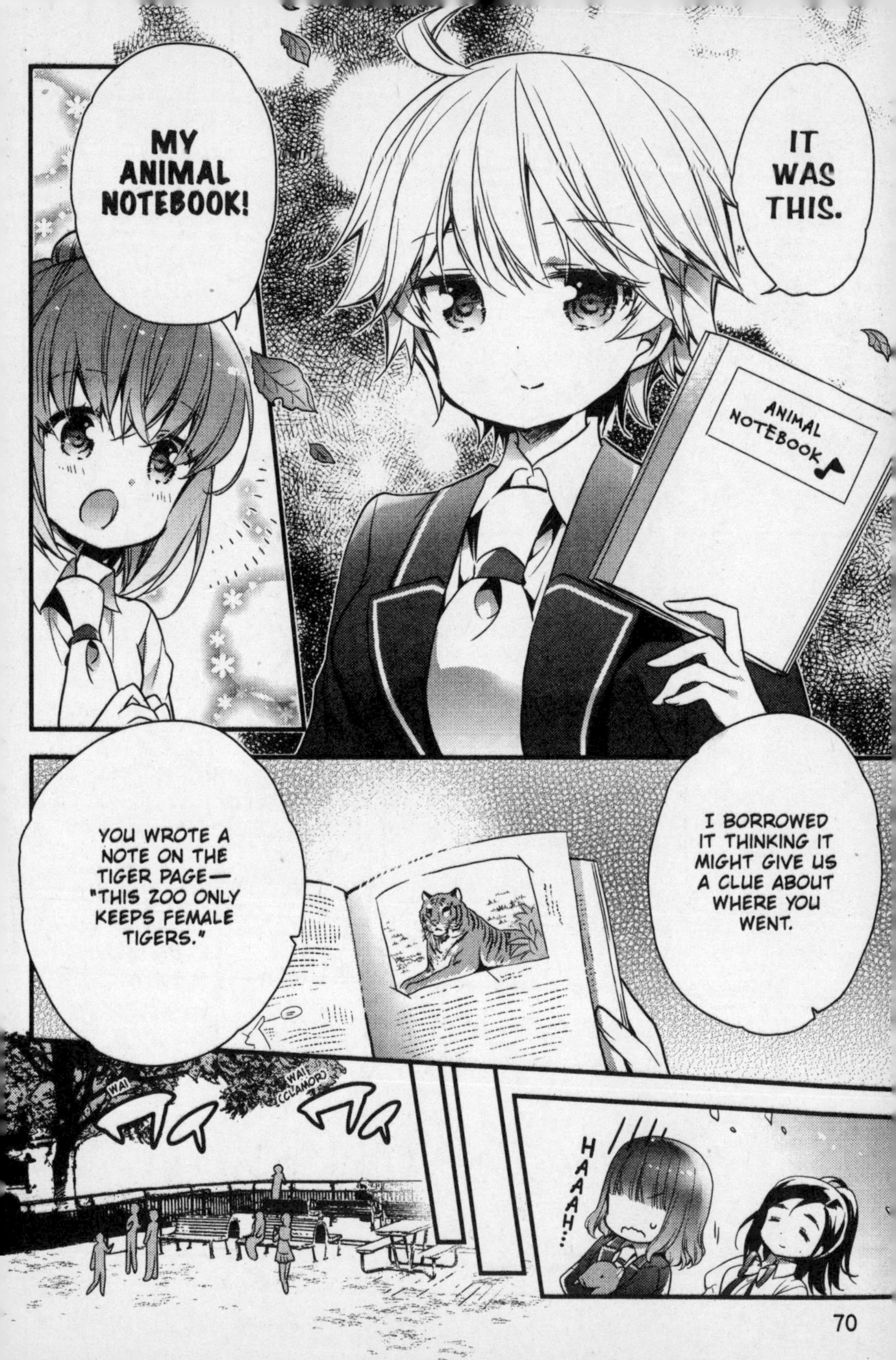
IT WAS THIS.
MY ANIMAL NOTEBOOK!
ANIMAL NOTEBOOK♪
I BORROWED IT THINKING IT MIGHT GIVE US A CLUE ABOUT WHERE YOU WENT.
YOU WROTE A NOTE ON THE TIGER PAGE—"THIS ZOO ONLY KEEPS FEMALE TIGERS."
HAAAAH...
WAI
WAI (CLAMOR)

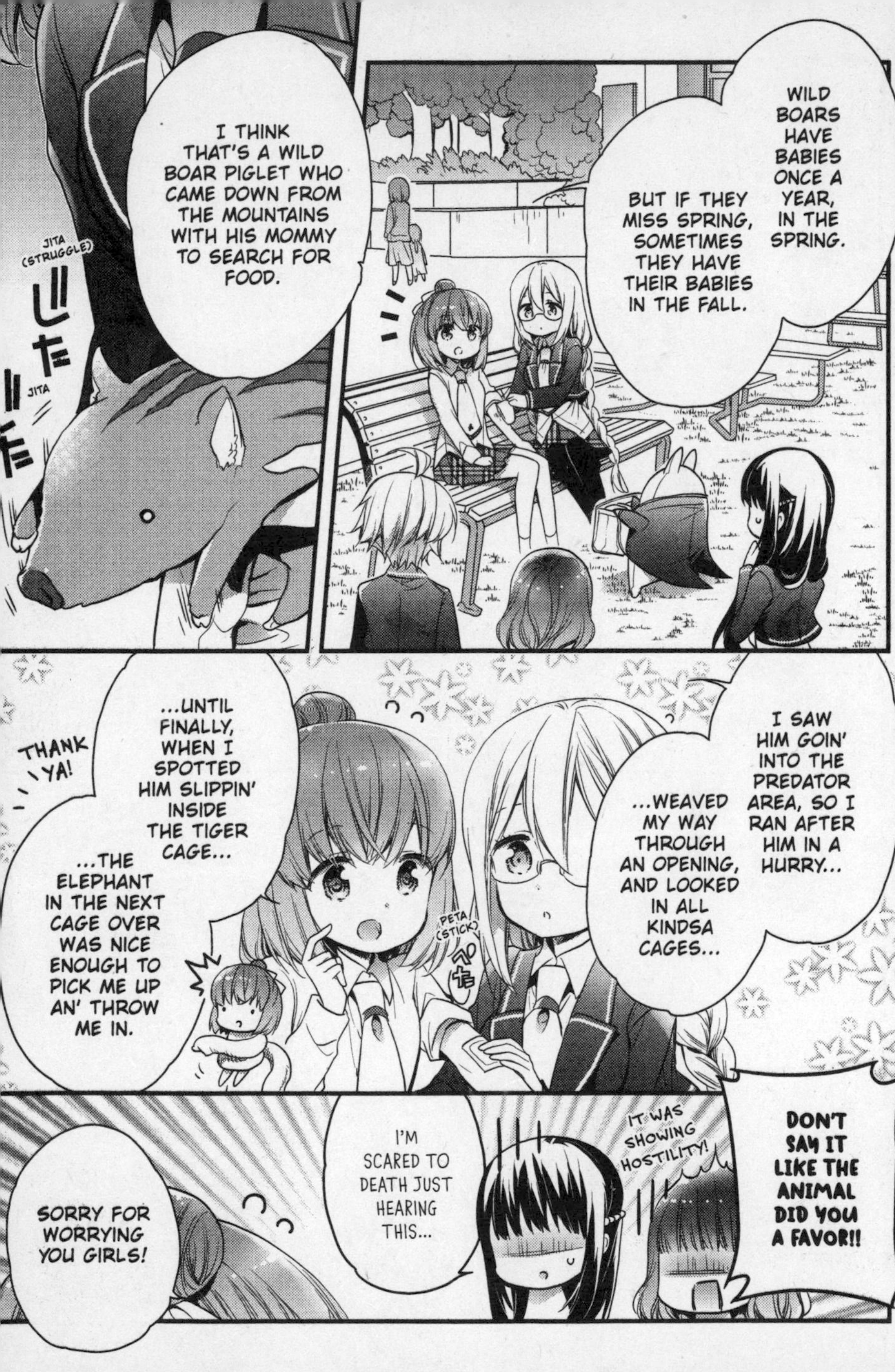
WILD BOARS HAVE BABIES ONCE A YEAR, IN THE SPRING.
BUT IF THEY MISS SPRING, SOMETIMES THEY HAVE THEIR BABIES IN THE FALL.
I THINK THAT'S A WILD BOAR PIGLET WHO CAME DOWN FROM THE MOUNTAINS WITH HIS MOMMY TO SEARCH FOR FOOD.
JITA (STRUGGLE)
JITA
I SAW HIM GOIN' INTO THE PREDATOR AREA, SO I RAN AFTER HIM IN A HURRY...
...WEAVED MY WAY THROUGH AN OPENING, AND LOOKED IN ALL KINDSA CAGES...
...UNTIL FINALLY, WHEN I SPOTTED HIM SLIPPIN' INSIDE THE TIGER CAGE...
PETA (STICK)
THANK YA!
...THE ELEPHANT IN THE NEXT CAGE OVER WAS NICE ENOUGH TO PICK ME UP AN' THROW ME IN.
DON'T SAY IT LIKE THE ANIMAL DID YOU A FAVOR!!
IT WAS SHOWING HOSTILITY!
I'M SCARED TO DEATH JUST HEARING THIS...
SORRY FOR WORRYING YOU GIRLS!

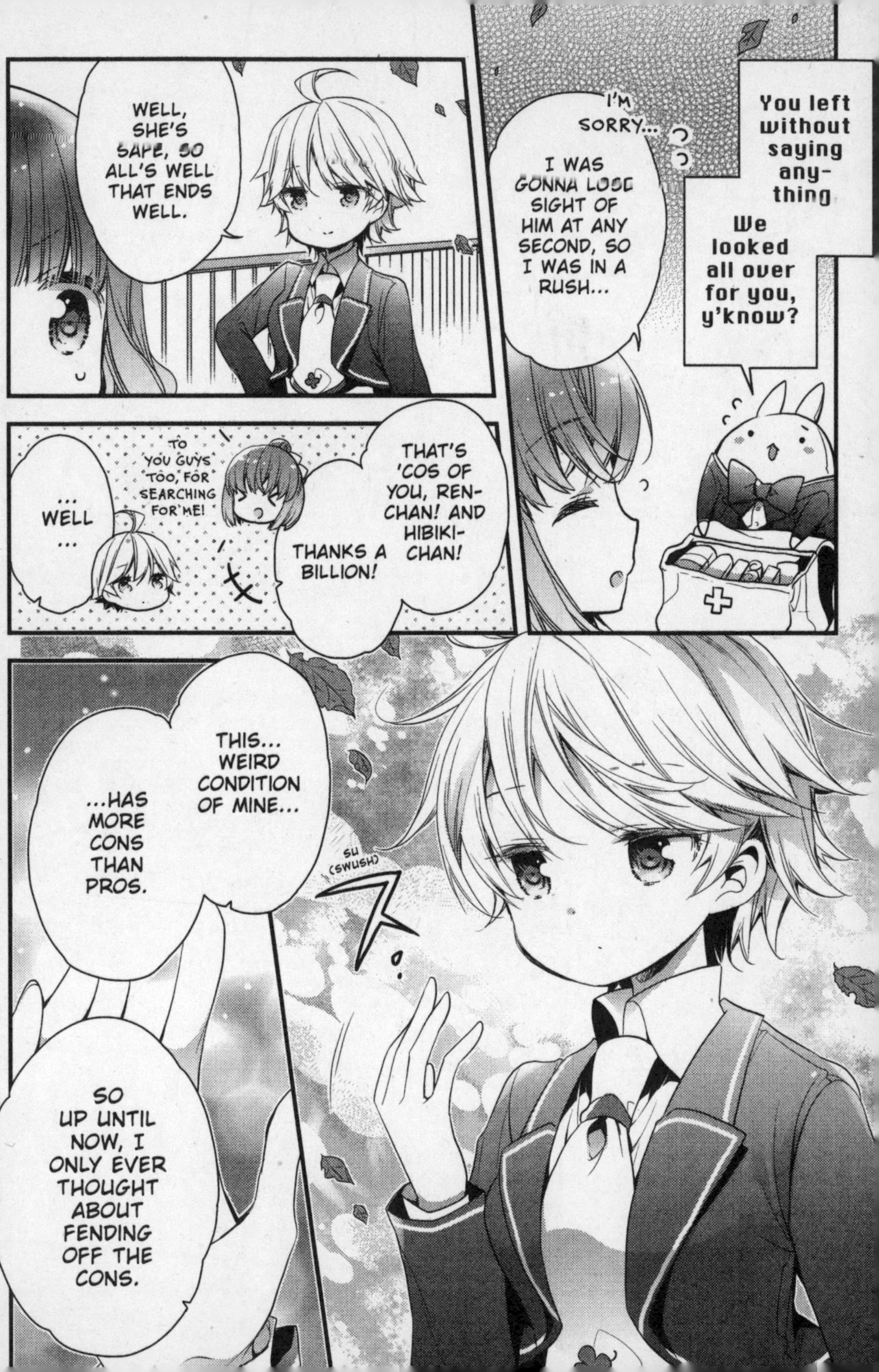
You left without saying anything.
We looked all over for you, y'know?
I'M SORRY...
I WAS GONNA LOSE SIGHT OF HIM AT ANY SECOND, SO I WAS IN A RUSH...
WELL, SHE'S SAFE, SO ALL'S WELL THAT ENDS WELL.
THAT'S 'COS OF YOU, REN-CHAN! AND HIBIKI-CHAN!
THANKS A BILLION!
TO YOU GUYS TOO, FOR SEARCHING FOR ME!
...WELL...
THIS... WEIRD CONDITION OF MINE...
...HAS MORE CONS THAN PROS.
SU (SWUSH)
SO UP UNTIL NOW, I ONLY EVER THOUGHT ABOUT FENDING OFF THE CONS.

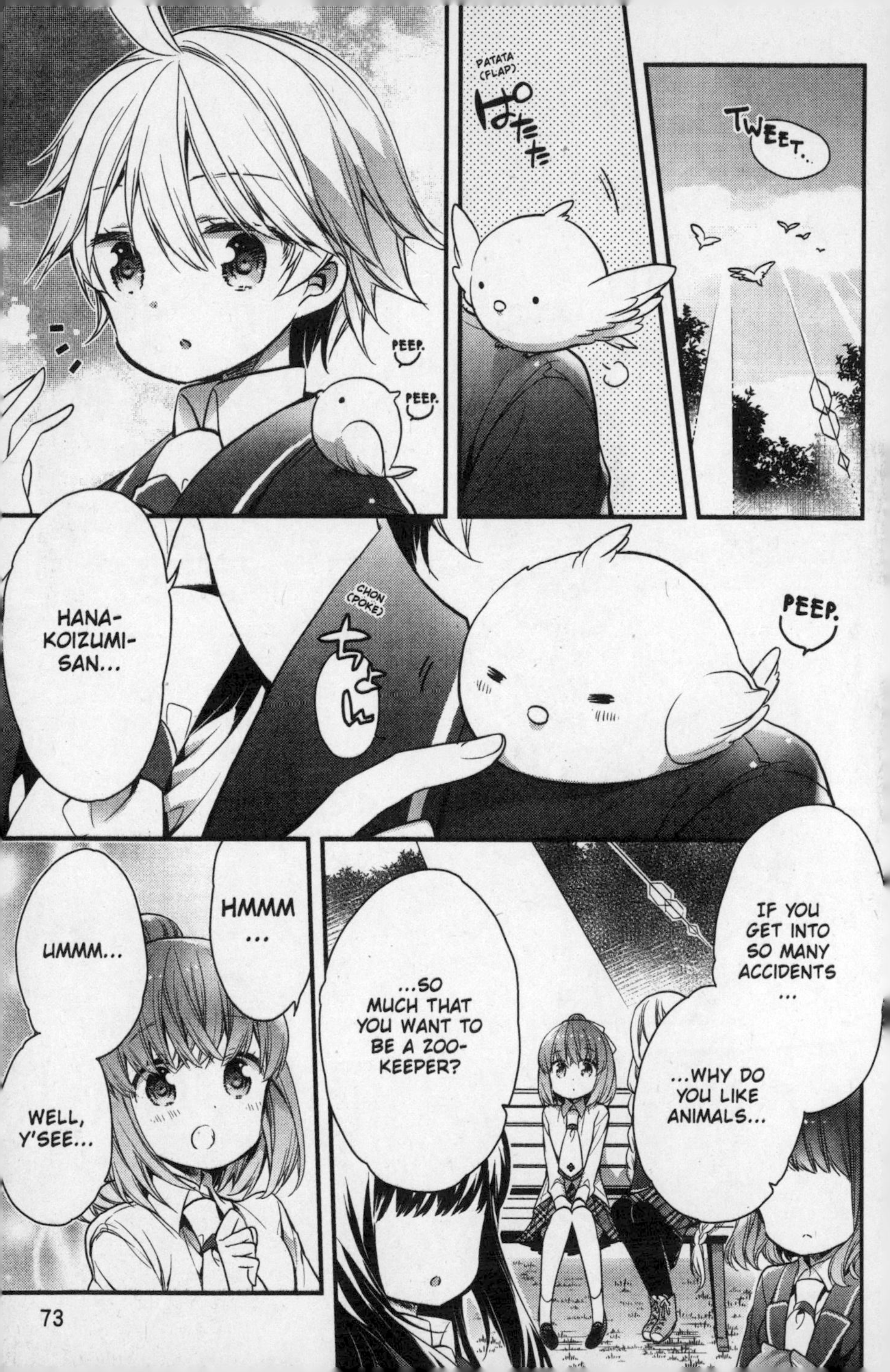
TWEET...
PATATA (FLAP)
ぱたた
PEEP.
PEEP.
PEEP.
CHON (POKE)
ちょん
HANA-KOIZUMI-SAN...
IF YOU GET INTO SO MANY ACCIDENTS...
...WHY DO YOU LIKE ANIMALS...
...SO MUCH THAT YOU WANT TO BE A ZOO-KEEPER?
HMMM...
UMMM...
WELL, Y'SEE...

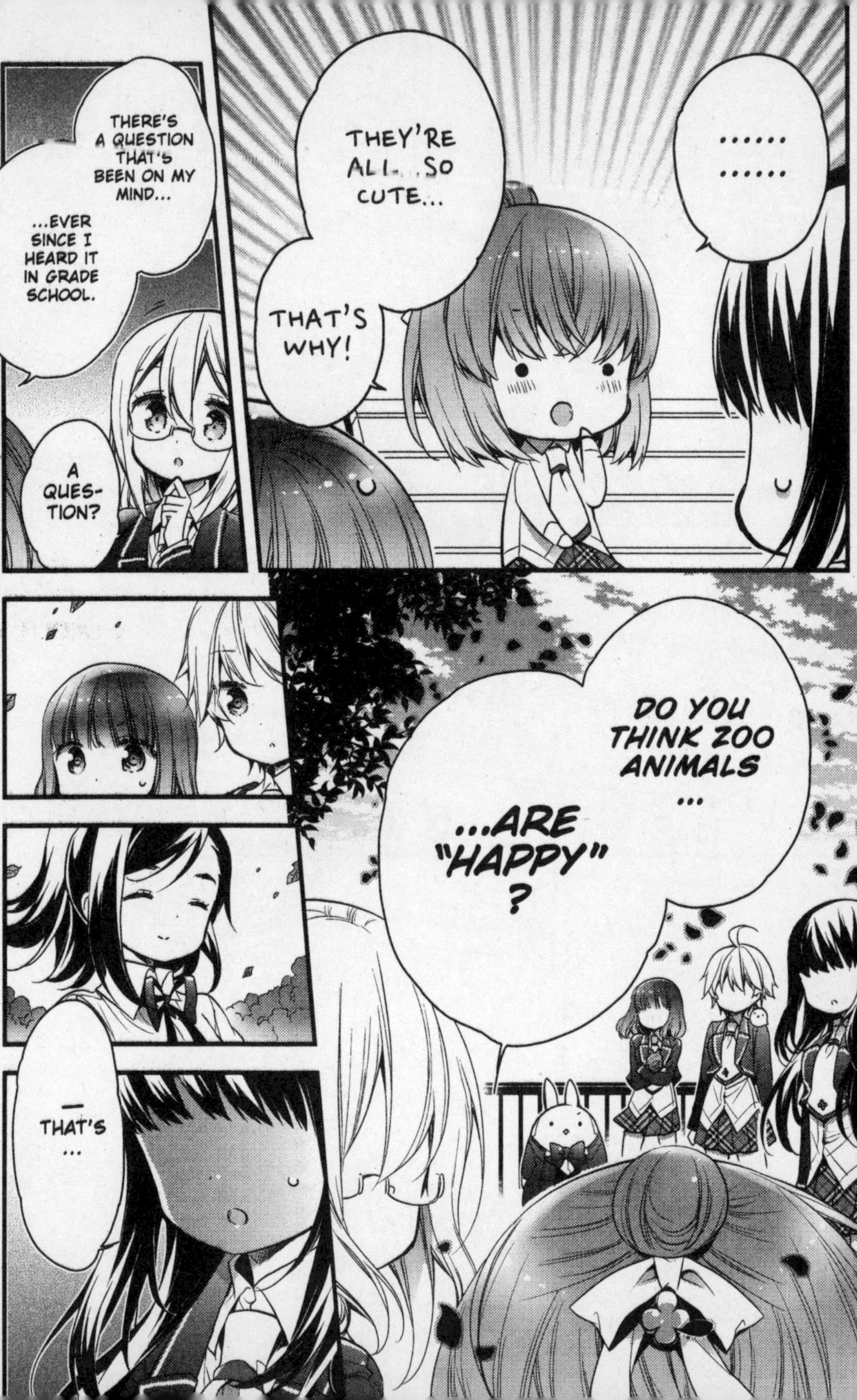
......
......
THEY'RE ALL... SO CUTE...
THAT'S WHY!
THERE'S A QUESTION THAT'S BEEN ON MY MIND...
...EVER SINCE I HEARD IT IN GRADE SCHOOL.
A QUESTION?
DO YOU THINK ZOO ANIMALS ...
...ARE "HAPPY"?
—THAT'S ...

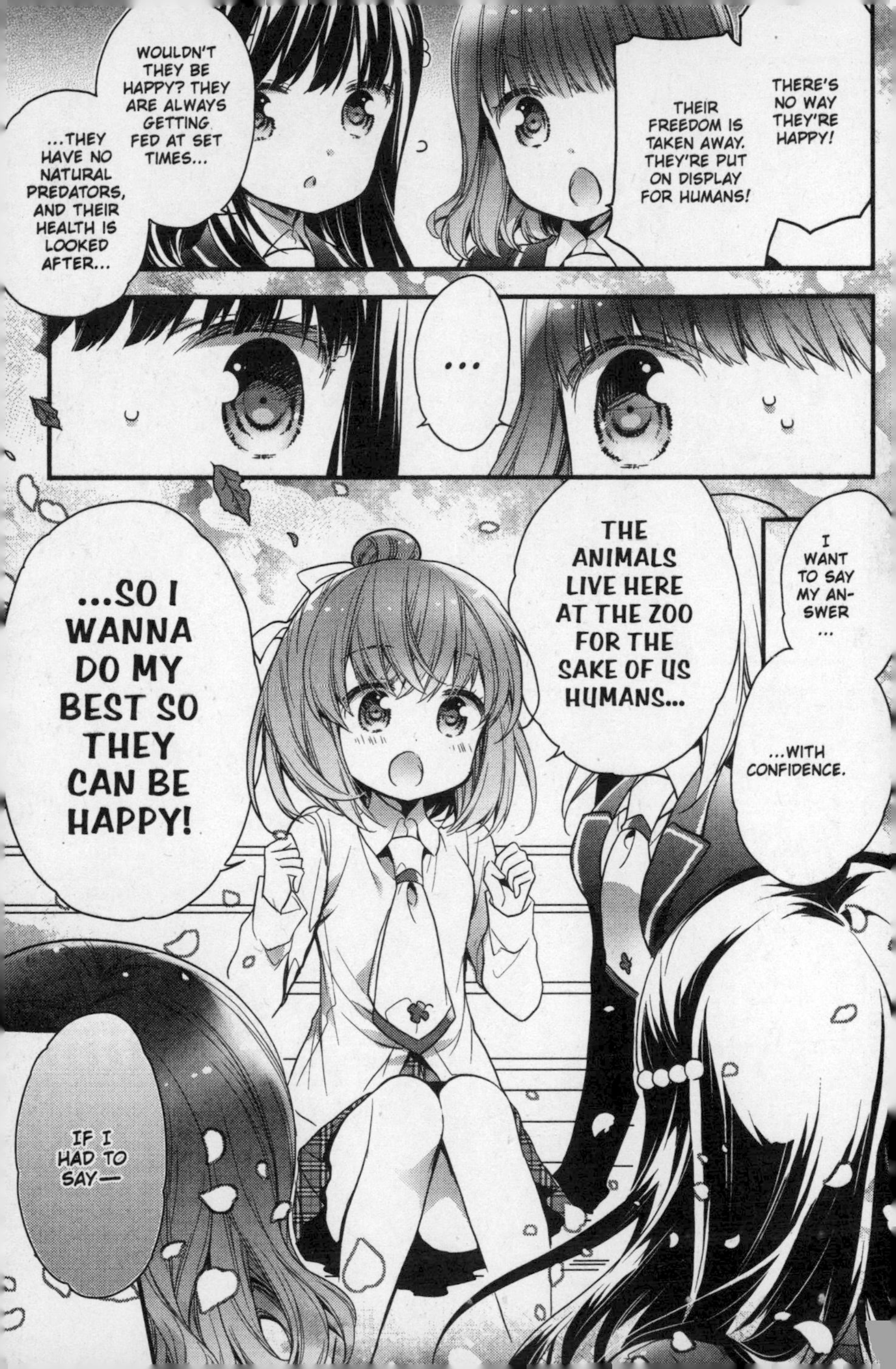
THERE'S NO WAY THEY'RE HAPPY!
THEIR FREEDOM IS TAKEN AWAY. THEY'RE PUT ON DISPLAY FOR HUMANS!
WOULDN'T THEY BE HAPPY? THEY ARE ALWAYS GETTING FED AT SET TIMES...
...THEY HAVE NO NATURAL PREDATORS, AND THEIR HEALTH IS LOOKED AFTER...
...
I WANT TO SAY MY AN-SWER...
...WITH CONFIDENCE.
THE ANIMALS LIVE HERE AT THE ZOO FOR THE SAKE OF US HUMANS...
...SO I WANNA DO MY BEST SO THEY CAN BE HAPPY!
IF I HAD TO SAY—

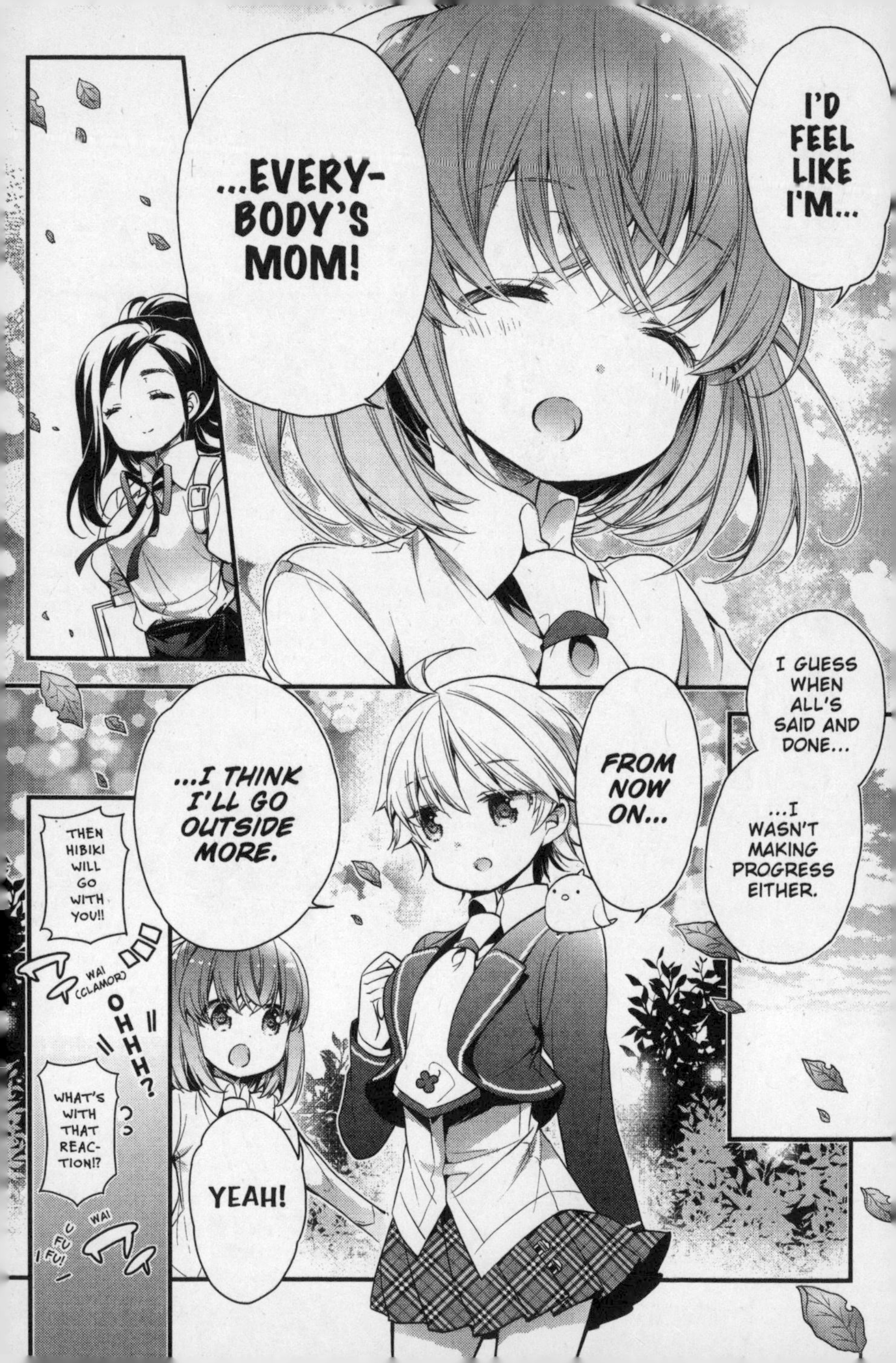
I'D FEEL LIKE I'M...
...EVERY-BODY'S MOM!
I GUESS WHEN ALL'S SAID AND DONE...
...I WASN'T MAKING PROGRESS EITHER.
FROM NOW ON...
...I THINK I'LL GO OUTSIDE MORE.
THEN HIBIKI WILL GO WITH YOU!!
WAI (CLAMOR)
OHHH?
WHAT'S WITH THAT REAC-TION!?
YEAH!
WAI
U FU FU!

Anne Happy
unhappy go lucky!

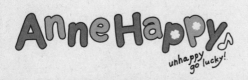

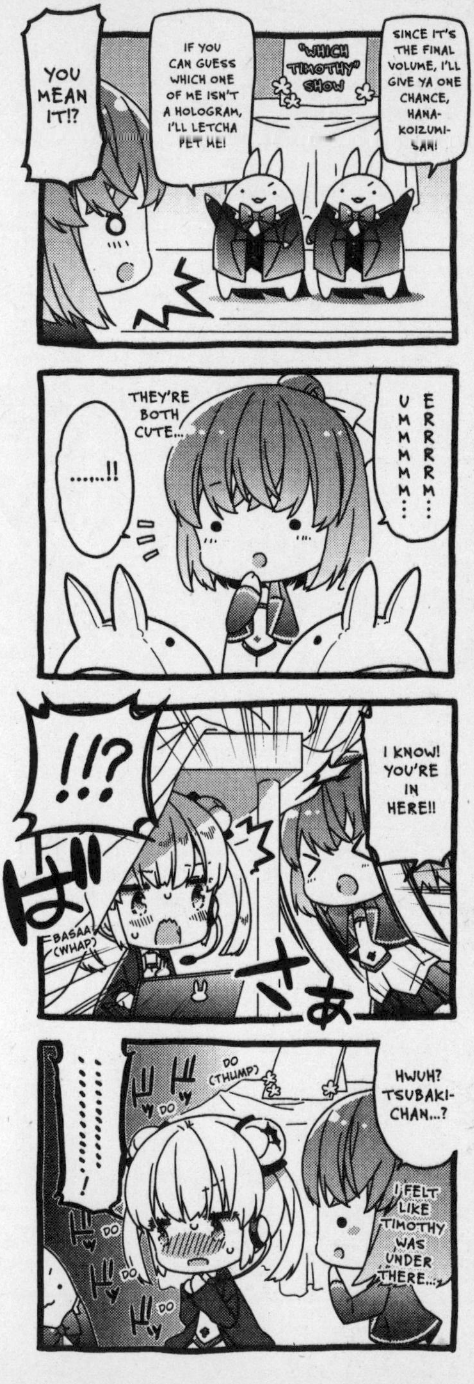
SINCE IT'S THE FINAL VOLUME, I'LL GIVE YA ONE CHANCE, HANA-KOIZUMI-SAN!
"WHICH TIMOTHY" SHOW
IF YOU CAN GUESS WHICH ONE OF ME ISN'T A HOLOGRAM, I'LL LETCHA PET ME!
YOU MEAN IT!?
ERRRRM... UMMMMM...
THEY'RE BOTH CUTE...
......!!
I KNOW! YOU'RE IN HERE!!
!!?
BASAA (WHAP)
HWUH? TSUBAKI-CHAN...?
I FELT LIKE TIMOTHY WAS UNDER THERE...
DO (THUMP)
..........!

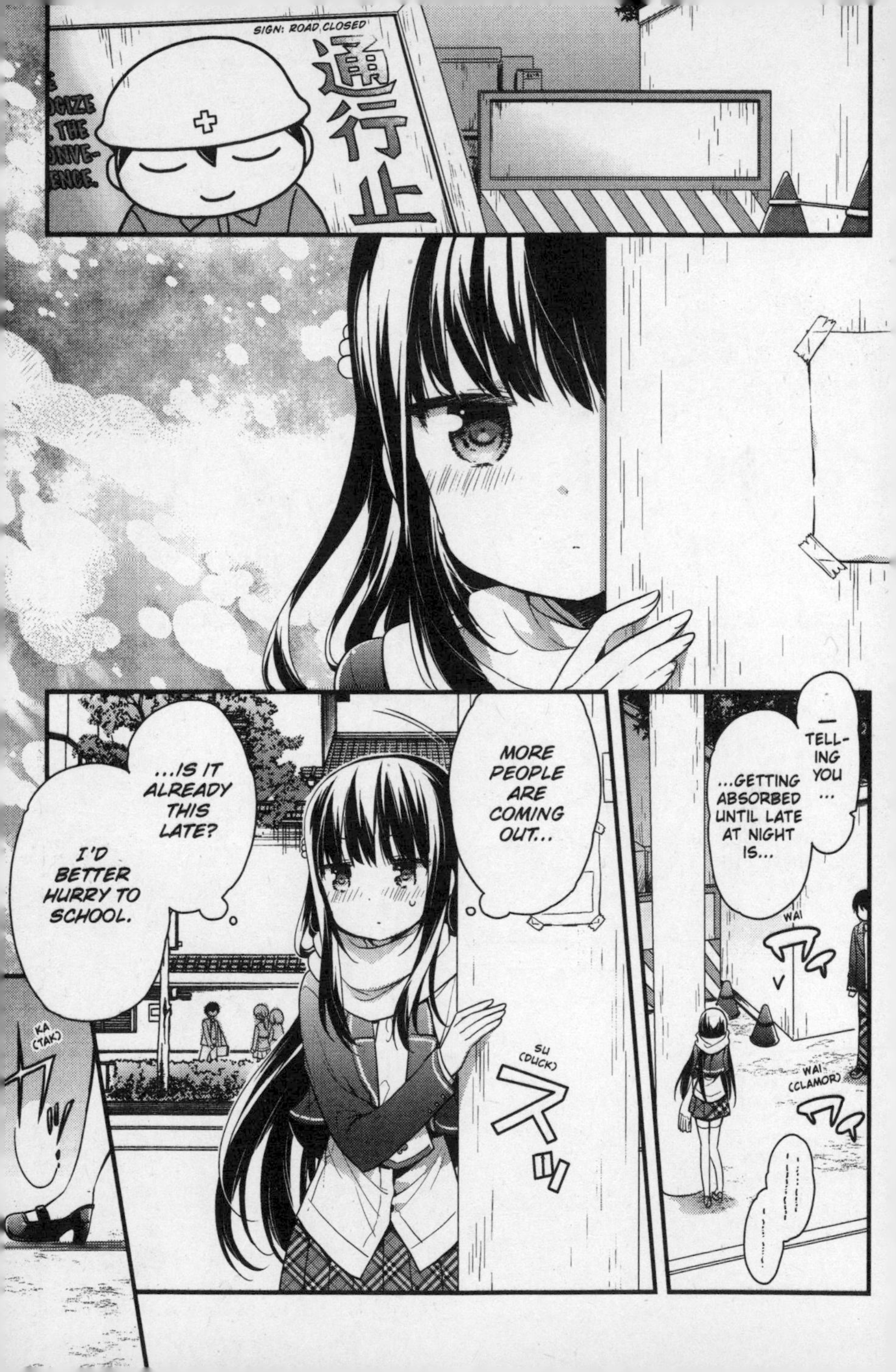
SIGN: ROAD CLOSED
通行止
— TELL-ING YOU ...
...GETTING ABSORBED UNTIL LATE AT NIGHT IS...
WAI
WAI (CLAMOR)
......
MORE PEOPLE ARE COMING OUT...
SU (DUCK)
...IS IT ALREADY THIS LATE?
I'D BETTER HURRY TO SCHOOL.
KA (TAK)

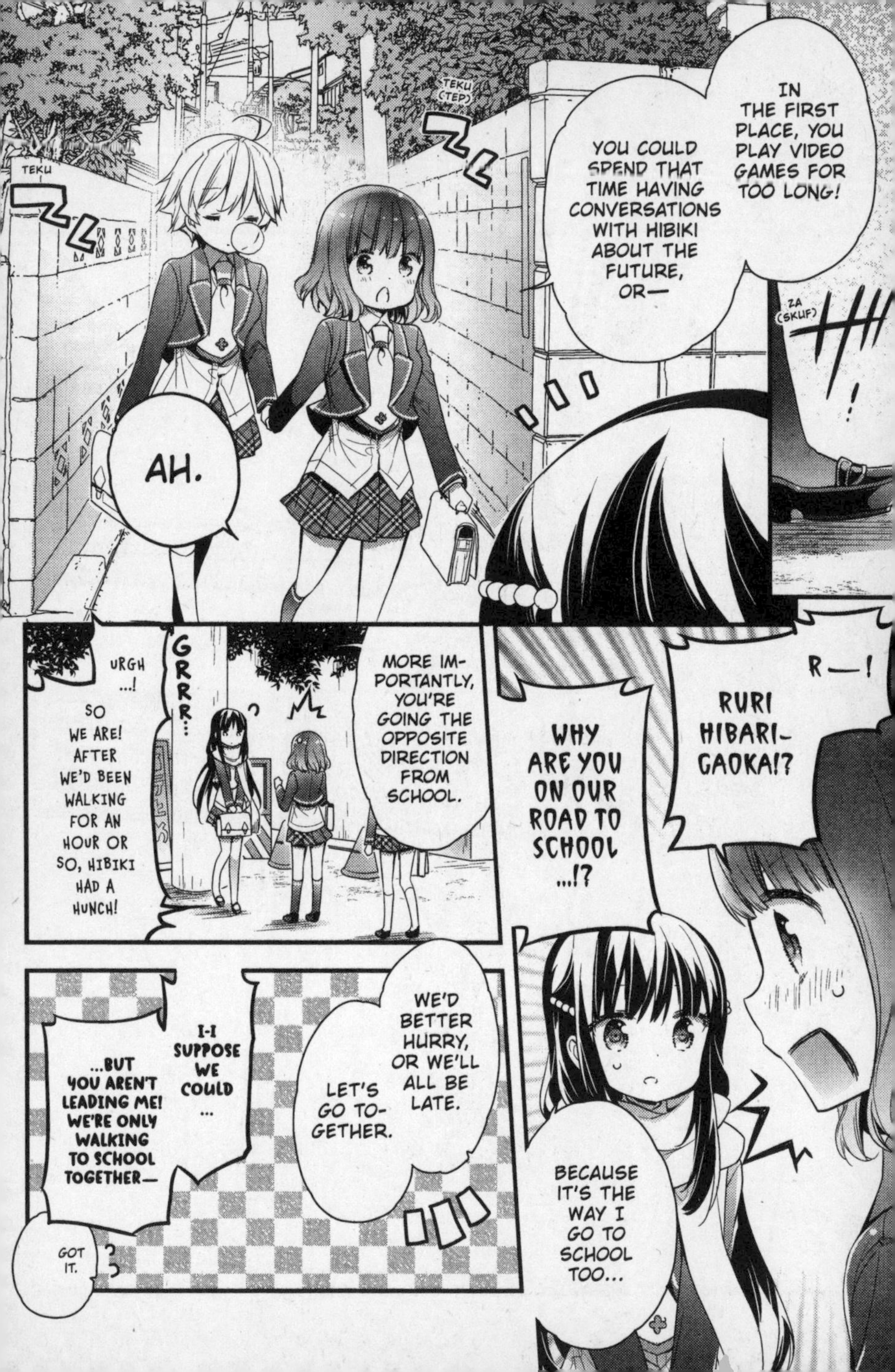
IN THE FIRST PLACE, YOU PLAY VIDEO GAMES FOR TOO LONG!
YOU COULD SPEND THAT TIME HAVING CONVERSATIONS WITH HIBIKI ABOUT THE FUTURE, OR—
TEKU (TEP)
TEKU
AH.
ZA (SKUF)
!
R—!
RURI HIBARI-GAOKA!?
WHY ARE YOU ON OUR ROAD TO SCHOOL ...!?
BECAUSE IT'S THE WAY I GO TO SCHOOL TOO...
MORE IM-PORTANTLY, YOU'RE GOING THE OPPOSITE DIRECTION FROM SCHOOL.
GRRR...
URGH ...!
SO WE ARE! AFTER WE'D BEEN WALKING FOR AN HOUR OR SO, HIBIKI HAD A HUNCH!
WE'D BETTER HURRY, OR WE'LL ALL BE LATE.
LET'S GO TO-GETHER.
I-I SUPPOSE WE COULD ...
...BUT YOU AREN'T LEADING ME! WE'RE ONLY WALKING TO SCHOOL TOGETHER—
GOT IT.

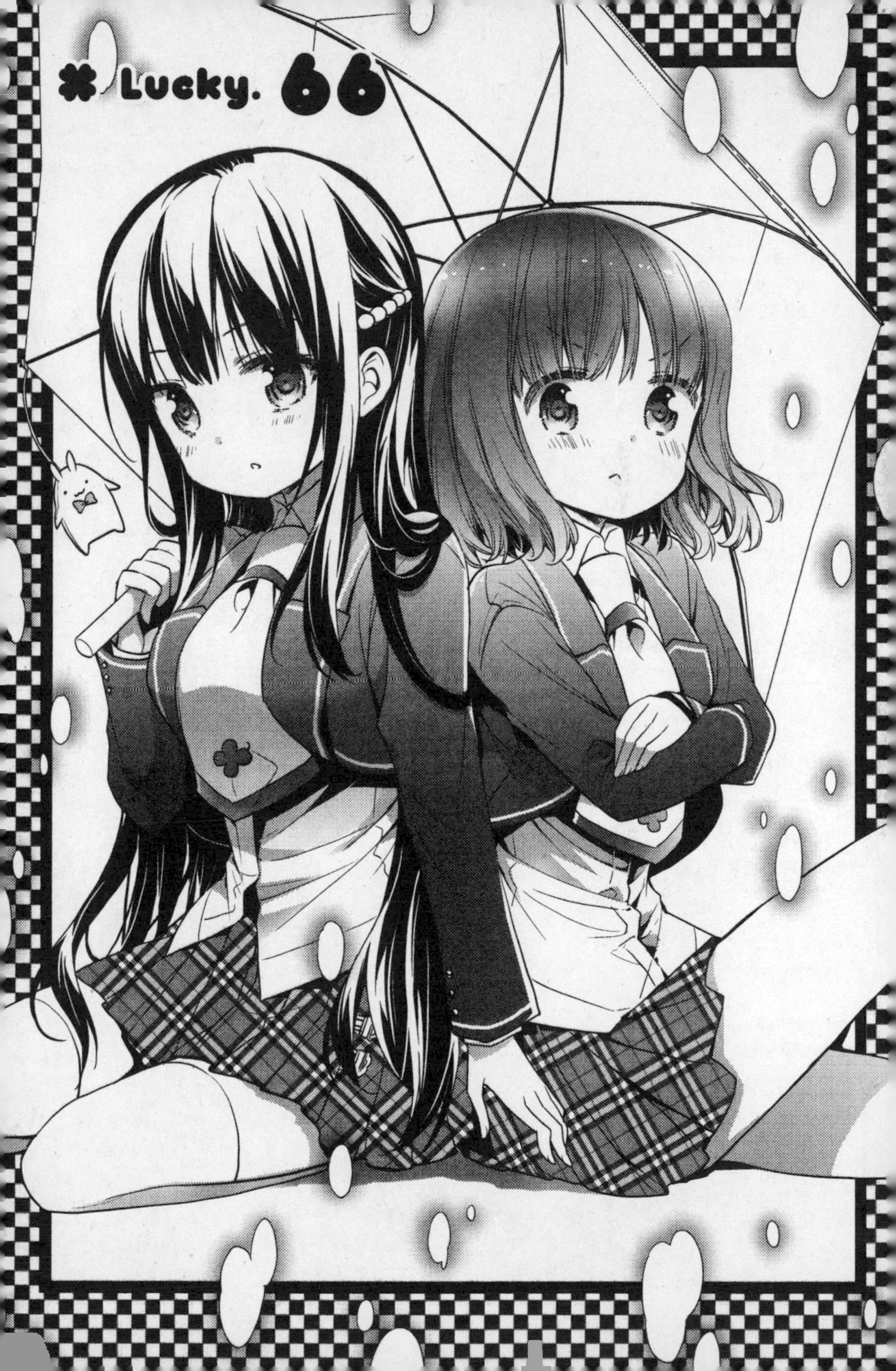
Lucky. 66

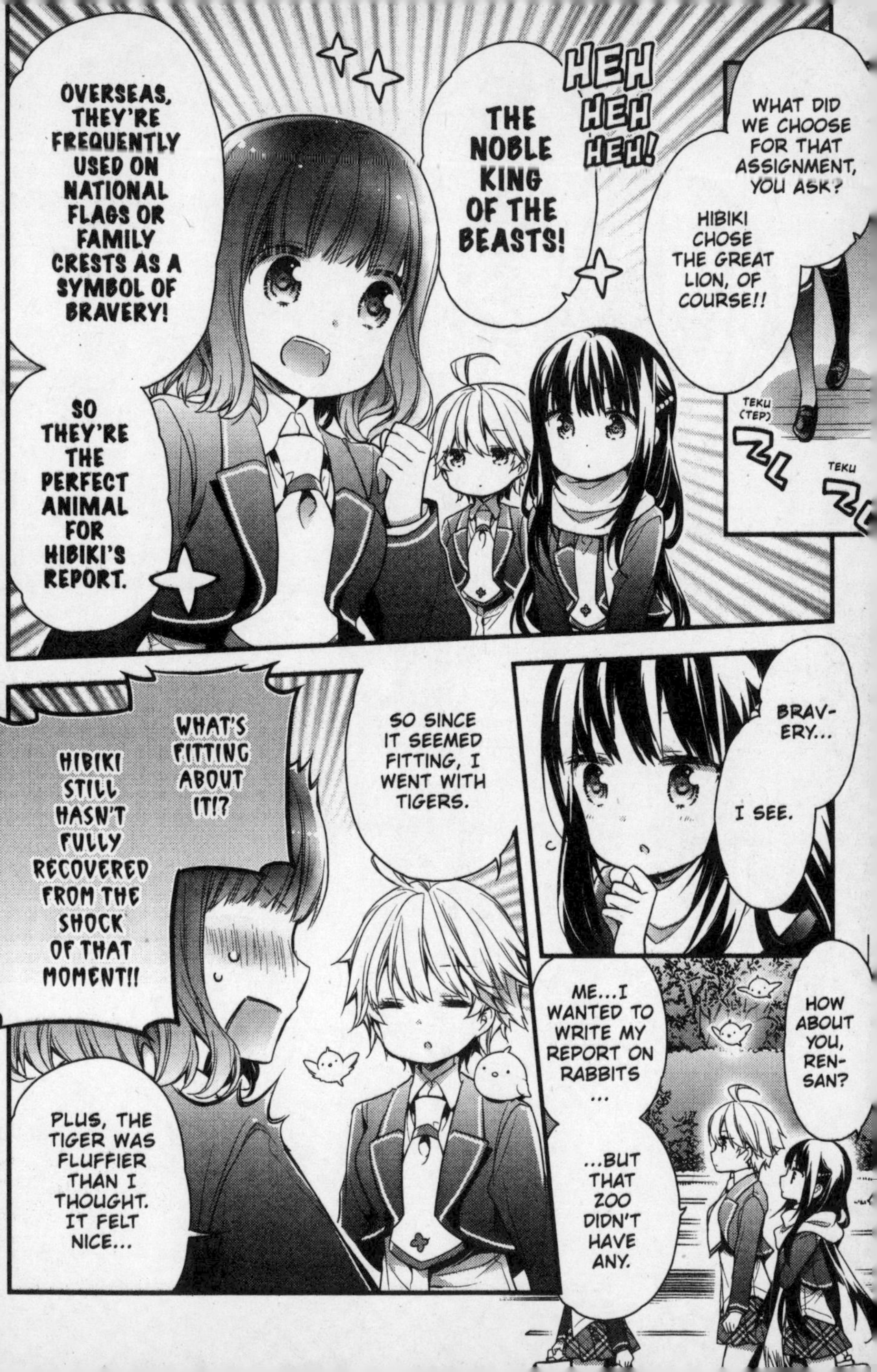
WHAT DID WE CHOOSE FOR THAT ASSIGNMENT, YOU ASK?
HIBIKI CHOSE THE GREAT LION, OF COURSE!!
TEKU (TEP)
TEKU
HEH HEH HEH!
THE NOBLE KING OF THE BEASTS!
OVERSEAS, THEY'RE FREQUENTLY USED ON NATIONAL FLAGS OR FAMILY CRESTS AS A SYMBOL OF BRAVERY!
SO THEY'RE THE PERFECT ANIMAL FOR HIBIKI'S REPORT.
BRAV-ERY...
I SEE.
HOW ABOUT YOU, REN-SAN?
ME...I WANTED TO WRITE MY REPORT ON RABBITS...
...BUT THAT ZOO DIDN'T HAVE ANY.
SO SINCE IT SEEMED FITTING, I WENT WITH TIGERS.
WHAT'S FITTING ABOUT IT!?
HIBIKI STILL HASN'T FULLY RECOVERED FROM THE SHOCK OF THAT MOMENT!!
PLUS, THE TIGER WAS FLUFFIER THAN I THOUGHT. IT FELT NICE...

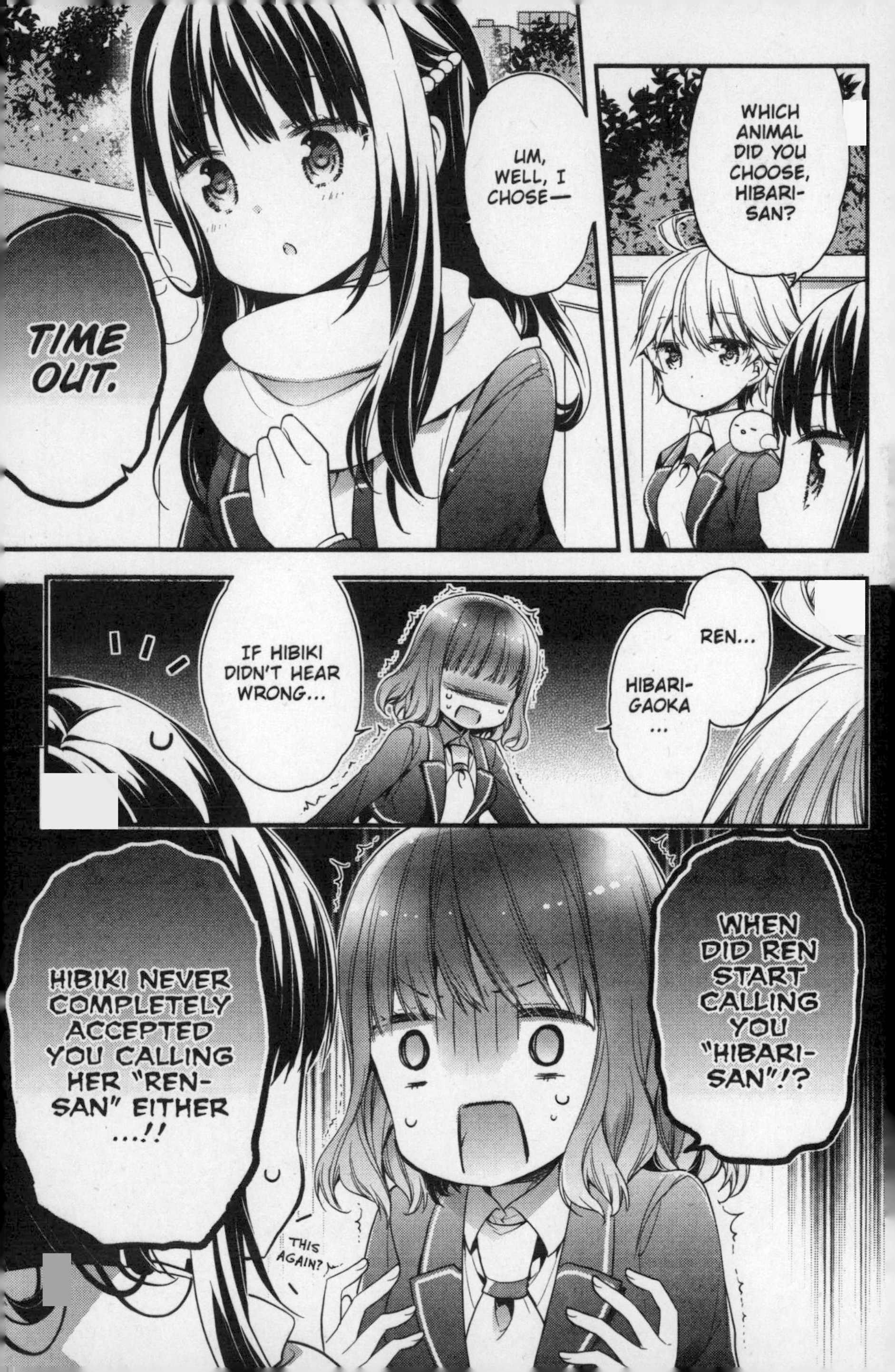
WHICH ANIMAL DID YOU CHOOSE, HIBARI-SAN?
UM, WELL, I CHOSE—
TIME OUT.
REN... HIBARI-GAOKA...
IF HIBIKI DIDN'T HEAR WRONG...
WHEN DID REN START CALLING YOU "HIBARI-SAN"!?
HIBIKI NEVER COMPLETELY ACCEPTED YOU CALLING HER "REN-SAN" EITHER ...!!
THIS AGAIN?

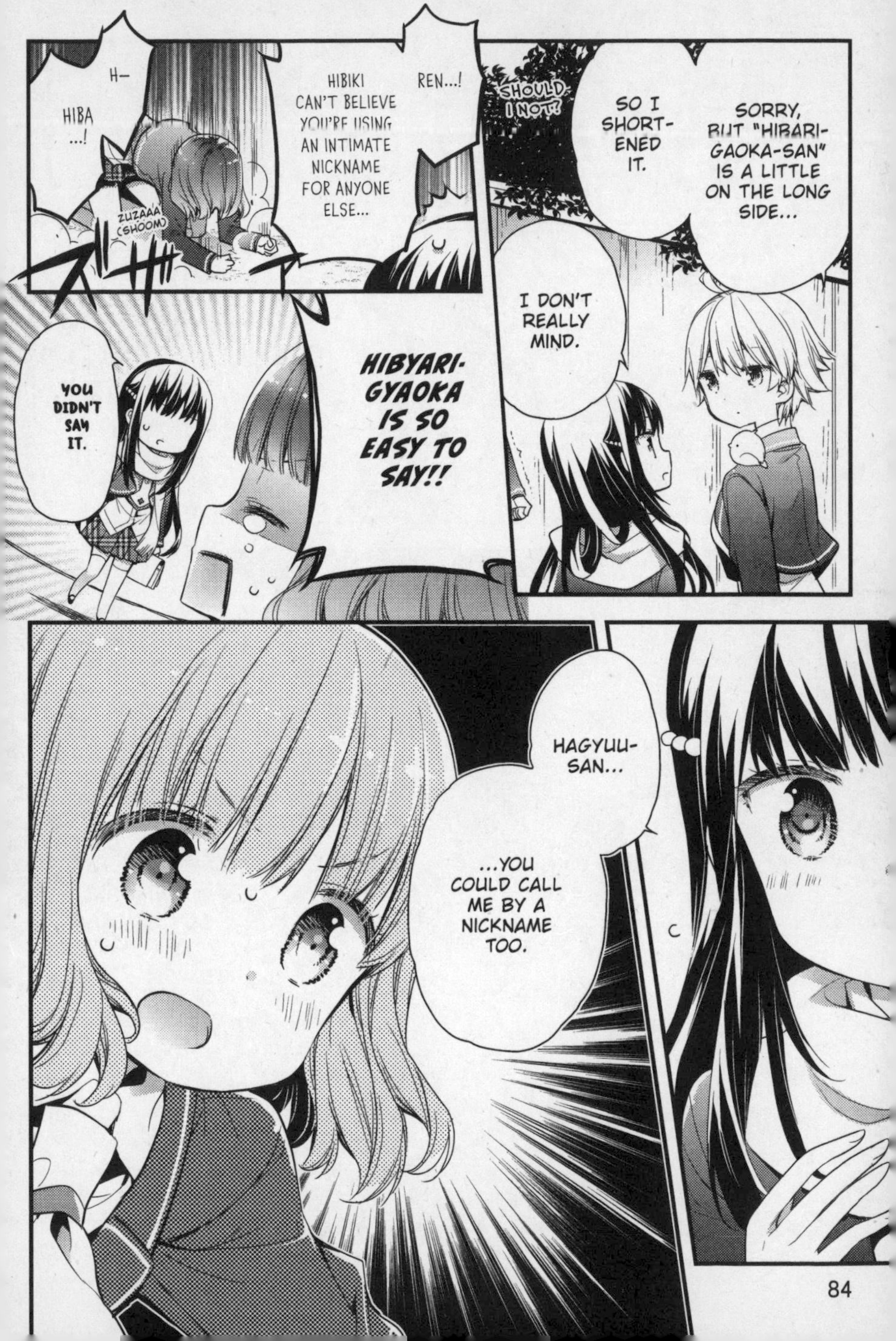
SORRY, BUT "HIBARI-GAOKA-SAN" IS A LITTLE ON THE LONG SIDE...
SO I SHORTENED IT.
SHOULD I NOT?
I DON'T REALLY MIND.
REN...!
HIBIKI CAN'T BELIEVE YOU'RE USING AN INTIMATE NICKNAME FOR ANYONE ELSE...
H—
HIBA...!
ZUZAAA (SHOOM)
HIBYARI-GYAOKA IS SO EASY TO SAY!!
YOU DIDN'T SAY IT.
HAGYUU-SAN...
...YOU COULD CALL ME BY A NICKNAME TOO.

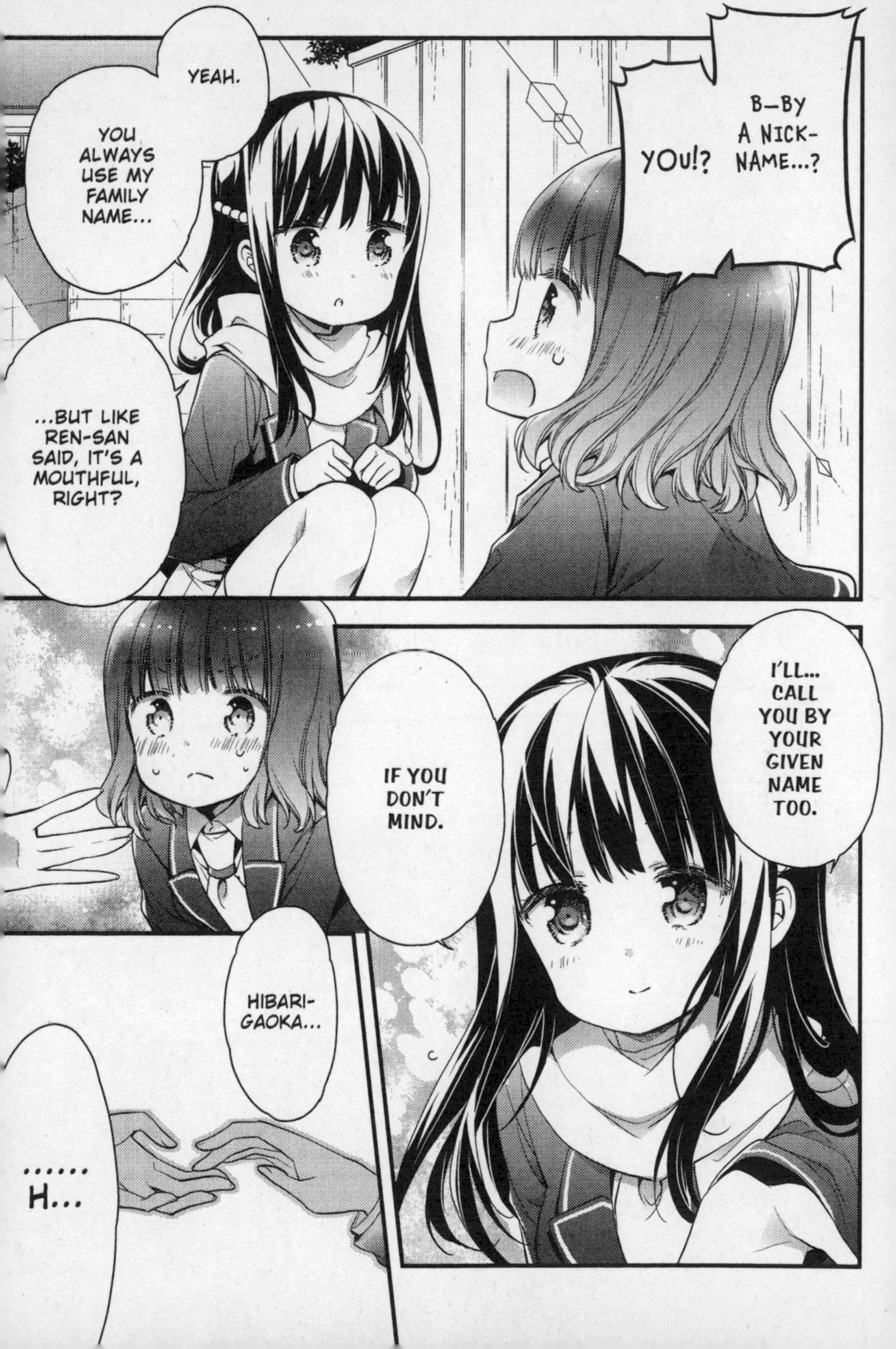
B—BY A NICK-NAME...?
YOU!?
YEAH.
YOU ALWAYS USE MY FAMILY NAME...
...BUT LIKE REN-SAN SAID, IT'S A MOUTHFUL, RIGHT?
I'LL... CALL YOU BY YOUR GIVEN NAME TOO.
IF YOU DON'T MIND.
HIBARI-GAOKA...
...... H...

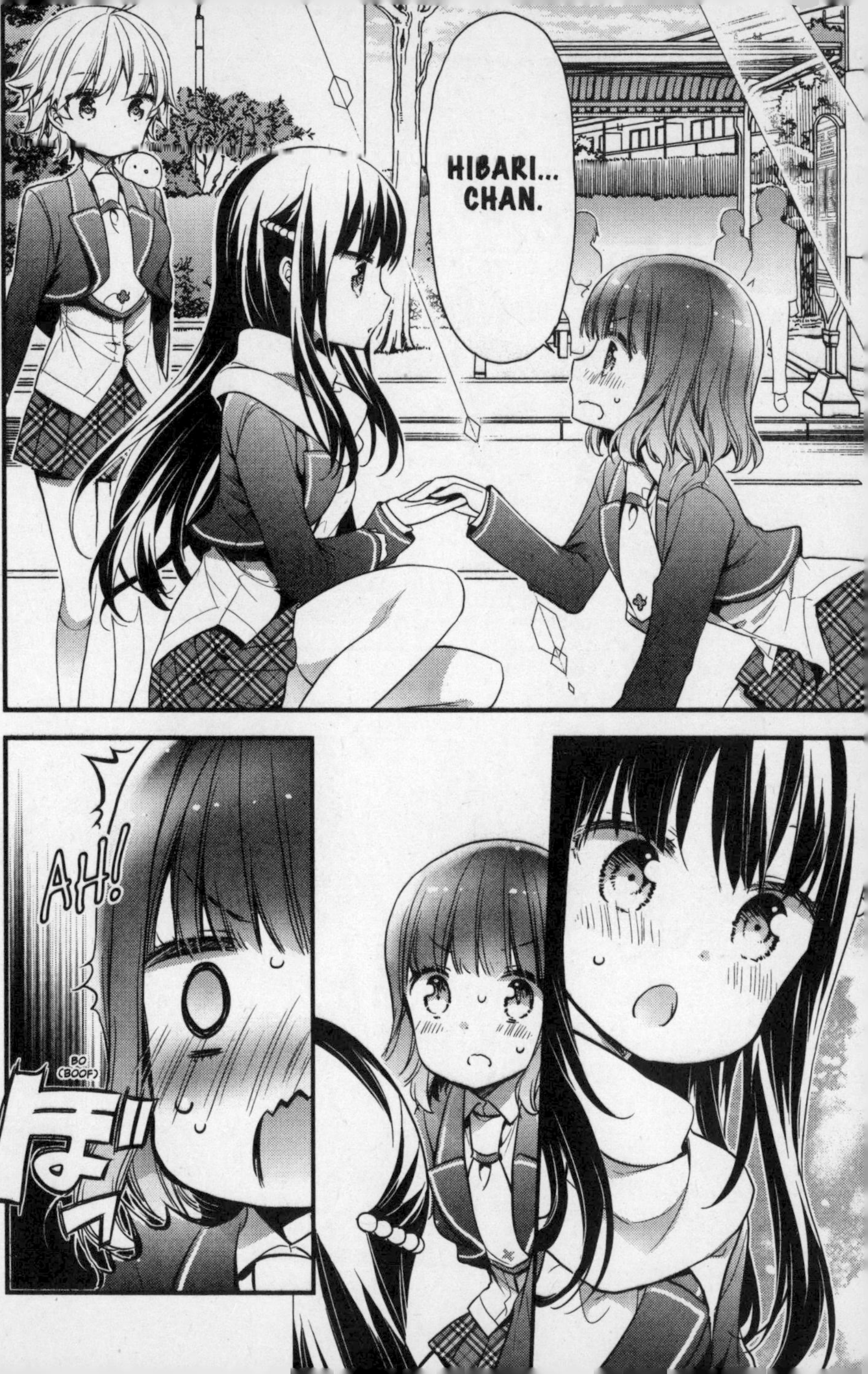
HIBARI... CHAN.
AH!
BO (BOOF)
ぼっ

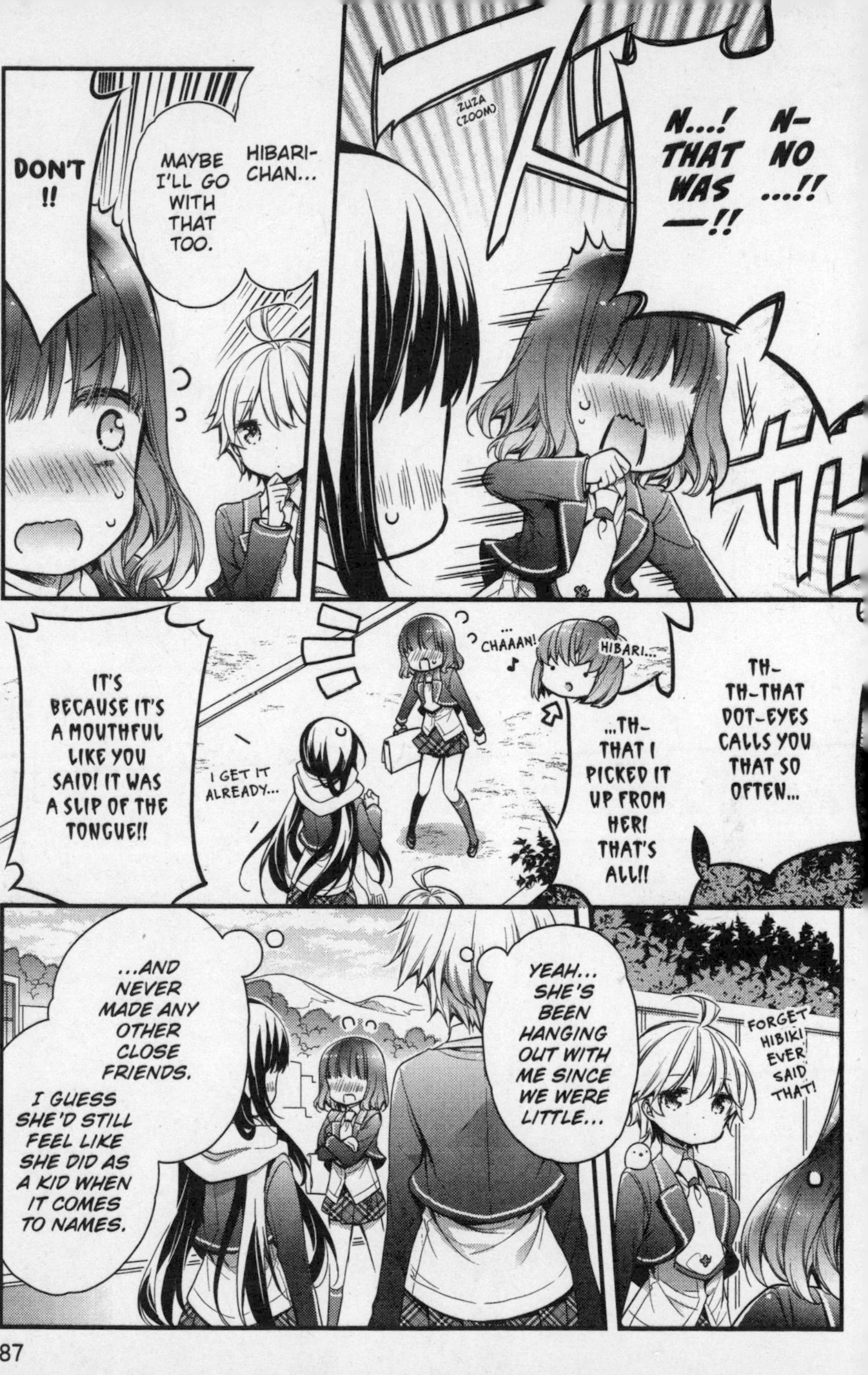
N-NO...!!
N...! THAT WAS—!!
ZUZA (ZOOM)
HIBARI-CHAN...
MAYBE I'LL GO WITH THAT TOO.
DON'T!!
TH-TH-THAT DOT-EYES CALLS YOU THAT SO OFTEN...
HIBARI...
...CHAAAN!
...TH-THAT I PICKED IT UP FROM HER! THAT'S ALL!!
I GET IT ALREADY...
IT'S BECAUSE IT'S A MOUTHFUL LIKE YOU SAID! IT WAS A SLIP OF THE TONGUE!!
FORGET HIBIKI EVER SAID THAT!
YEAH... SHE'S BEEN HANGING OUT WITH ME SINCE WE WERE LITTLE...
...AND NEVER MADE ANY OTHER CLOSE FRIENDS.
I GUESS SHE'D STILL FEEL LIKE SHE DID AS A KID WHEN IT COMES TO NAMES.

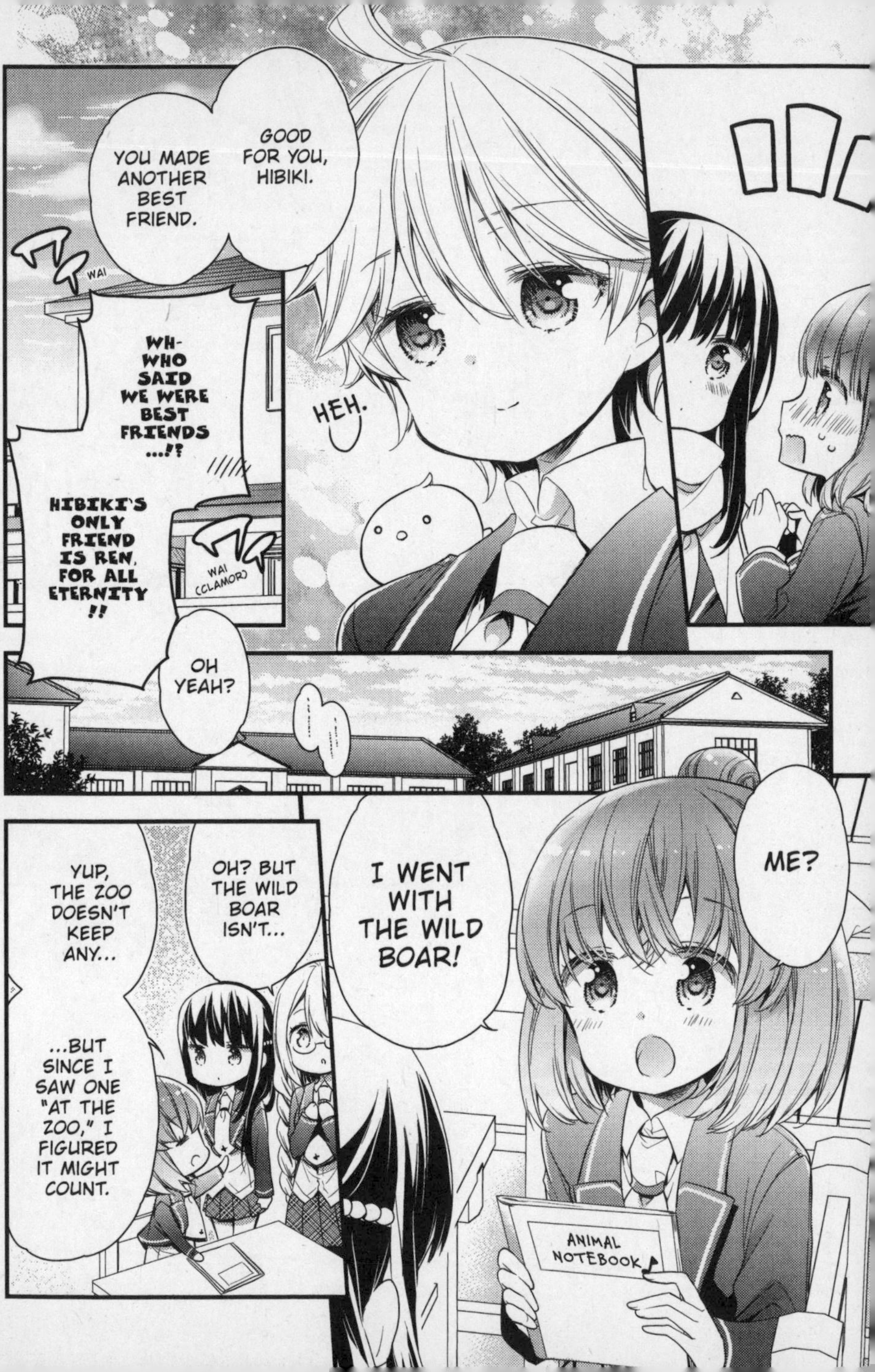
GOOD FOR YOU, HIBIKI.
YOU MADE ANOTHER BEST FRIEND.
HEH.
WAI
WH-WHO SAID WE WERE BEST FRIENDS...!?
HIBIKI'S ONLY FRIEND IS REN, FOR ALL ETERNITY!!
WAI (CLAMOR)
OH YEAH?
ME?
ANIMAL NOTEBOOK
I WENT WITH THE WILD BOAR!
OH? BUT THE WILD BOAR ISN'T...
YUP, THE ZOO DOESN'T KEEP ANY...
...BUT SINCE I SAW ONE "AT THE ZOO," I FIGURED IT MIGHT COUNT.

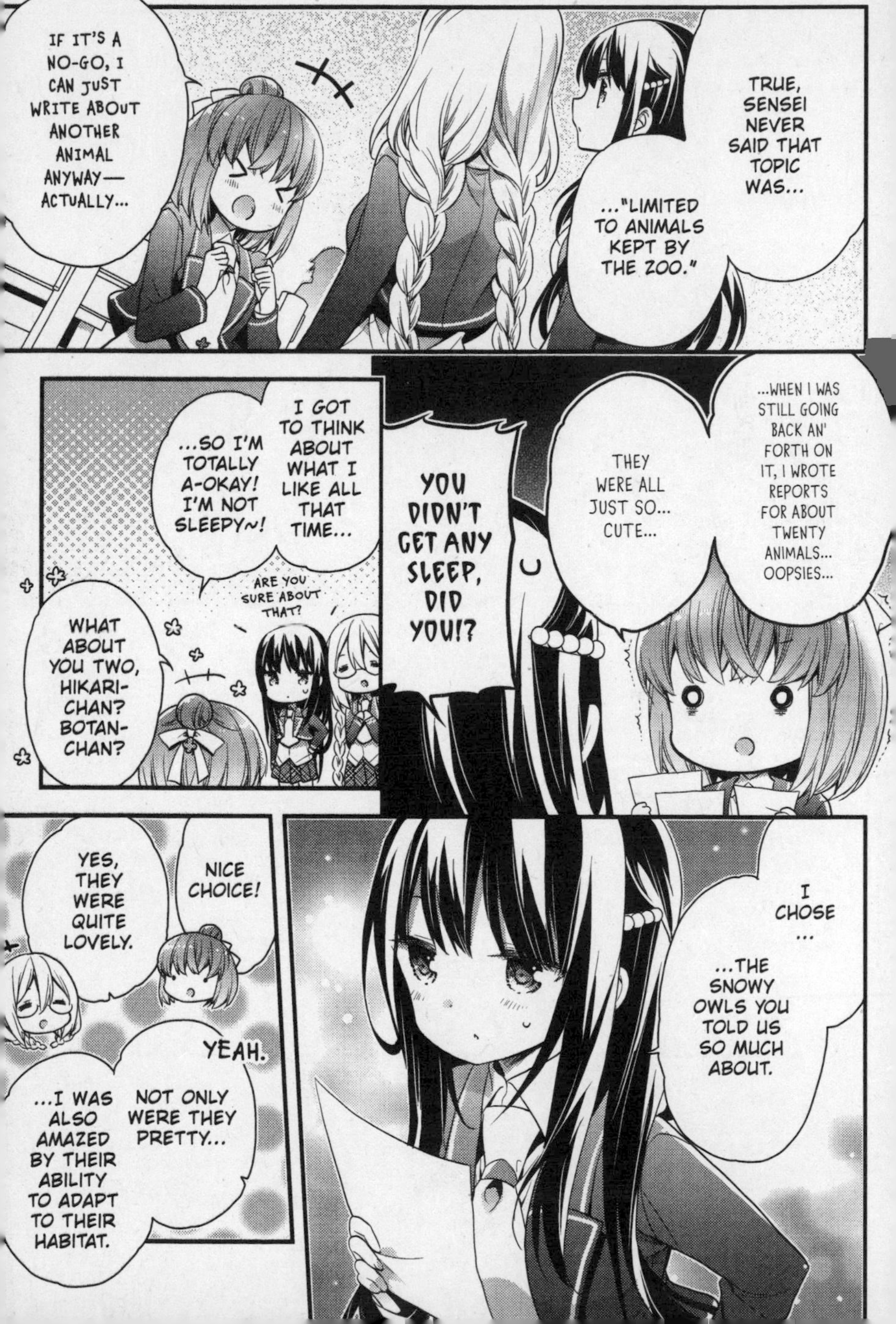
TRUE, SENSEI NEVER SAID THAT TOPIC WAS...
..."LIMITED TO ANIMALS KEPT BY THE ZOO."
IF IT'S A NO-GO, I CAN JUST WRITE ABOUT ANOTHER ANIMAL ANYWAY— ACTUALLY...
...WHEN I WAS STILL GOING BACK AN' FORTH ON IT, I WROTE REPORTS FOR ABOUT TWENTY ANIMALS... OOPSIES...
THEY WERE ALL JUST SO... CUTE...
YOU DIDN'T GET ANY SLEEP, DID YOU!?
I GOT TO THINK ABOUT WHAT I LIKE ALL THAT TIME...
...SO I'M TOTALLY A-OKAY! I'M NOT SLEEPY~!
ARE YOU SURE ABOUT THAT?
WHAT ABOUT YOU TWO, HIKARI-CHAN? BOTAN-CHAN?
I CHOSE...
...THE SNOWY OWLS YOU TOLD US SO MUCH ABOUT.
NICE CHOICE!
YES, THEY WERE QUITE LOVELY.
YEAH.
NOT ONLY WERE THEY PRETTY...
...I WAS ALSO AMAZED BY THEIR ABILITY TO ADAPT TO THEIR HABITAT.

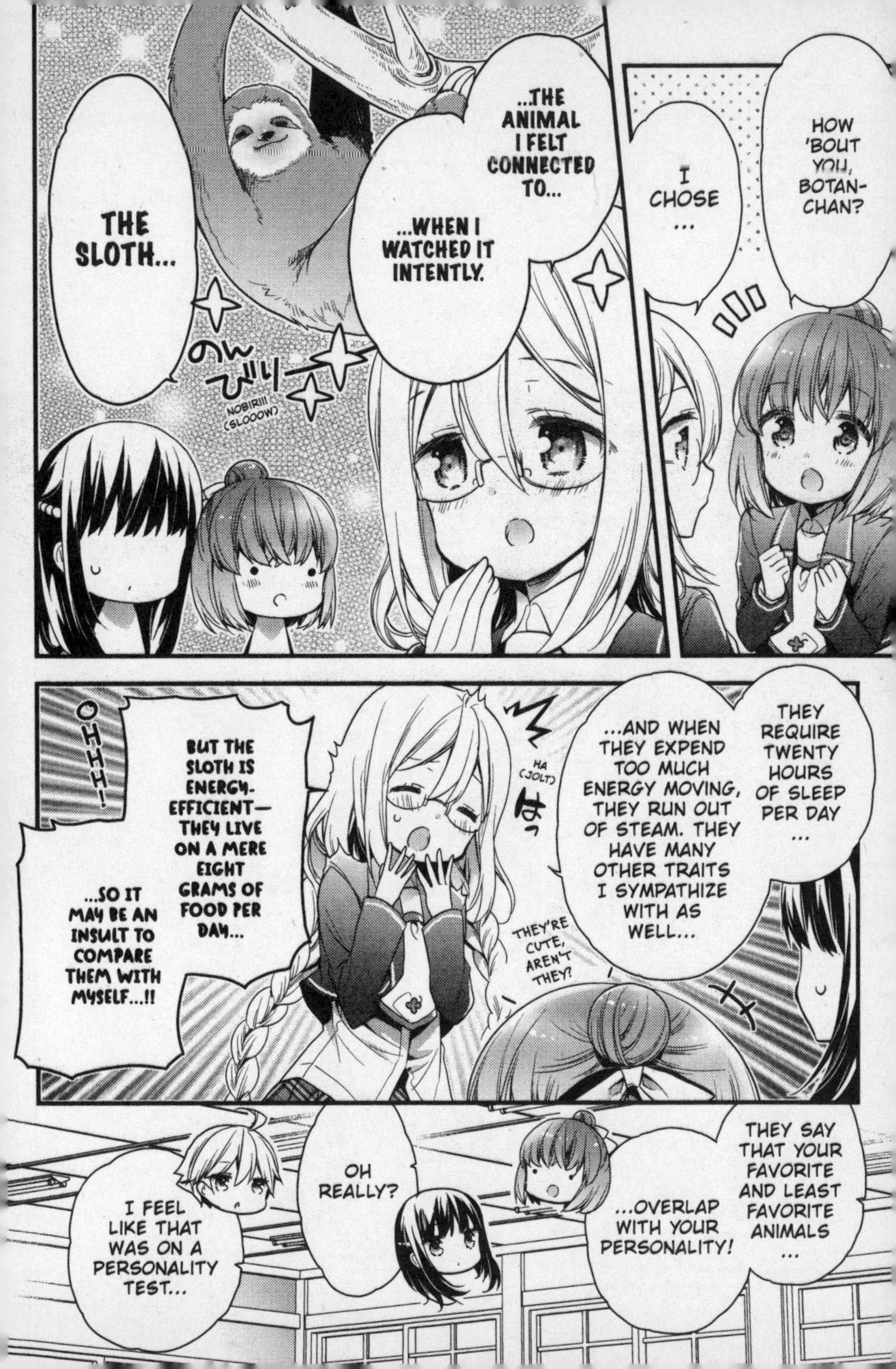
HOW 'BOUT YOU, BOTAN-CHAN?
I CHOSE...
...THE ANIMAL I FELT CONNECTED TO...
...WHEN I WATCHED IT INTENTLY.
THE SLOTH...
のんびり
NOBIRIII (SLOOOW)
THEY REQUIRE TWENTY HOURS OF SLEEP PER DAY...
...AND WHEN THEY EXPEND TOO MUCH ENERGY MOVING, THEY RUN OUT OF STEAM. THEY HAVE MANY OTHER TRAITS I SYMPATHIZE WITH AS WELL...
THEY'RE CUTE, AREN'T THEY?
はっ
HA (JOLT)
BUT THE SLOTH IS ENERGY-EFFICIENT—THEY LIVE ON A MERE EIGHT GRAMS OF FOOD PER DAY...
...SO IT MAY BE AN INSULT TO COMPARE THEM WITH MYSELF...!!
OHHH!
THEY SAY THAT YOUR FAVORITE AND LEAST FAVORITE ANIMALS...
...OVERLAP WITH YOUR PERSONALITY!
OH REALLY?
I FEEL LIKE THAT WAS ON A PERSONALITY TEST...

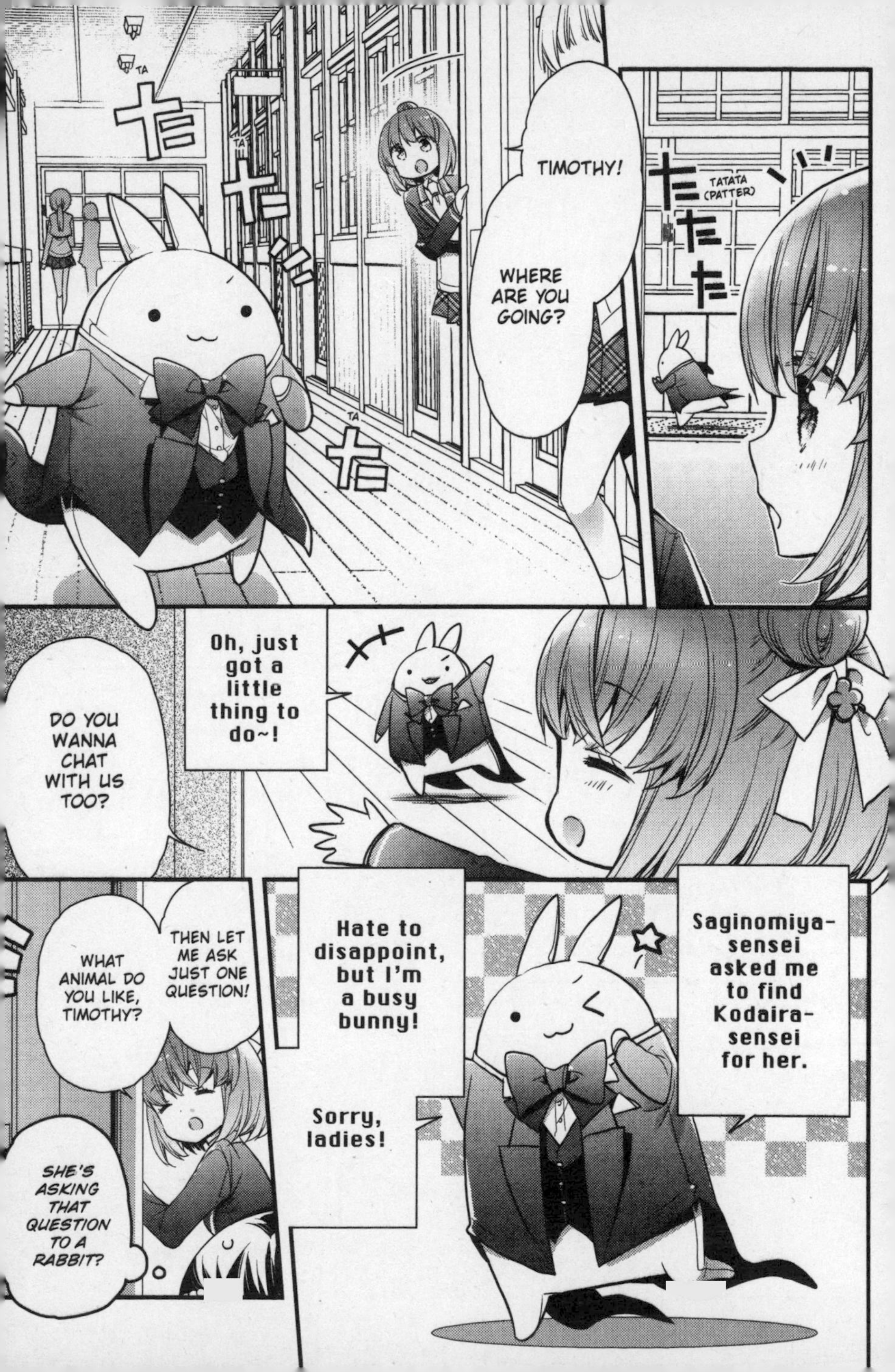

TATATA (PATTER)
TIMOTHY!
WHERE ARE YOU GOING?
TA
TA
TA
Oh, just got a little thing to do~!
DO YOU WANNA CHAT WITH US TOO?
Saginomiya-sensei asked me to find Kodaira-sensei for her.
Hate to disappoint, but I'm a busy bunny!
Sorry, ladies!
THEN LET ME ASK JUST ONE QUESTION!
WHAT ANIMAL DO YOU LIKE, TIMOTHY?
SHE'S ASKING THAT QUESTION TO A RABBIT?

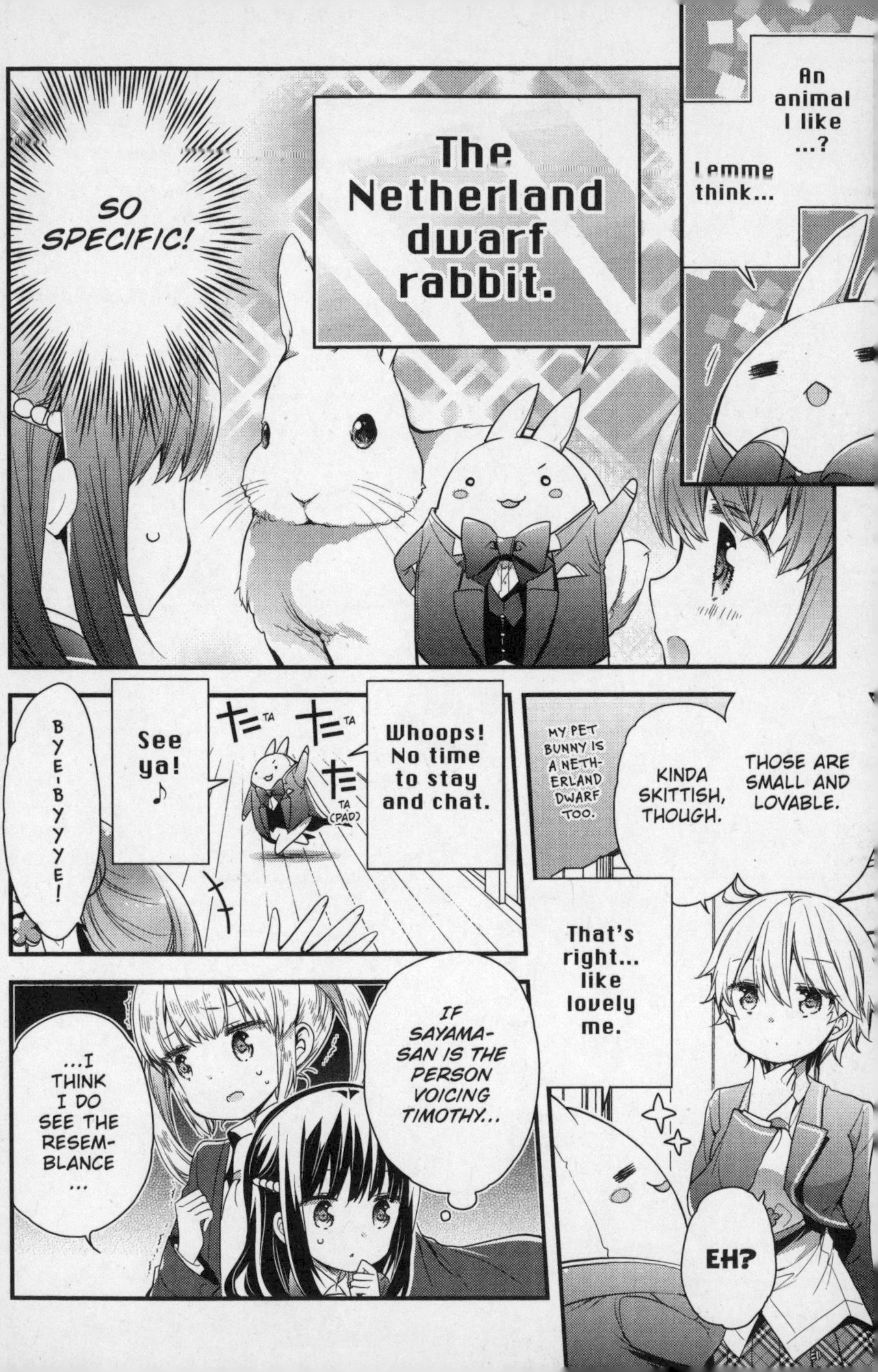
An animal I like ...?
Lemme think...
The Netherland dwarf rabbit.
SO SPECIFIC!
THOSE ARE SMALL AND LOVABLE.
KINDA SKITTISH, THOUGH.
MY PET BUNNY IS A NETH-ERLAND DWARF TOO.
Whoops! No time to stay and chat.
TA
TA
TA (PAD)
See ya! ♪
BYE-BYYYYE!
That's right... like lovely me.
EH?
IF SAYAMA-SAN IS THE PERSON VOICING TIMOTHY...
...I THINK I DO SEE THE RESEM-BLANCE ...

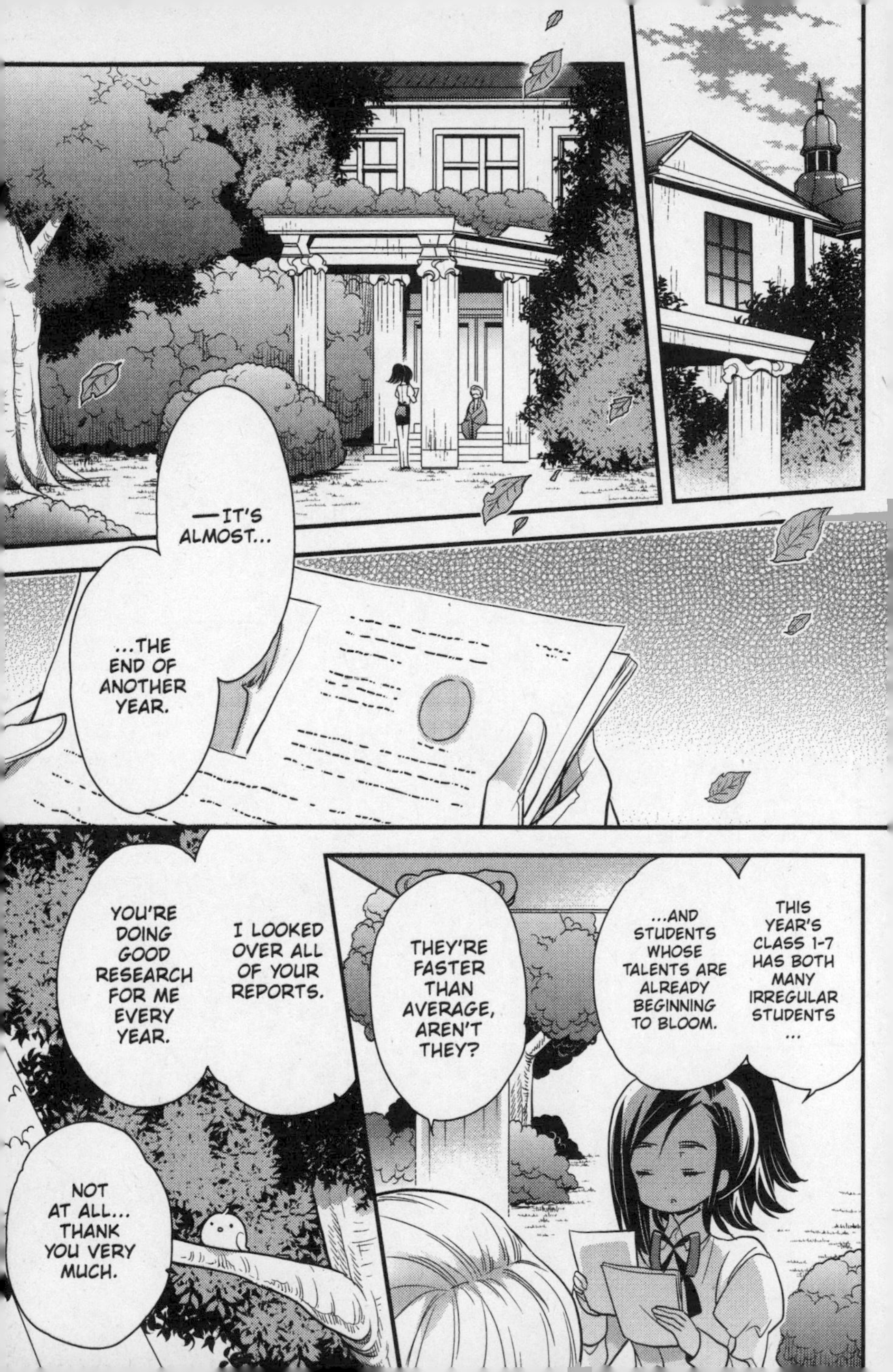
—IT'S ALMOST...
...THE END OF ANOTHER YEAR.
THIS YEAR'S CLASS 1-7 HAS BOTH MANY IRREGULAR STUDENTS ...
...AND STUDENTS WHOSE TALENTS ARE ALREADY BEGINNING TO BLOOM.
THEY'RE FASTER THAN AVERAGE, AREN'T THEY?
I LOOKED OVER ALL OF YOUR REPORTS.
YOU'RE DOING GOOD RESEARCH FOR ME EVERY YEAR.
NOT AT ALL... THANK YOU VERY MUCH.

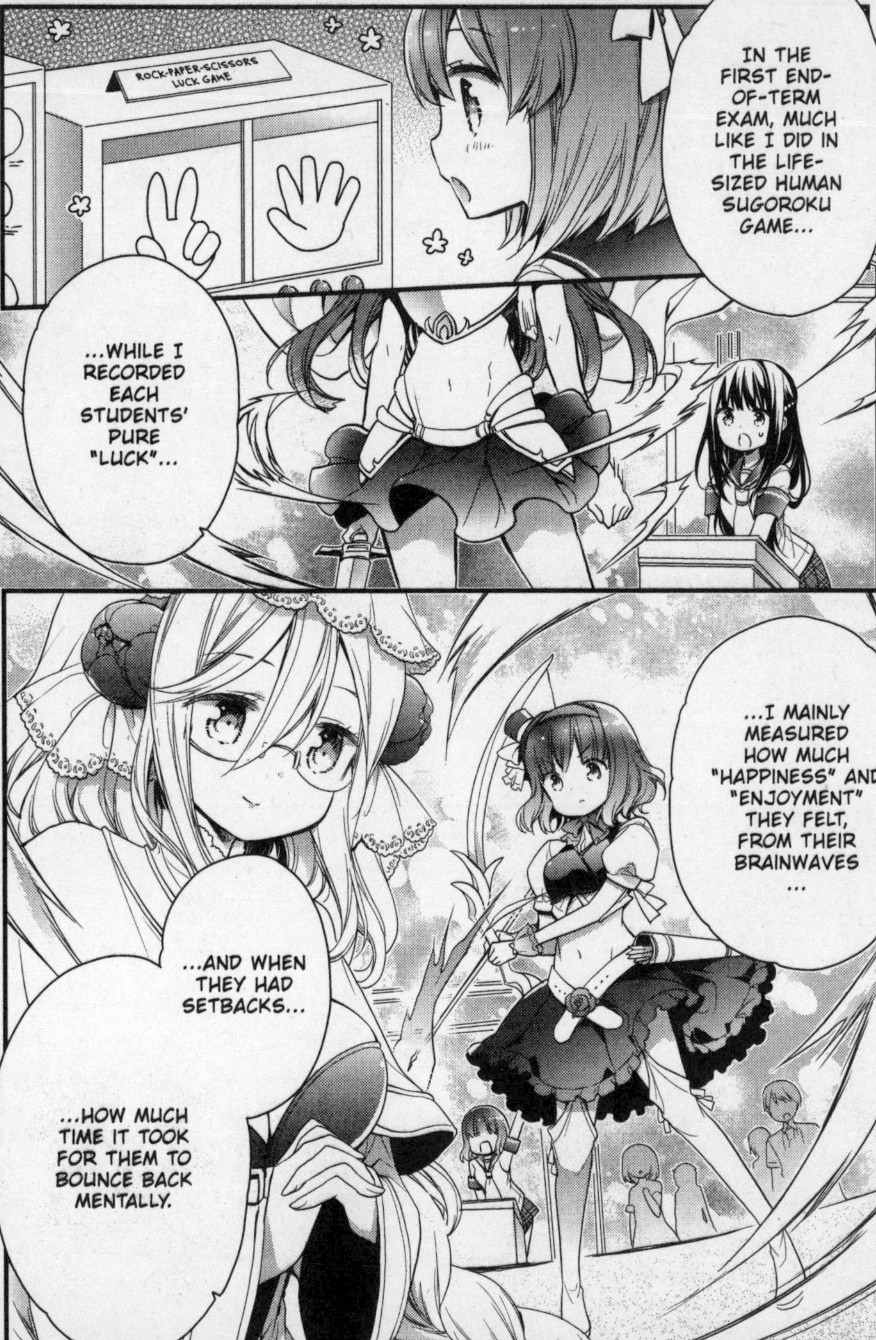
ROCK-PAPER-SCISSORS LUCK GAME
IN THE FIRST END-OF-TERM EXAM, MUCH LIKE I DID IN THE LIFE-SIZED HUMAN SUGOROKU GAME...
...WHILE I RECORDED EACH STUDENTS' PURE "LUCK"...
...I MAINLY MEASURED HOW MUCH "HAPPINESS" AND "ENJOYMENT" THEY FELT, FROM THEIR BRAINWAVES ...
...AND WHEN THEY HAD SETBACKS...
...HOW MUCH TIME IT TOOK FOR THEM TO BOUNCE BACK MENTALLY.

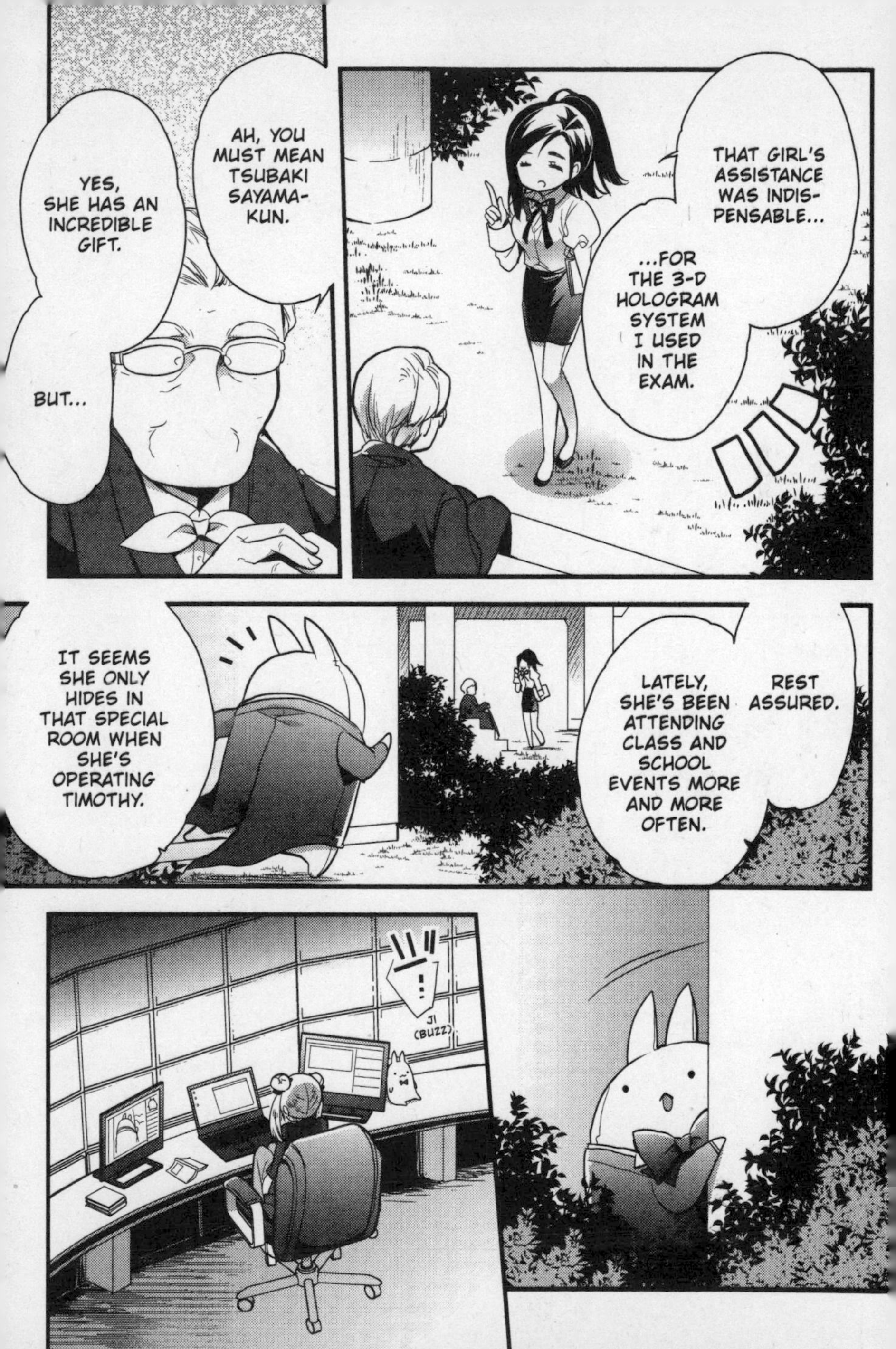
THAT GIRL'S ASSISTANCE WAS INDIS-PENSABLE...
...FOR THE 3-D HOLOGRAM SYSTEM I USED IN THE EXAM.
AH, YOU MUST MEAN TSUBAKI SAYAMA-KUN.
YES, SHE HAS AN INCREDIBLE GIFT.
BUT...
REST ASSURED.
LATELY, SHE'S BEEN ATTENDING CLASS AND SCHOOL EVENTS MORE AND MORE OFTEN.
IT SEEMS SHE ONLY HIDES IN THAT SPECIAL ROOM WHEN SHE'S OPERATING TIMOTHY.
JI (BUZZ)

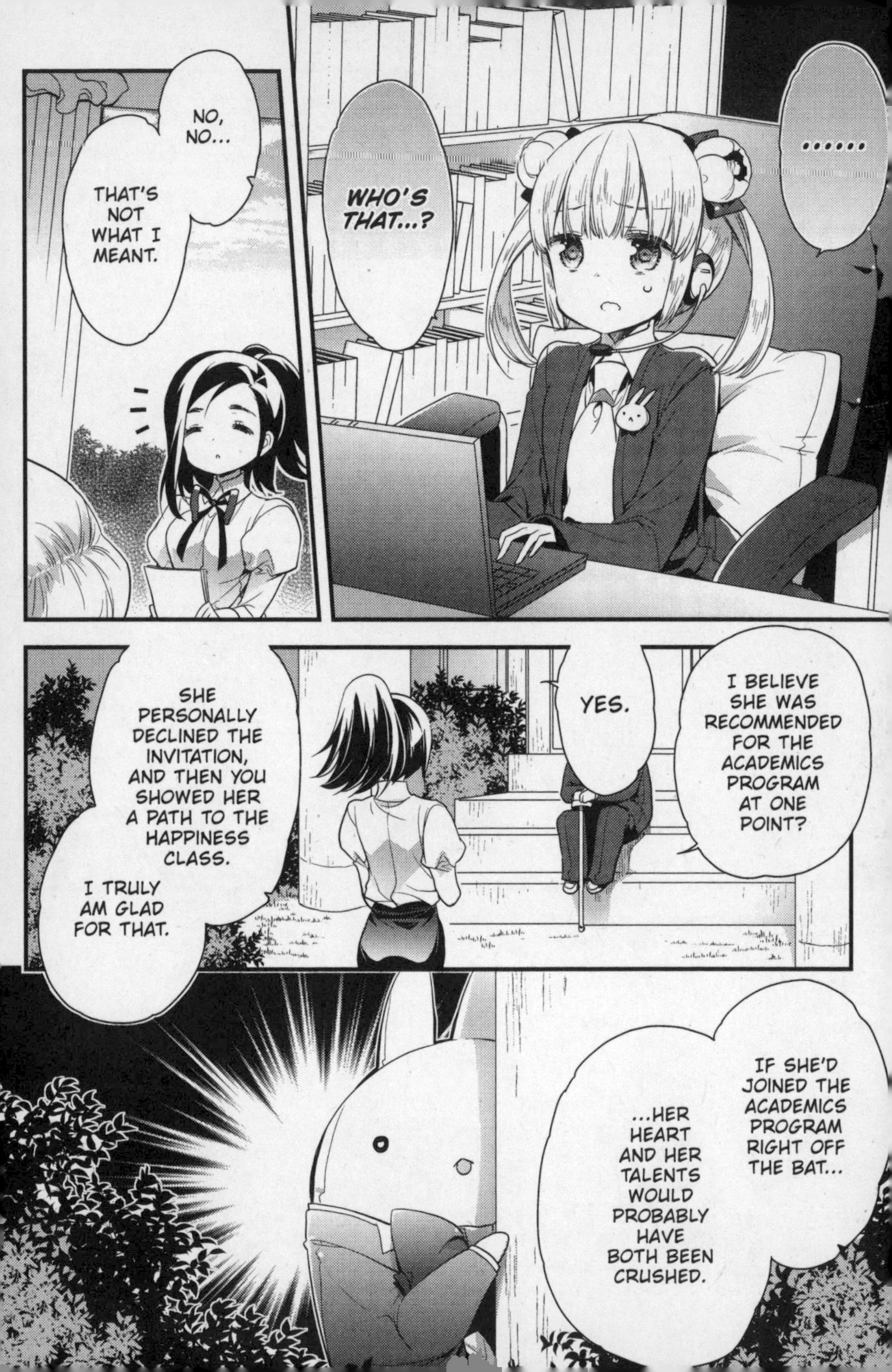
......
WHO'S THAT...?
NO, NO...
THAT'S NOT WHAT I MEANT.
I BELIEVE SHE WAS RECOMMENDED FOR THE ACADEMICS PROGRAM AT ONE POINT?
YES.
SHE PERSONALLY DECLINED THE INVITATION, AND THEN YOU SHOWED HER A PATH TO THE HAPPINESS CLASS.
I TRULY AM GLAD FOR THAT.
IF SHE'D JOINED THE ACADEMICS PROGRAM RIGHT OFF THE BAT...
...HER HEART AND HER TALENTS WOULD PROBABLY HAVE BOTH BEEN CRUSHED.

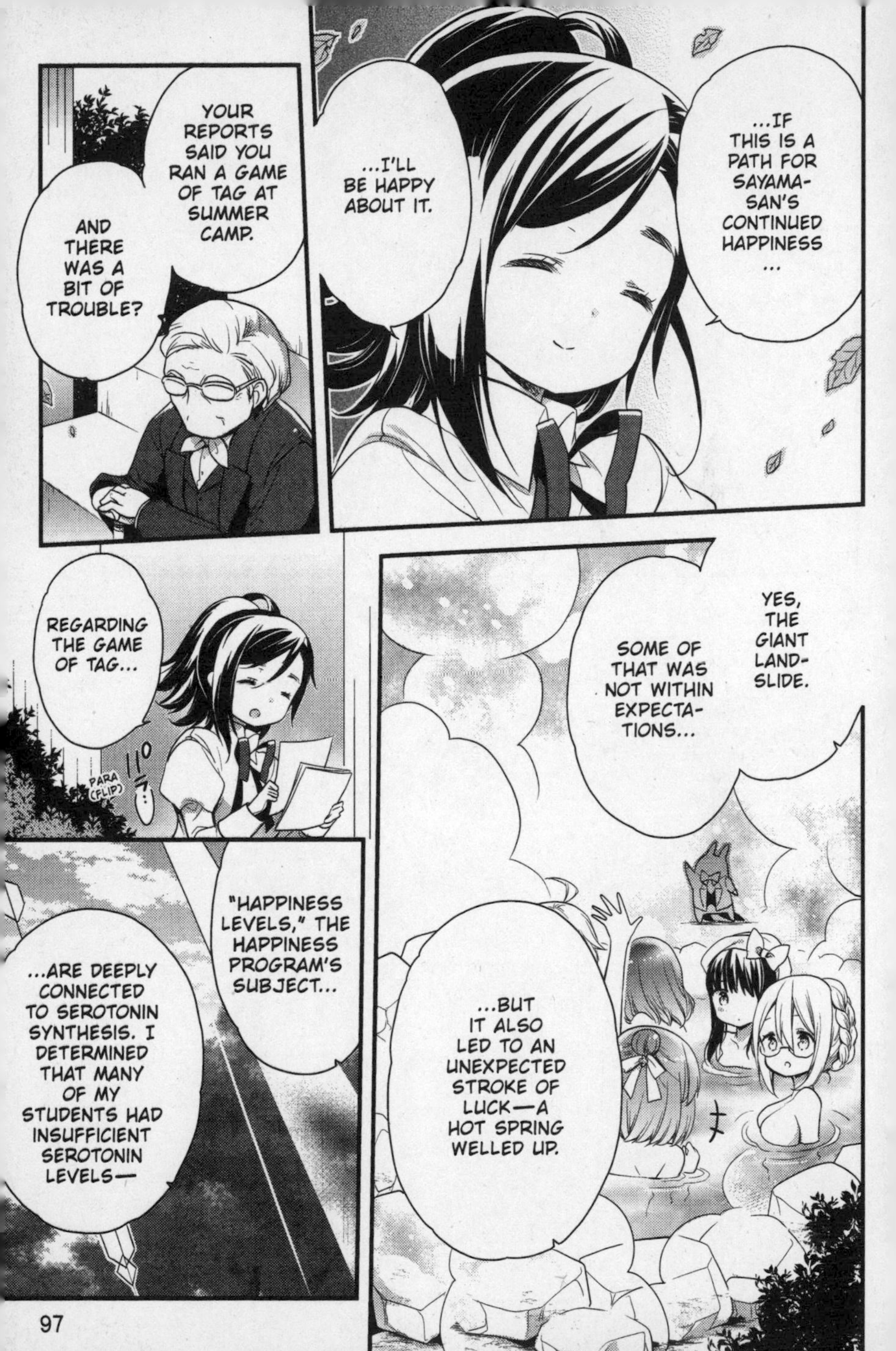
...IF THIS IS A PATH FOR SAYAMA-SAN'S CONTINUED HAPPINESS ...
...I'LL BE HAPPY ABOUT IT.
YOUR REPORTS SAID YOU RAN A GAME OF TAG AT SUMMER CAMP.
AND THERE WAS A BIT OF TROUBLE?
YES, THE GIANT LAND-SLIDE.
SOME OF THAT WAS NOT WITHIN EXPECTA-TIONS...
...BUT IT ALSO LED TO AN UNEXPECTED STROKE OF LUCK—A HOT SPRING WELLED UP.
REGARDING THE GAME OF TAG...
PARA (FLIP)
"HAPPINESS LEVELS," THE HAPPINESS PROGRAM'S SUBJECT...
...ARE DEEPLY CONNECTED TO SEROTONIN SYNTHESIS. I DETERMINED THAT MANY OF MY STUDENTS HAD INSUFFICIENT SEROTONIN LEVELS—

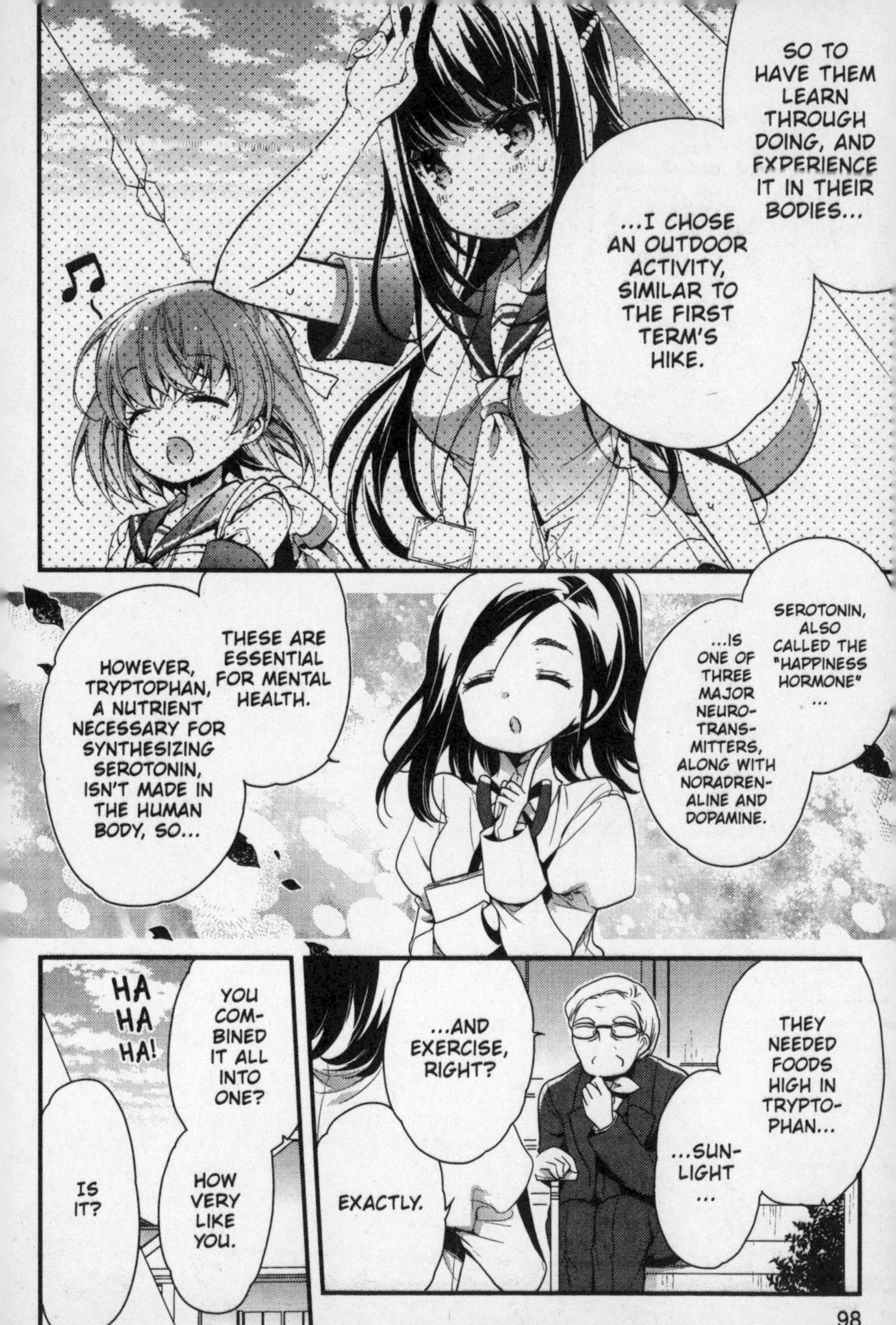
SO TO HAVE THEM LEARN THROUGH DOING, AND EXPERIENCE IT IN THEIR BODIES...
...I CHOSE AN OUTDOOR ACTIVITY, SIMILAR TO THE FIRST TERM'S HIKE.
SEROTONIN, ALSO CALLED THE "HAPPINESS HORMONE"...
...IS ONE OF THREE MAJOR NEURO-TRANS-MITTERS, ALONG WITH NORADREN-ALINE AND DOPAMINE.
THESE ARE ESSENTIAL FOR MENTAL HEALTH.
HOWEVER, TRYPTOPHAN, A NUTRIENT NECESSARY FOR SYNTHESIZING SEROTONIN, ISN'T MADE IN THE HUMAN BODY, SO...
THEY NEEDED FOODS HIGH IN TRYPTO-PHAN...
...SUN-LIGHT...
...AND EXERCISE, RIGHT?
EXACTLY.
YOU COM-BINED IT ALL INTO ONE?
HA HA HA!
HOW VERY LIKE YOU.
IS IT?

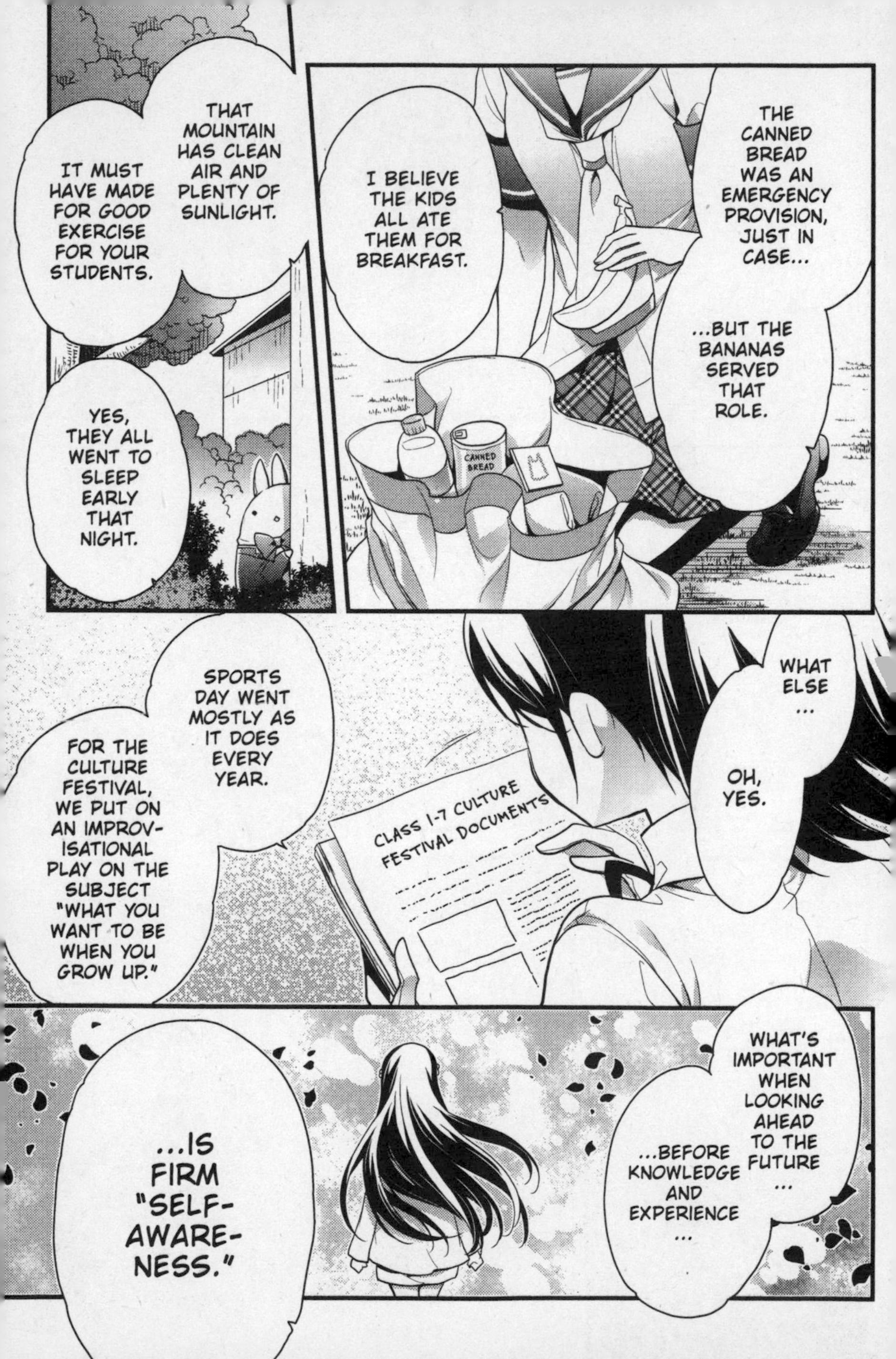
THE CANNED BREAD WAS AN EMERGENCY PROVISION, JUST IN CASE...
...BUT THE BANANAS SERVED THAT ROLE.
CANNED BREAD
I BELIEVE THE KIDS ALL ATE THEM FOR BREAKFAST.
THAT MOUNTAIN HAS CLEAN AIR AND PLENTY OF SUNLIGHT.
IT MUST HAVE MADE FOR GOOD EXERCISE FOR YOUR STUDENTS.
YES, THEY ALL WENT TO SLEEP EARLY THAT NIGHT.
WHAT ELSE ...
OH, YES.
CLASS 1-7 CULTURE FESTIVAL DOCUMENTS
SPORTS DAY WENT MOSTLY AS IT DOES EVERY YEAR.
FOR THE CULTURE FESTIVAL, WE PUT ON AN IMPROV-ISATIONAL PLAY ON THE SUBJECT "WHAT YOU WANT TO BE WHEN YOU GROW UP."
WHAT'S IMPORTANT WHEN LOOKING AHEAD TO THE FUTURE ...
...BEFORE KNOWLEDGE AND EXPERIENCE ...
...IS FIRM "SELF-AWARENESS."

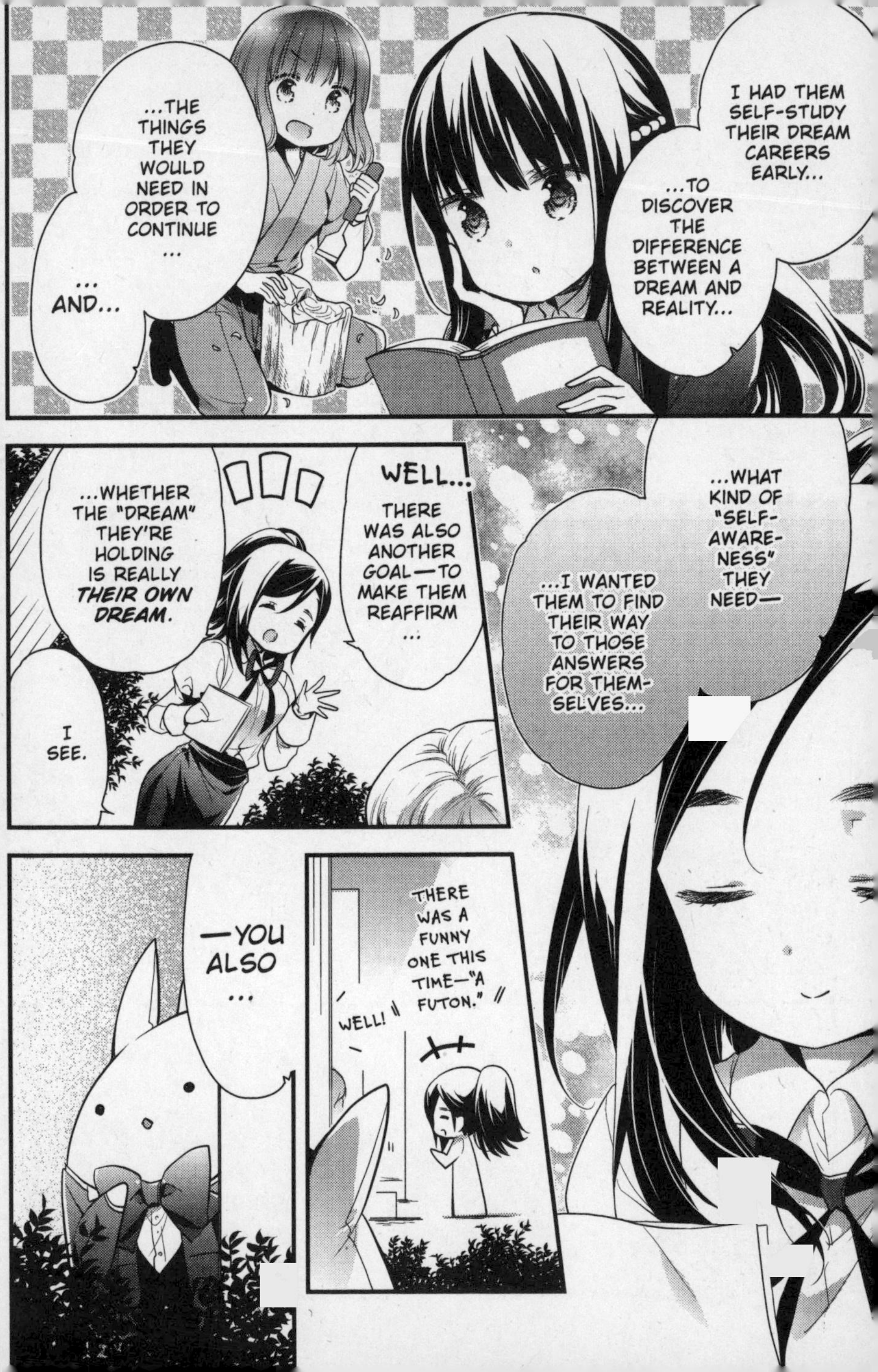
I HAD THEM SELF-STUDY THEIR DREAM CAREERS EARLY...
...TO DISCOVER THE DIFFERENCE BETWEEN A DREAM AND REALITY...
...THE THINGS THEY WOULD NEED IN ORDER TO CONTINUE ...
... AND...
...WHAT KIND OF "SELF-AWARENESS" THEY NEED—
...I WANTED THEM TO FIND THEIR WAY TO THOSE ANSWERS FOR THEMSELVES...
WELL...
THERE WAS ALSO ANOTHER GOAL—TO MAKE THEM REAFFIRM ...
...WHETHER THE "DREAM" THEY'RE HOLDING IS REALLY *THEIR OWN DREAM*.
I SEE.
THERE WAS A FUNNY ONE THIS TIME—"A FUTON."
WELL!
—YOU ALSO ...

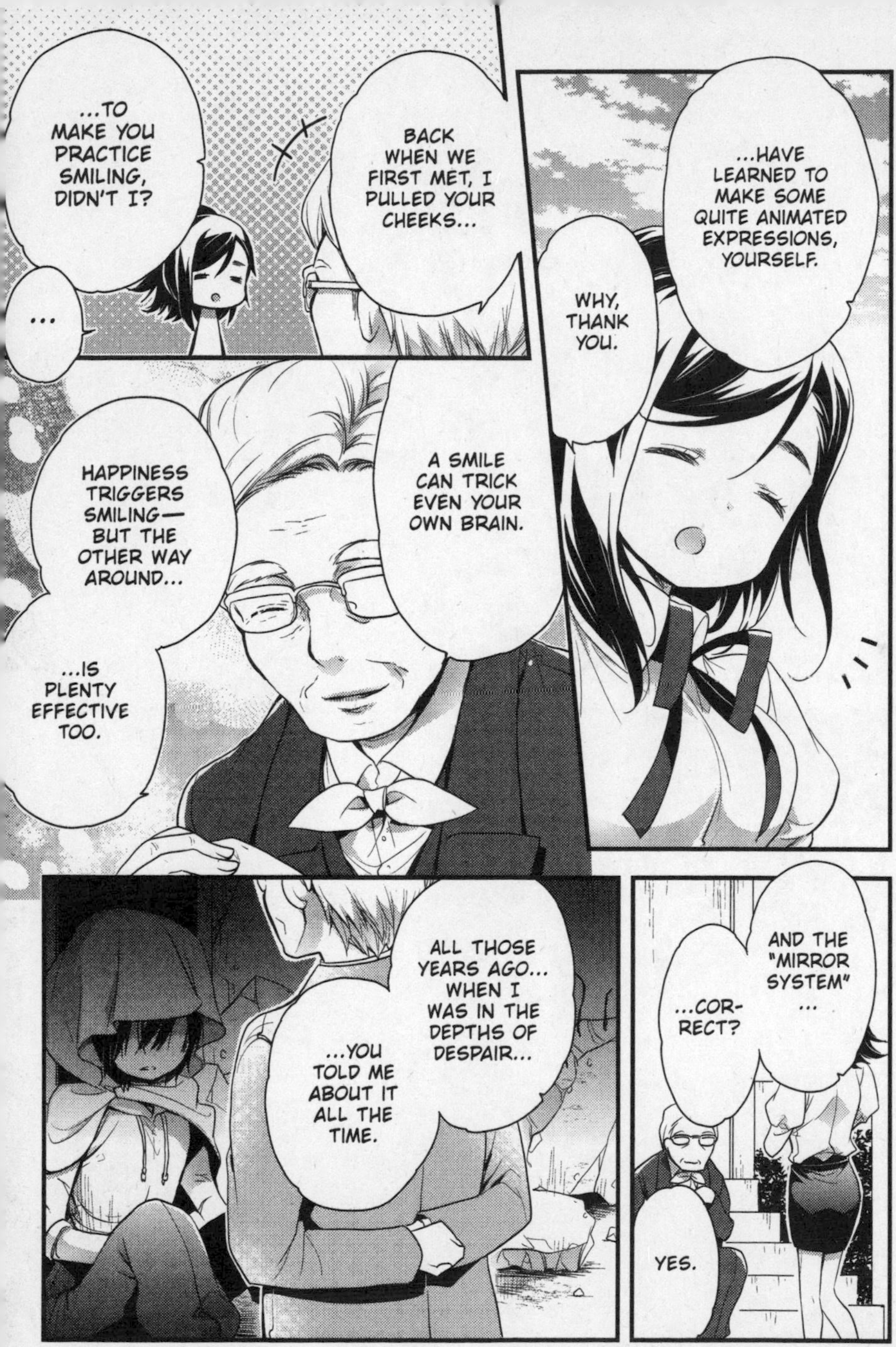
...HAVE LEARNED TO MAKE SOME QUITE ANIMATED EXPRESSIONS, YOURSELF.
WHY, THANK YOU.
BACK WHEN WE FIRST MET, I PULLED YOUR CHEEKS...
...TO MAKE YOU PRACTICE SMILING, DIDN'T I?
...
A SMILE CAN TRICK EVEN YOUR OWN BRAIN.
HAPPINESS TRIGGERS SMILING— BUT THE OTHER WAY AROUND...
...IS PLENTY EFFECTIVE TOO.
AND THE "MIRROR SYSTEM"...
...COR-RECT?
YES.
ALL THOSE YEARS AGO... WHEN I WAS IN THE DEPTHS OF DESPAIR...
...YOU TOLD ME ABOUT IT ALL THE TIME.

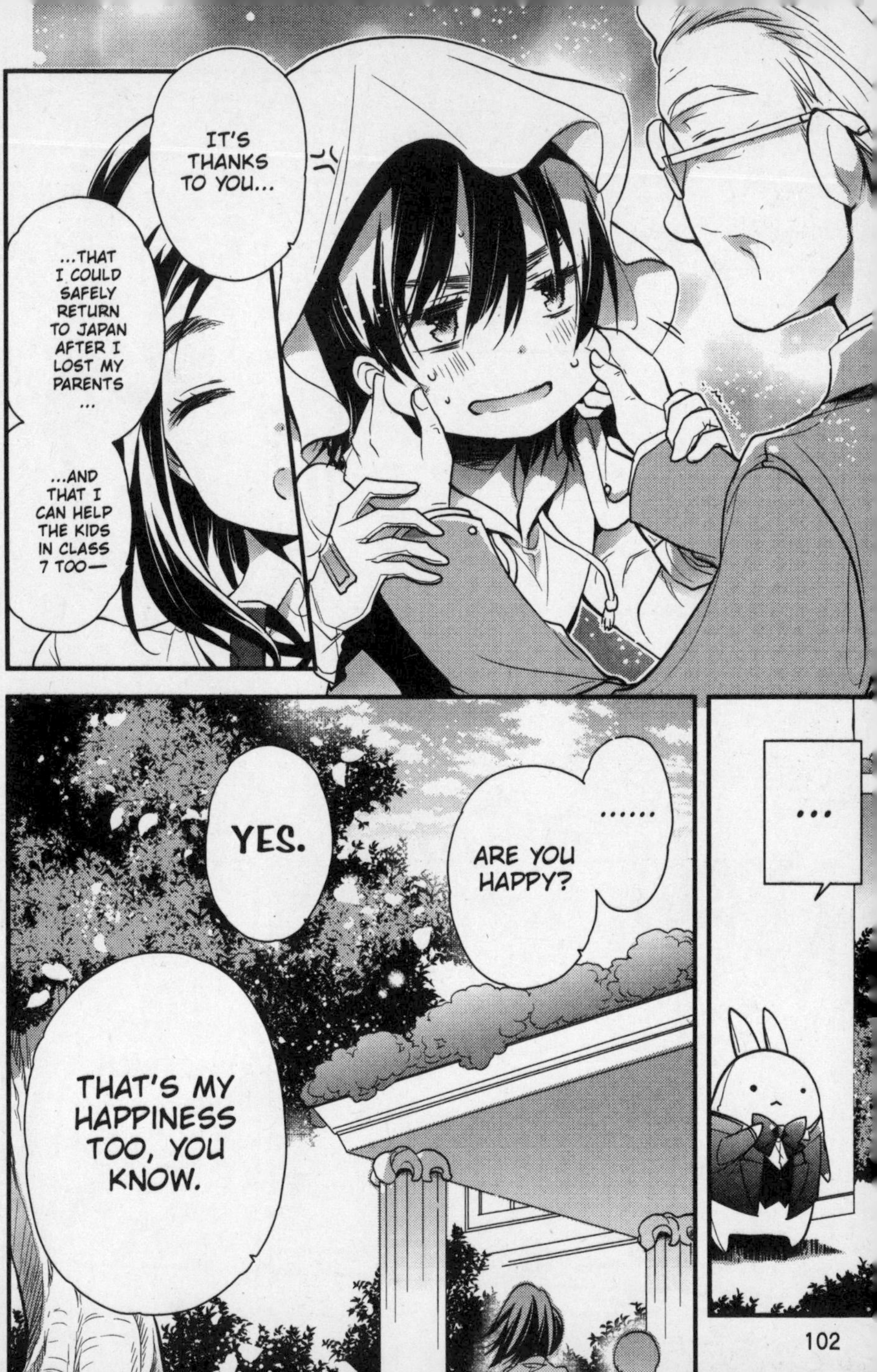
IT'S THANKS TO YOU...
...THAT I COULD SAFELY RETURN TO JAPAN AFTER I LOST MY PARENTS ...
...AND THAT I CAN HELP THE KIDS IN CLASS 7 TOO—
...
......
ARE YOU HAPPY?
YES.
THAT'S MY HAPPINESS TOO, YOU KNOW.

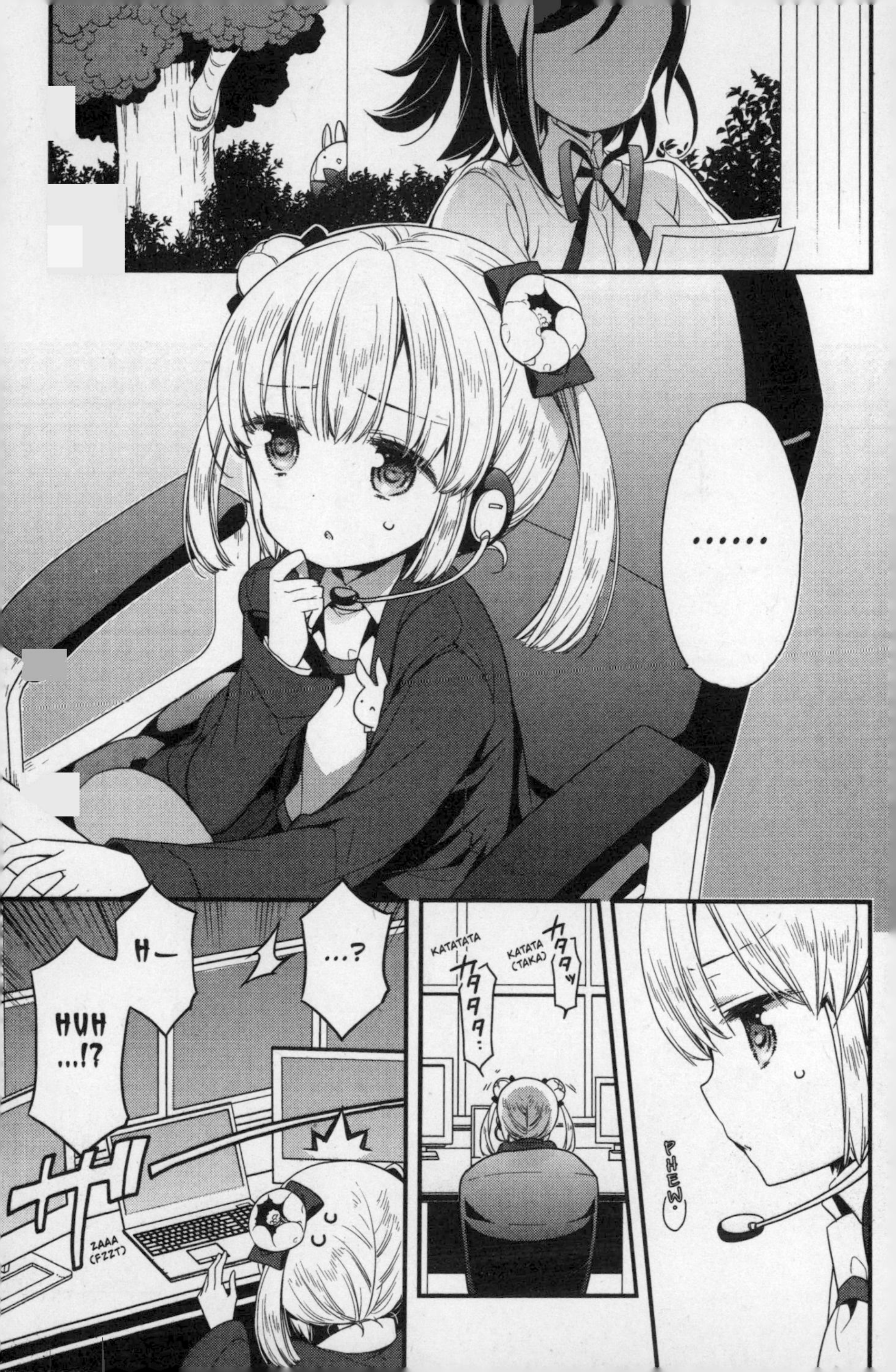

......
PHEW
KATATA (TAKA)
カタタッ
KATATATA
カタタタ…
...?
H—
HUH ...!?
ZAAA (FZZT)

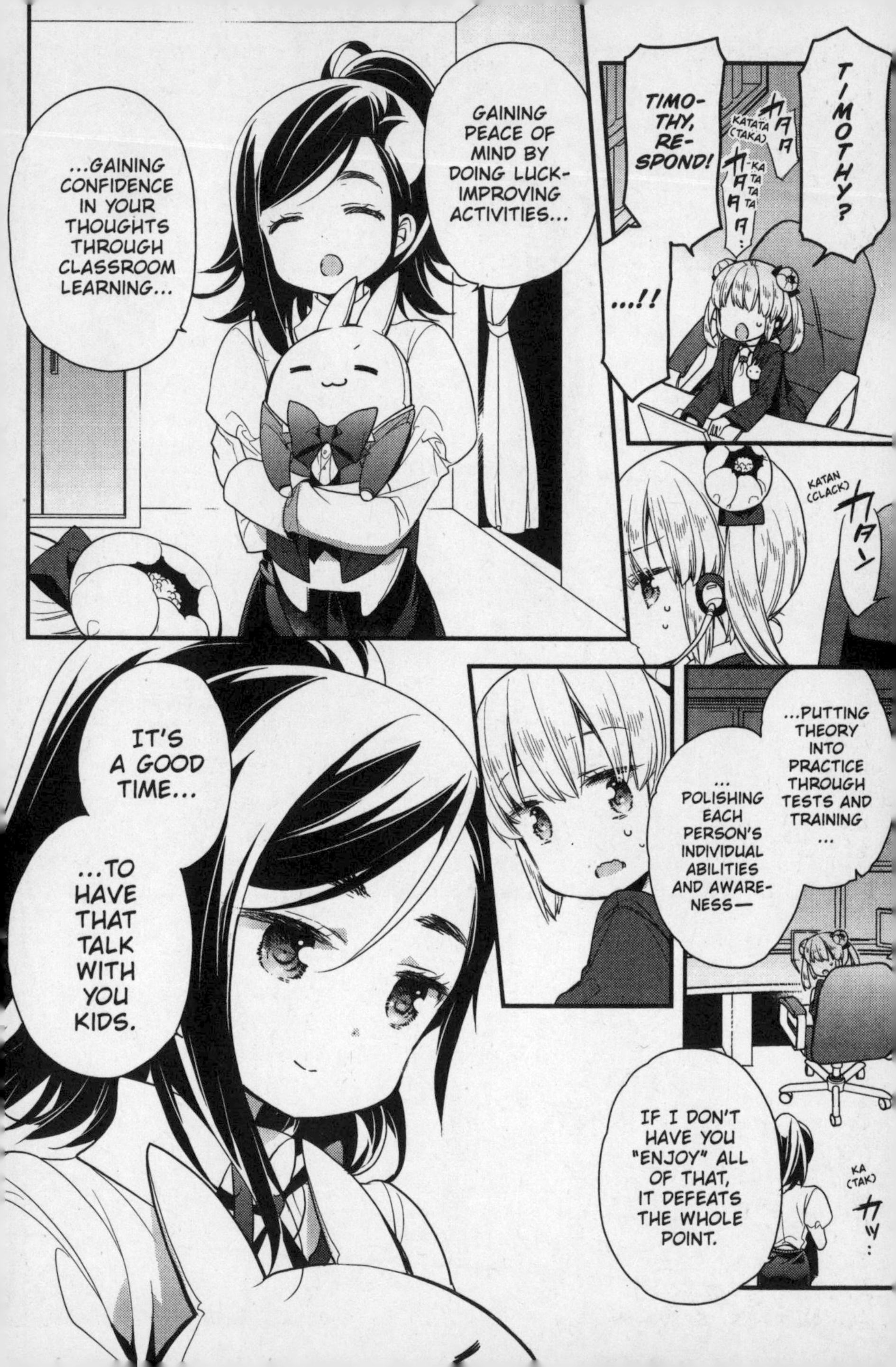
TIMOTHY?
TIMOTHY, RESPOND!
KATATA (TAKA)
KA TA TA TA
...!!
KATAN (CLACK)
GAINING PEACE OF MIND BY DOING LUCK-IMPROVING ACTIVITIES...
...GAINING CONFIDENCE IN YOUR THOUGHTS THROUGH CLASSROOM LEARNING...
...PUTTING THEORY INTO PRACTICE THROUGH TESTS AND TRAINING...
... POLISHING EACH PERSON'S INDIVIDUAL ABILITIES AND AWARENESS—
IF I DON'T HAVE YOU "ENJOY" ALL OF THAT, IT DEFEATS THE WHOLE POINT.
KA (TAK)
IT'S A GOOD TIME...
...TO HAVE THAT TALK WITH YOU KIDS.

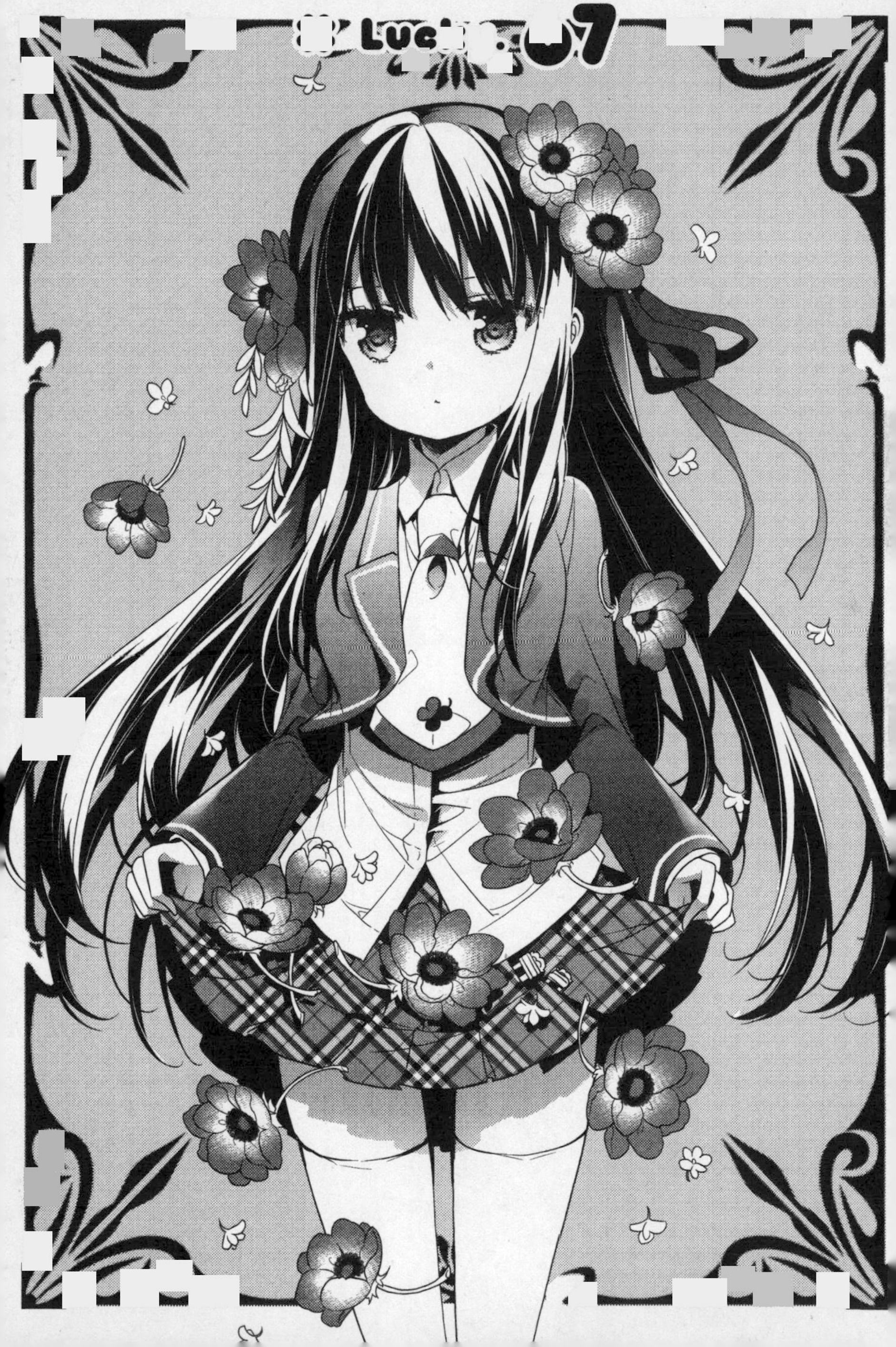

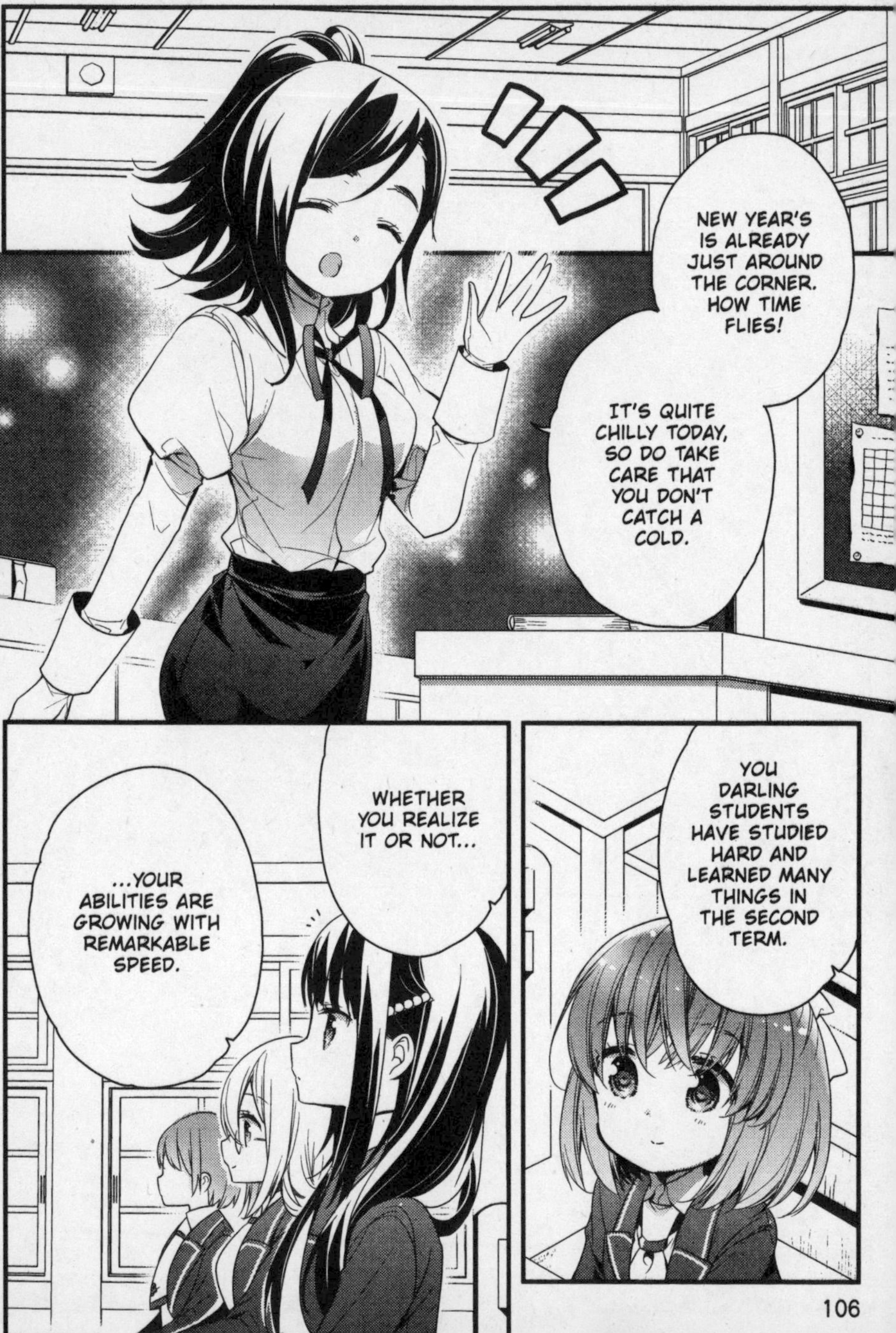
NEW YEAR'S IS ALREADY JUST AROUND THE CORNER. HOW TIME FLIES!
IT'S QUITE CHILLY TODAY, SO DO TAKE CARE THAT YOU DON'T CATCH A COLD.
YOU DARLING STUDENTS HAVE STUDIED HARD AND LEARNED MANY THINGS IN THE SECOND TERM.
WHETHER YOU REALIZE IT OR NOT...
...YOUR ABILITIES ARE GROWING WITH REMARKABLE SPEED.

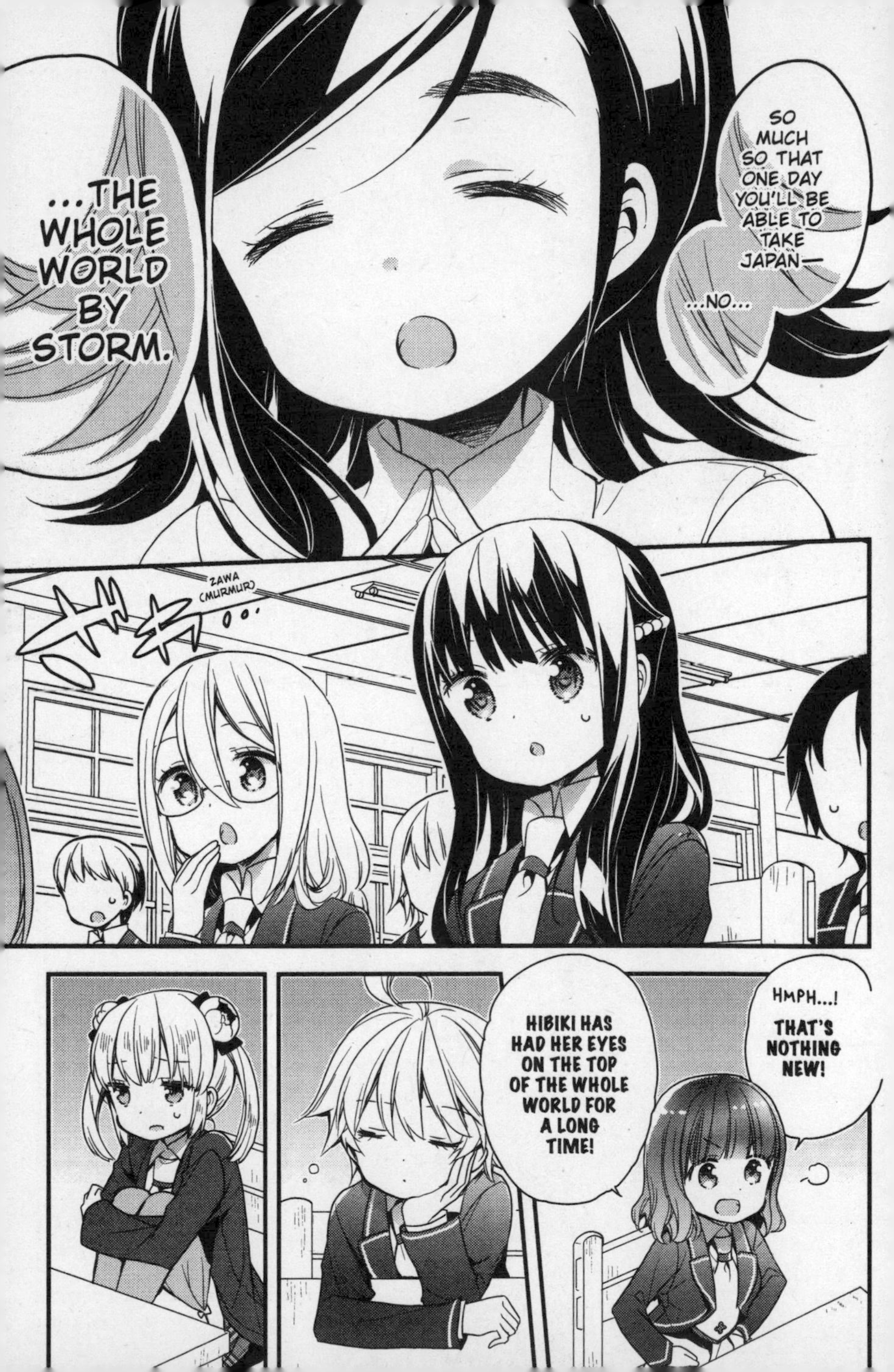
SO MUCH SO THAT ONE DAY YOU'LL BE ABLE TO TAKE JAPAN—
...NO...
...THE WHOLE WORLD BY STORM.
ZAWA (MURMUR)
HMPH...!
THAT'S NOTHING NEW!
HIBIKI HAS HAD HER EYES ON THE TOP OF THE WHOLE WORLD FOR A LONG TIME!

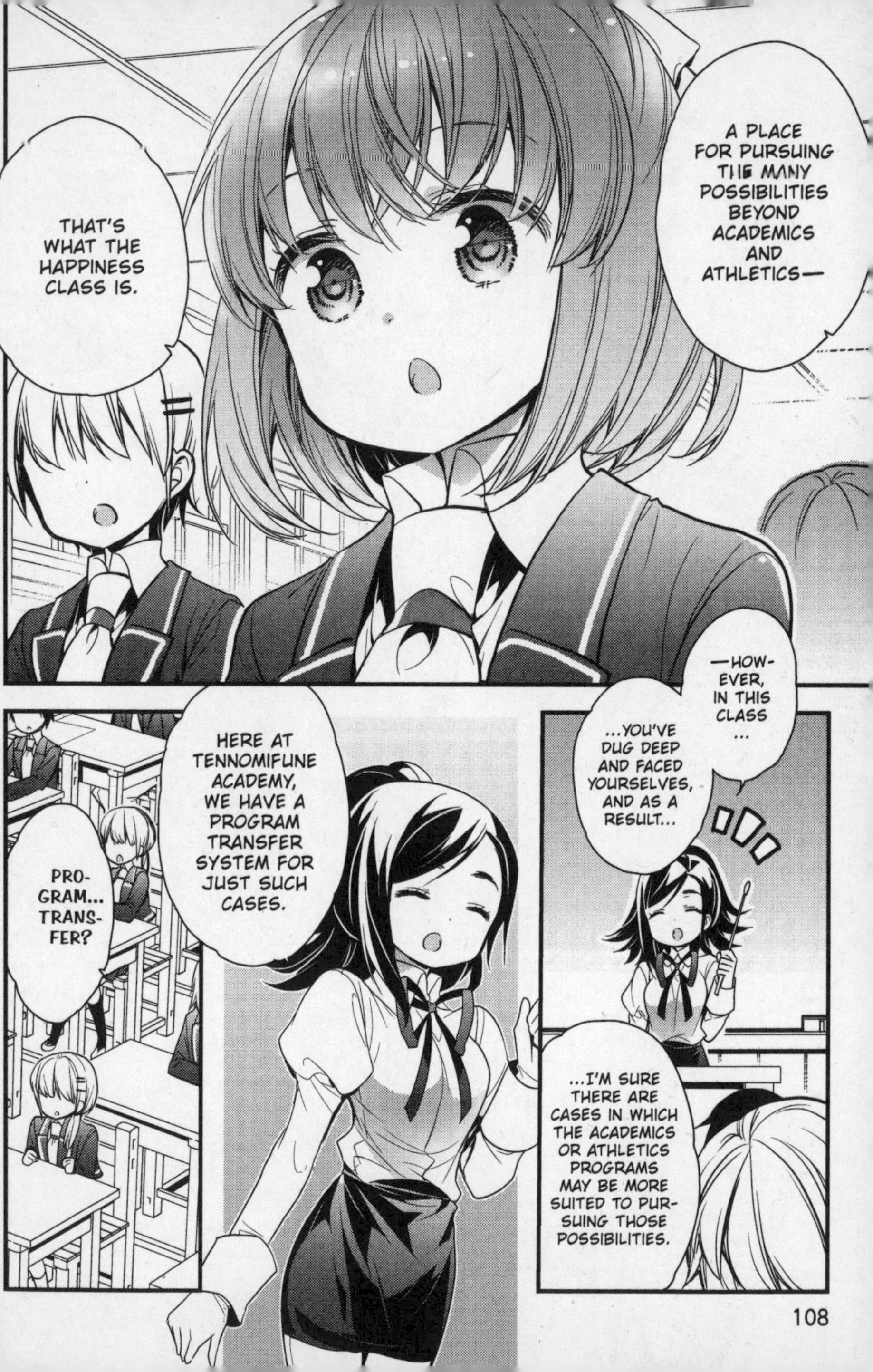
A PLACE FOR PURSUING THE MANY POSSIBILITIES BEYOND ACADEMICS AND ATHLETICS—
THAT'S WHAT THE HAPPINESS CLASS IS.
—HOW-EVER, IN THIS CLASS ...
...YOU'VE DUG DEEP AND FACED YOURSELVES, AND AS A RESULT...
...I'M SURE THERE ARE CASES IN WHICH THE ACADEMICS OR ATHLETICS PROGRAMS MAY BE MORE SUITED TO PUR-SUING THOSE POSSIBILITIES.
HERE AT TENNOMIFUNE ACADEMY, WE HAVE A PROGRAM TRANSFER SYSTEM FOR JUST SUCH CASES.
PRO-GRAM... TRANS-FER?

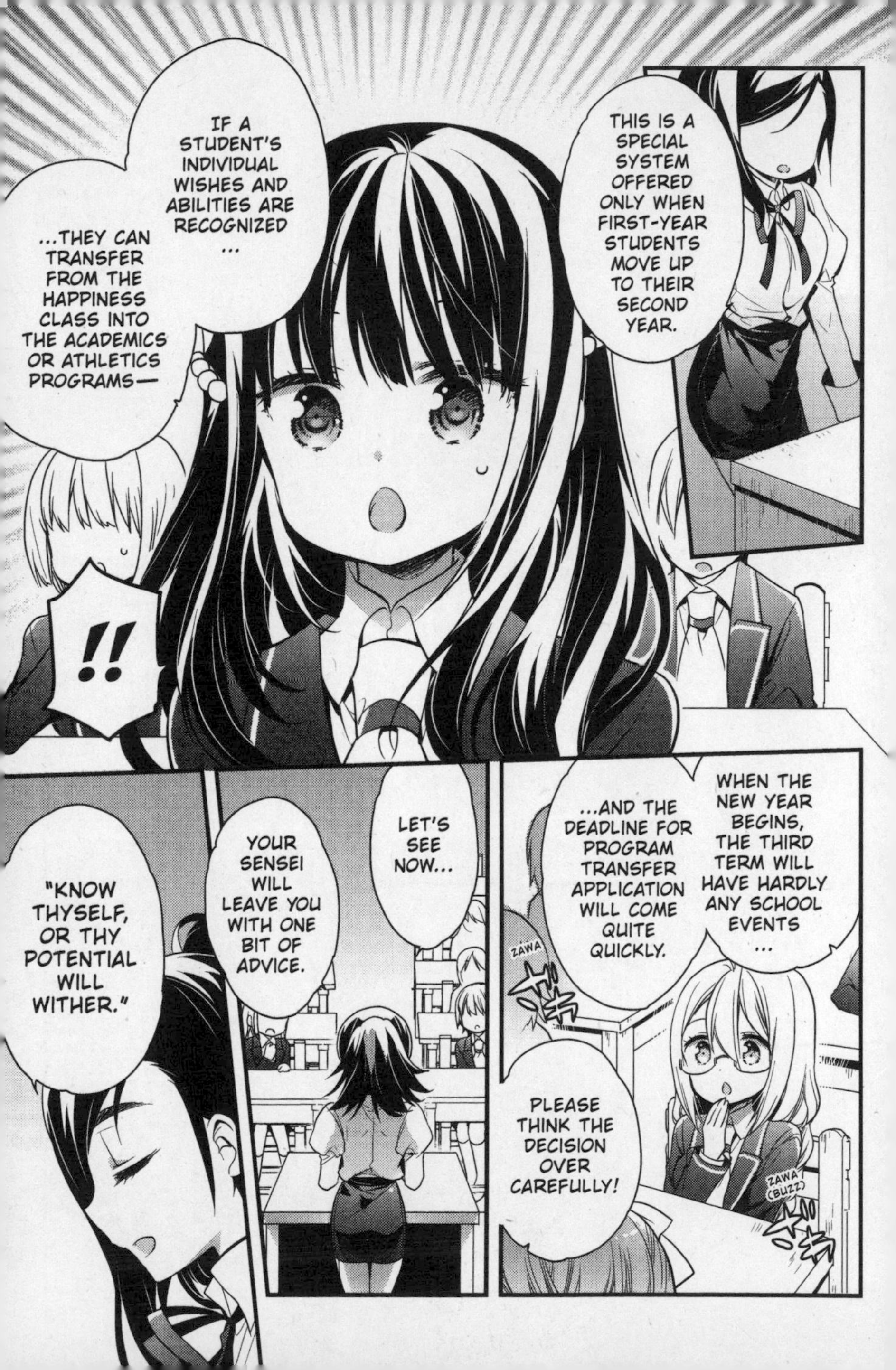
THIS IS A SPECIAL SYSTEM OFFERED ONLY WHEN FIRST-YEAR STUDENTS MOVE UP TO THEIR SECOND YEAR.
IF A STUDENT'S INDIVIDUAL WISHES AND ABILITIES ARE RECOGNIZED...
...THEY CAN TRANSFER FROM THE HAPPINESS CLASS INTO THE ACADEMICS OR ATHLETICS PROGRAMS—
!!
WHEN THE NEW YEAR BEGINS, THE THIRD TERM WILL HAVE HARDLY ANY SCHOOL EVENTS...
...AND THE DEADLINE FOR PROGRAM TRANSFER APPLICATION WILL COME QUITE QUICKLY.
ZAWA
PLEASE THINK THE DECISION OVER CAREFULLY!
ZAWA (BUZZ)
LET'S SEE NOW...
YOUR SENSEI WILL LEAVE YOU WITH ONE BIT OF ADVICE.
"KNOW THYSELF, OR THY POTENTIAL WILL WITHER."

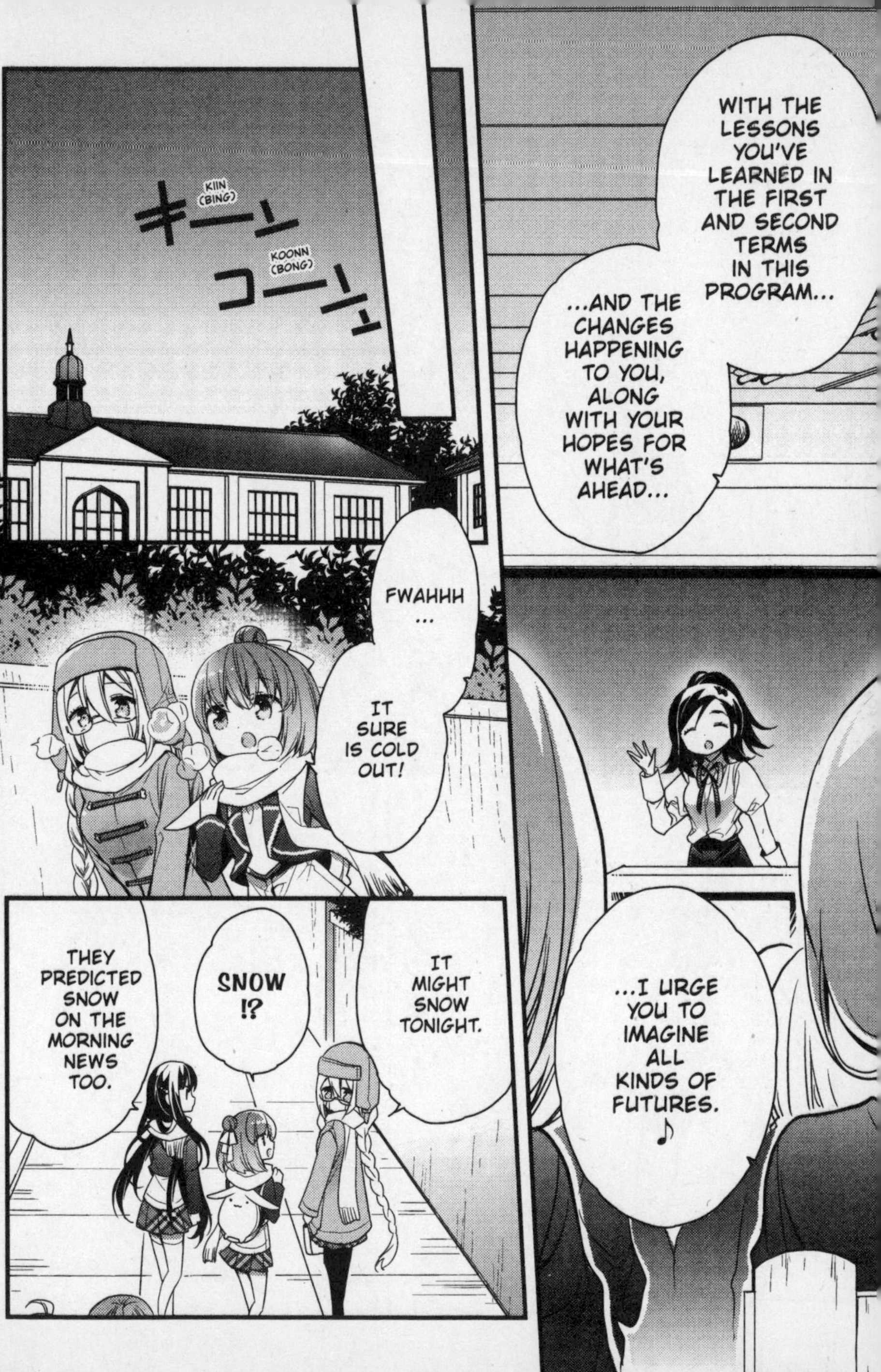
WITH THE LESSONS YOU'VE LEARNED IN THE FIRST AND SECOND TERMS IN THIS PROGRAM...
...AND THE CHANGES HAPPENING TO YOU, ALONG WITH YOUR HOPES FOR WHAT'S AHEAD...
...I URGE YOU TO IMAGINE ALL KINDS OF FUTURES. ♪
キーン
KIIN (BING)
コーン
KOONN (BONG)
FWAHHH...
IT SURE IS COLD OUT!
IT MIGHT SNOW TONIGHT.
SNOW!?
THEY PREDICTED SNOW ON THE MORNING NEWS TOO.

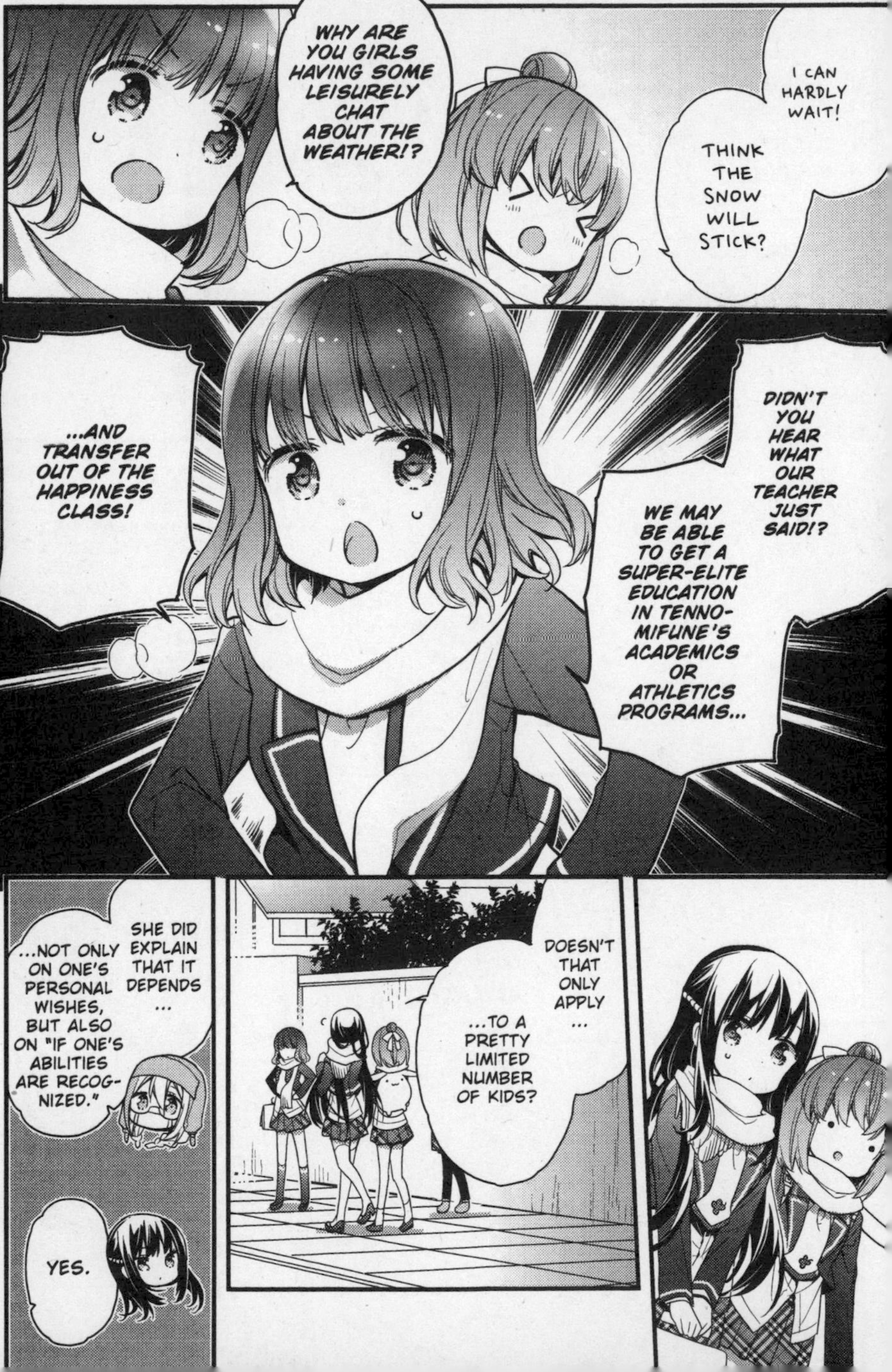

I CAN HARDLY WAIT!
THINK THE SNOW WILL STICK?
WHY ARE YOU GIRLS HAVING SOME LEISURELY CHAT ABOUT THE WEATHER!?
DIDN'T YOU HEAR WHAT OUR TEACHER JUST SAID!?
WE MAY BE ABLE TO GET A SUPER-ELITE EDUCATION IN TENNO-MIFUNE'S ACADEMICS OR ATHLETICS PROGRAMS...
...AND TRANSFER OUT OF THE HAPPINESS CLASS!
DOESN'T THAT ONLY APPLY...
...TO A PRETTY LIMITED NUMBER OF KIDS?
SHE DID EXPLAIN THAT IT DEPENDS...
...NOT ONLY ON ONE'S PERSONAL WISHES, BUT ALSO ON "IF ONE'S ABILITIES ARE RECOG-NIZED."
YES.

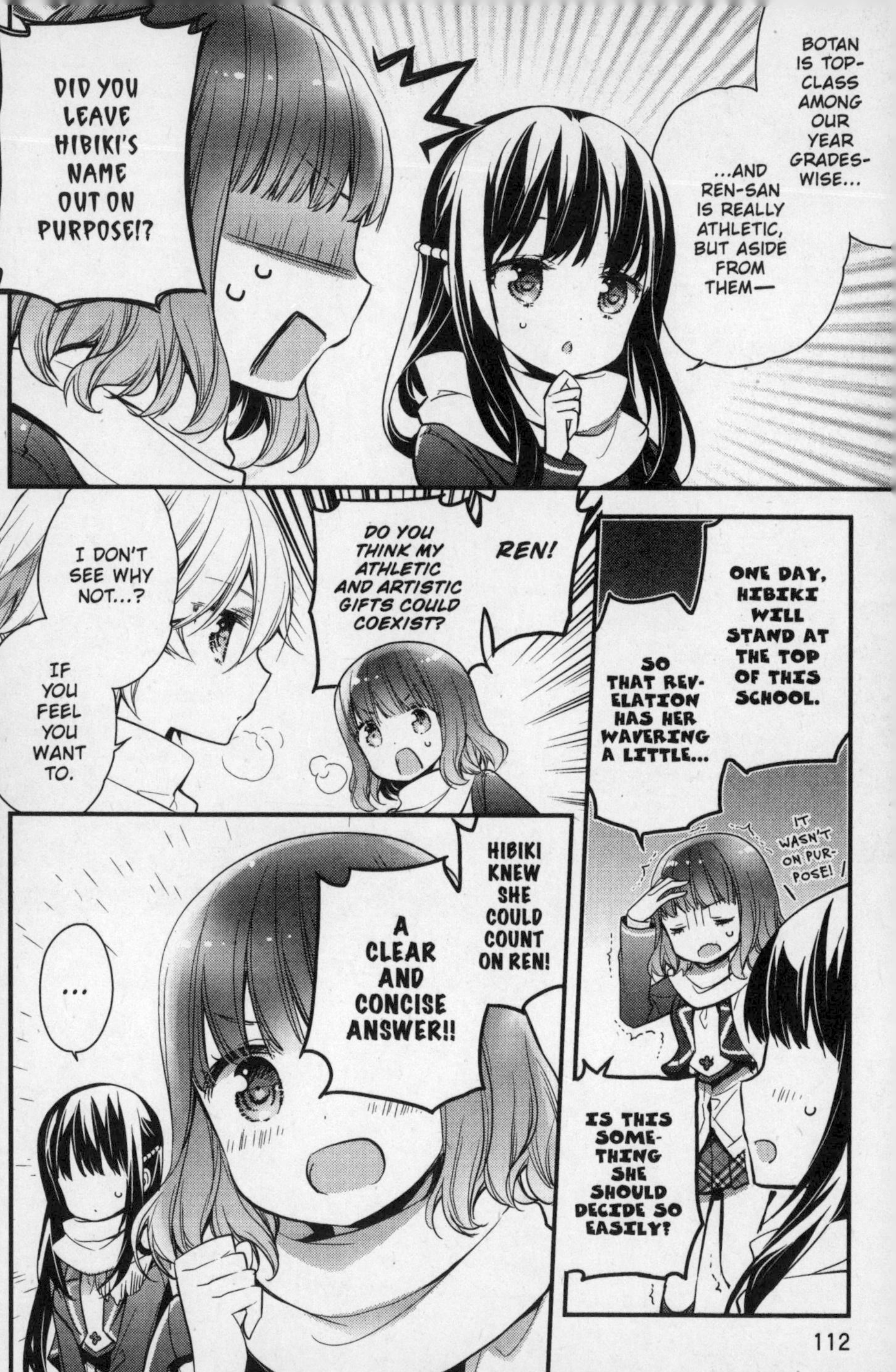
BOTAN IS TOP-CLASS AMONG OUR YEAR GRADES-WISE...
...AND REN-SAN IS REALLY ATHLETIC, BUT ASIDE FROM THEM—
DID YOU LEAVE HIBIKI'S NAME OUT ON PURPOSE!?
ONE DAY, HIBIKI WILL STAND AT THE TOP OF THIS SCHOOL.
SO THAT REVELATION HAS HER WAVERING A LITTLE...
IT WASN'T ON PURPOSE!
IS THIS SOMETHING SHE SHOULD DECIDE SO EASILY?
REN!
DO YOU THINK MY ATHLETIC AND ARTISTIC GIFTS COULD COEXIST?
I DON'T SEE WHY NOT...?
IF YOU FEEL YOU WANT TO.
HIBIKI KNEW SHE COULD COUNT ON REN!
A CLEAR AND CONCISE ANSWER!!
...

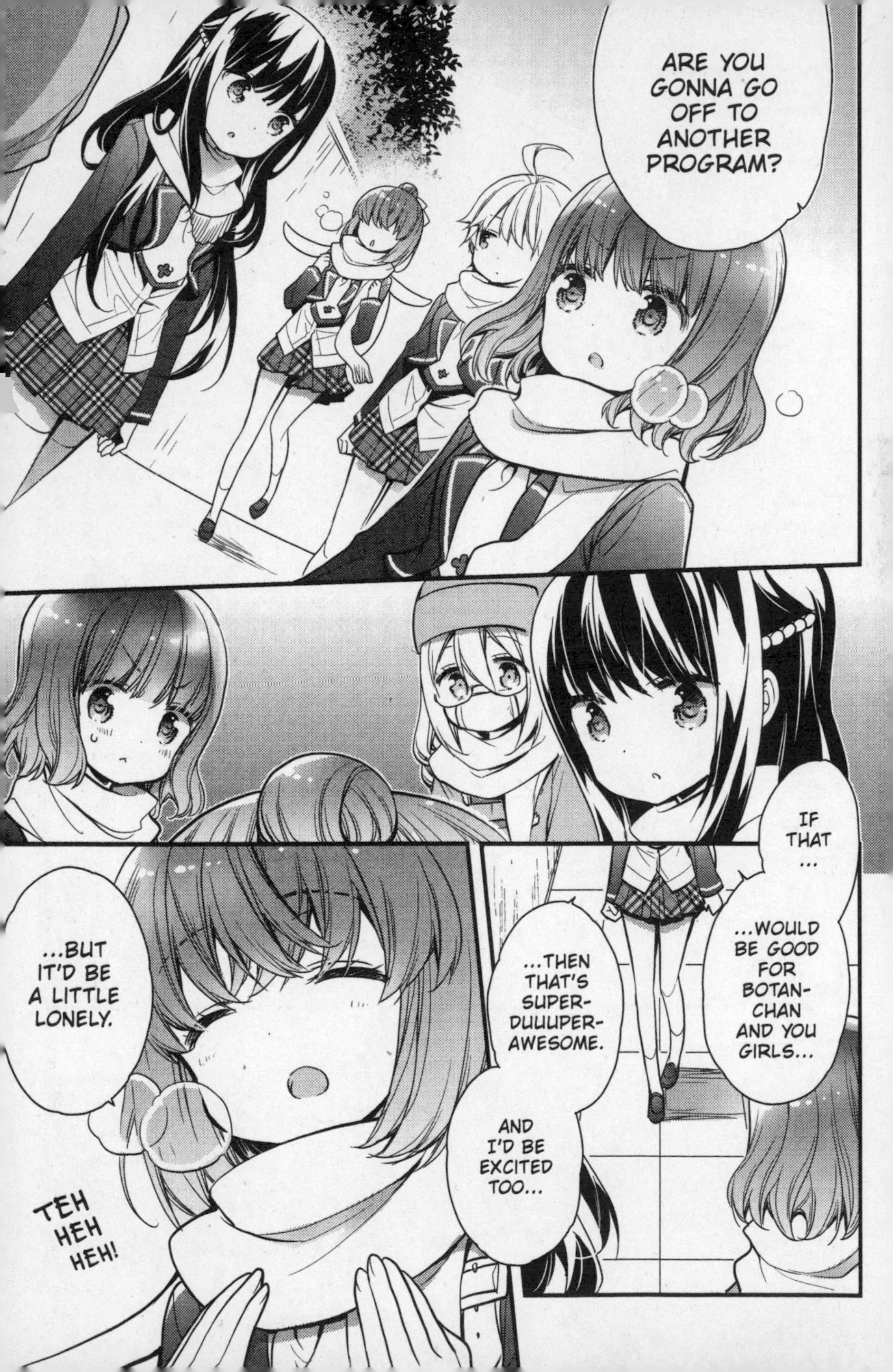
ARE YOU GONNA GO OFF TO ANOTHER PROGRAM?
IF THAT...
...WOULD BE GOOD FOR BOTAN-CHAN AND YOU GIRLS...
...THEN THAT'S SUPER-DUUUPER-AWESOME.
AND I'D BE EXCITED TOO...
...BUT IT'D BE A LITTLE LONELY.
TEH HEH HEH!

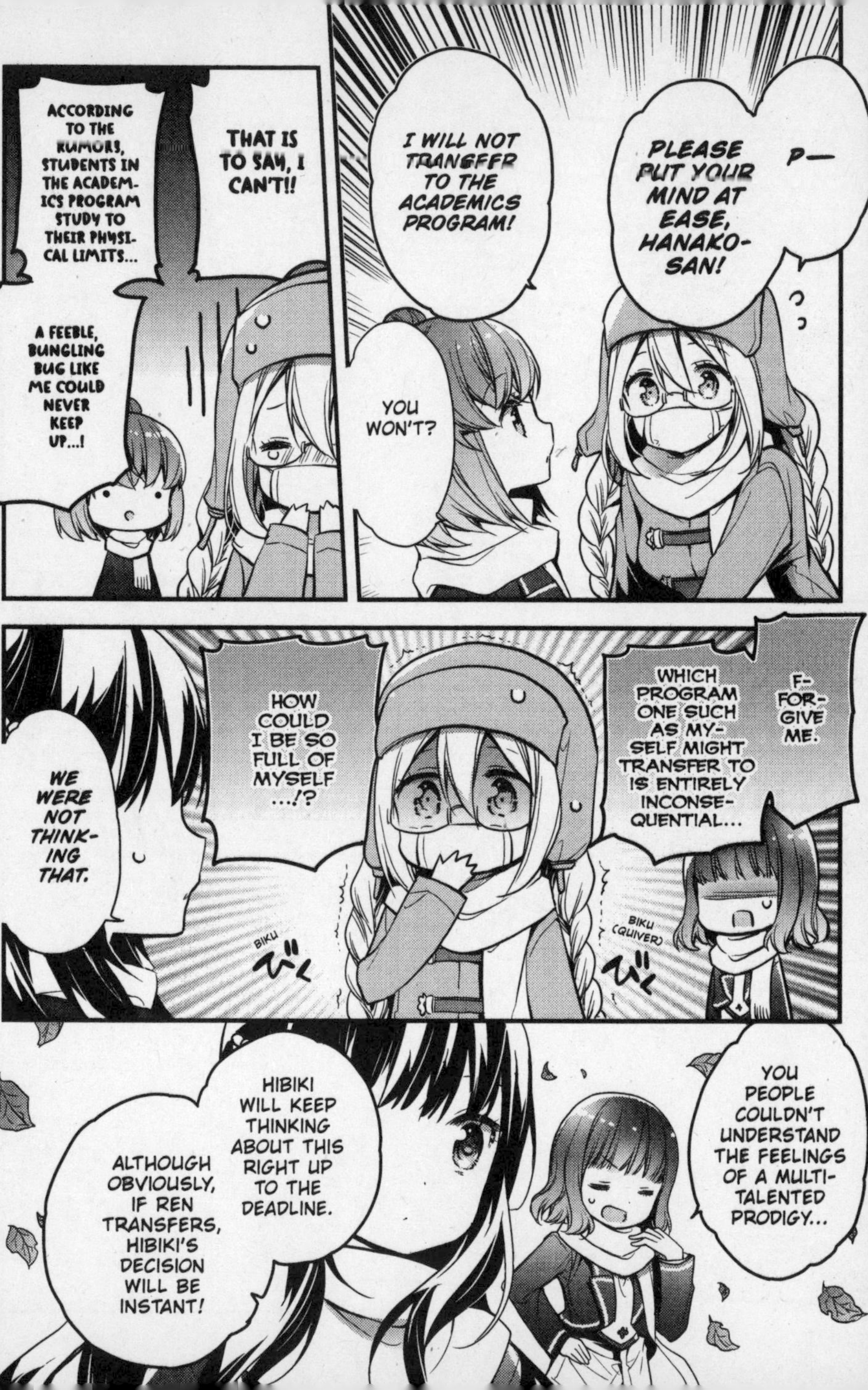
P—
PLEASE PUT YOUR MIND AT EASE, HANAKO-SAN!
I WILL NOT TRANSFER TO THE ACADEMICS PROGRAM!
YOU WON'T?
THAT IS TO SAY, I CAN'T!!
ACCORDING TO THE RUMORS, STUDENTS IN THE ACADEMICS PROGRAM STUDY TO THEIR PHYSICAL LIMITS...
A FEEBLE, BUNGLING BUG LIKE ME COULD NEVER KEEP UP...!
F-FORGIVE ME.
WHICH PROGRAM ONE SUCH AS MYSELF MIGHT TRANSFER TO IS ENTIRELY INCONSEQUENTIAL...
BIKU (QUIVER)
HOW COULD I BE SO FULL OF MYSELF...!?
BIKU
WE WERE NOT THINKING THAT.
YOU PEOPLE COULDN'T UNDERSTAND THE FEELINGS OF A MULTI-TALENTED PRODIGY...
HIBIKI WILL KEEP THINKING ABOUT THIS RIGHT UP TO THE DEADLINE.
ALTHOUGH OBVIOUSLY, IF REN TRANSFERS, HIBIKI'S DECISION WILL BE INSTANT!

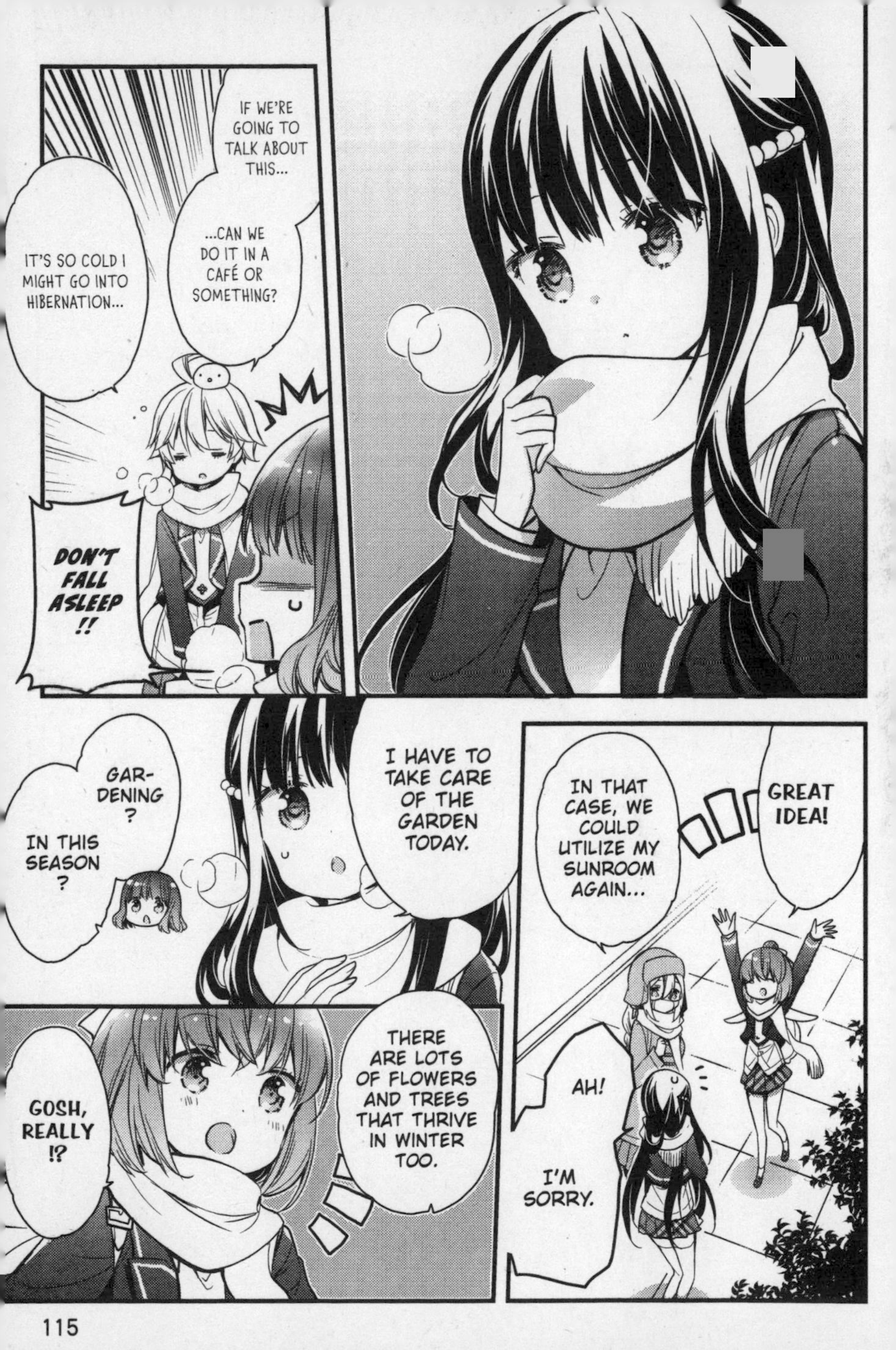
IF WE'RE GOING TO TALK ABOUT THIS...
...CAN WE DO IT IN A CAFÉ OR SOMETHING?
IT'S SO COLD I MIGHT GO INTO HIBERNATION...
DON'T FALL ASLEEP!!
I HAVE TO TAKE CARE OF THE GARDEN TODAY.
GAR-DENING?
IN THIS SEASON?
THERE ARE LOTS OF FLOWERS AND TREES THAT THRIVE IN WINTER TOO.
GOSH, REALLY!?
IN THAT CASE, WE COULD UTILIZE MY SUNROOM AGAIN...
GREAT IDEA!
AH!
I'M SORRY.

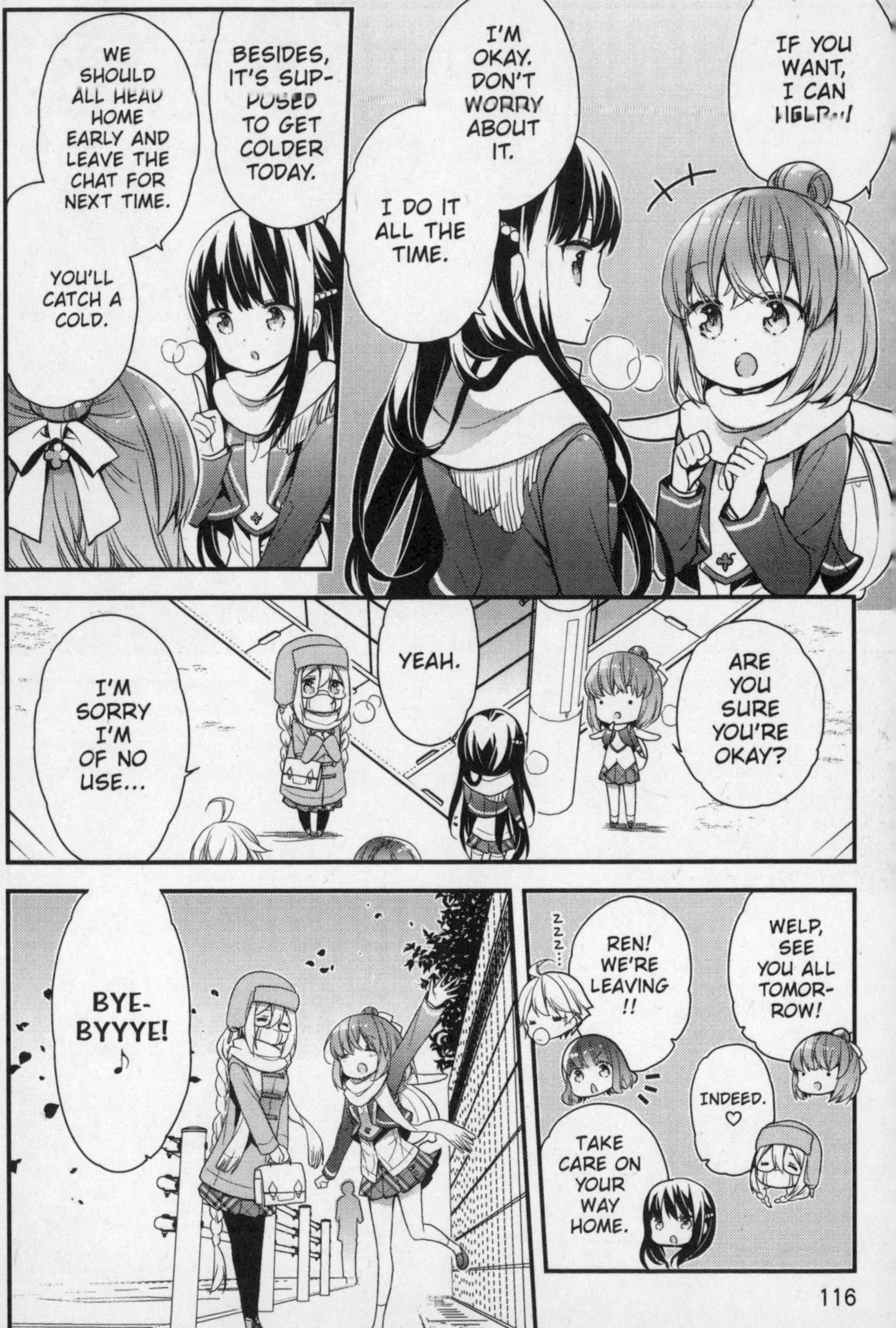
IF YOU WANT, I CAN HELP...!
I'M OKAY. DON'T WORRY ABOUT IT.
I DO IT ALL THE TIME.
BESIDES, IT'S SUP-POSED TO GET COLDER TODAY.
WE SHOULD ALL HEAD HOME EARLY AND LEAVE THE CHAT FOR NEXT TIME.
YOU'LL CATCH A COLD.
ARE YOU SURE YOU'RE OKAY?
YEAH.
I'M SORRY I'M OF NO USE...
WELP, SEE YOU ALL TOMOR-ROW!
REN! WE'RE LEAVING!!
ZZZ...
INDEED. ♡
TAKE CARE ON YOUR WAY HOME.
BYE-BYYYE! ♪

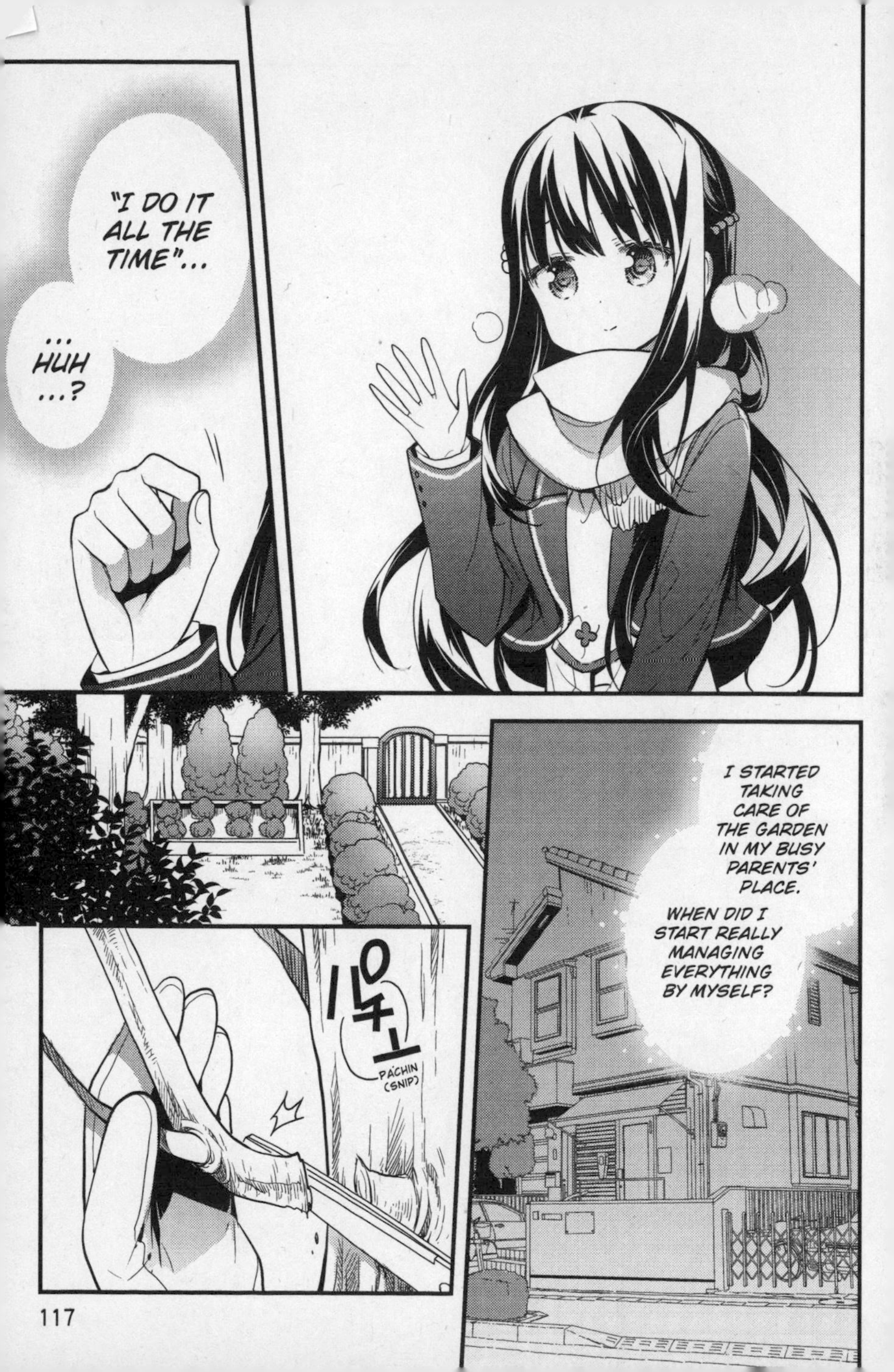
"I DO IT ALL THE TIME"...
... HUH ...?
I STARTED TAKING CARE OF THE GARDEN IN MY BUSY PARENTS' PLACE.
WHEN DID I START REALLY MANAGING EVERYTHING BY MYSELF?
パチン
PACHIN (SNIP)

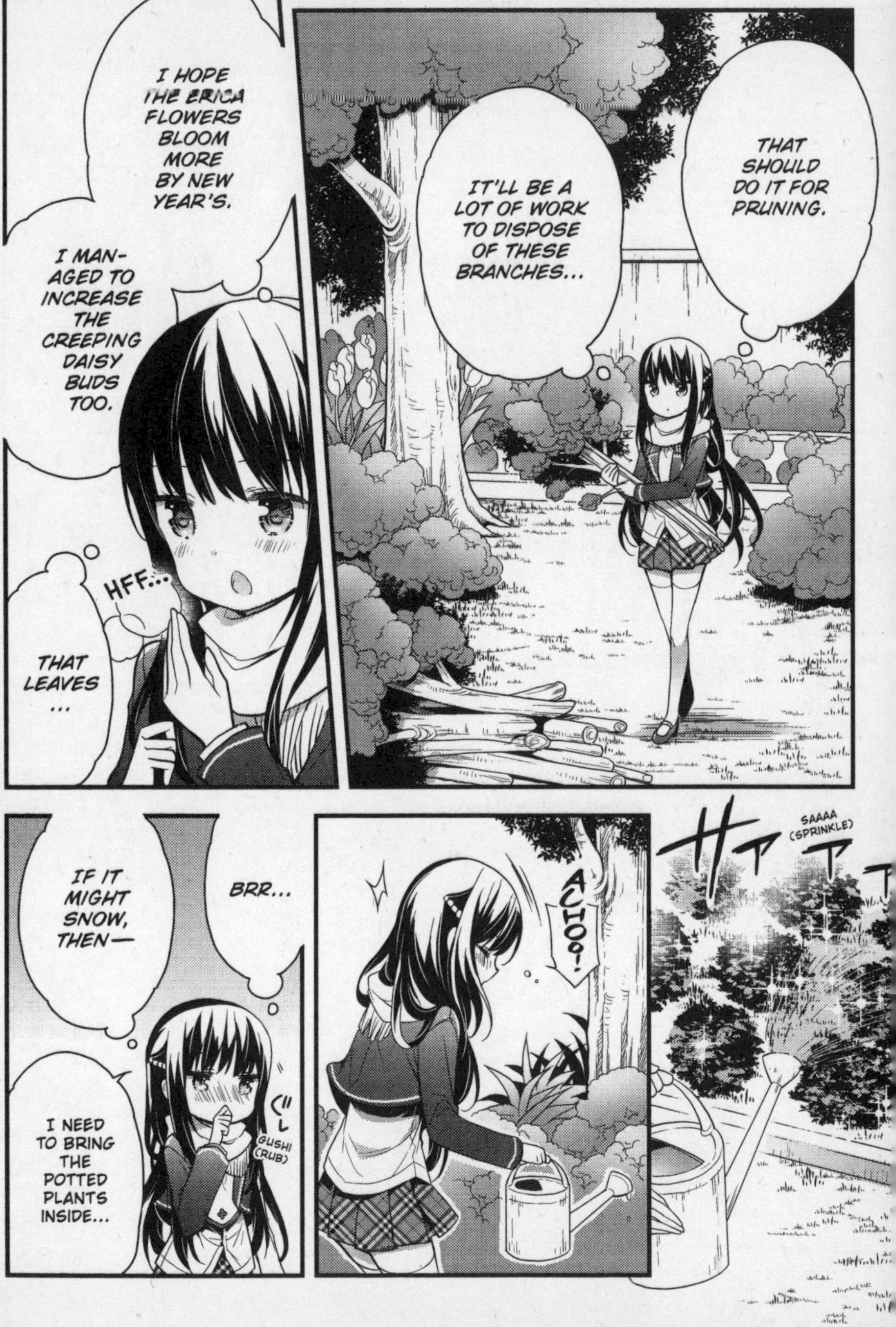

THAT SHOULD DO IT FOR PRUNING.
IT'LL BE A LOT OF WORK TO DISPOSE OF THESE BRANCHES...
I HOPE THE ERICA FLOWERS BLOOM MORE BY NEW YEAR'S.
I MAN-AGED TO INCREASE THE CREEPING DAISY BUDS TOO.
HFF...
THAT LEAVES ...
SAAAA (SPRINKLE)
ACHOO!
BRR...
IF IT MIGHT SNOW, THEN—
GUSHI (RUB)
I NEED TO BRING THE POTTED PLANTS INSIDE...

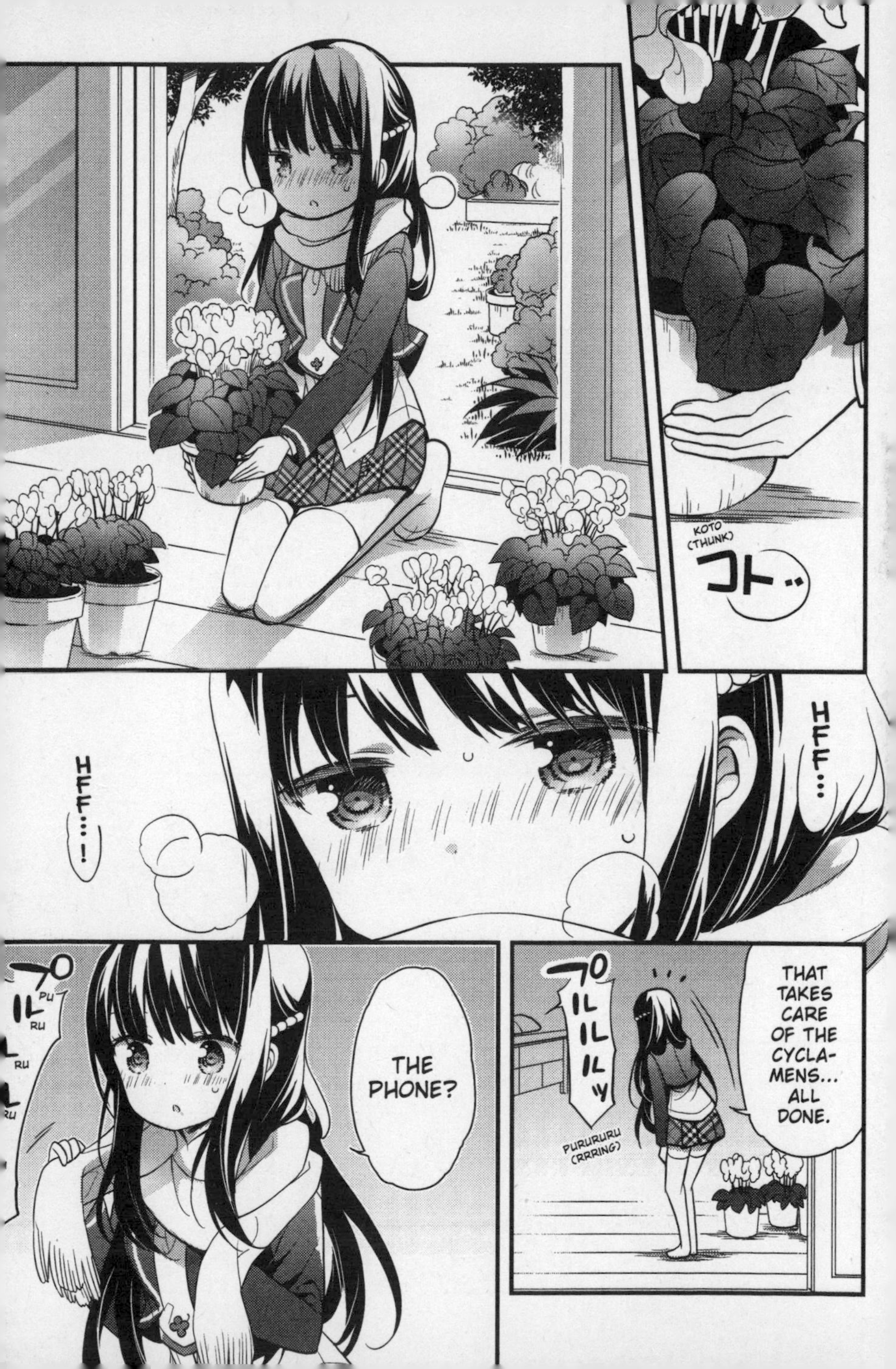
KOTO (THUNK)
コト‥
HFF...
HFF...!
THAT TAKES CARE OF THE CYCLAMENS... ALL DONE.
プルルルッ
PURURURU (RRRING)
プルル
PU RU RU RU
THE PHONE?

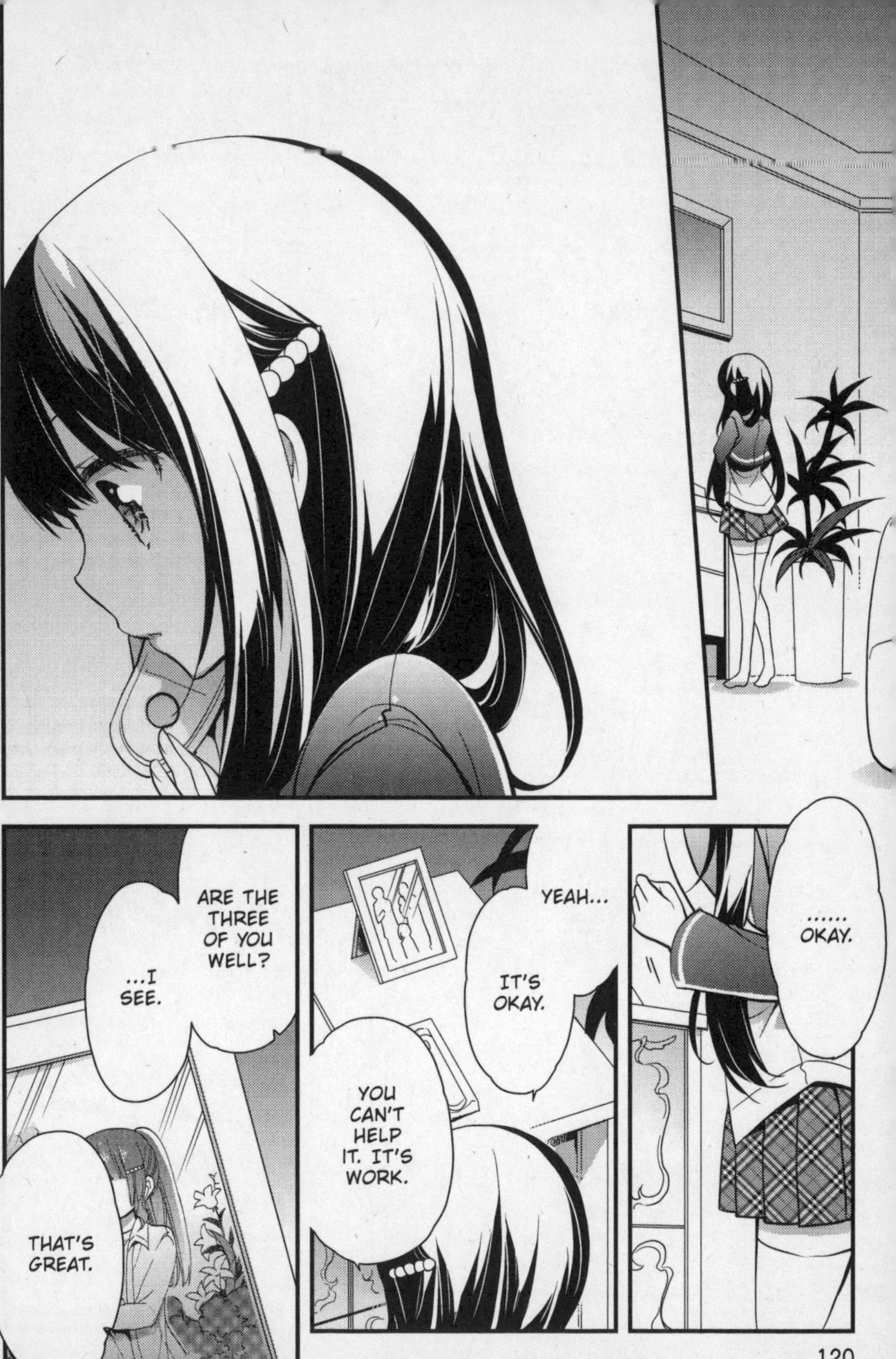

......
OKAY.
YEAH...
IT'S OKAY.
YOU CAN'T HELP IT. IT'S WORK.
ARE THE THREE OF YOU WELL?
...I SEE.
THAT'S GREAT.

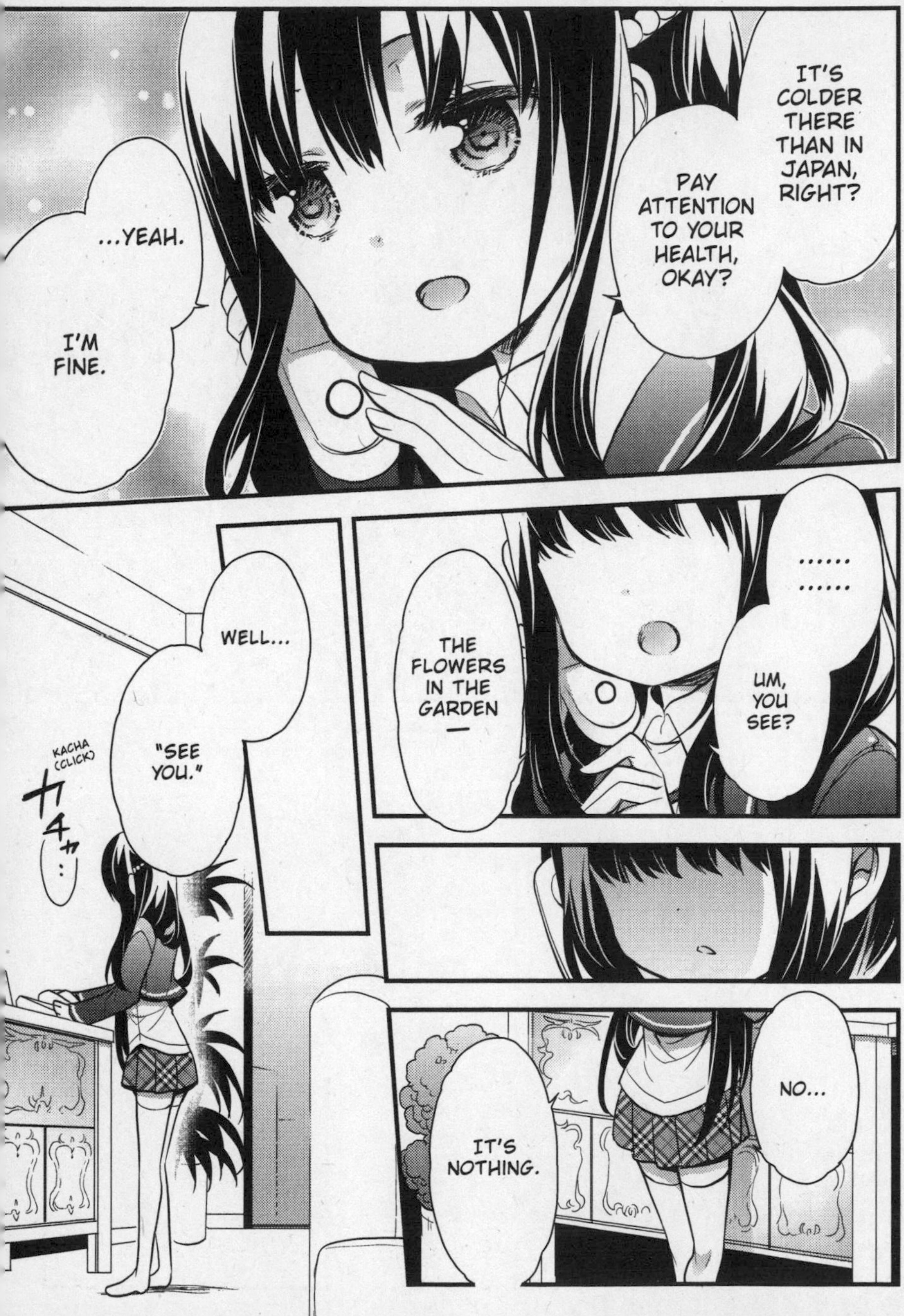
IT'S COLDER THERE THAN IN JAPAN, RIGHT?
PAY ATTENTION TO YOUR HEALTH, OKAY?
...YEAH.
I'M FINE.
......
......
UM, YOU SEE?
THE FLOWERS IN THE GARDEN—
NO...
IT'S NOTHING.
WELL...
"SEE YOU."
KACHA (CLICK)

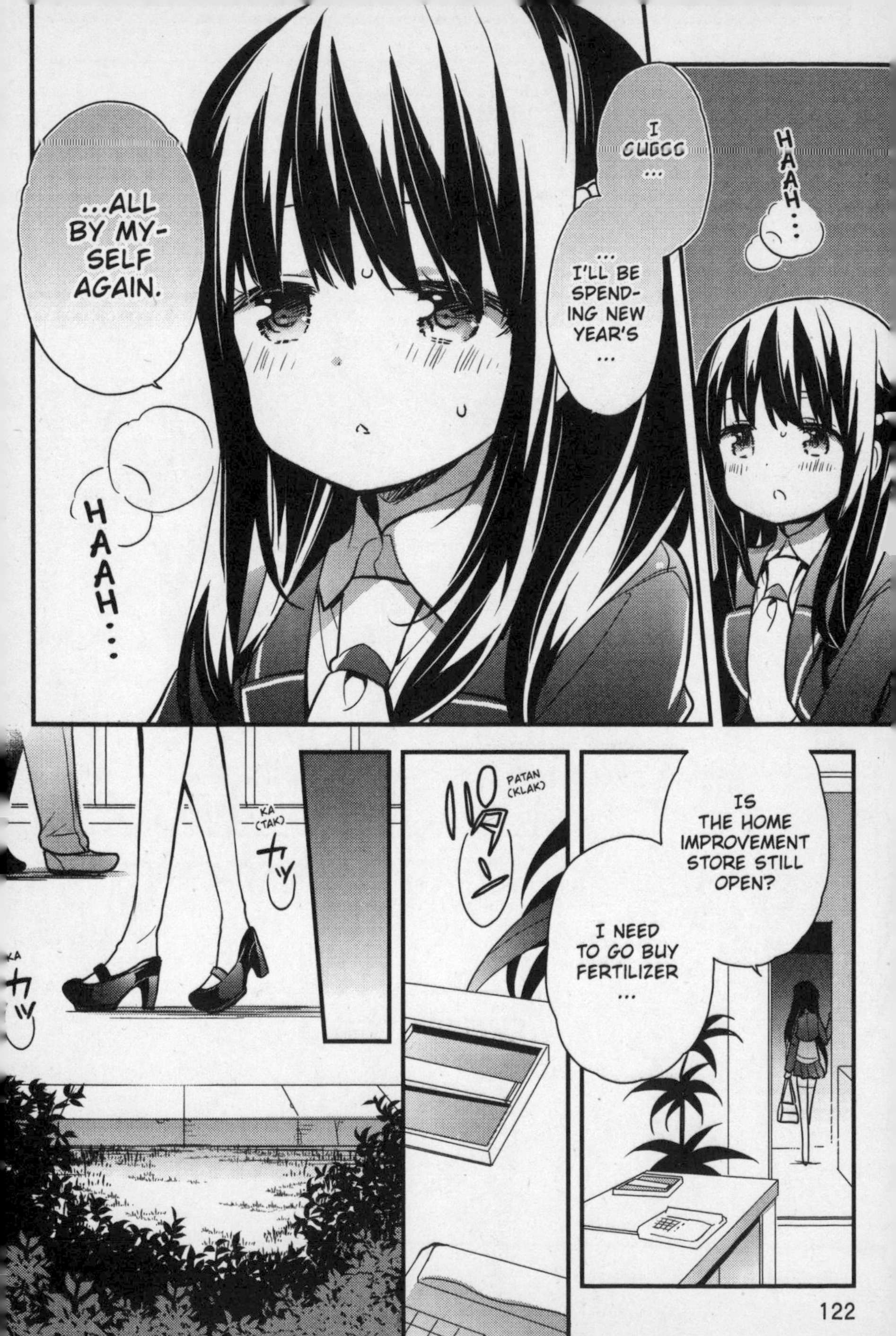
HAAAH...
I GUESS...
...I'LL BE SPENDING NEW YEAR'S...
...ALL BY MY-SELF AGAIN.
HAAAH...
IS THE HOME IMPROVEMENT STORE STILL OPEN?
I NEED TO GO BUY FERTILIZER...
パタン
PATAN (KLAK)
カッ
KA (TAK)
カッ
KA

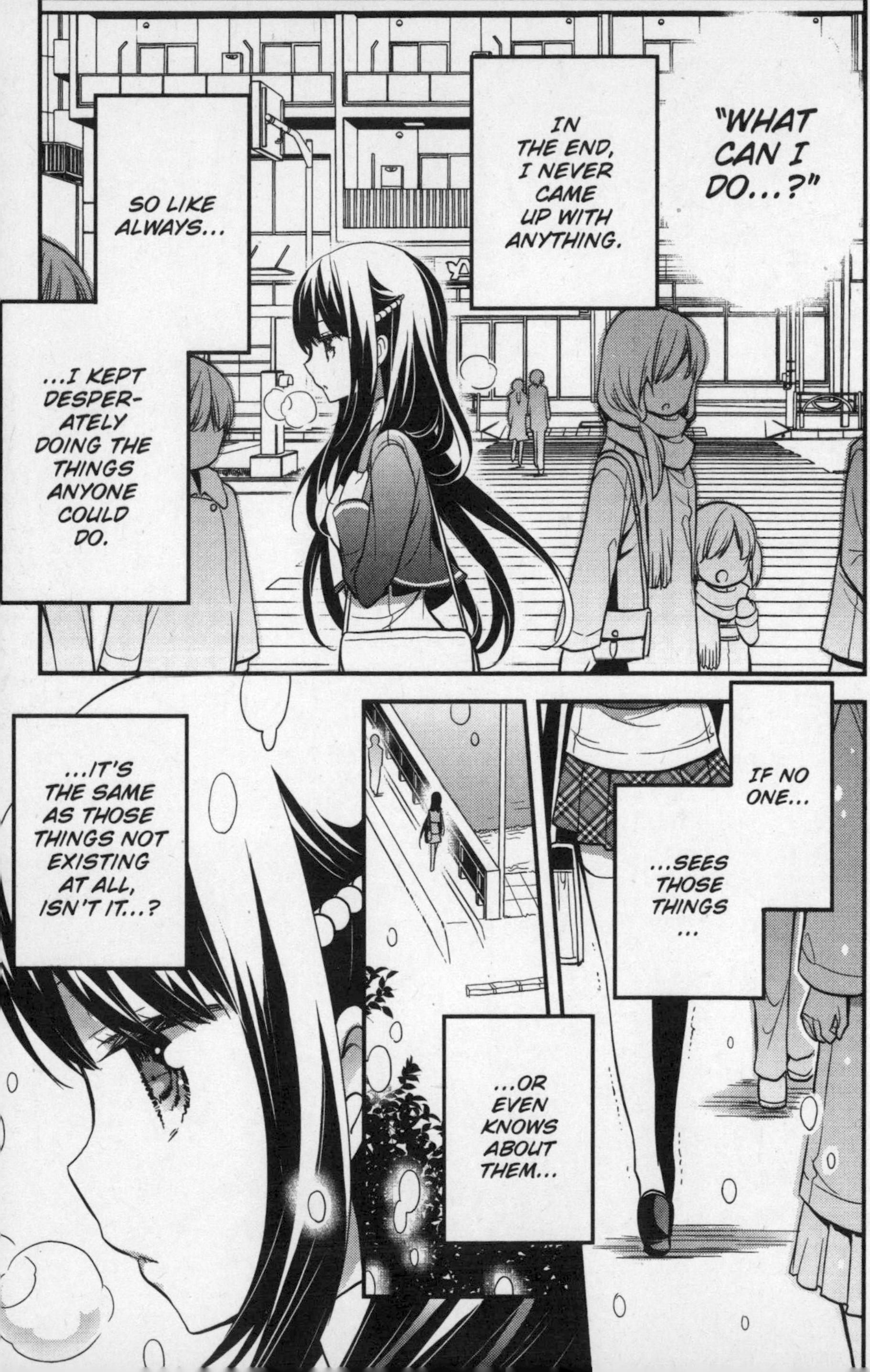
"WHAT CAN I DO...?"
IN THE END, I NEVER CAME UP WITH ANYTHING.
SO LIKE ALWAYS...
...I KEPT DESPER-ATELY DOING THE THINGS ANYONE COULD DO.
IF NO ONE...
...SEES THOSE THINGS...
...OR EVEN KNOWS ABOUT THEM...
...IT'S THE SAME AS THOSE THINGS NOT EXISTING AT ALL, ISN'T IT...?

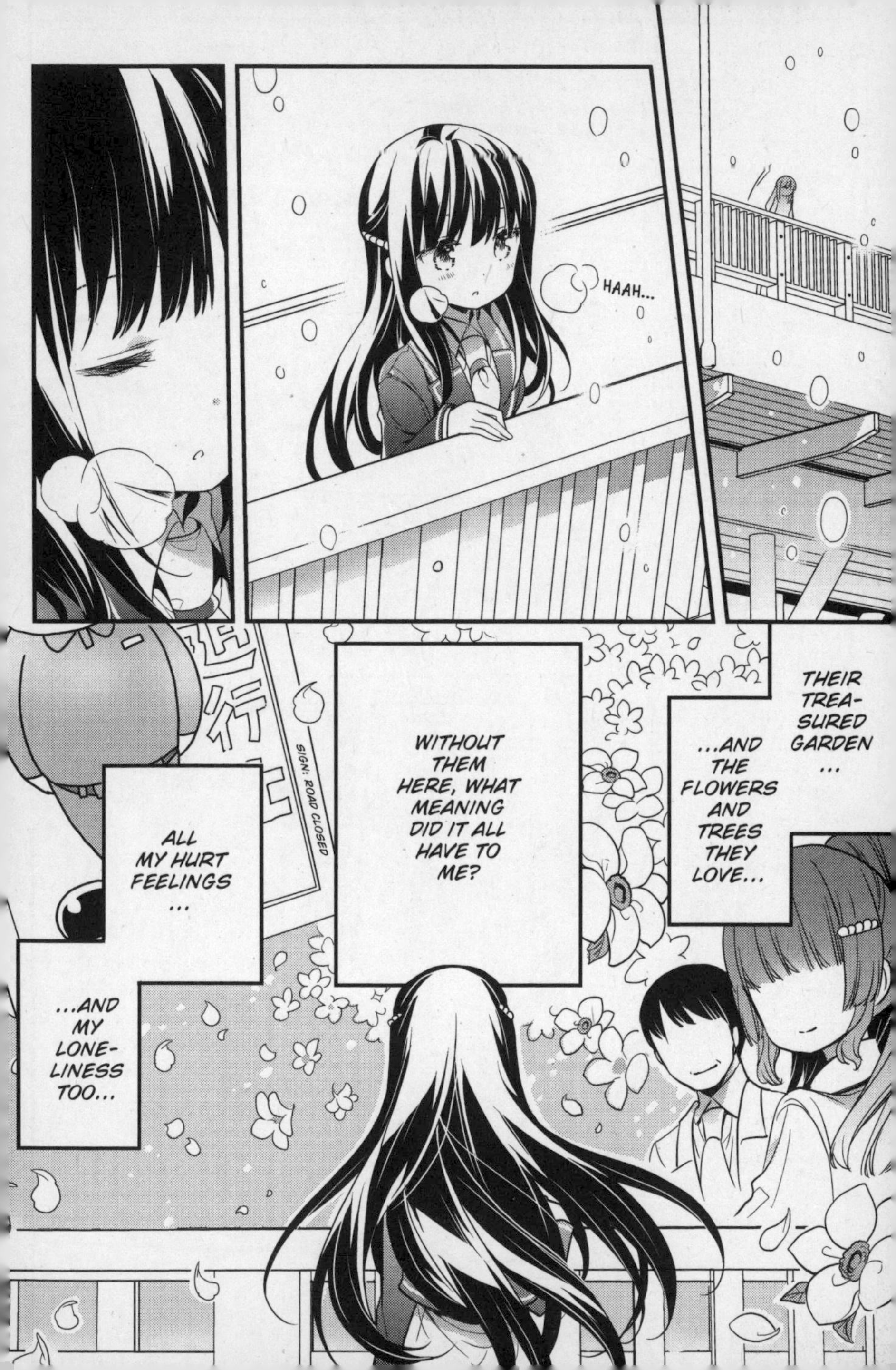
HAAH...
THEIR TREA-SURED GARDEN...
...AND THE FLOWERS AND TREES THEY LOVE...
WITHOUT THEM HERE, WHAT MEANING DID IT ALL HAVE TO ME?
SIGN: ROAD CLOSED
ALL MY HURT FEELINGS...
...AND MY LONE-LINESS TOO...

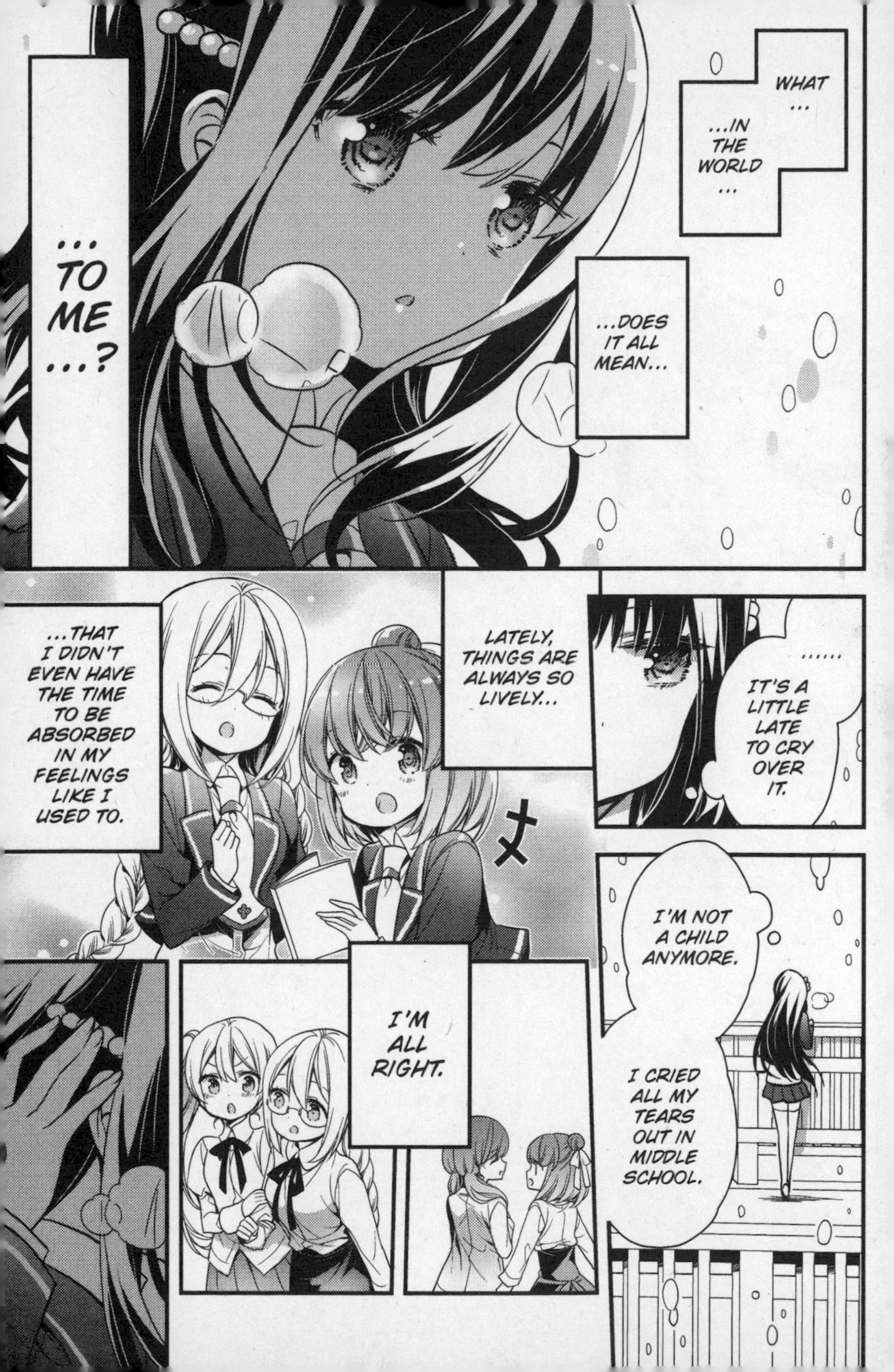
WHAT… …IN THE WORLD…
…DOES IT ALL MEAN…
…TO ME…?
……
IT'S A LITTLE LATE TO CRY OVER IT.
LATELY, THINGS ARE ALWAYS SO LIVELY…
…THAT I DIDN'T EVEN HAVE THE TIME TO BE ABSORBED IN MY FEELINGS LIKE I USED TO.
I'M NOT A CHILD ANYMORE.
I CRIED ALL MY TEARS OUT IN MIDDLE SCHOOL.
I'M ALL RIGHT.

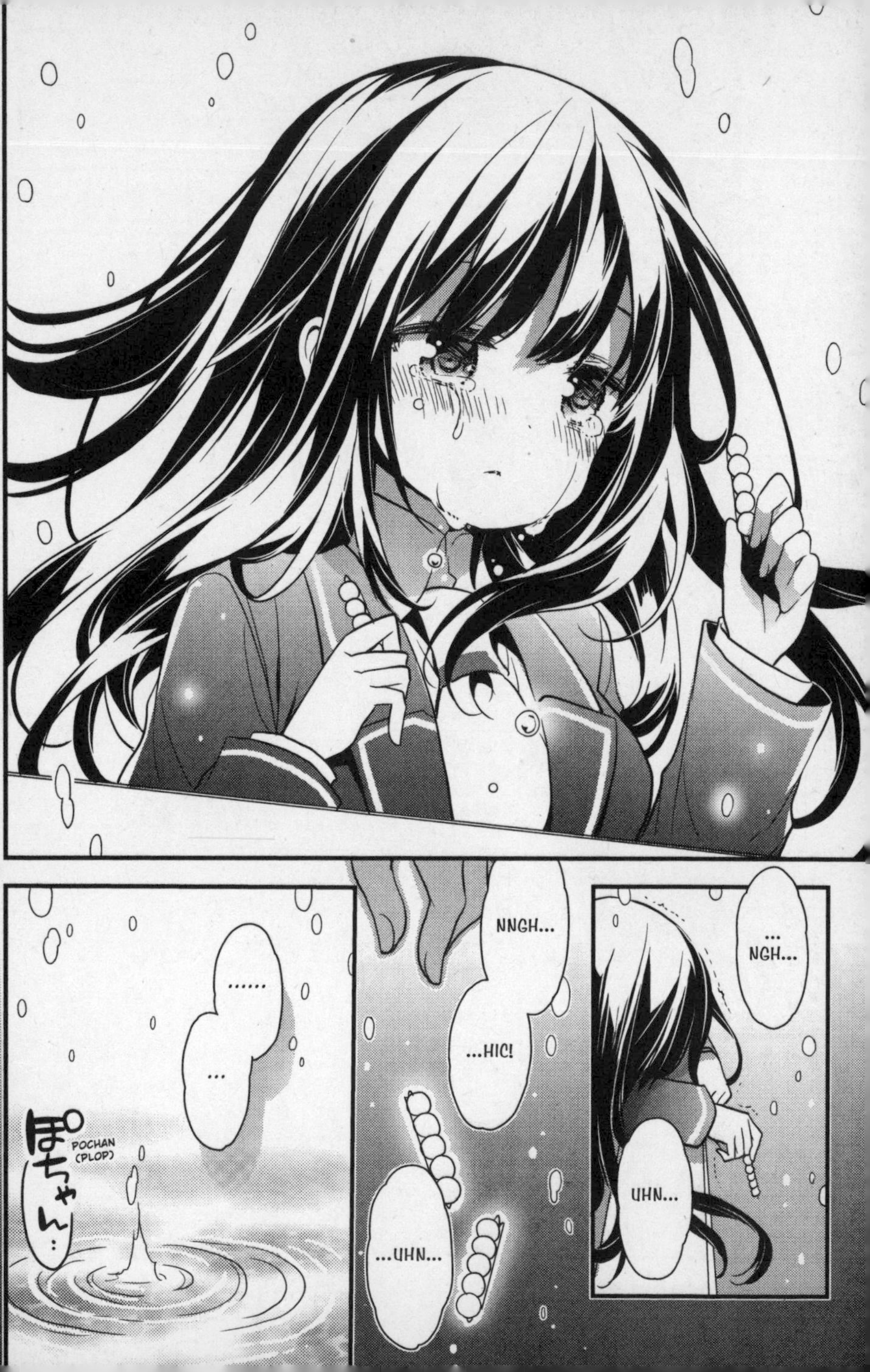
... NGH...
UHN...
NNGH...
...HIC!
...UHN...
......
...
ぽちゃん..
POCHAN (PLOP)

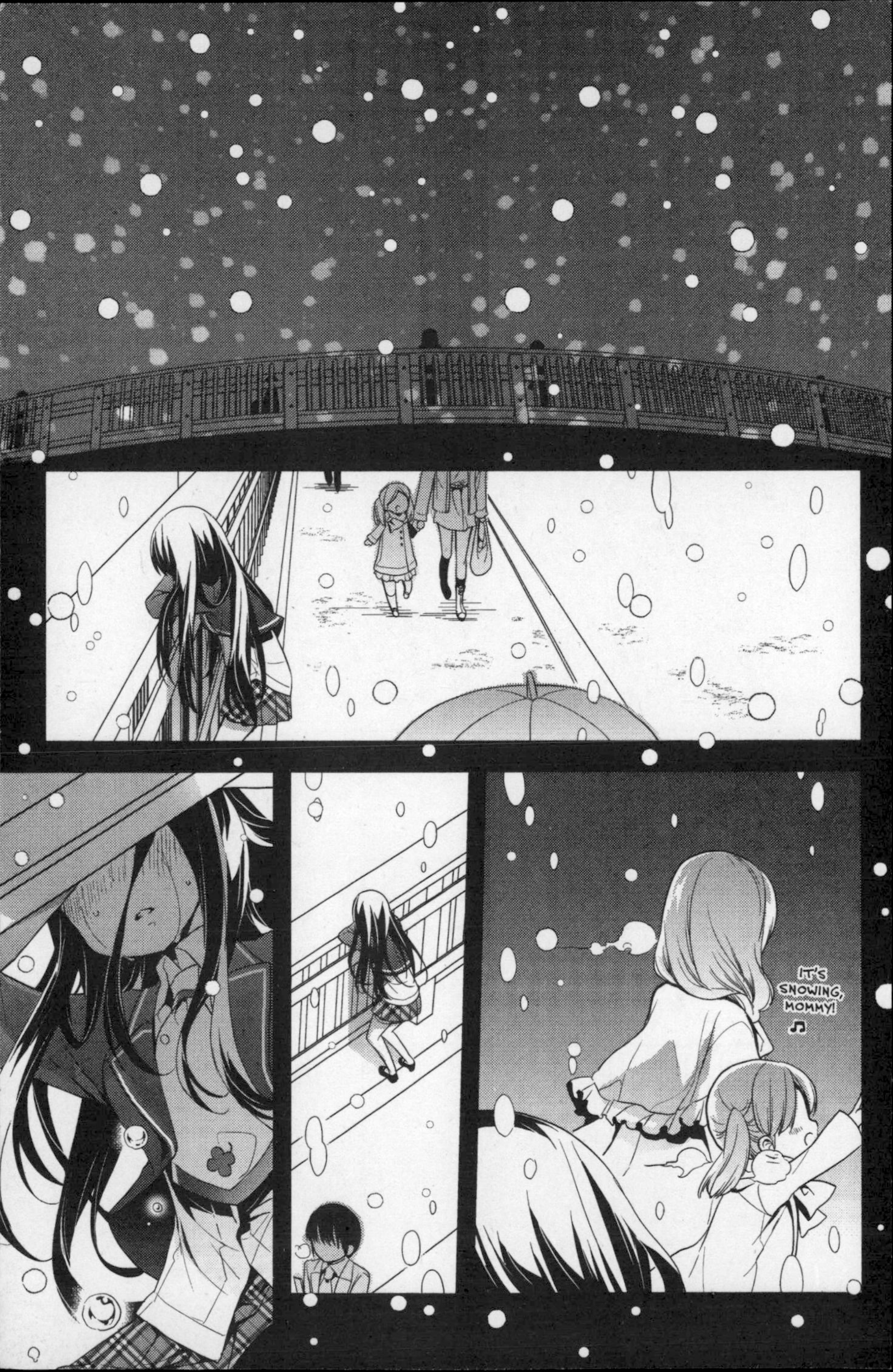
IT'S SNOWING, MOMMY! ♫

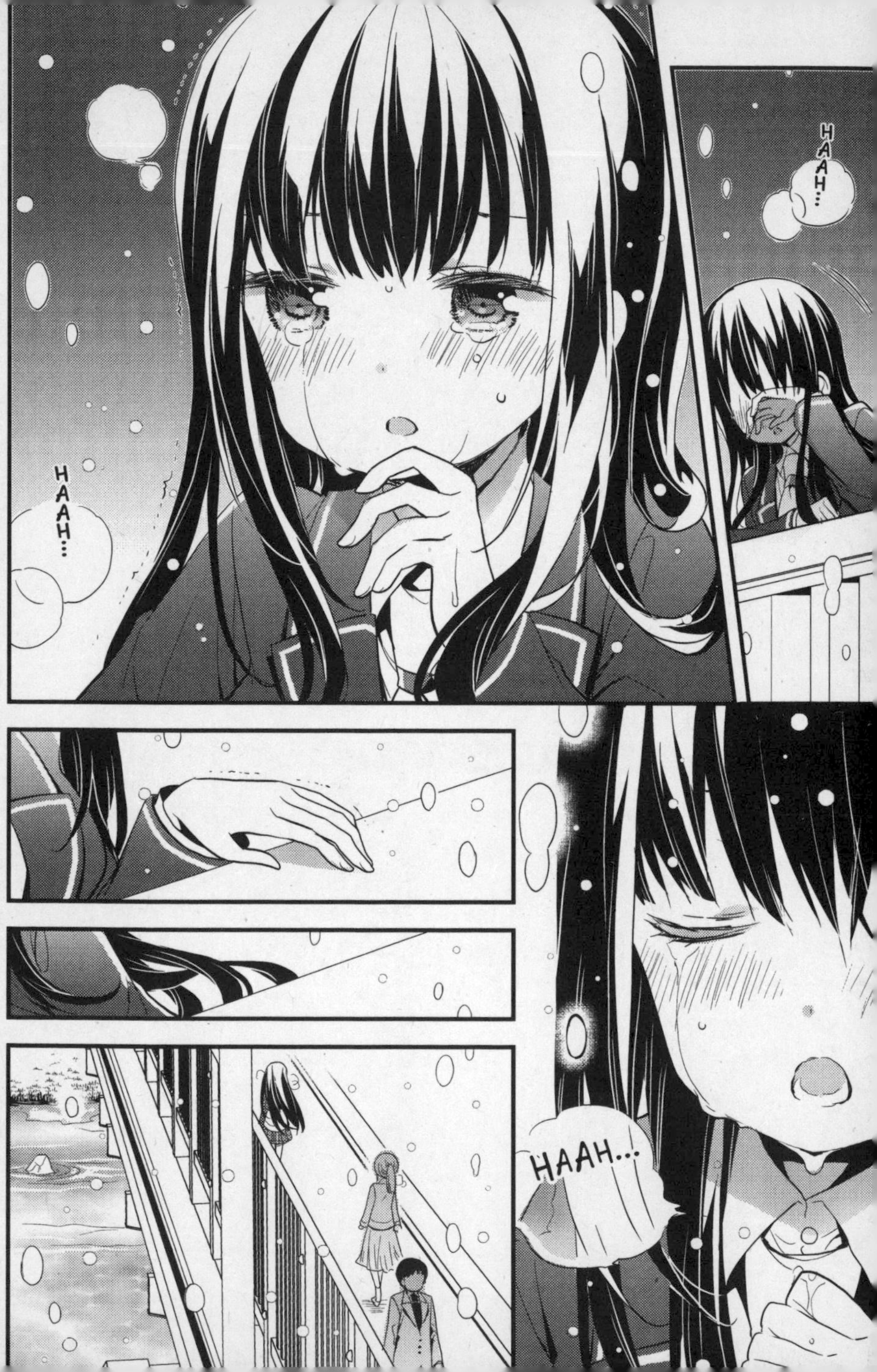
HAAAH...
HAAH...
HAAH...

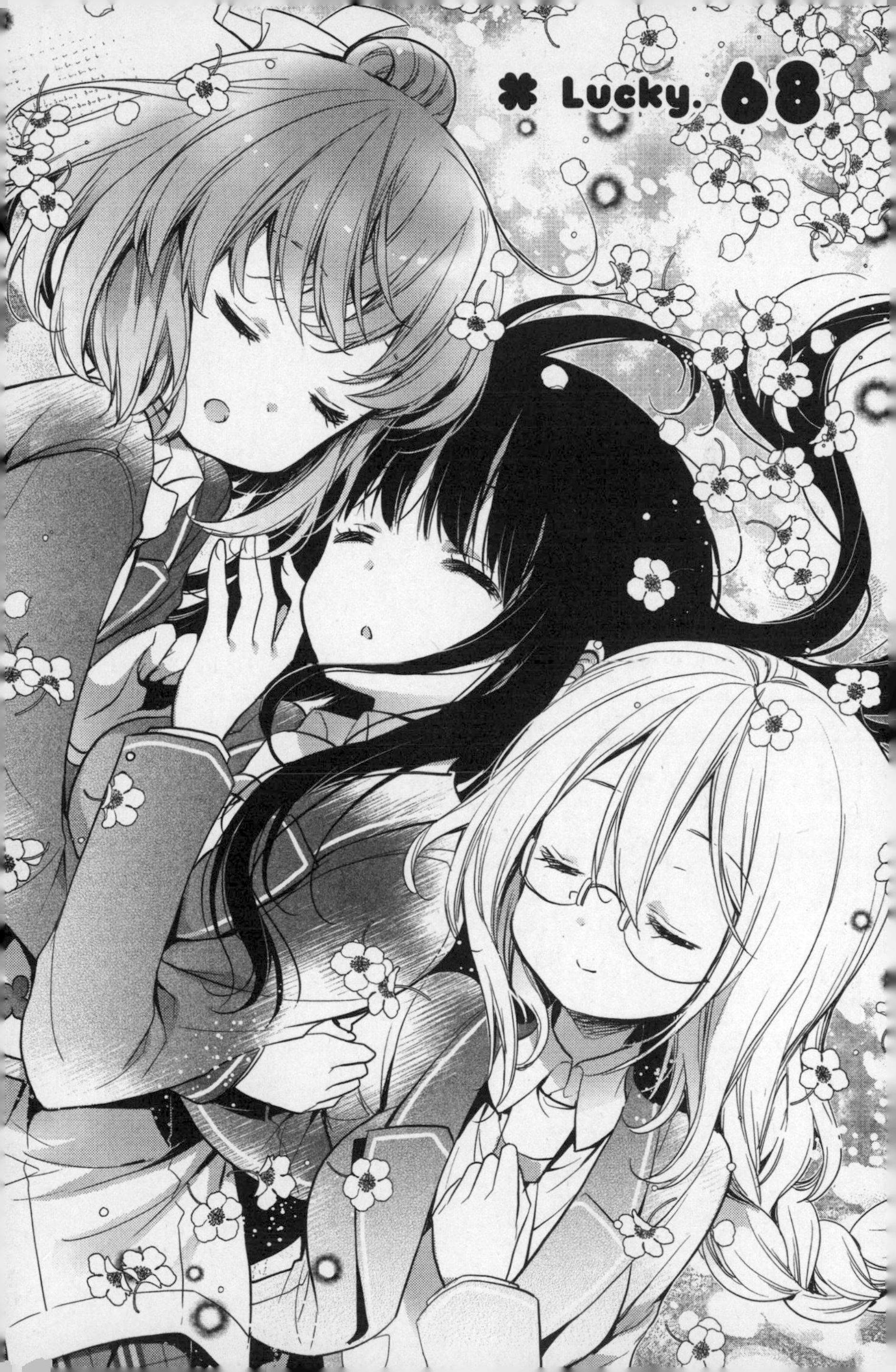

Lucky. 68

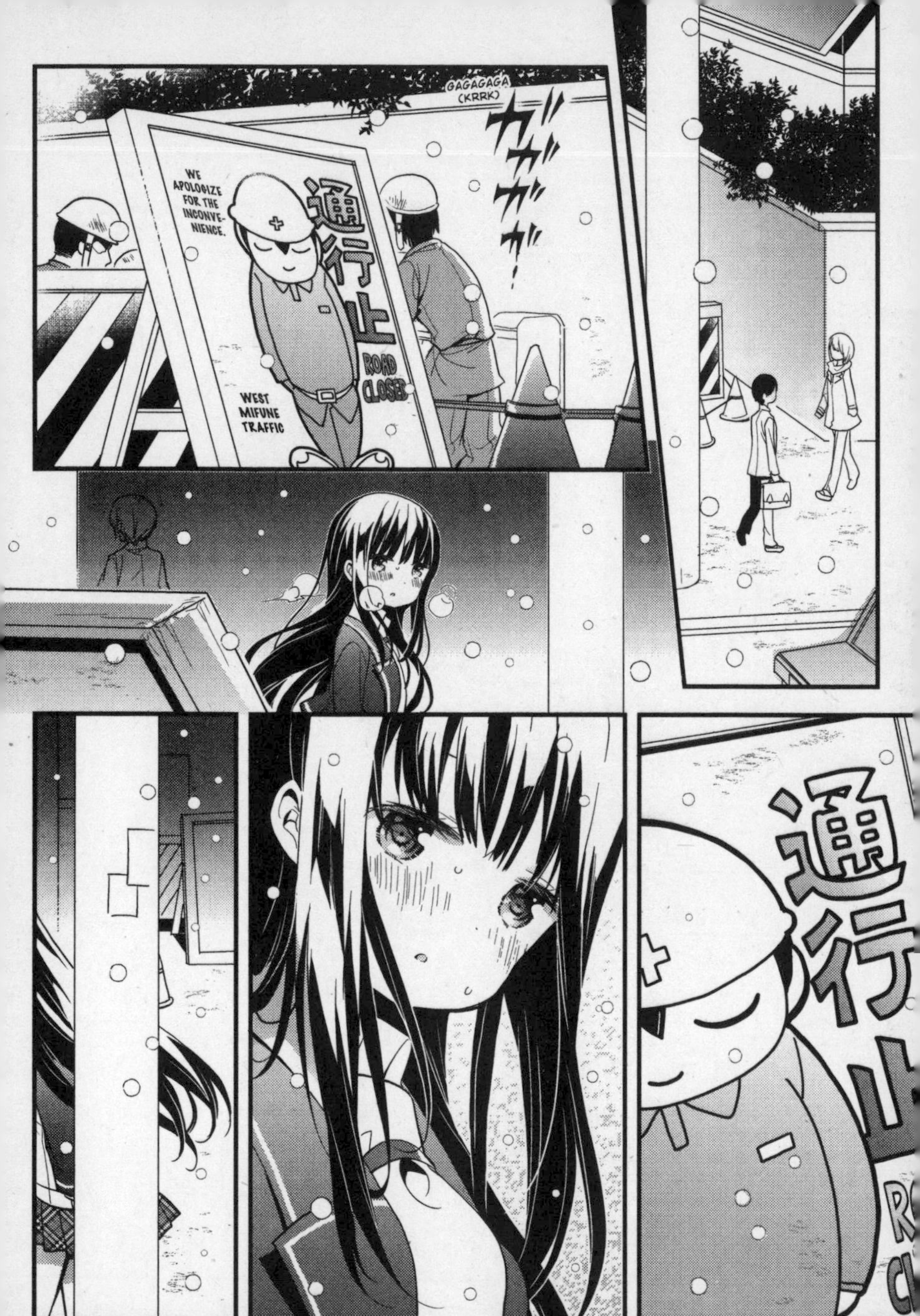
GAGAGAGA
(KRRK)
ガガガガ!
WE APOLOGIZE FOR THE INCONVE-NIENCE.
通行止
ROAD CLOSED
WEST MIFUNE TRAFFIC
通行止

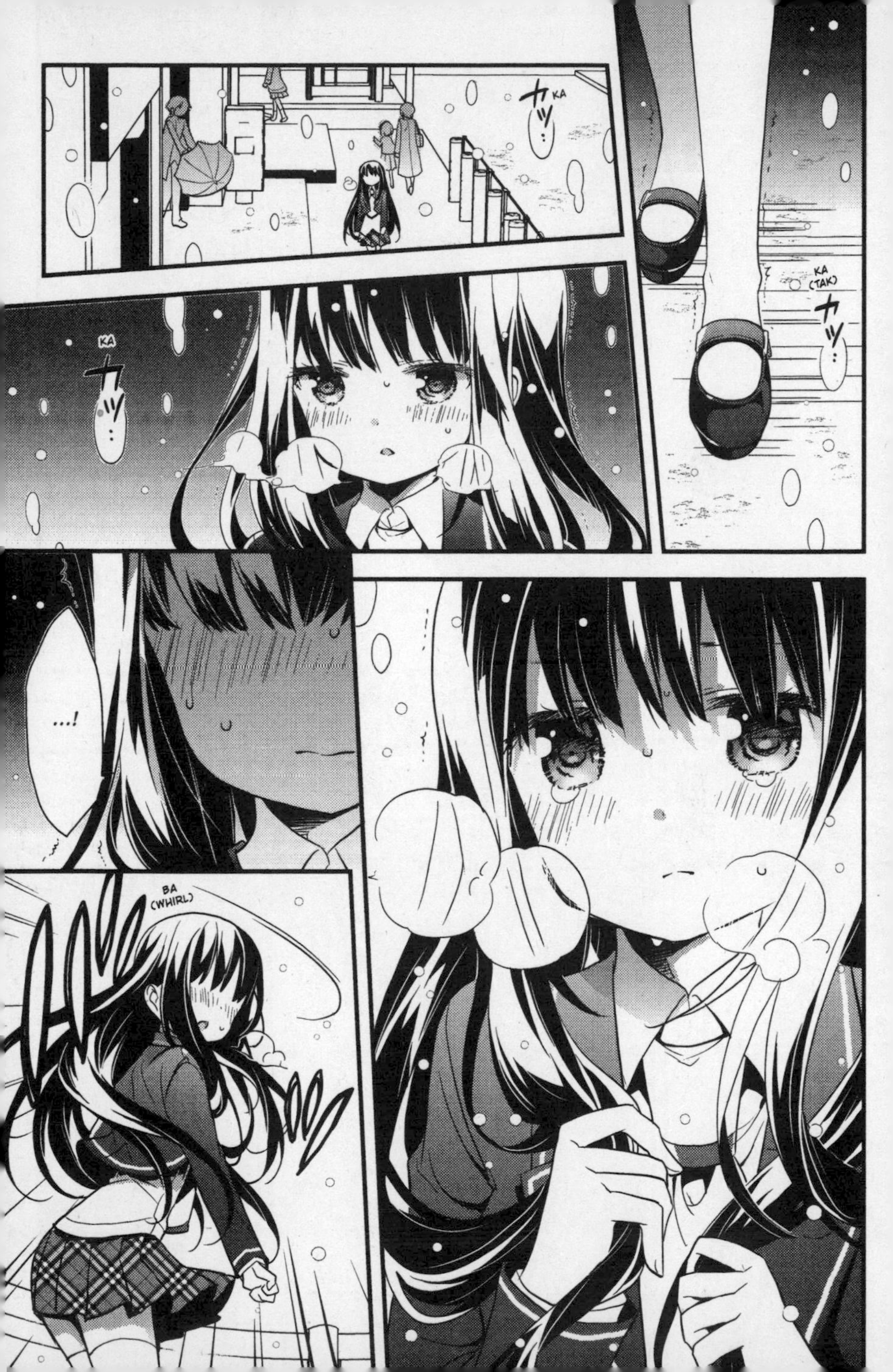
KA
(TAK)
KA
KA
...!
BA
(WHIRL)

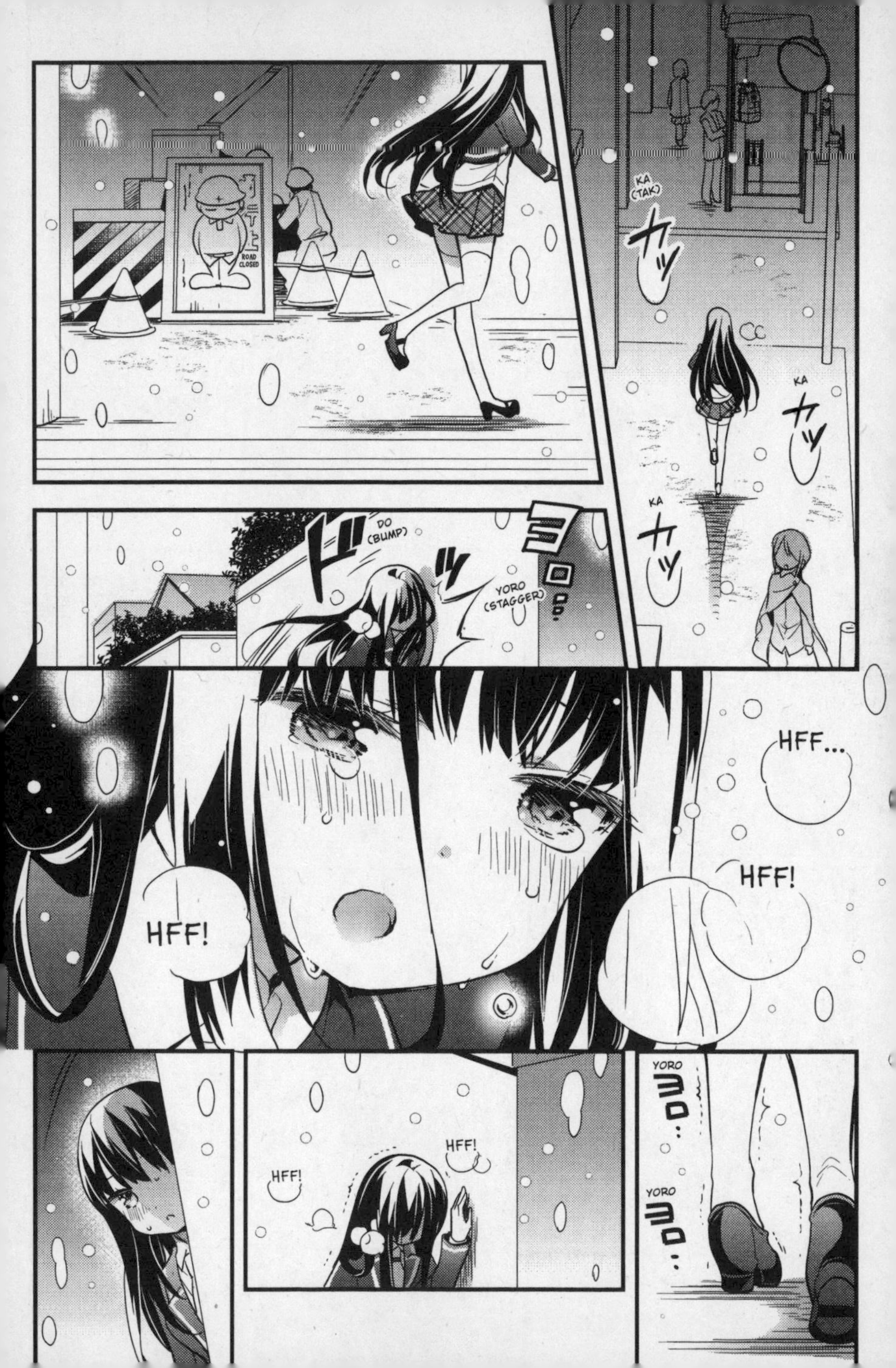
KA (TAK)
カッ
KA
カッ
KA
カッ
ROAD CLOSED
DO (BUMP)
ドッ
YORO (STAGGER)
ヨロ
HFF...
HFF!
HFF!
YORO
ヨロ..
YORO
ヨロ..
HFF!
HFF!

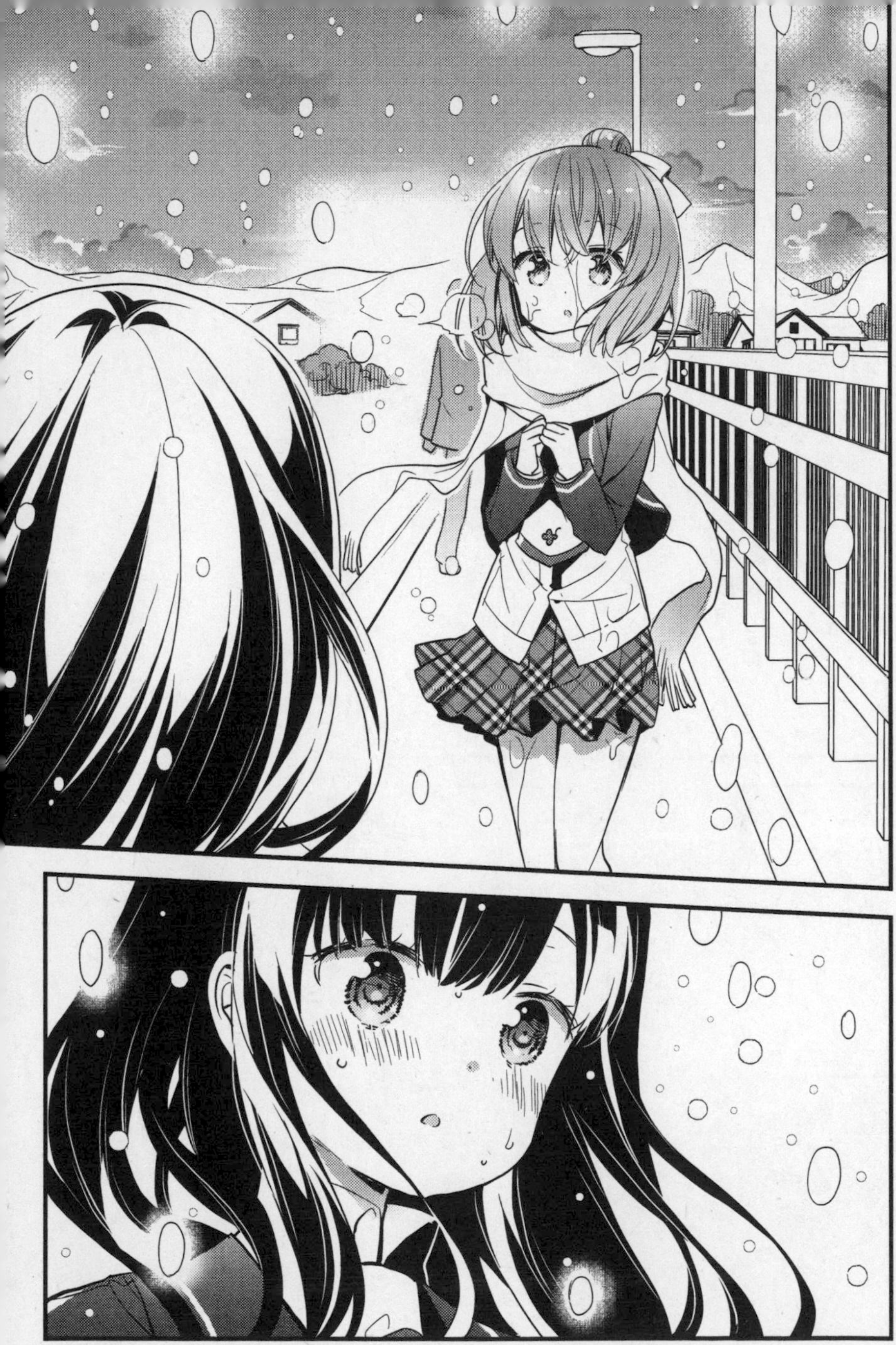

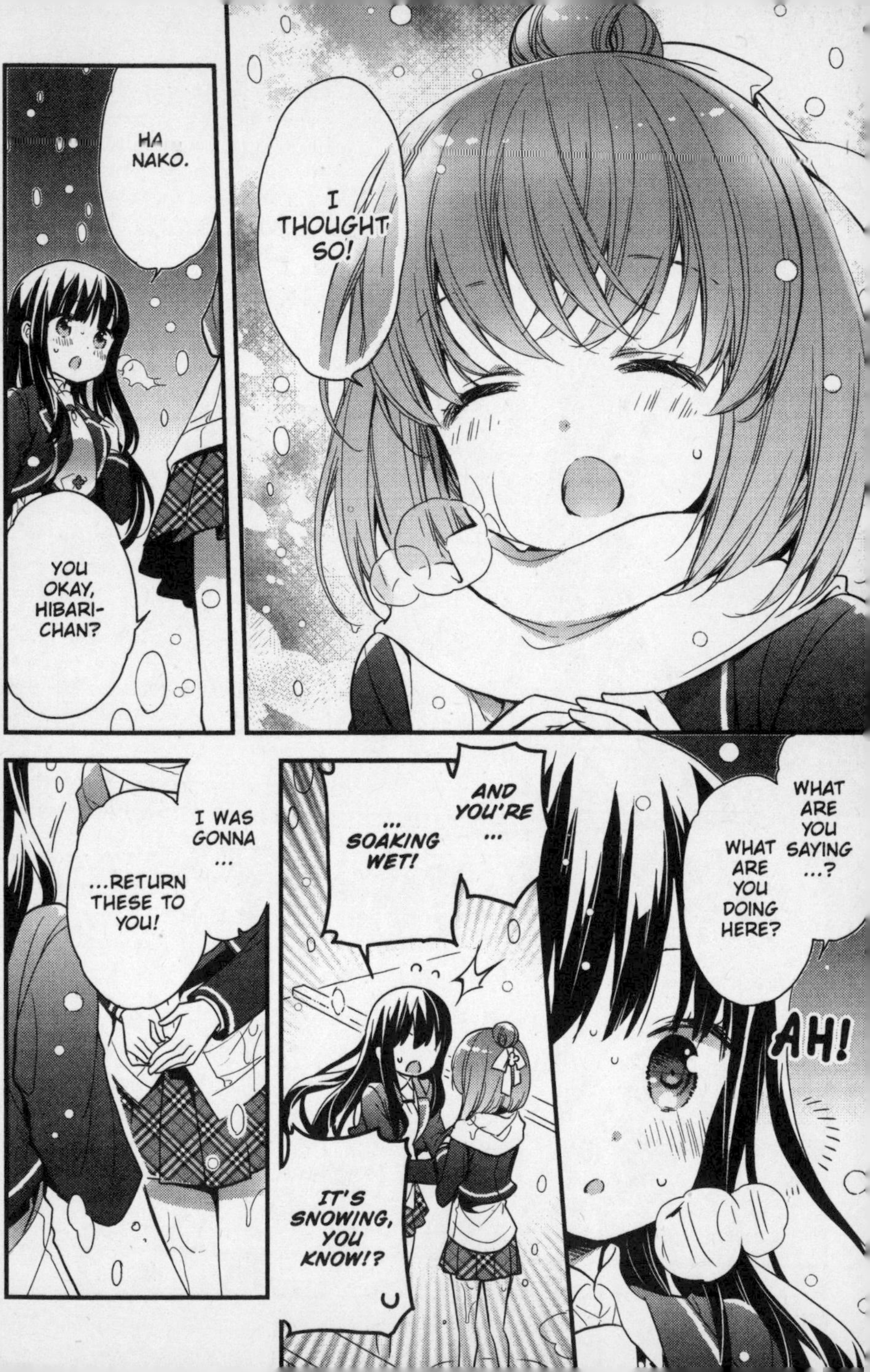
I THOUGHT SO!
HA NAKO.
YOU OKAY, HIBARI-CHAN?
WHAT ARE YOU SAYING ...?
WHAT ARE YOU DOING HERE?
AH!
AND YOU'RE ...
... SOAKING WET!
IT'S SNOWING, YOU KNOW!?
I WAS GONNA ...
...RETURN THESE TO YOU!

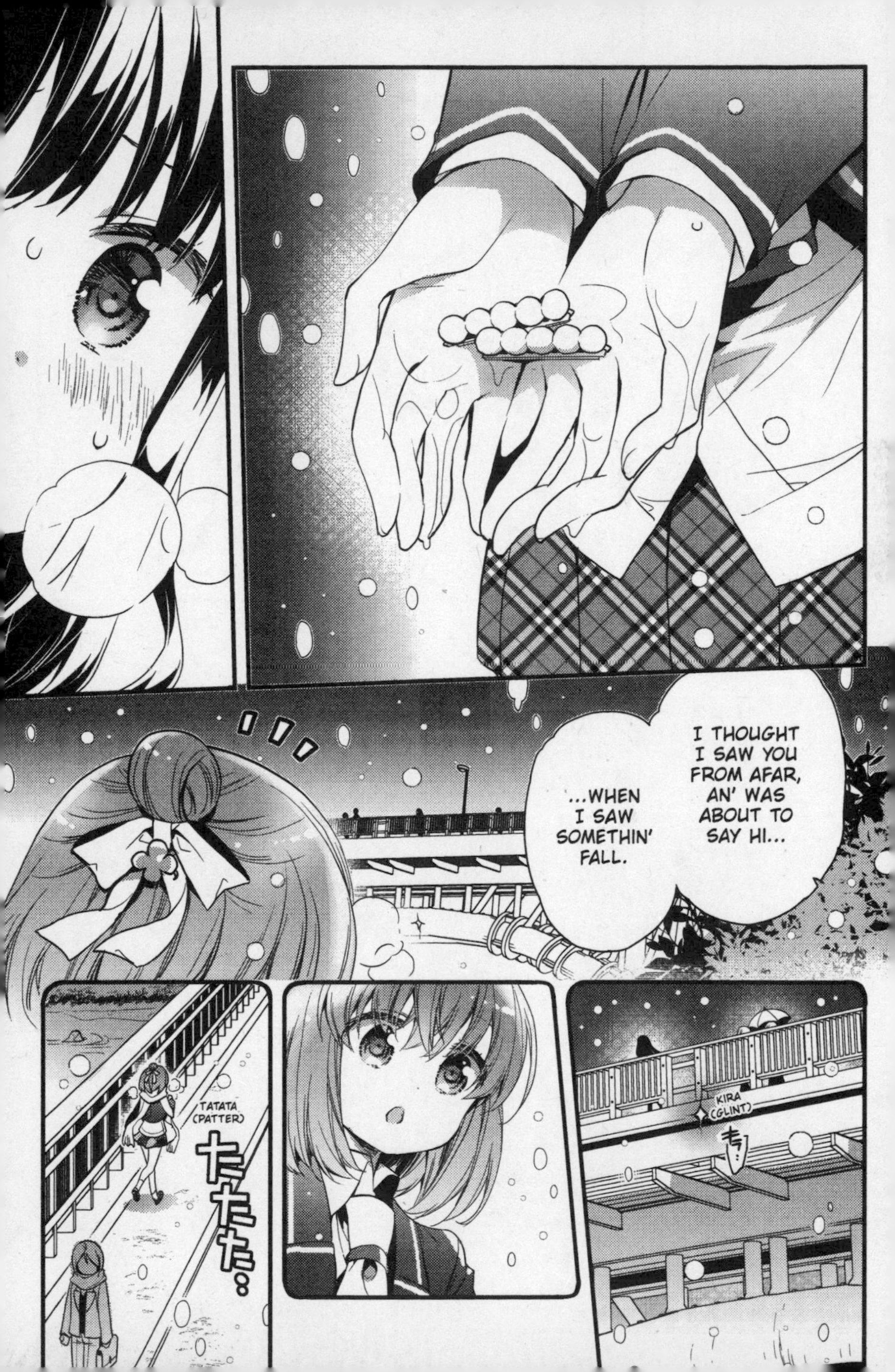
I THOUGHT I SAW YOU FROM AFAR, AN' WAS ABOUT TO SAY HI...
...WHEN I SAW SOMETHIN' FALL.
KIRA (GLINT)
キラ…
TATATA (PATTER)
たたた。

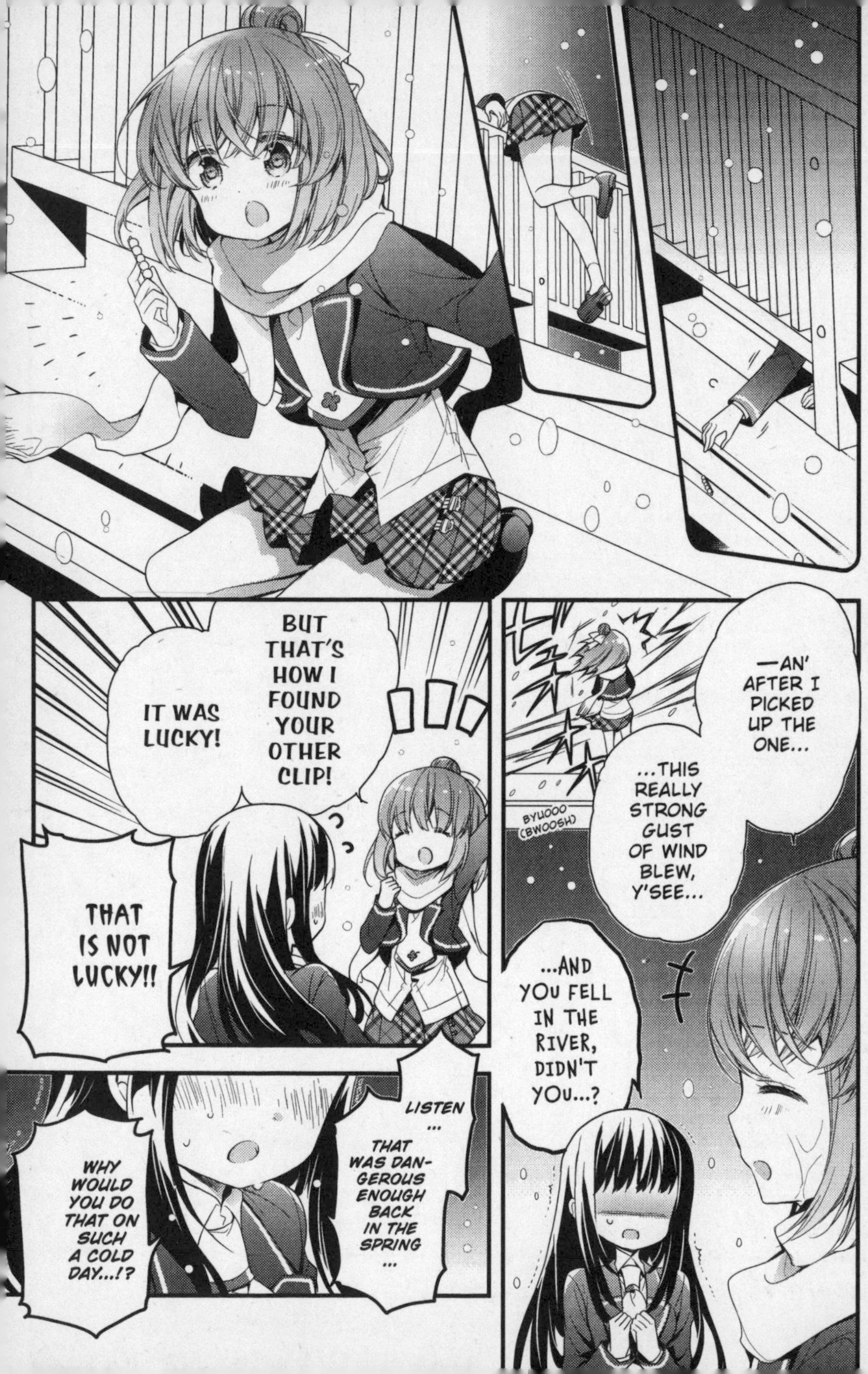
—AN' AFTER I PICKED UP THE ONE...
...THIS REALLY STRONG GUST OF WIND BLEW, Y'SEE...
BYUOOO (BWOOSH)
...AND YOU FELL IN THE RIVER, DIDN'T YOU...?
BUT THAT'S HOW I FOUND YOUR OTHER CLIP!
IT WAS LUCKY!
THAT IS NOT LUCKY!!
LISTEN... THAT WAS DANGEROUS ENOUGH BACK IN THE SPRING...
WHY WOULD YOU DO THAT ON SUCH A COLD DAY...!?

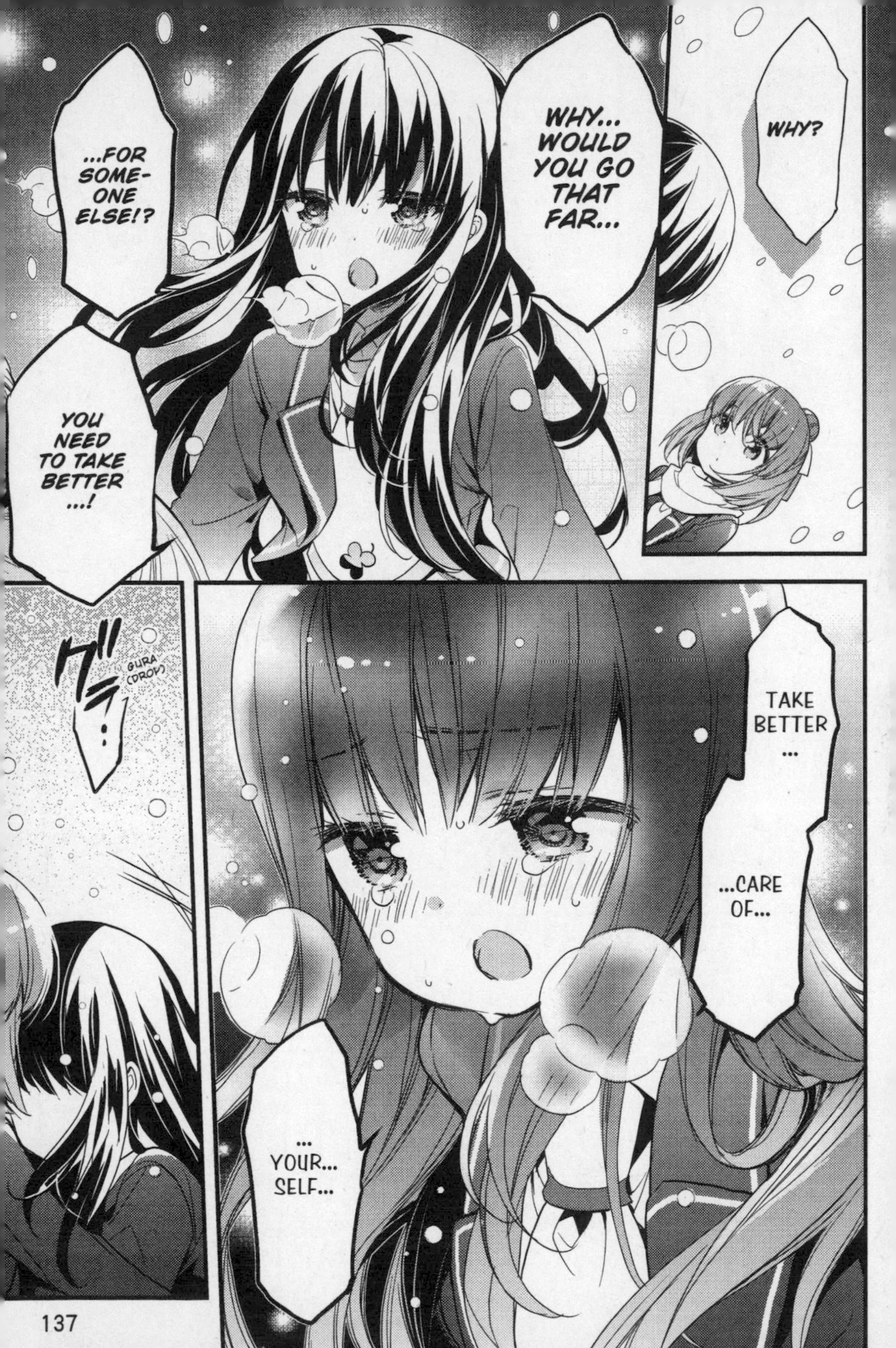
WHY?
WHY... WOULD YOU GO THAT FAR...
...FOR SOME-ONE ELSE!?
YOU NEED TO TAKE BETTER ...!
TAKE BETTER ...
...CARE OF...
... YOUR... SELF...
GURA (DROP)

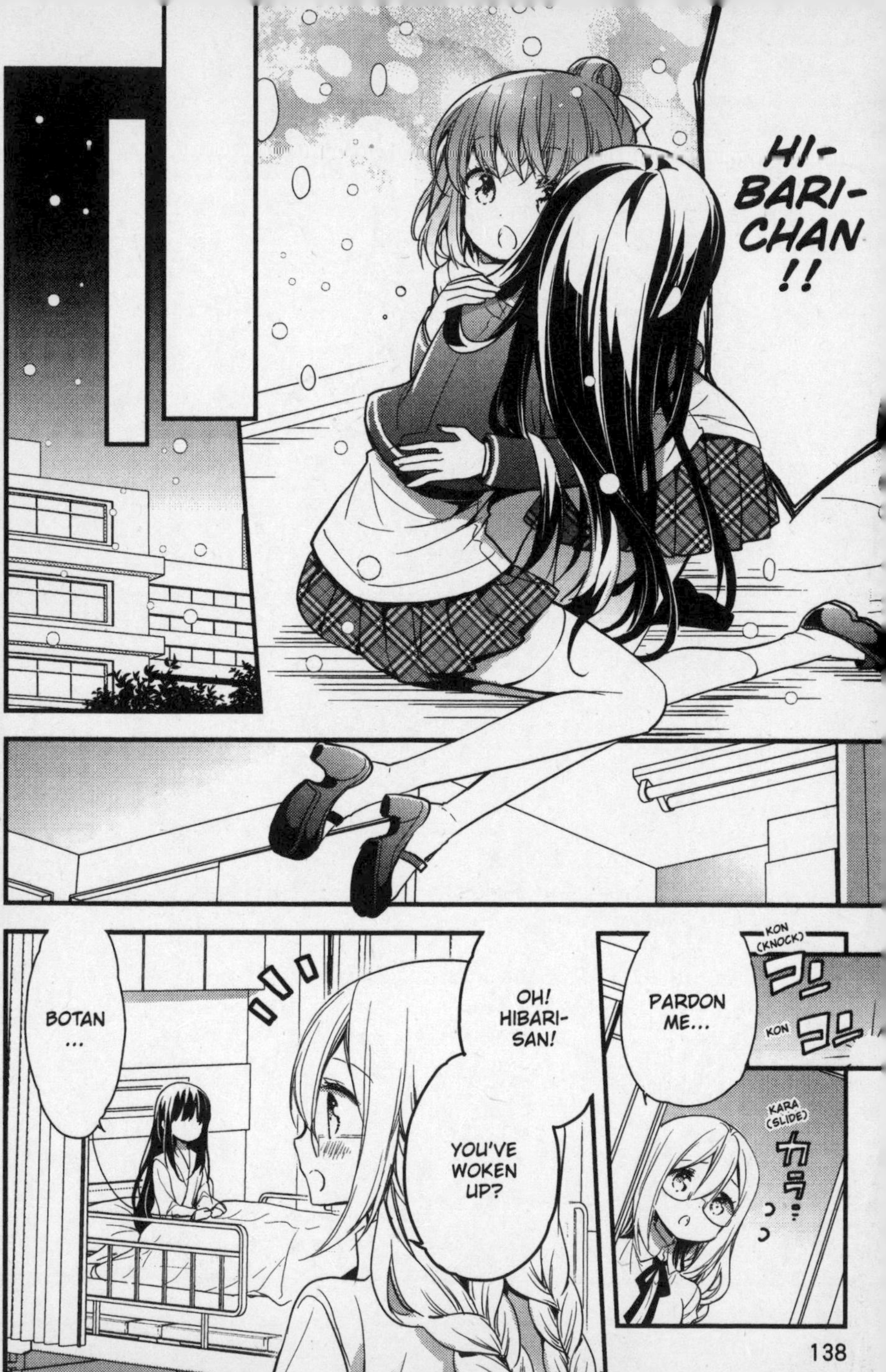
HI-BARI-CHAN!!
KON (KNOCK)
KON
PARDON ME...
KARA (SLIDE)
OH! HIBARI-SAN!
YOU'VE WOKEN UP?
BOTAN...

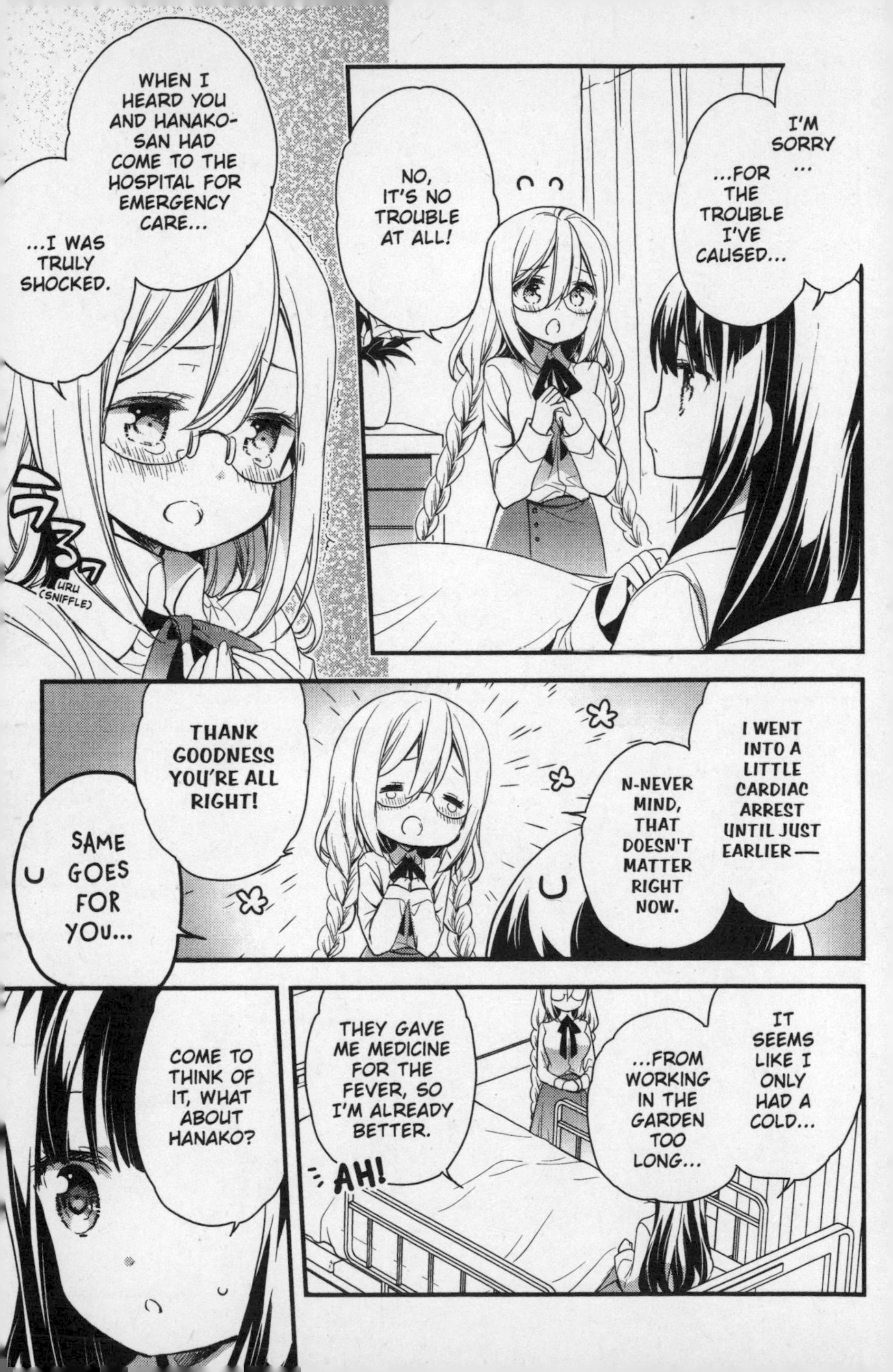
I'M SORRY...
...FOR THE TROUBLE I'VE CAUSED...
NO, IT'S NO TROUBLE AT ALL!
WHEN I HEARD YOU AND HANAKO-SAN HAD COME TO THE HOSPITAL FOR EMERGENCY CARE...
...I WAS TRULY SHOCKED.
URU (SNIFFLE)
I WENT INTO A LITTLE CARDIAC ARREST UNTIL JUST EARLIER—
N-NEVER MIND, THAT DOESN'T MATTER RIGHT NOW.
THANK GOODNESS YOU'RE ALL RIGHT!
SAME GOES FOR YOU...
IT SEEMS LIKE I ONLY HAD A COLD...
...FROM WORKING IN THE GARDEN TOO LONG...
THEY GAVE ME MEDICINE FOR THE FEVER, SO I'M ALREADY BETTER.
AH!
COME TO THINK OF IT, WHAT ABOUT HANAKO?

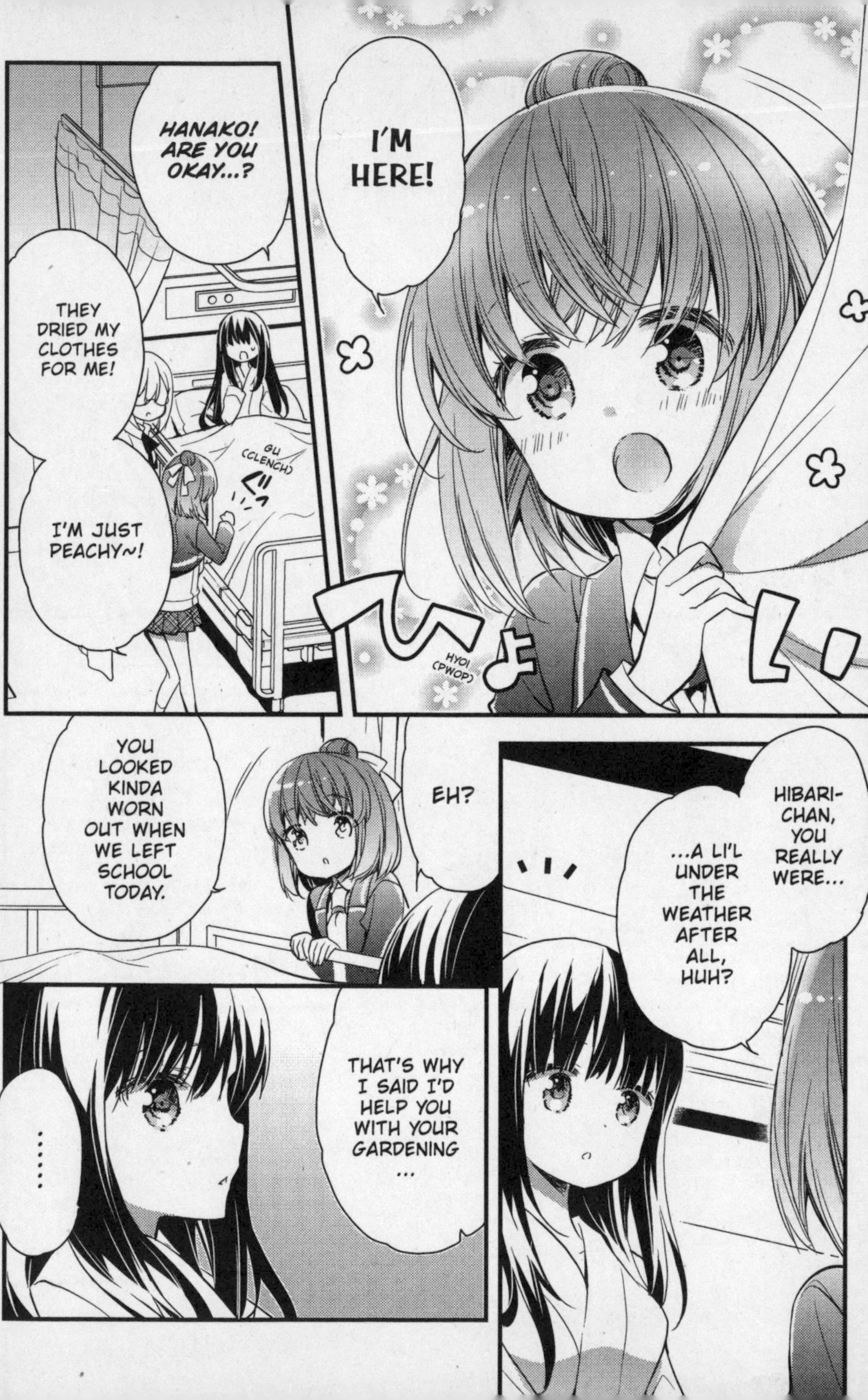
I'M HERE!
HYOI (PWOP)
HANAKO! ARE YOU OKAY...?
THEY DRIED MY CLOTHES FOR ME!
GU (CLENCH)
I'M JUST PEACHY~!
HIBARI-CHAN, YOU REALLY WERE...
...A LI'L UNDER THE WEATHER AFTER ALL, HUH?
EH?
YOU LOOKED KINDA WORN OUT WHEN WE LEFT SCHOOL TODAY.
THAT'S WHY I SAID I'D HELP YOU WITH YOUR GARDENING...
......

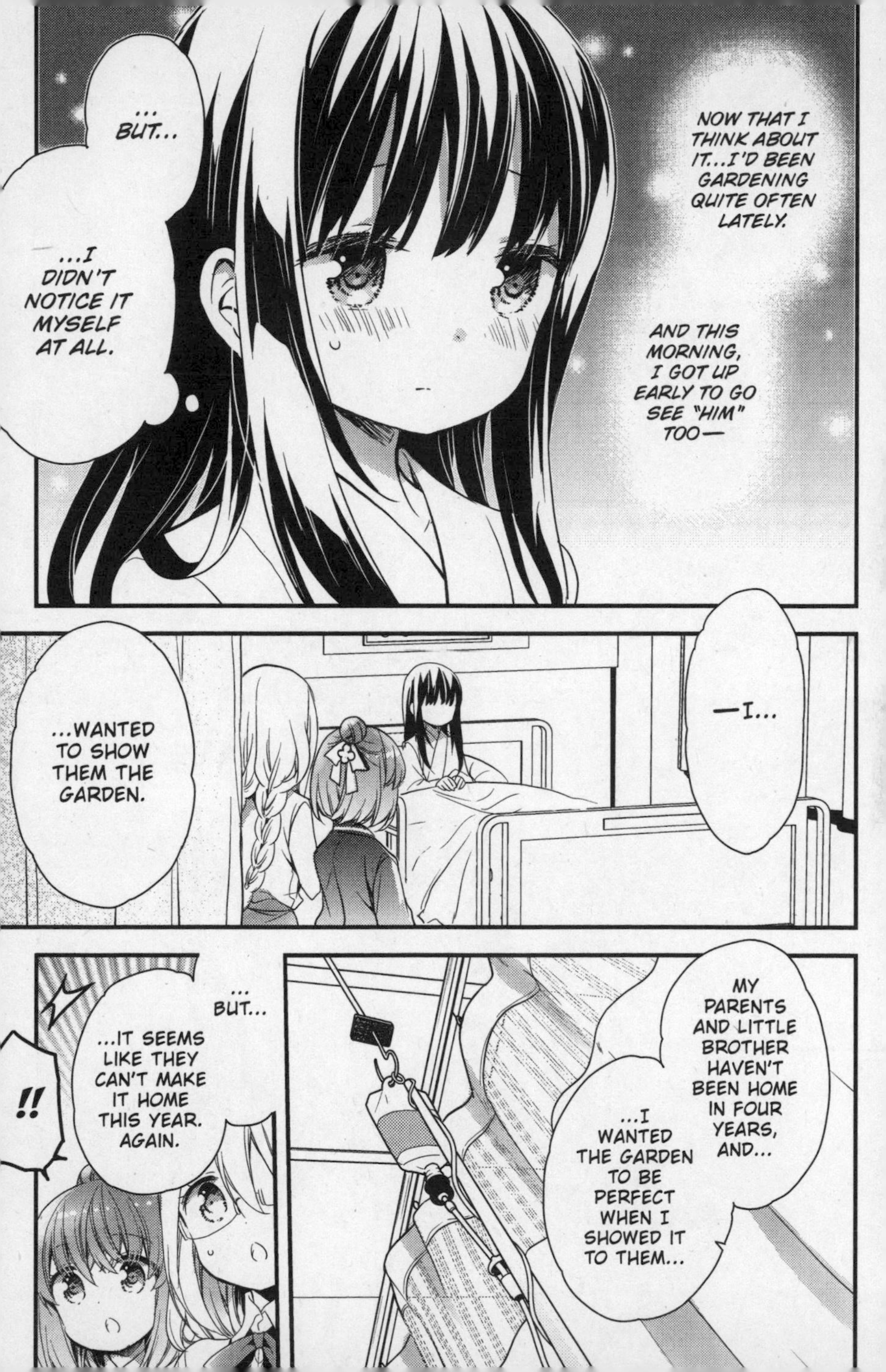
NOW THAT I THINK ABOUT IT...I'D BEEN GARDENING QUITE OFTEN LATELY.
AND THIS MORNING, I GOT UP EARLY TO GO SEE "HIM" TOO—
... BUT...
...I DIDN'T NOTICE IT MYSELF AT ALL.
—I...
...WANTED TO SHOW THEM THE GARDEN.
MY PARENTS AND LITTLE BROTHER HAVEN'T BEEN HOME IN FOUR YEARS, AND...
...I WANTED THE GARDEN TO BE PERFECT WHEN I SHOWED IT TO THEM...
... BUT...
...IT SEEMS LIKE THEY CAN'T MAKE IT HOME THIS YEAR. AGAIN.
!!

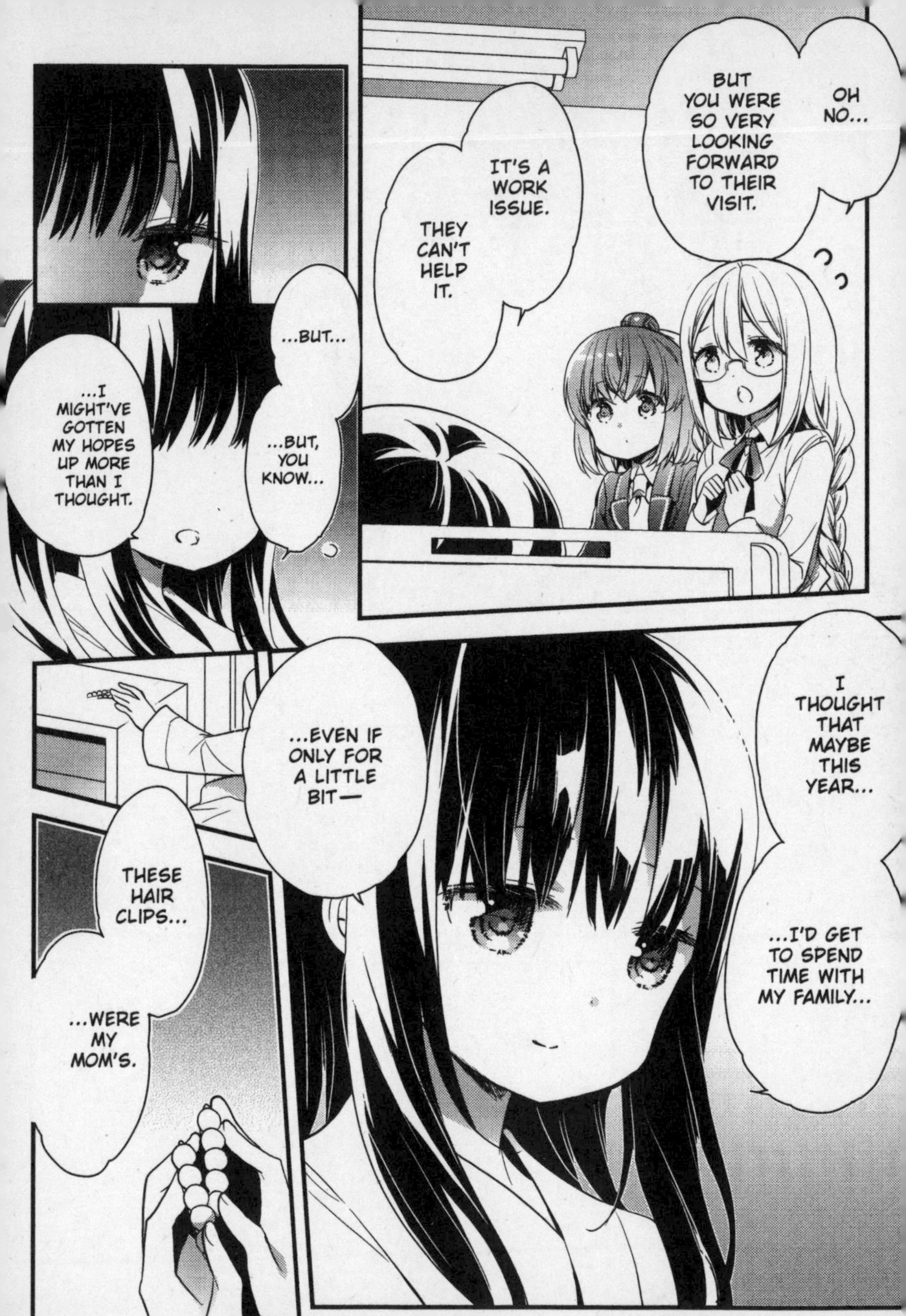
OH NO...
BUT YOU WERE SO VERY LOOKING FORWARD TO THEIR VISIT.
IT'S A WORK ISSUE.
THEY CAN'T HELP IT.
...BUT...
...BUT, YOU KNOW...
...I MIGHT'VE GOTTEN MY HOPES UP MORE THAN I THOUGHT.
I THOUGHT THAT MAYBE THIS YEAR...
...I'D GET TO SPEND TIME WITH MY FAMILY...
...EVEN IF ONLY FOR A LITTLE BIT—
THESE HAIR CLIPS...
...WERE MY MOM'S.

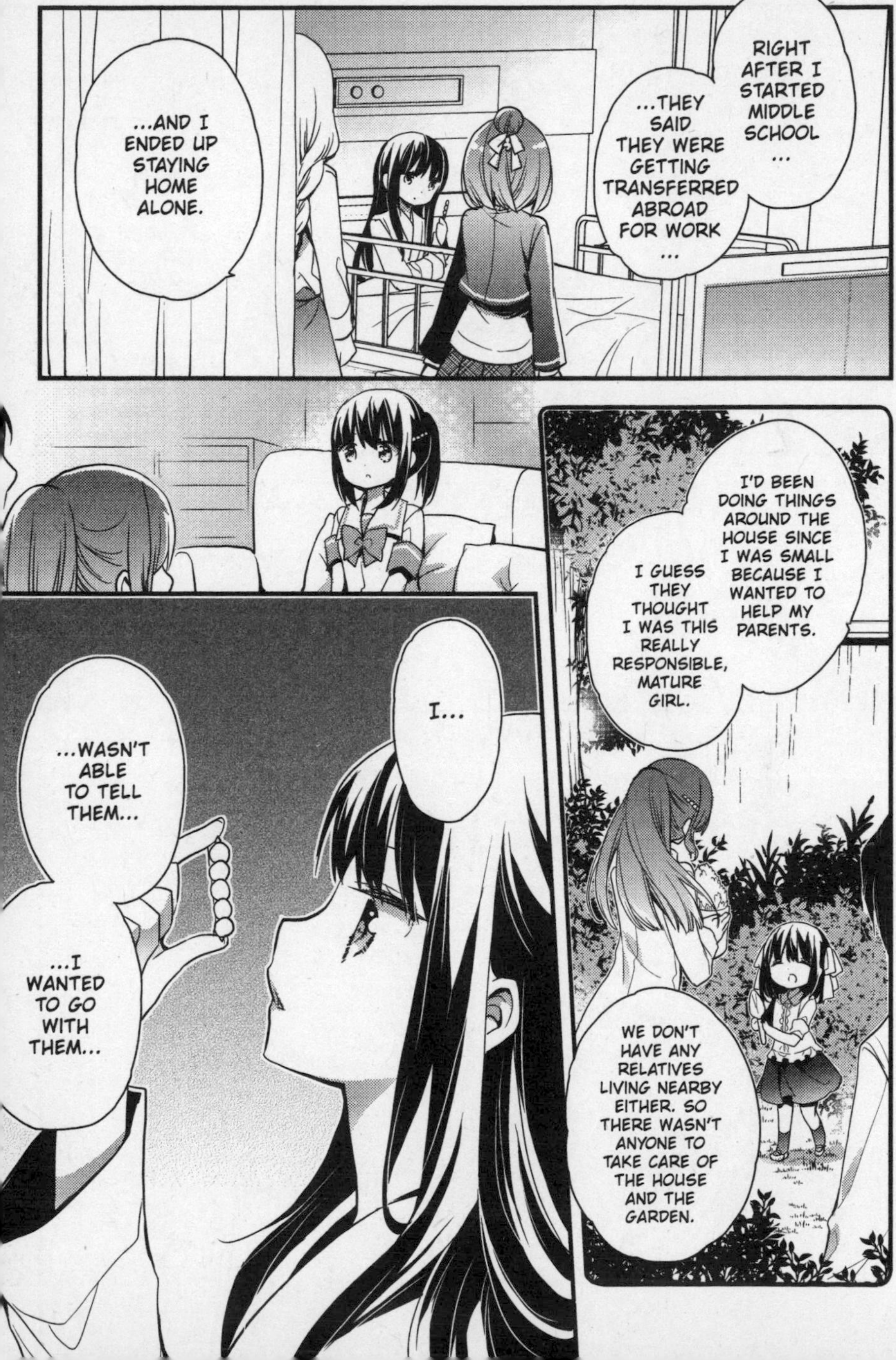
RIGHT AFTER I STARTED MIDDLE SCHOOL ...
...THEY SAID THEY WERE GETTING TRANSFERRED ABROAD FOR WORK ...
...AND I ENDED UP STAYING HOME ALONE.
I'D BEEN DOING THINGS AROUND THE HOUSE SINCE I WAS SMALL BECAUSE I WANTED TO HELP MY PARENTS.
I GUESS THEY THOUGHT I WAS THIS REALLY RESPONSIBLE, MATURE GIRL.
WE DON'T HAVE ANY RELATIVES LIVING NEARBY EITHER. SO THERE WASN'T ANYONE TO TAKE CARE OF THE HOUSE AND THE GARDEN.
I...
...WASN'T ABLE TO TELL THEM...
...I WANTED TO GO WITH THEM...

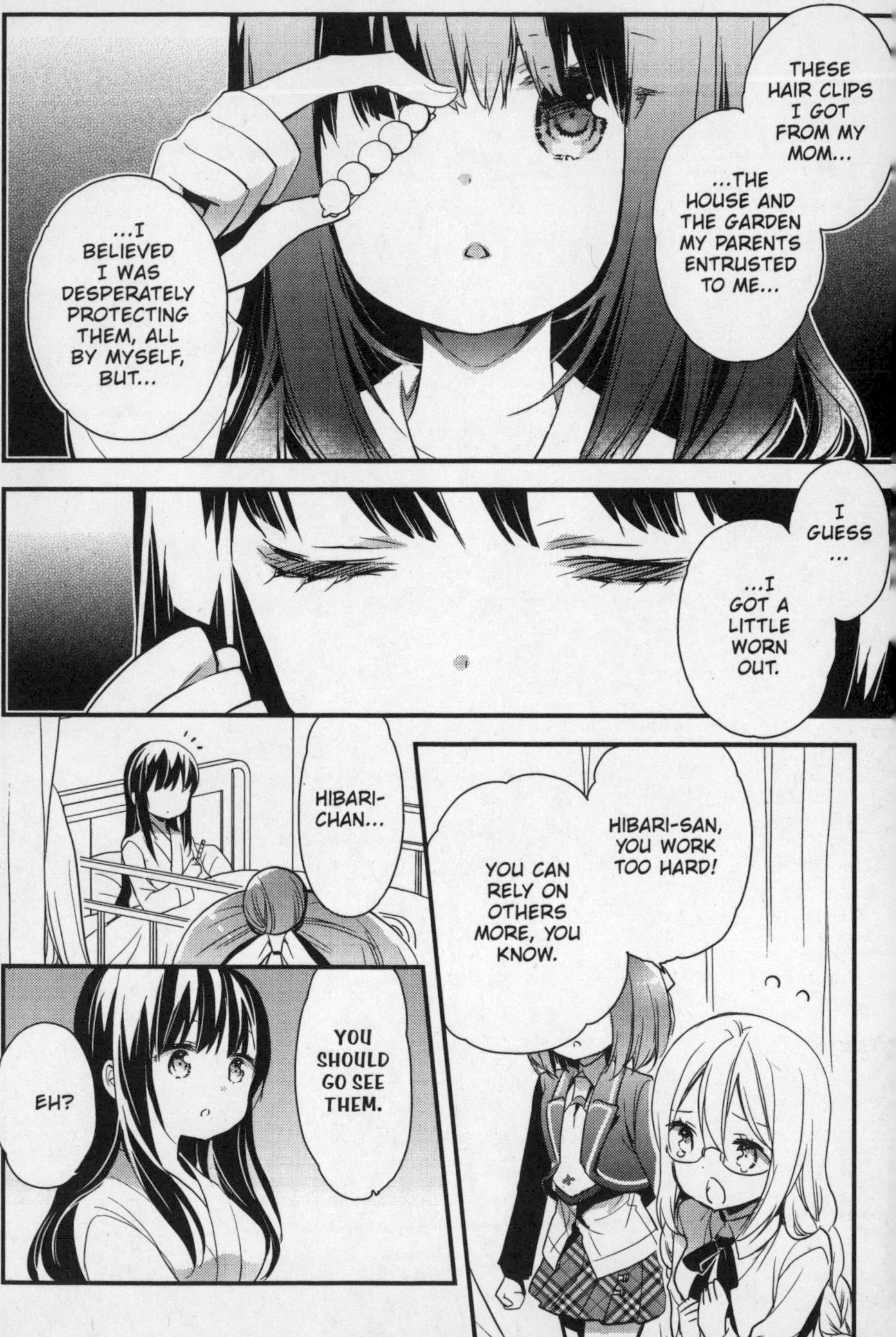
THESE HAIR CLIPS I GOT FROM MY MOM...
...THE HOUSE AND THE GARDEN MY PARENTS ENTRUSTED TO ME...
...I BELIEVED I WAS DESPERATELY PROTECTING THEM, ALL BY MYSELF, BUT...
I GUESS...
...I GOT A LITTLE WORN OUT.
HIBARI-SAN, YOU WORK TOO HARD!
YOU CAN RELY ON OTHERS MORE, YOU KNOW.
HIBARI-CHAN...
YOU SHOULD GO SEE THEM.
EH?

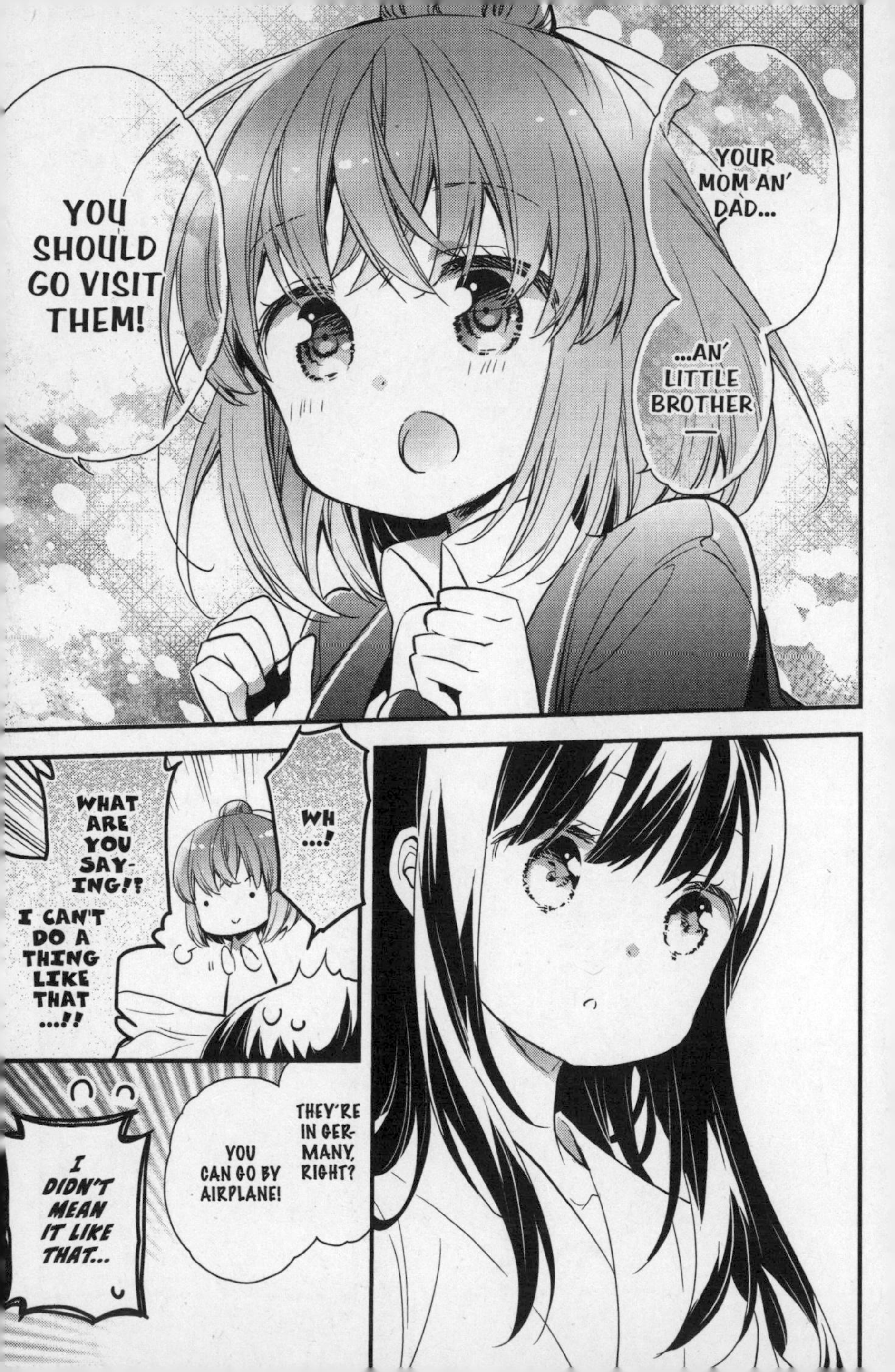
YOUR MOM AN' DAD...
...AN' LITTLE BROTHER—
YOU SHOULD GO VISIT THEM!
WH...!
WHAT ARE YOU SAYING!? I CAN'T DO A THING LIKE THAT...!!
THEY'RE IN GERMANY, RIGHT?
YOU CAN GO BY AIRPLANE!
I DIDN'T MEAN IT LIKE THAT...

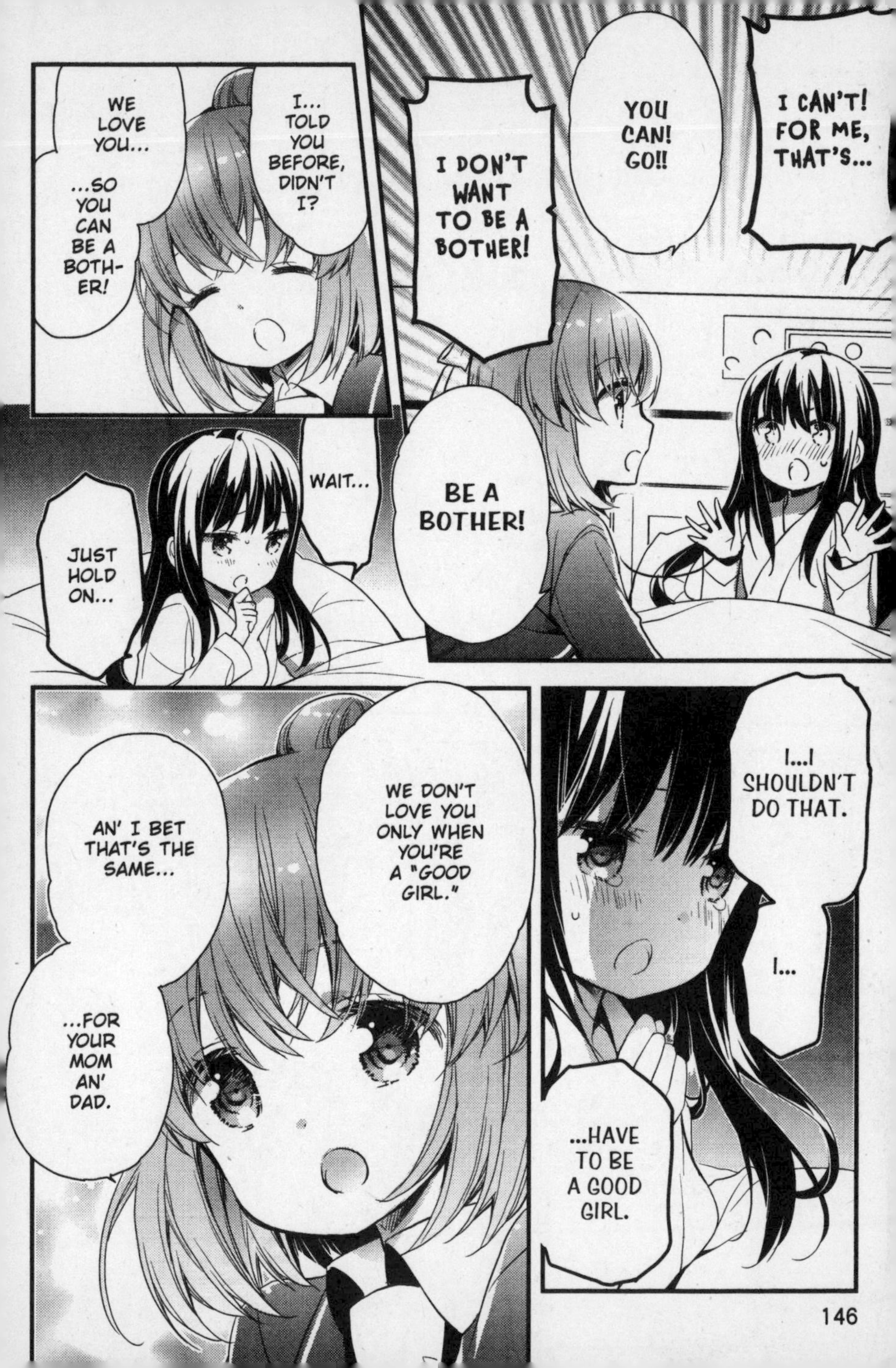

I CAN'T! FOR ME, THAT'S...
YOU CAN! GO!!
I DON'T WANT TO BE A BOTHER!
BE A BOTHER!
I... TOLD YOU BEFORE, DIDN'T I?
WE LOVE YOU...
...SO YOU CAN BE A BOTH-ER!
WAIT...
JUST HOLD ON...
I...I SHOULDN'T DO THAT.
I...
...HAVE TO BE A GOOD GIRL.
WE DON'T LOVE YOU ONLY WHEN YOU'RE A "GOOD GIRL."
AN' I BET THAT'S THE SAME...
...FOR YOUR MOM AN' DAD.

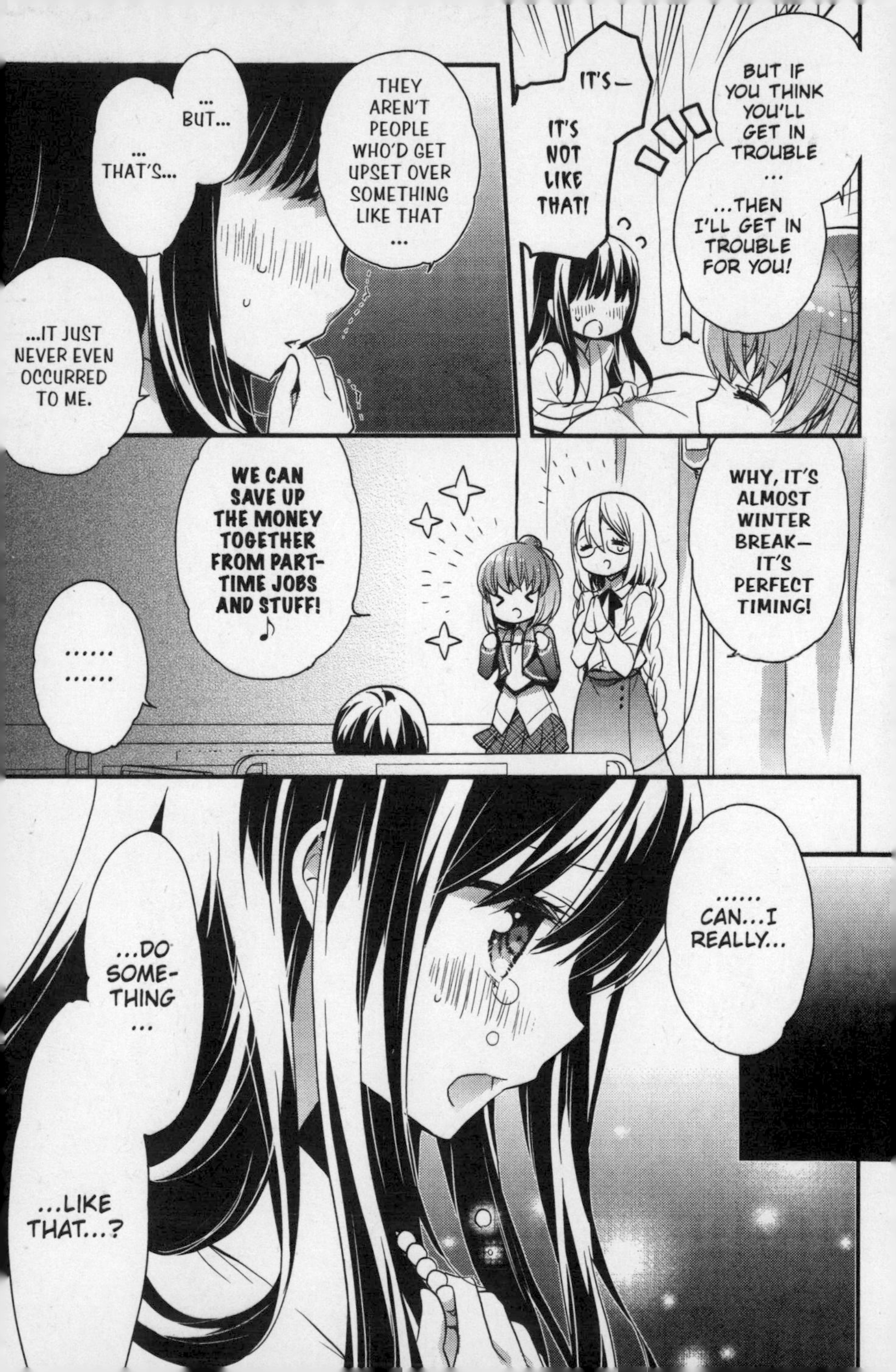
BUT IF YOU THINK YOU'LL GET IN TROUBLE ...
...THEN I'LL GET IN TROUBLE FOR YOU!
IT'S—
IT'S NOT LIKE THAT!
THEY AREN'T PEOPLE WHO'D GET UPSET OVER SOMETHING LIKE THAT ...
... BUT...
... THAT'S...
...IT JUST NEVER EVEN OCCURRED TO ME.
WHY, IT'S ALMOST WINTER BREAK—IT'S PERFECT TIMING!
WE CAN SAVE UP THE MONEY TOGETHER FROM PART-TIME JOBS AND STUFF! ♪
....
...... CAN...I REALLY...
...DO SOME-THING ...
...LIKE THAT...?

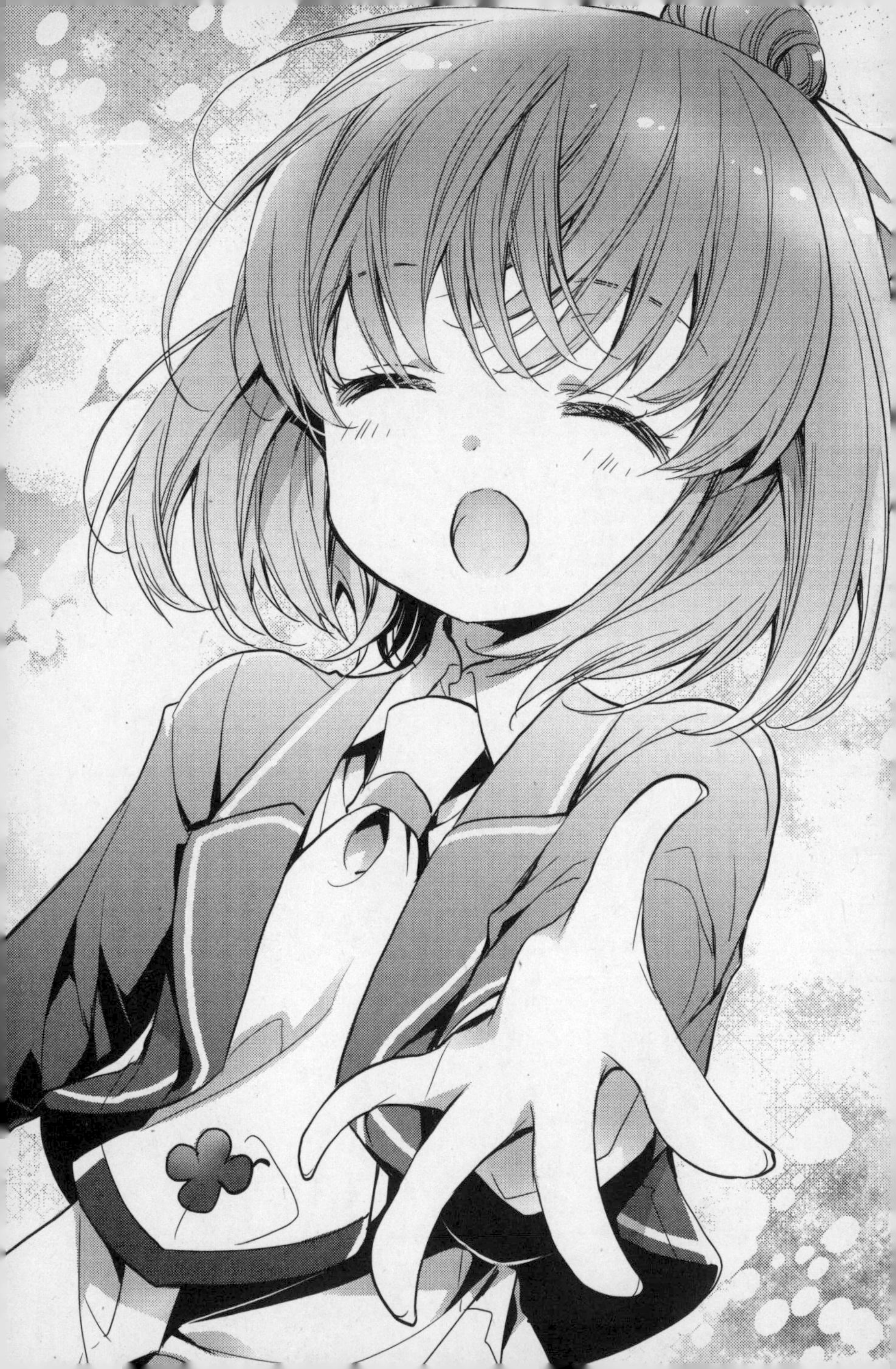

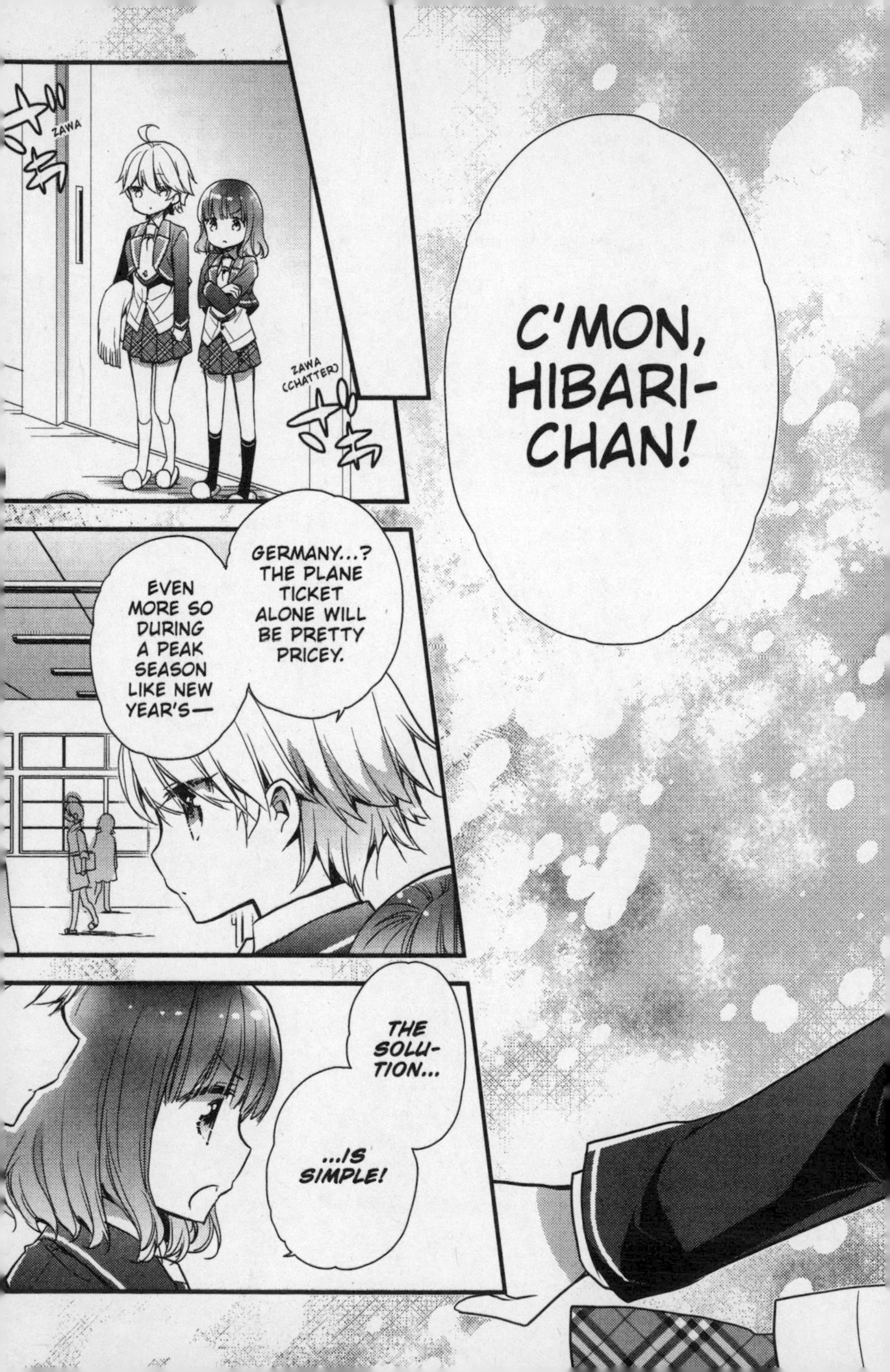
C'MON, HIBARI-CHAN!
ZAWA
ZAWA (CHATTER)
GERMANY...? THE PLANE TICKET ALONE WILL BE PRETTY PRICEY.
EVEN MORE SO DURING A PEAK SEASON LIKE NEW YEAR'S—
THE SOLUTION...
...IS SIMPLE!

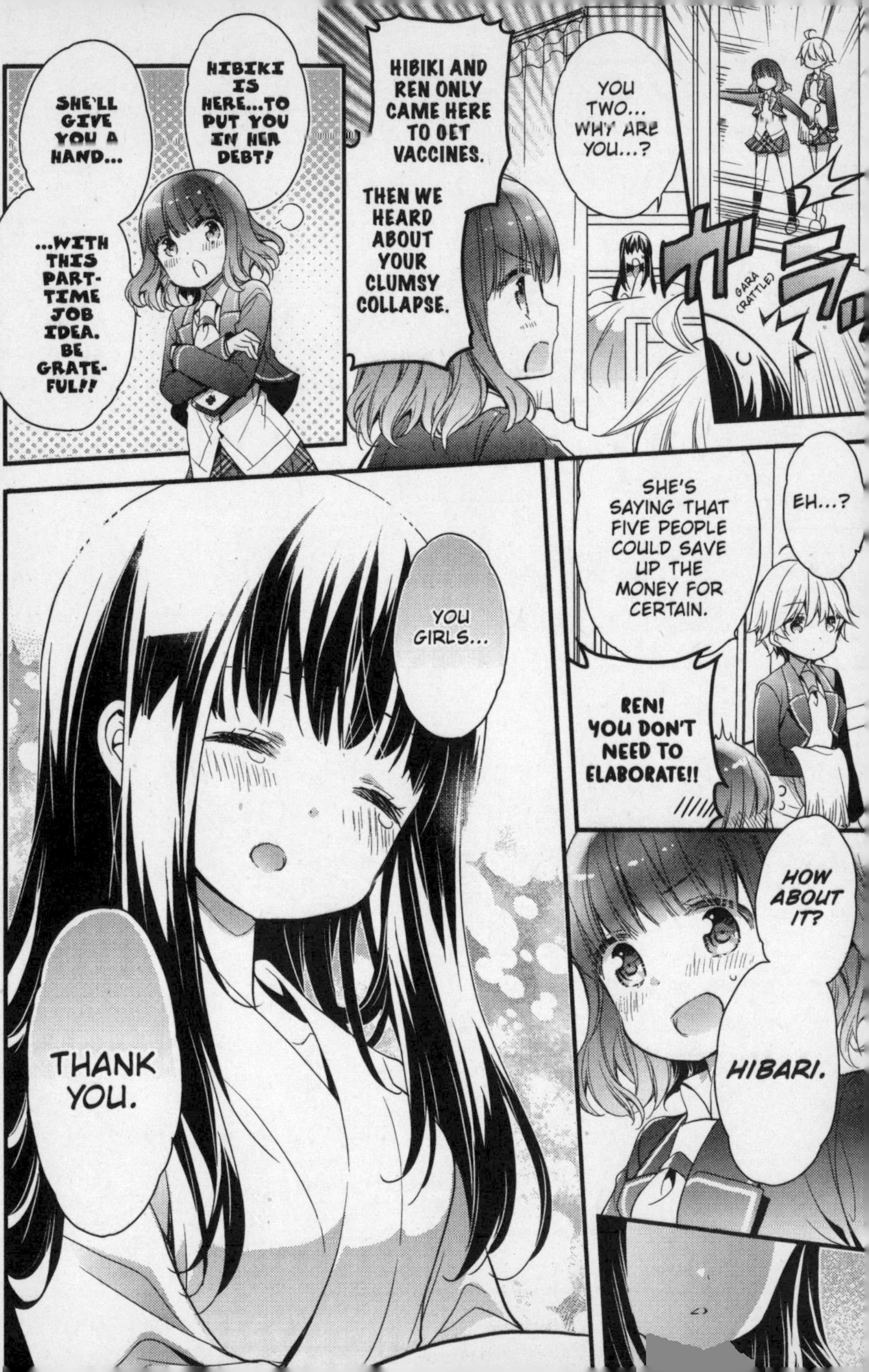
GARA (RATTLE)
YOU TWO... WHY ARE YOU...?
HIBIKI AND REN ONLY CAME HERE TO GET VACCINES.
THEN WE HEARD ABOUT YOUR CLUMSY COLLAPSE.
HIBIKI IS HERE...TO PUT YOU IN HER DEBT!
SHE'LL GIVE YOU A HAND...
...WITH THIS PART-TIME JOB IDEA. BE GRATEFUL!!
EH...?
SHE'S SAYING THAT FIVE PEOPLE COULD SAVE UP THE MONEY FOR CERTAIN.
REN! YOU DON'T NEED TO ELABORATE!!
HOW ABOUT IT?
HIBARI.
YOU GIRLS...
THANK YOU.

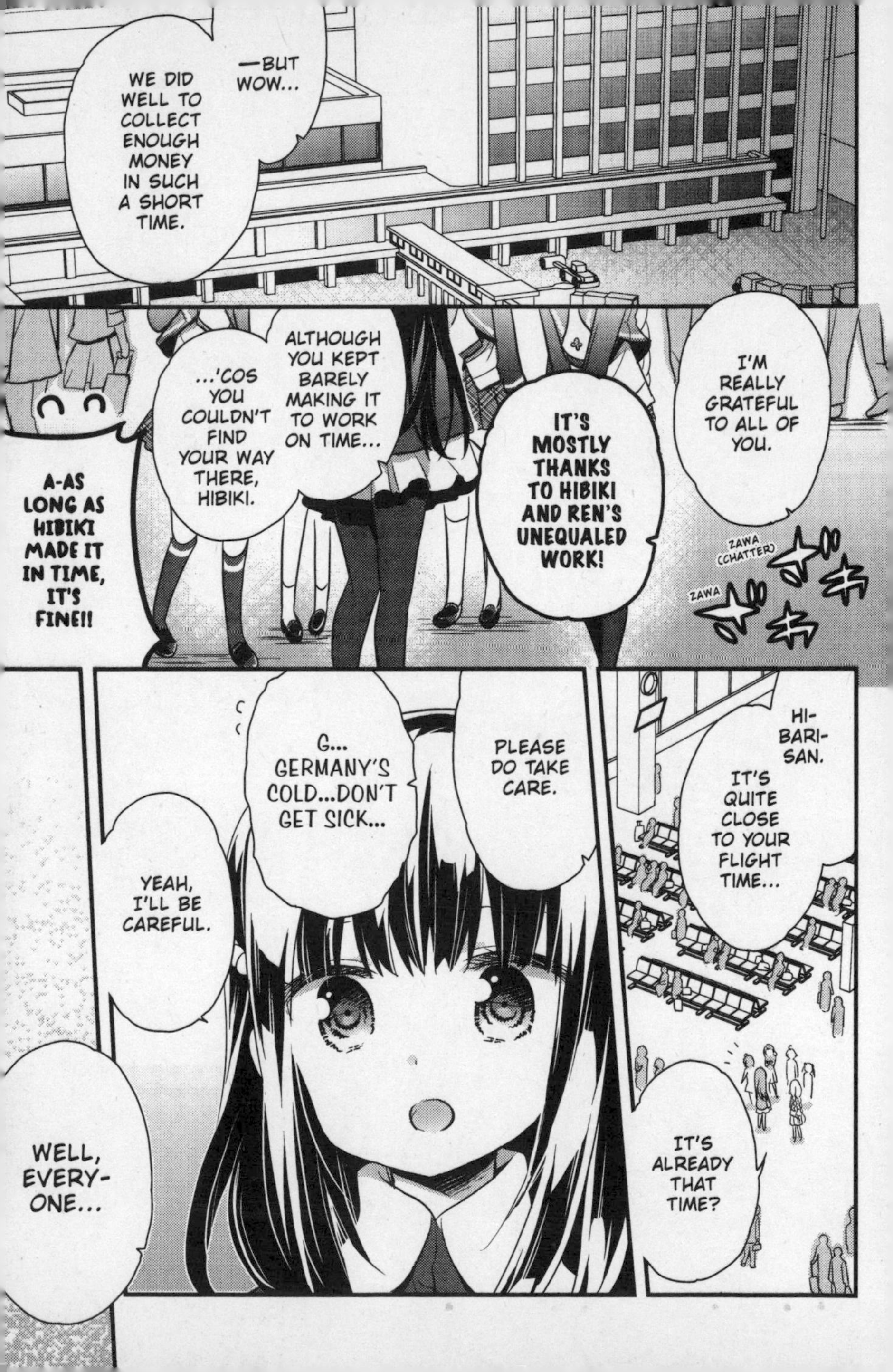
—BUT WOW...
WE DID WELL TO COLLECT ENOUGH MONEY IN SUCH A SHORT TIME.
I'M REALLY GRATEFUL TO ALL OF YOU.
ZAWA (CHATTER)
ZAWA
IT'S MOSTLY THANKS TO HIBIKI AND REN'S UNEQUALED WORK!
ALTHOUGH YOU KEPT BARELY MAKING IT TO WORK ON TIME...
...'COS YOU COULDN'T FIND YOUR WAY THERE, HIBIKI.
A-AS LONG AS HIBIKI MADE IT IN TIME, IT'S FINE!!
HI-BARI-SAN.
IT'S QUITE CLOSE TO YOUR FLIGHT TIME...
IT'S ALREADY THAT TIME?
PLEASE DO TAKE CARE.
G... GERMANY'S COLD...DON'T GET SICK...
YEAH, I'LL BE CAREFUL.
WELL, EVERY-ONE...

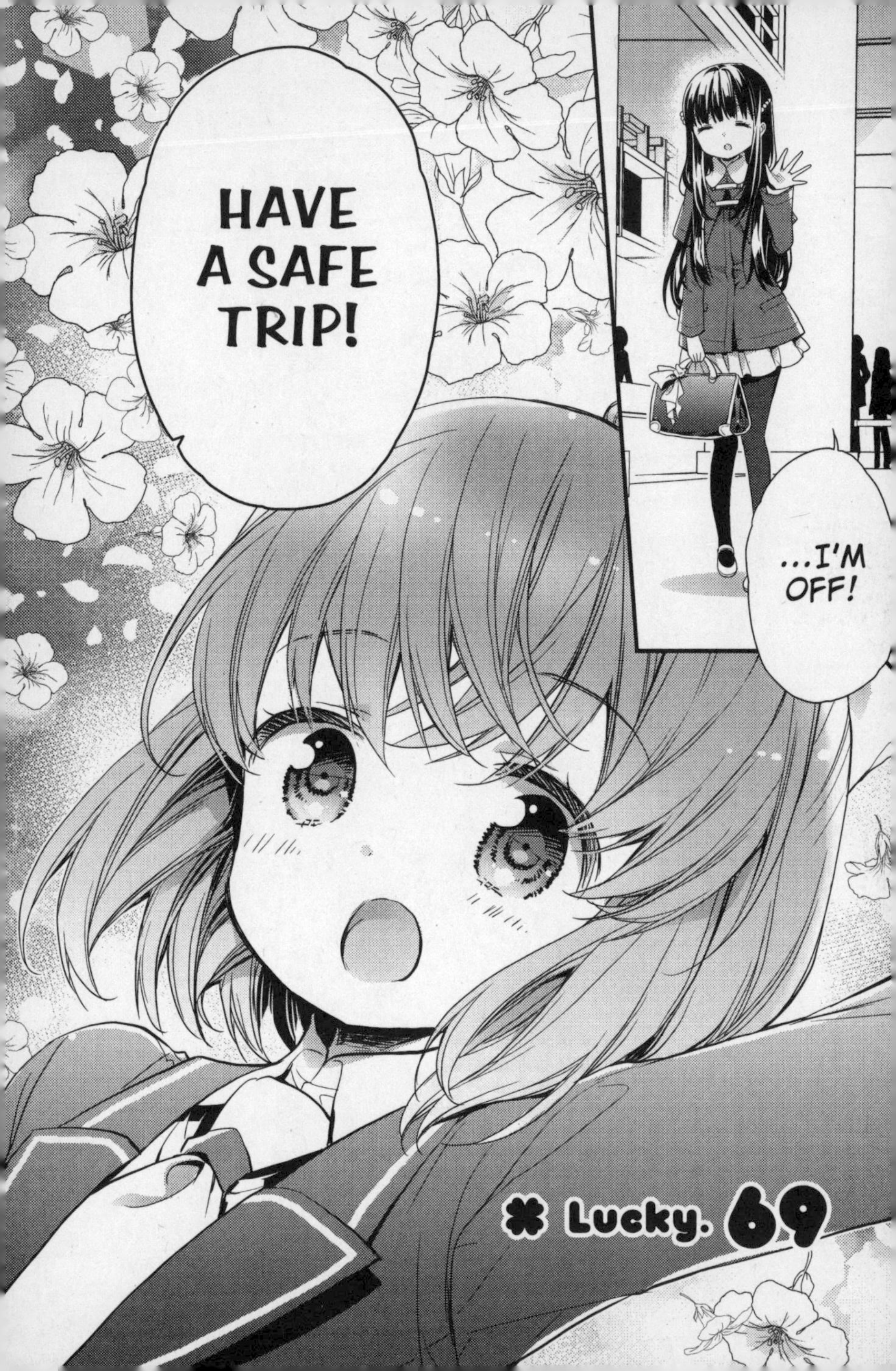
...I'M OFF!
HAVE A SAFE TRIP!
Lucky. 69

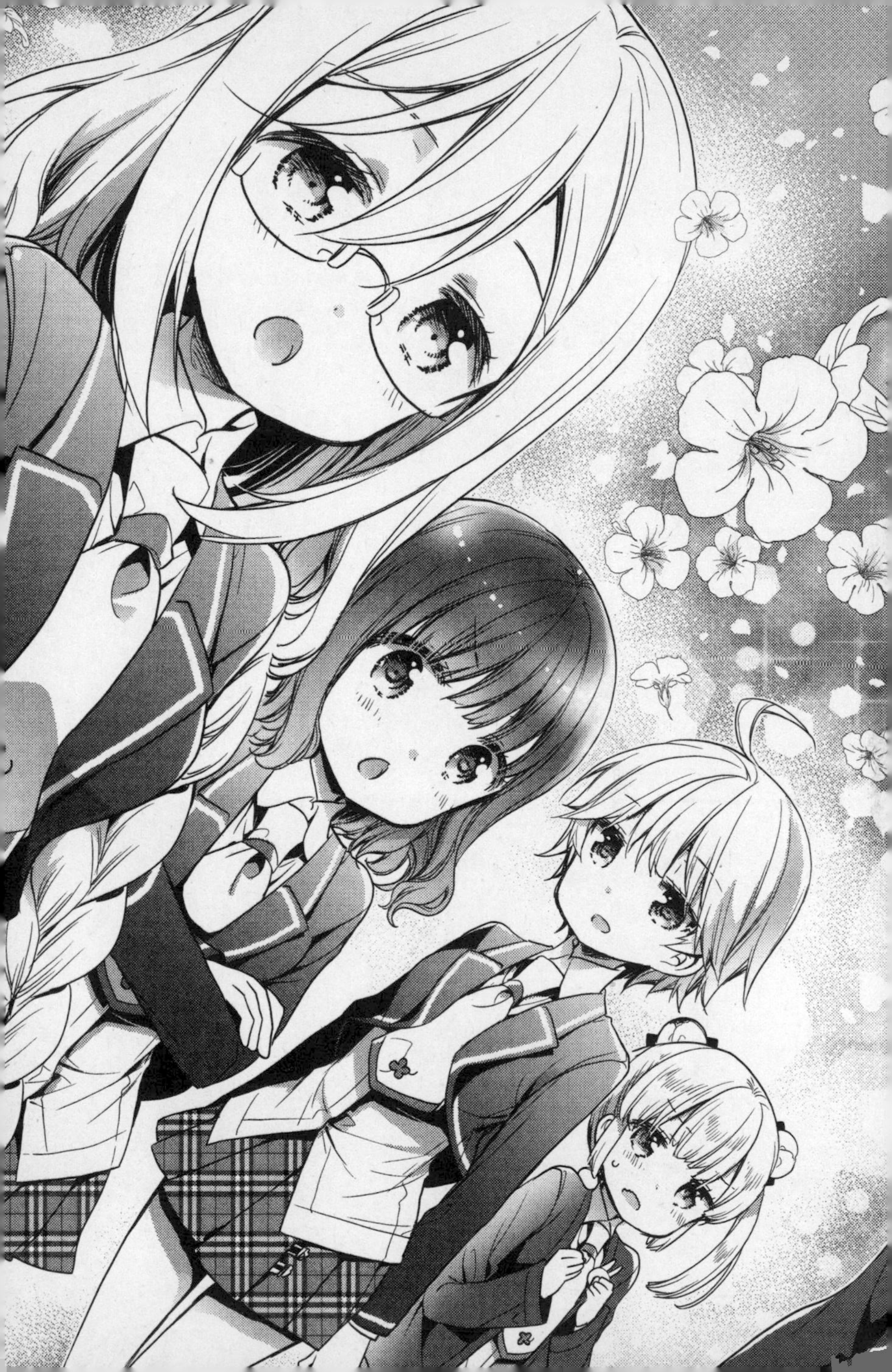

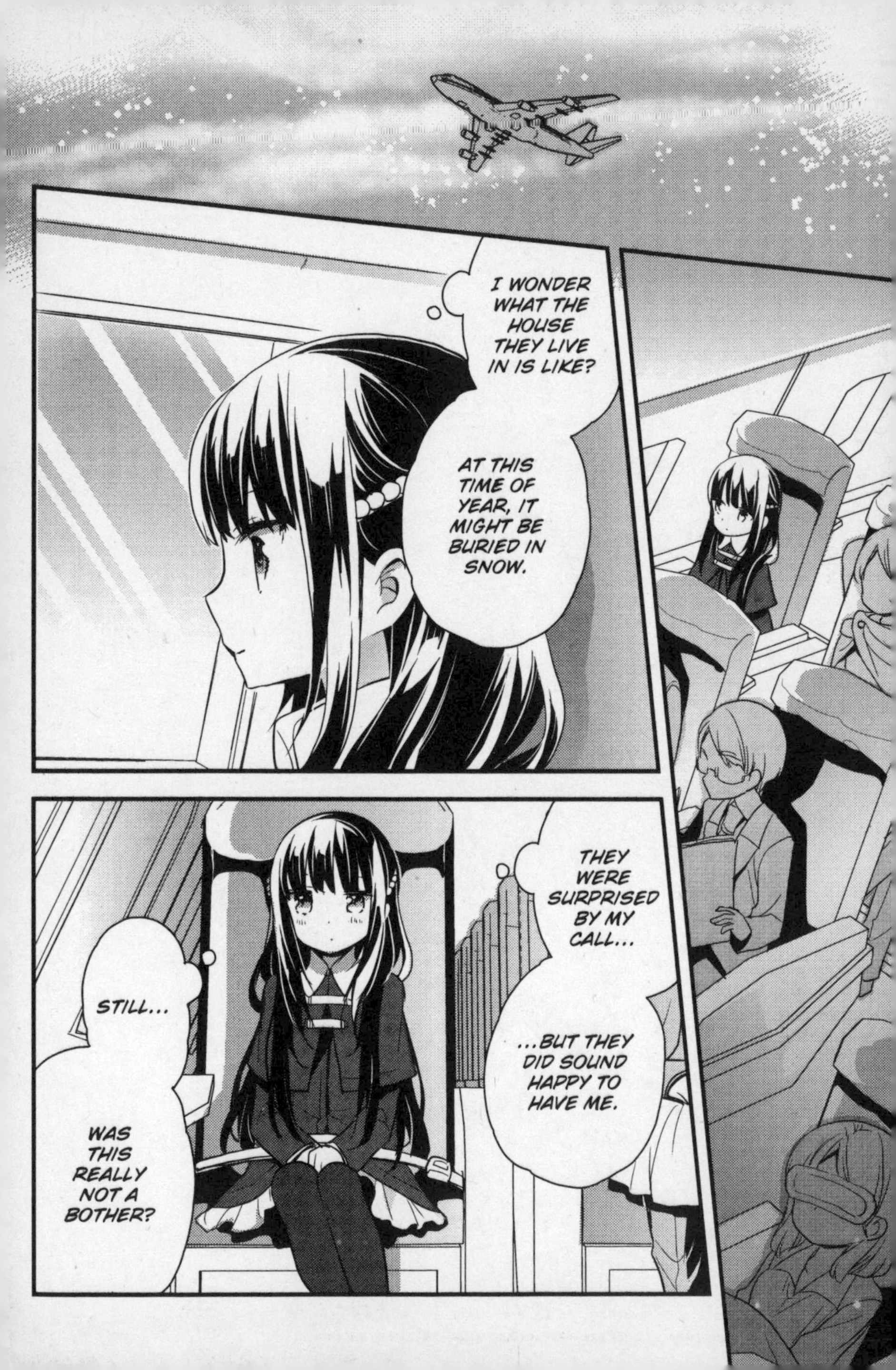
I WONDER WHAT THE HOUSE THEY LIVE IN IS LIKE?
AT THIS TIME OF YEAR, IT MIGHT BE BURIED IN SNOW.
THEY WERE SURPRISED BY MY CALL...
...BUT THEY DID SOUND HAPPY TO HAVE ME.
STILL...
WAS THIS REALLY NOT A BOTHER?

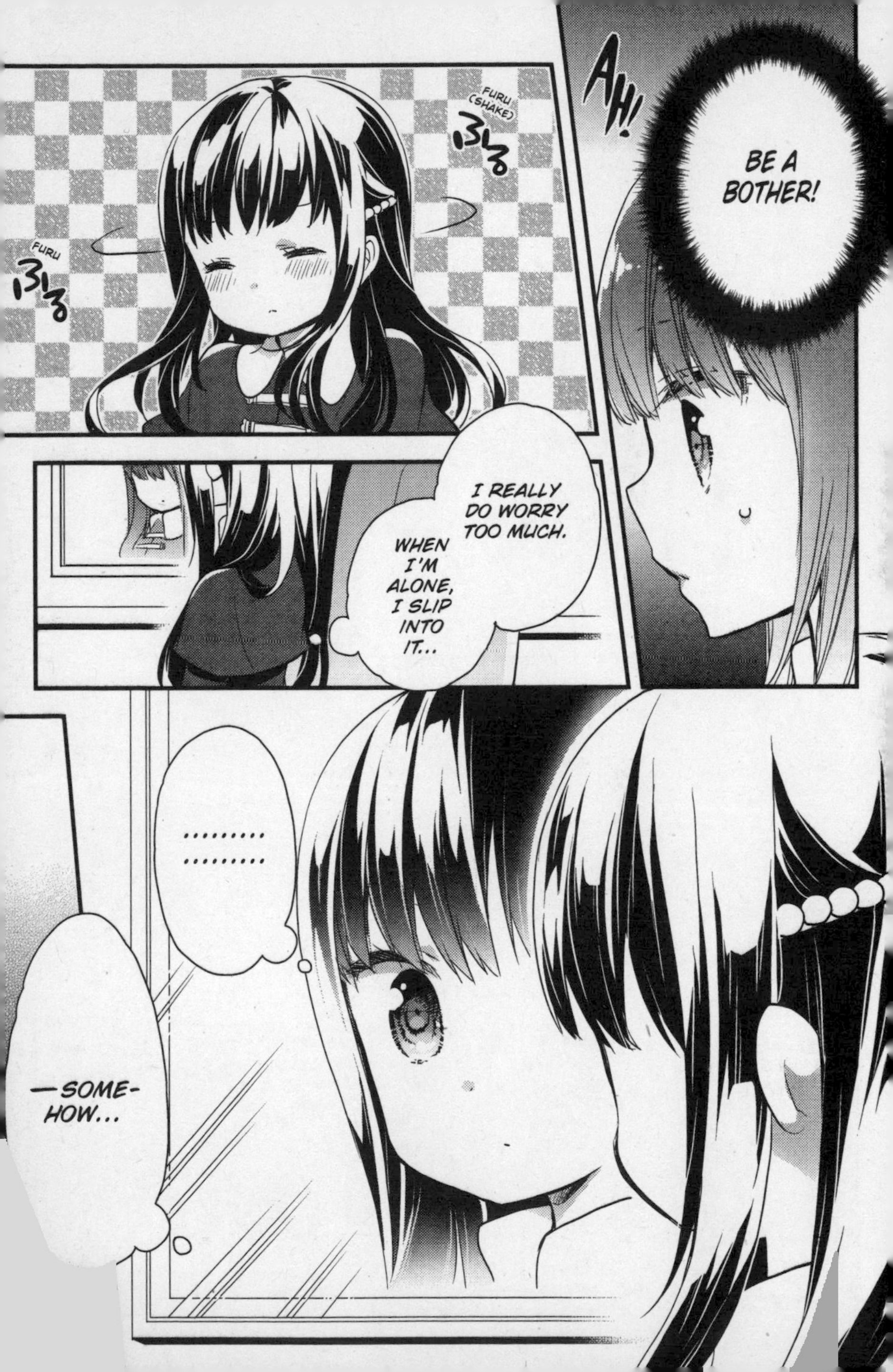
AH!
BE A BOTHER!
FURU (SHAKE)
FURU
I REALLY DO WORRY TOO MUCH.
WHEN I'M ALONE, I SLIP INTO IT...
....
....
—SOME-HOW...

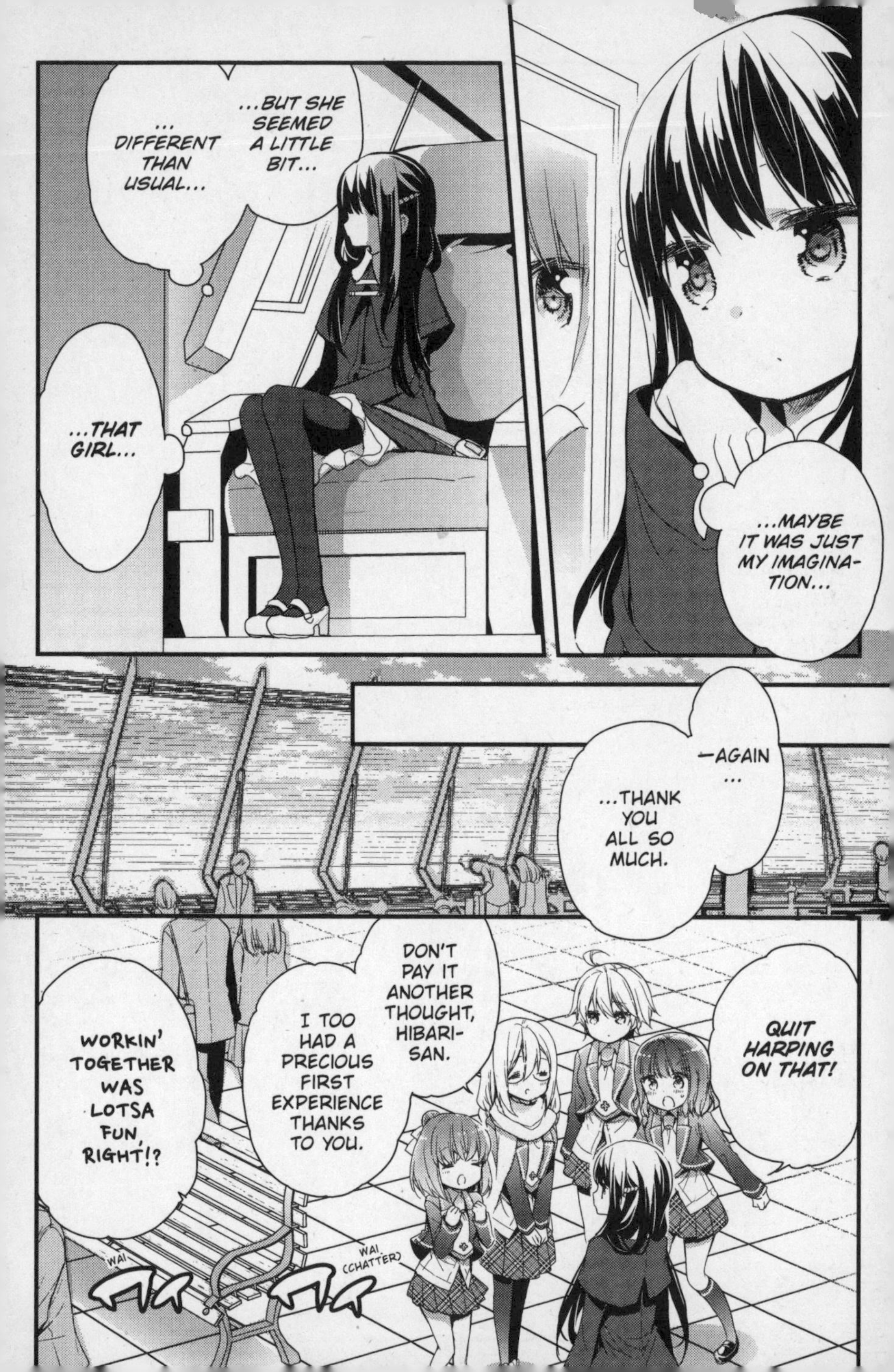
...MAYBE IT WAS JUST MY IMAGINATION...
...BUT SHE SEEMED A LITTLE BIT...
...DIFFERENT THAN USUAL...
...THAT GIRL...
—AGAIN...
...THANK YOU ALL SO MUCH.
QUIT HARPING ON THAT!
DON'T PAY IT ANOTHER THOUGHT, HIBARI-SAN.
I TOO HAD A PRECIOUS FIRST EXPERIENCE THANKS TO YOU.
WORKIN' TOGETHER WAS LOTSA FUN, RIGHT!?
WAI (CHATTER)
WAI

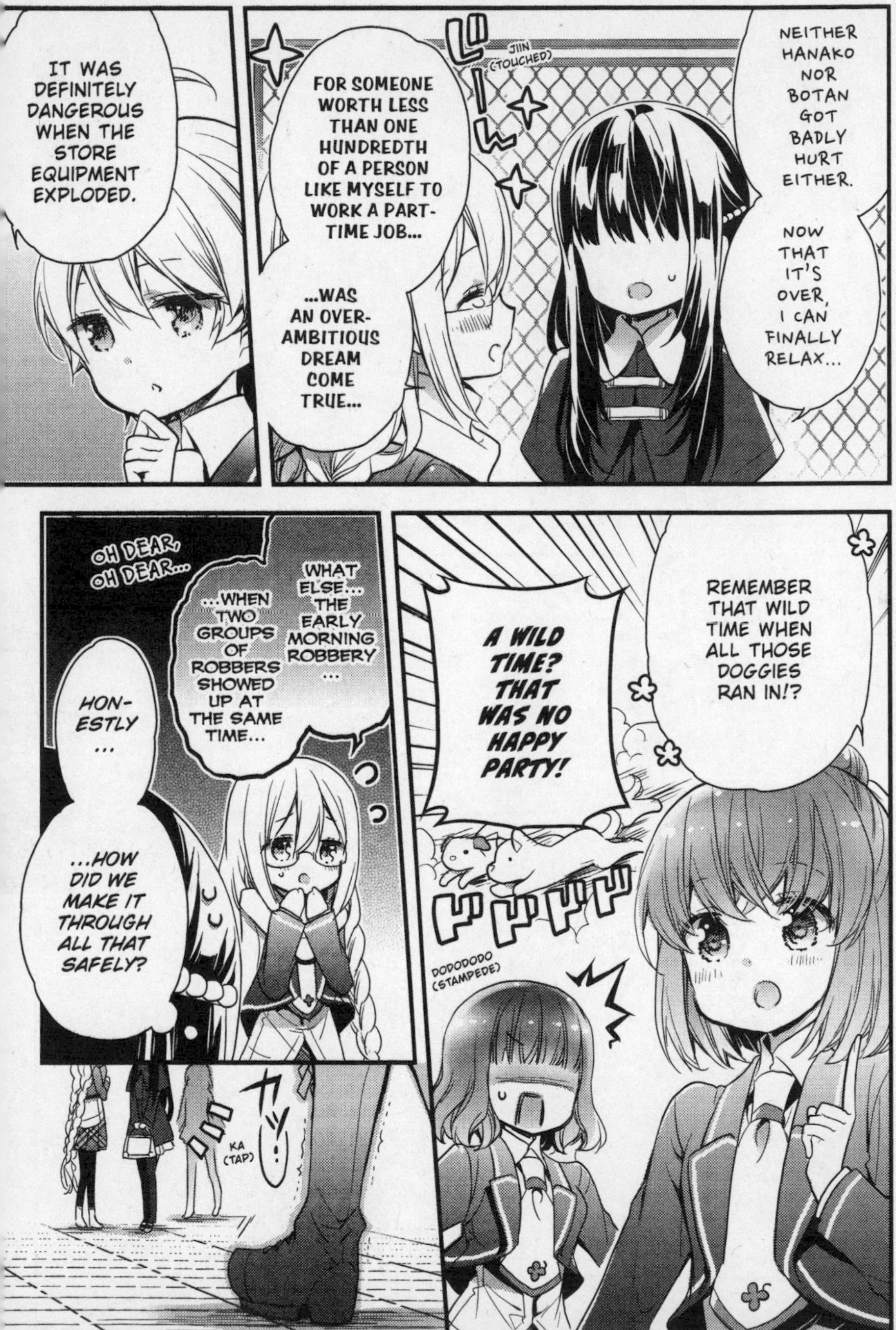
NEITHER HANAKO NOR BOTAN GOT BADLY HURT EITHER.
NOW THAT IT'S OVER, I CAN FINALLY RELAX...
JIIN (TOUCHED)
FOR SOMEONE WORTH LESS THAN ONE HUNDREDTH OF A PERSON LIKE MYSELF TO WORK A PART-TIME JOB...
...WAS AN OVER-AMBITIOUS DREAM COME TRUE...
IT WAS DEFINITELY DANGEROUS WHEN THE STORE EQUIPMENT EXPLODED.
REMEMBER THAT WILD TIME WHEN ALL THOSE DOGGIES RAN IN!?
A WILD TIME? THAT WAS NO HAPPY PARTY!
DODODODO (STAMPEDE)
OH DEAR, OH DEAR...
WHAT ELSE... THE EARLY MORNING ROBBERY...
...WHEN TWO GROUPS OF ROBBERS SHOWED UP AT THE SAME TIME...
HON-ESTLY...
...HOW DID WE MAKE IT THROUGH ALL THAT SAFELY?
KA (TAP)

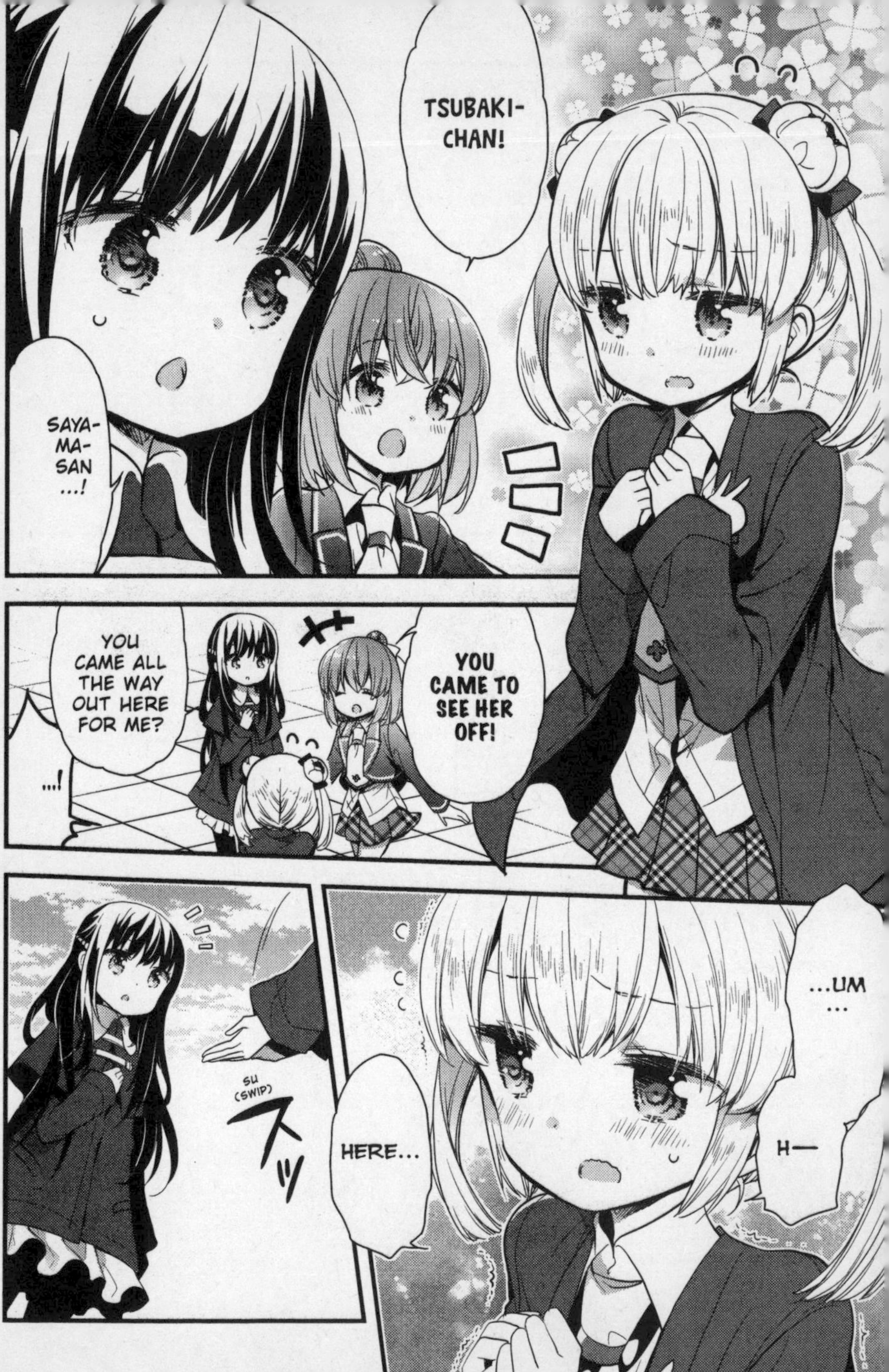

TSUBAKI-CHAN!
SAYAMA-SAN...!
YOU CAME TO SEE HER OFF!
YOU CAME ALL THE WAY OUT HERE FOR ME?
...!
...UM...
H—
HERE...
SU (SWIP)
スッ

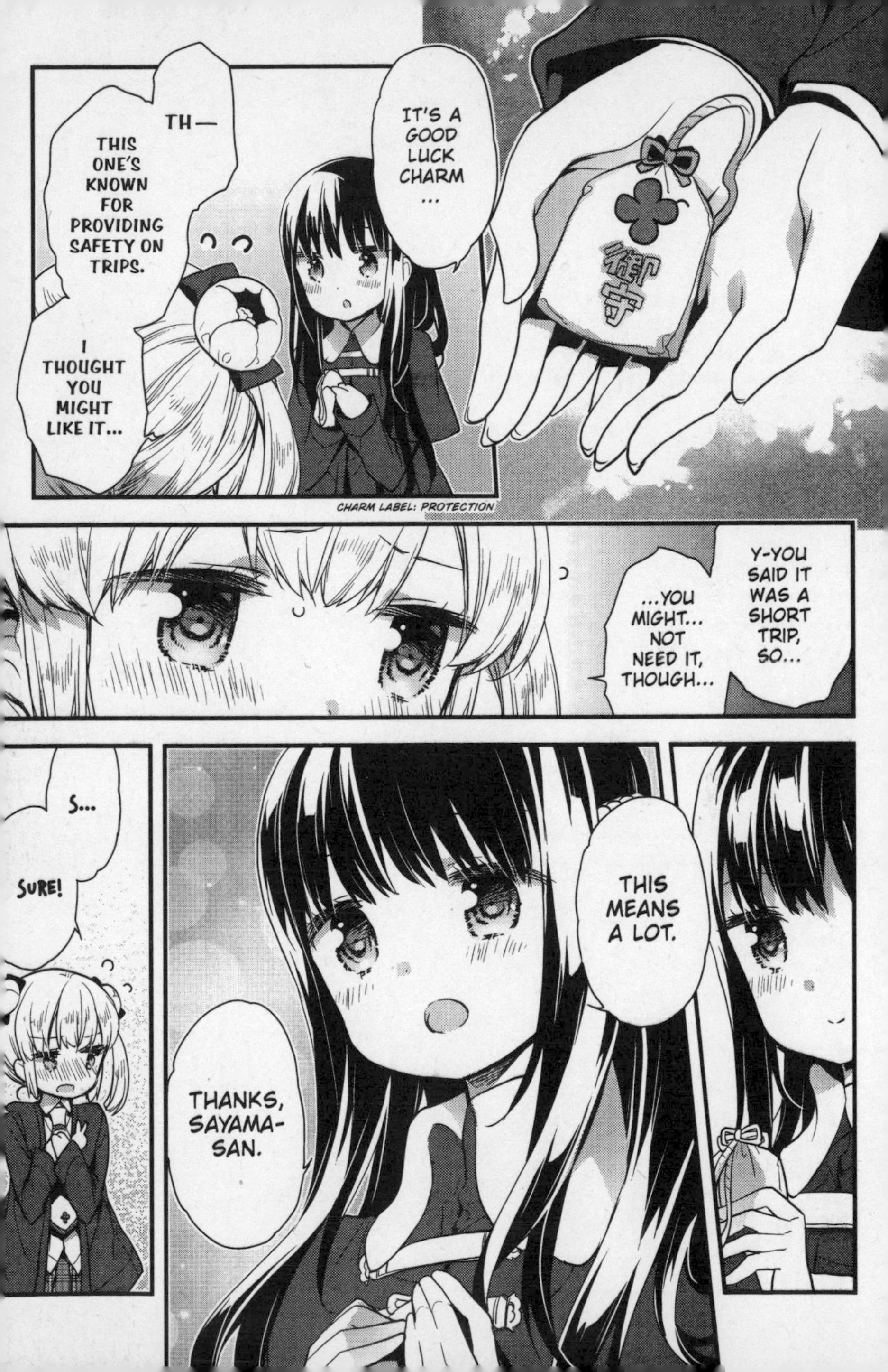
IT'S A GOOD LUCK CHARM ...
TH— THIS ONE'S KNOWN FOR PROVIDING SAFETY ON TRIPS.
I THOUGHT YOU MIGHT LIKE IT...
CHARM LABEL: PROTECTION
Y-YOU SAID IT WAS A SHORT TRIP, SO...
...YOU MIGHT... NOT NEED IT, THOUGH...
THIS MEANS A LOT.
THANKS, SAYAMA-SAN.
S... SURE!

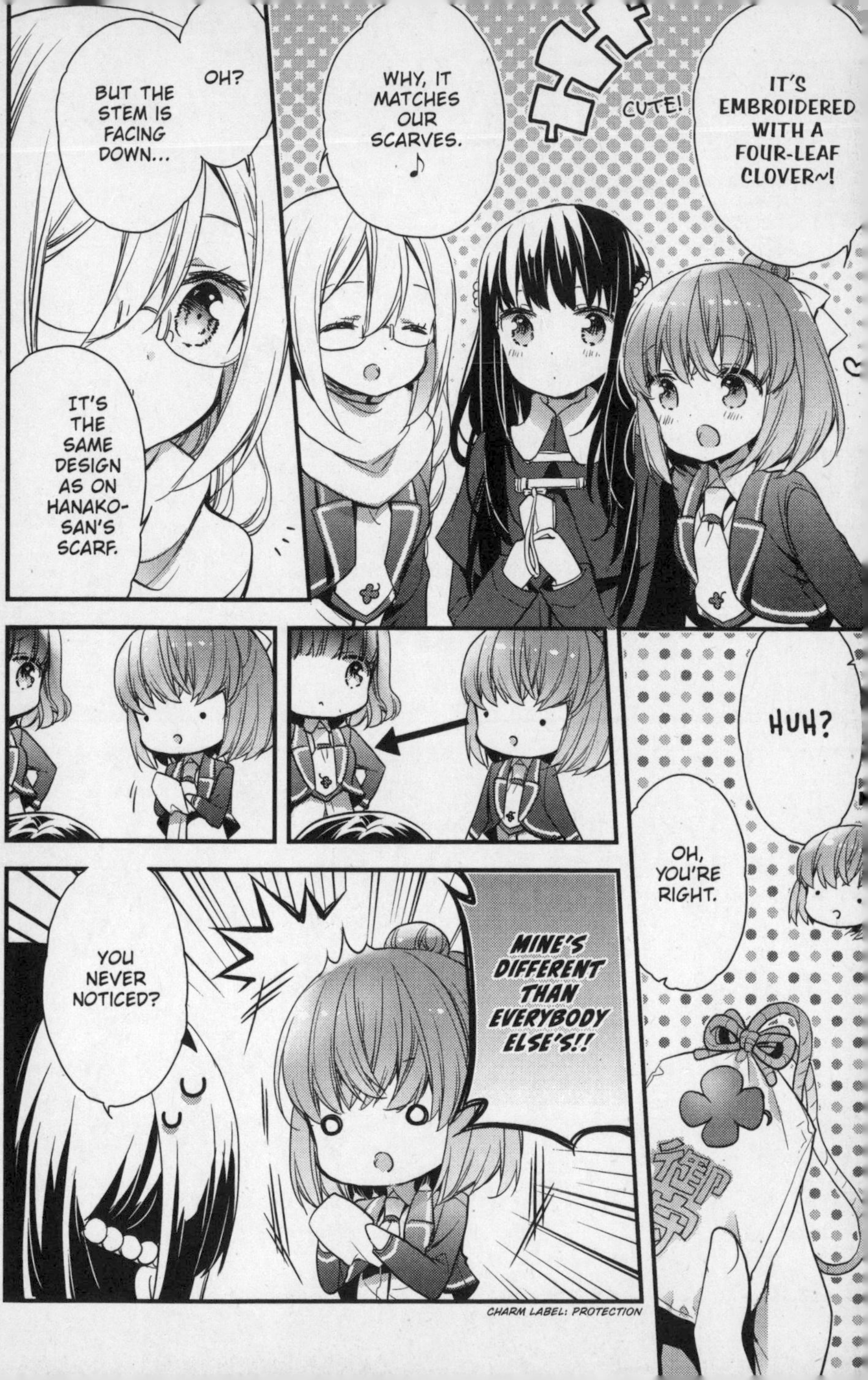
IT'S EMBROIDERED WITH A FOUR-LEAF CLOVER~!
CUTE!
WHY, IT MATCHES OUR SCARVES. ♪
OH?
BUT THE STEM IS FACING DOWN...
IT'S THE SAME DESIGN AS ON HANAKO-SAN'S SCARF.
HUH?
OH, YOU'RE RIGHT.
MINE'S DIFFERENT THAN EVERYBODY ELSE'S!!
YOU NEVER NOTICED?

CHARM LABEL: PROTECTION

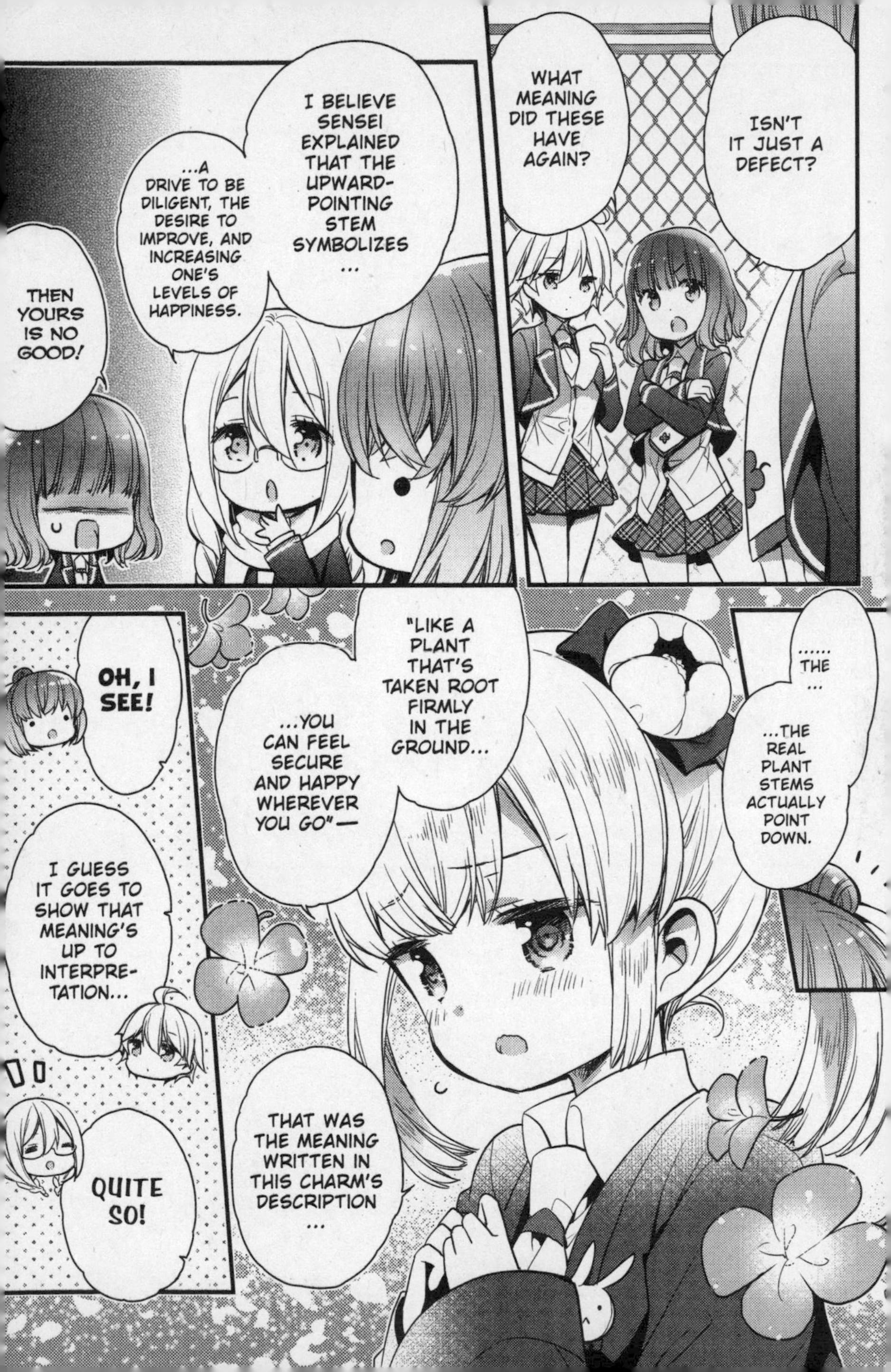
ISN'T IT JUST A DEFECT?
WHAT MEANING DID THESE HAVE AGAIN?
I BELIEVE SENSEI EXPLAINED THAT THE UPWARD-POINTING STEM SYMBOLIZES...
...A DRIVE TO BE DILIGENT, THE DESIRE TO IMPROVE, AND INCREASING ONE'S LEVELS OF HAPPINESS.
THEN YOURS IS NO GOOD!
......THE...
...THE REAL PLANT STEMS ACTUALLY POINT DOWN.
"LIKE A PLANT THAT'S TAKEN ROOT FIRMLY IN THE GROUND...
...YOU CAN FEEL SECURE AND HAPPY WHEREVER YOU GO"—
THAT WAS THE MEANING WRITTEN IN THIS CHARM'S DESCRIPTION...
OH, I SEE!
I GUESS IT GOES TO SHOW THAT MEANING'S UP TO INTERPRETATION...
QUITE SO!

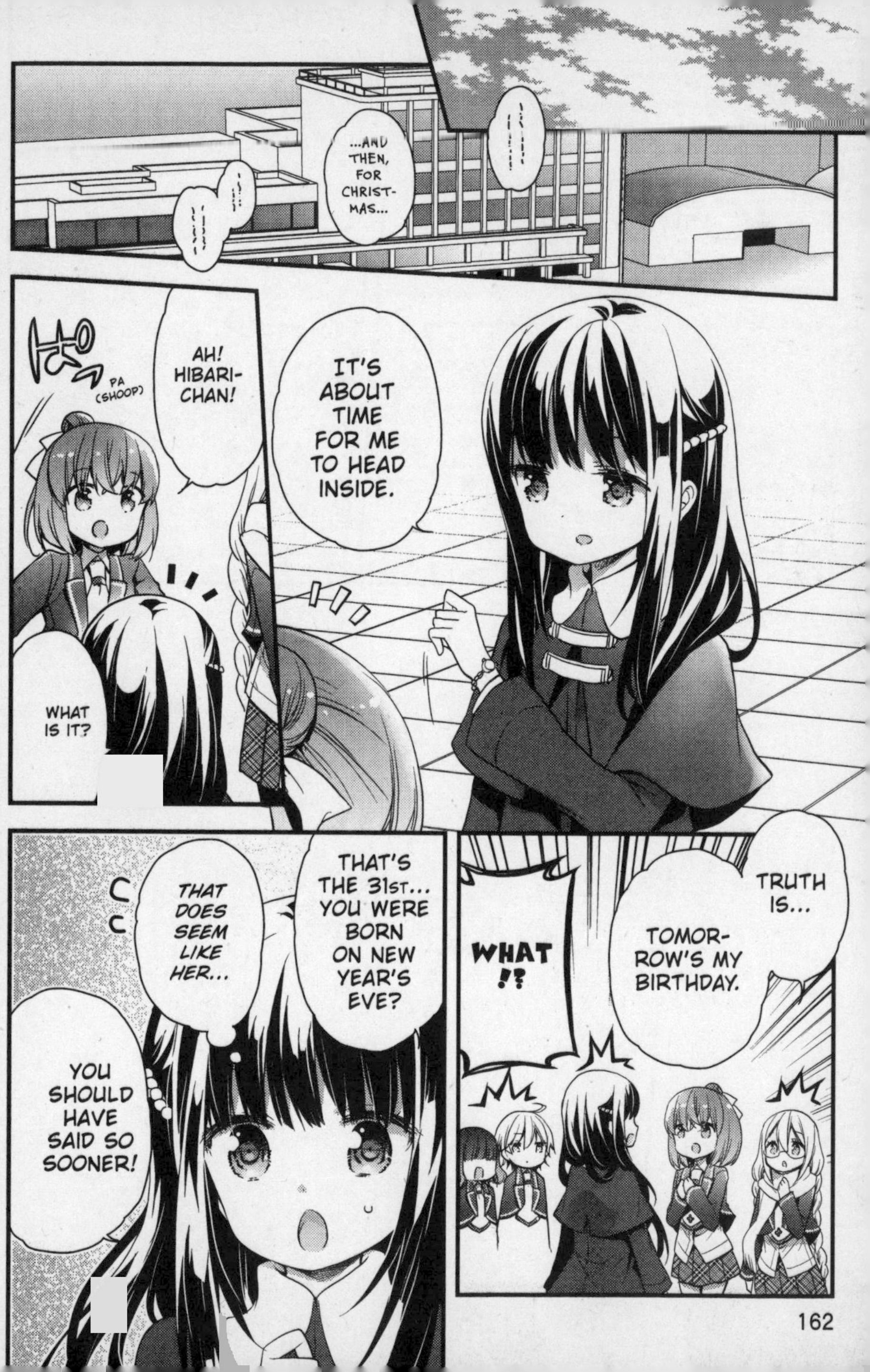
...AND THEN, FOR CHRIST-MAS...
IT'S ABOUT TIME FOR ME TO HEAD INSIDE.
AH! HIBARI-CHAN!
PA (SHOOP)
WHAT IS IT?
TRUTH IS...
TOMOR-ROW'S MY BIRTHDAY.
WHAT!?
THAT'S THE 31ST... YOU WERE BORN ON NEW YEAR'S EVE?
THAT DOES SEEM LIKE HER...
YOU SHOULD HAVE SAID SO SOONER!

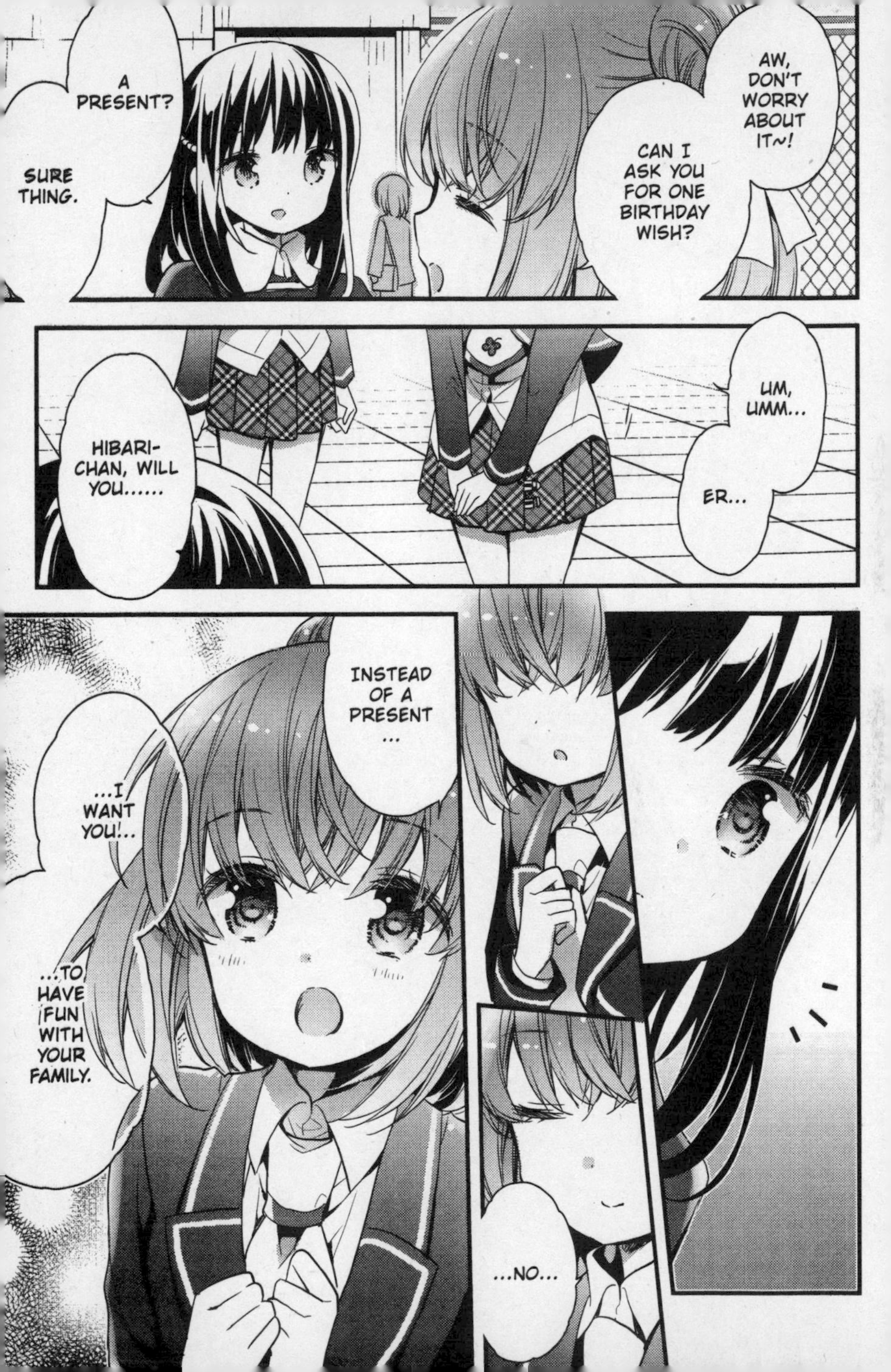
AW, DON'T WORRY ABOUT IT~!
CAN I ASK YOU FOR ONE BIRTHDAY WISH?
A PRESENT?
SURE THING.
UM, UMM...
ER...
HIBARI-CHAN, WILL YOU......
INSTEAD OF A PRESENT ...
...I WANT YOU!...
...TO HAVE FUN WITH YOUR FAMILY.
...NO...

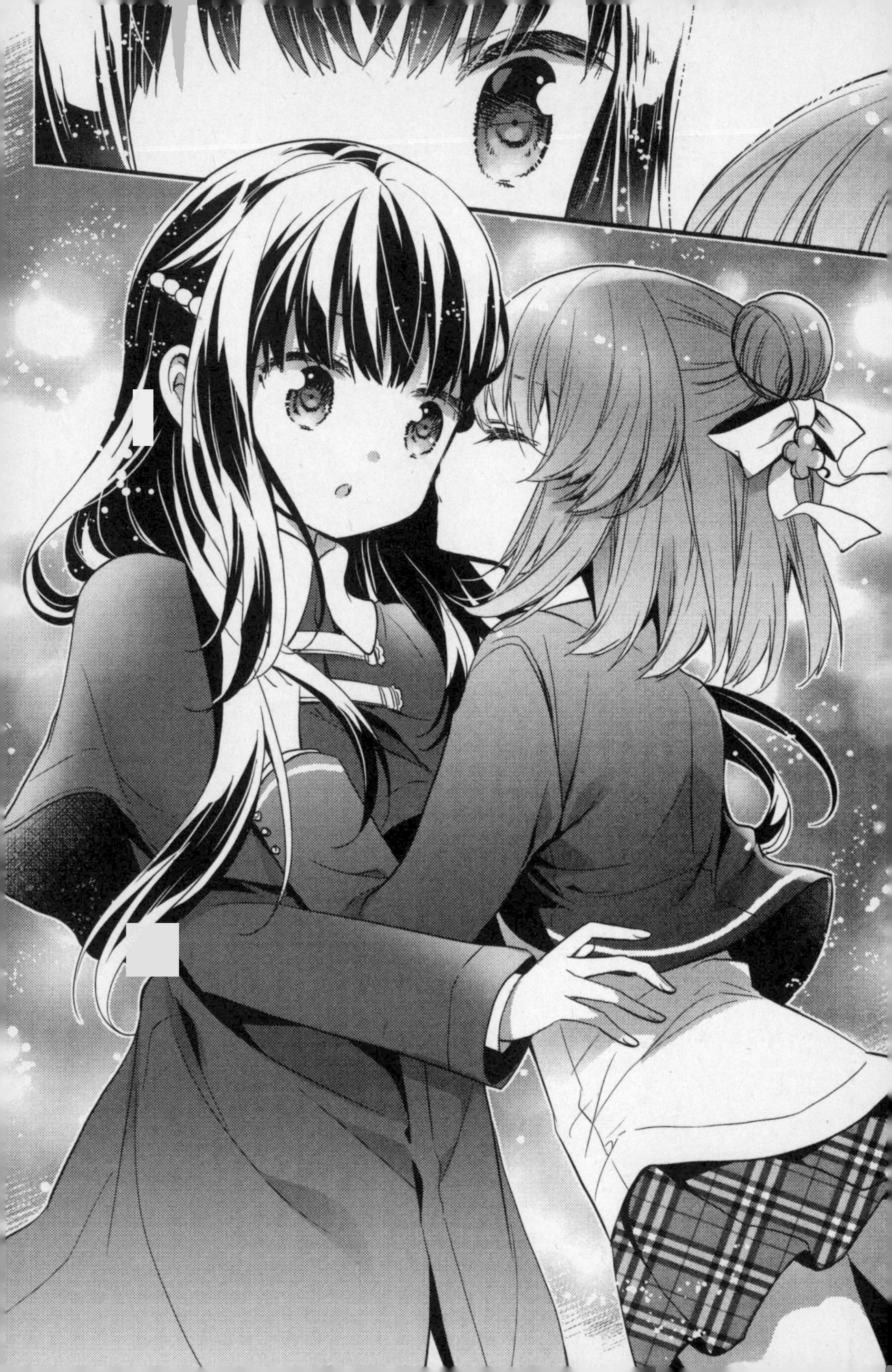

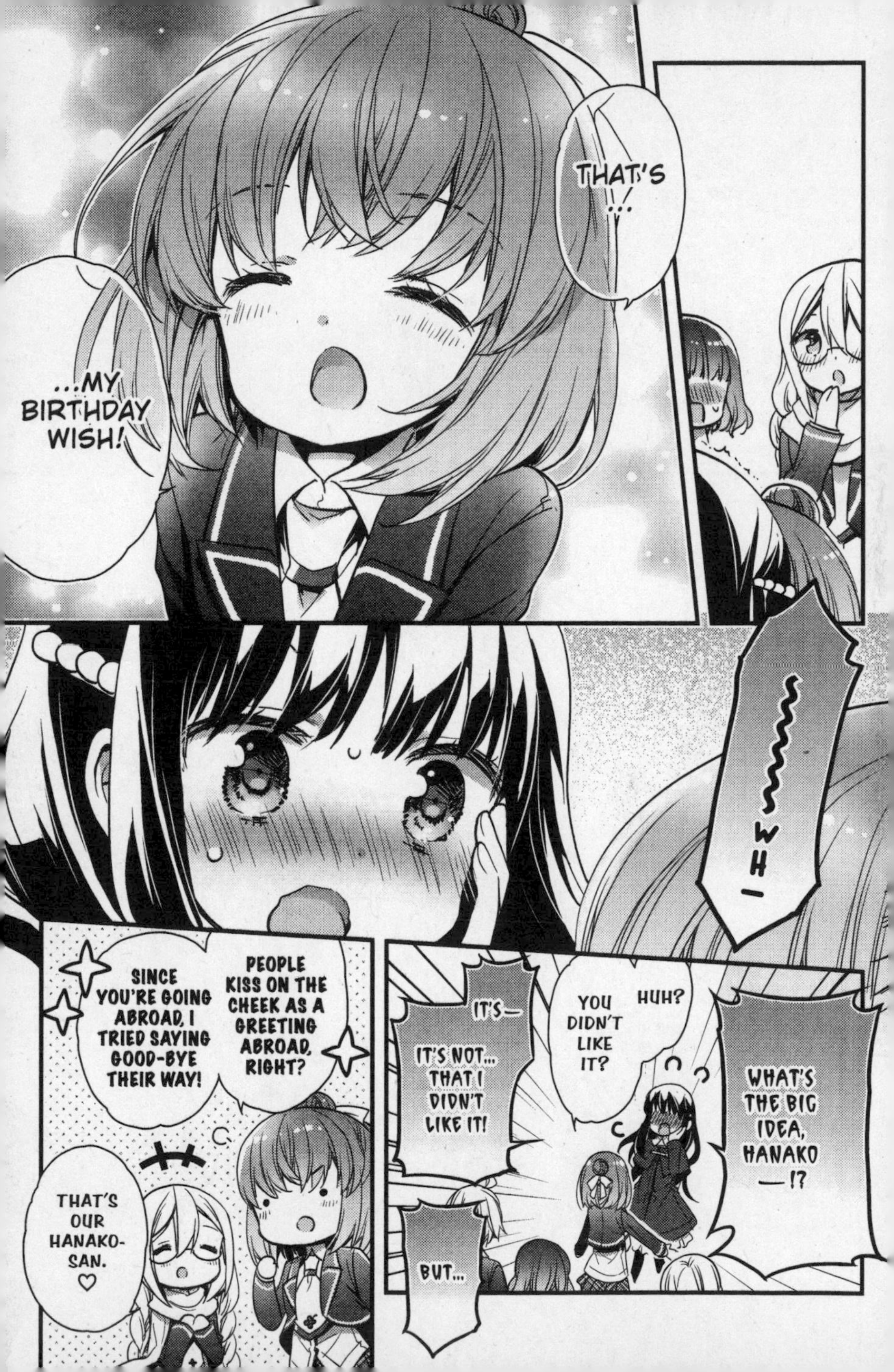
THAT'S...
...MY BIRTHDAY WISH!
WH—
WHAT'S THE BIG IDEA, HANAKO—!?
HUH?
YOU DIDN'T LIKE IT?
IT'S—
IT'S NOT... THAT I DIDN'T LIKE IT!
BUT...
PEOPLE KISS ON THE CHEEK AS A GREETING ABROAD, RIGHT?
SINCE YOU'RE GOING ABROAD, I TRIED SAYING GOOD-BYE THEIR WAY!
THAT'S OUR HANAKO-SAN. ♡

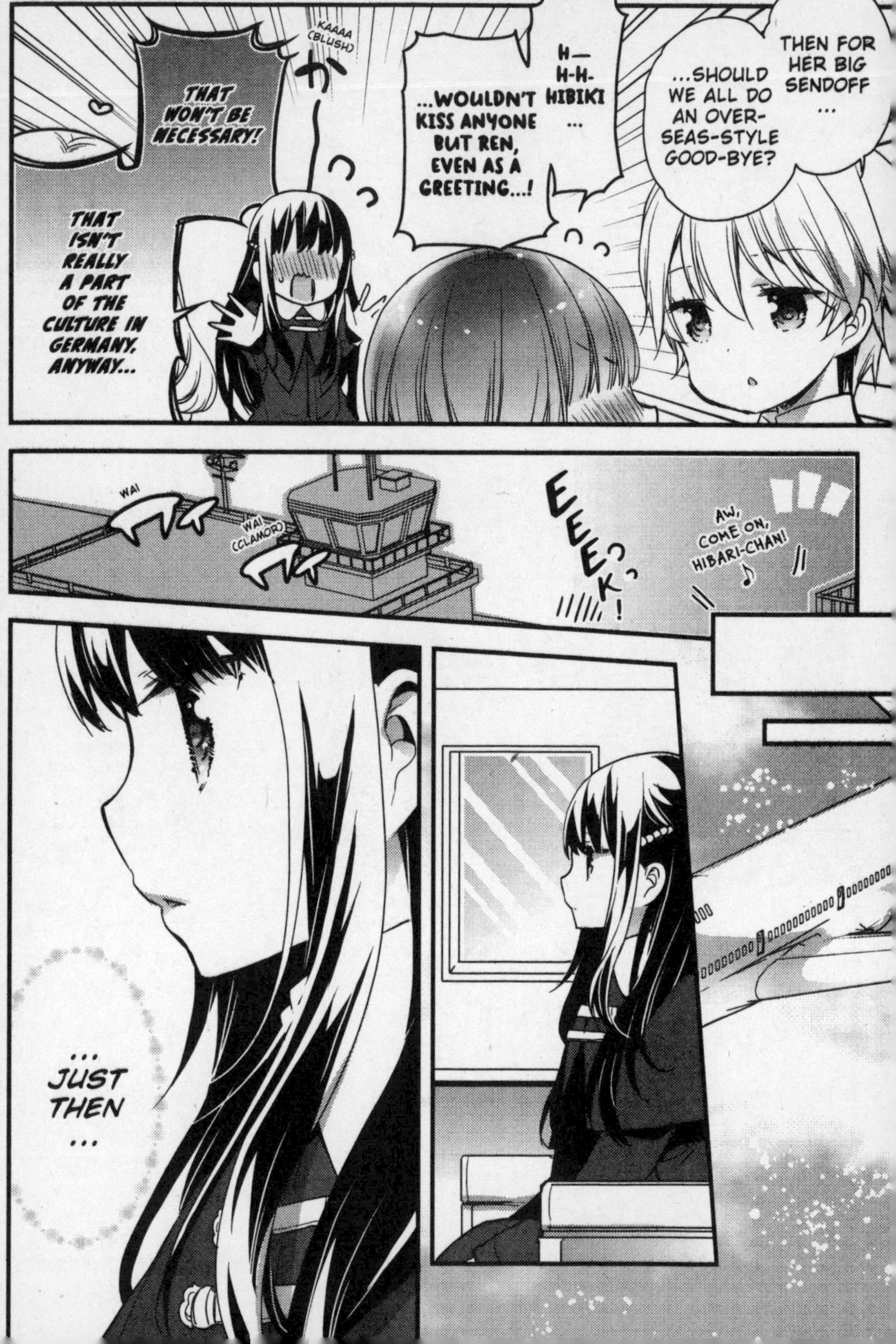

THEN FOR HER BIG SENDOFF ...
...SHOULD WE ALL DO AN OVER-SEAS-STYLE GOOD-BYE?
H— H-H- HIBIKI ...
...WOULDN'T KISS ANYONE BUT REN, EVEN AS A GREETING...!
KAAAA (BLUSH)
THAT WON'T BE NECESSARY!
THAT ISN'T REALLY A PART OF THE CULTURE IN GERMANY, ANYWAY...
AW, COME ON, HIBARI-CHAN! ♪
EEEEK!
WAI
WAI (CLAMOR)
... JUST THEN ...

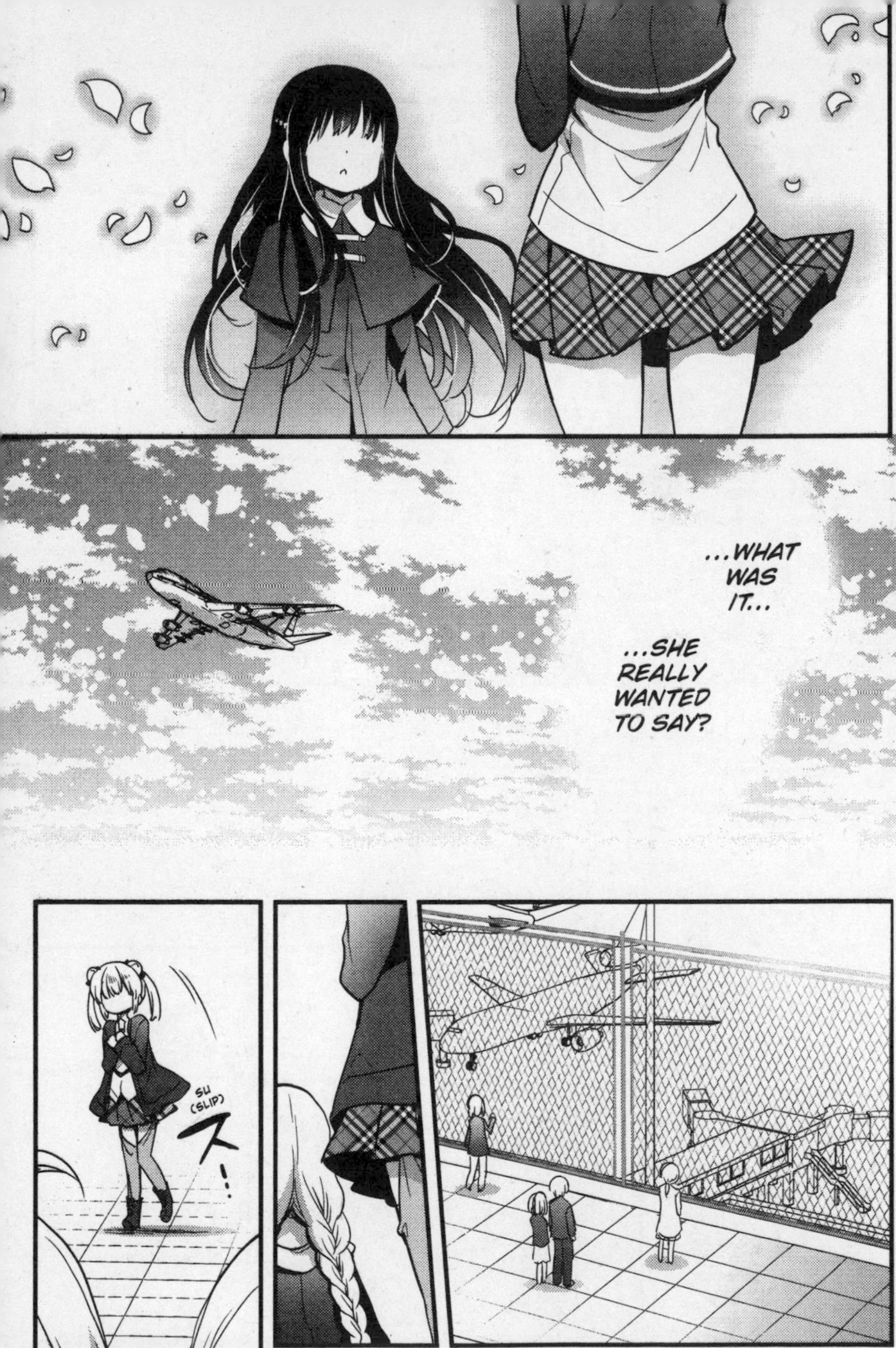
...WHAT WAS IT...
...SHE REALLY WANTED TO SAY?
SU (SLIP)
ス
!

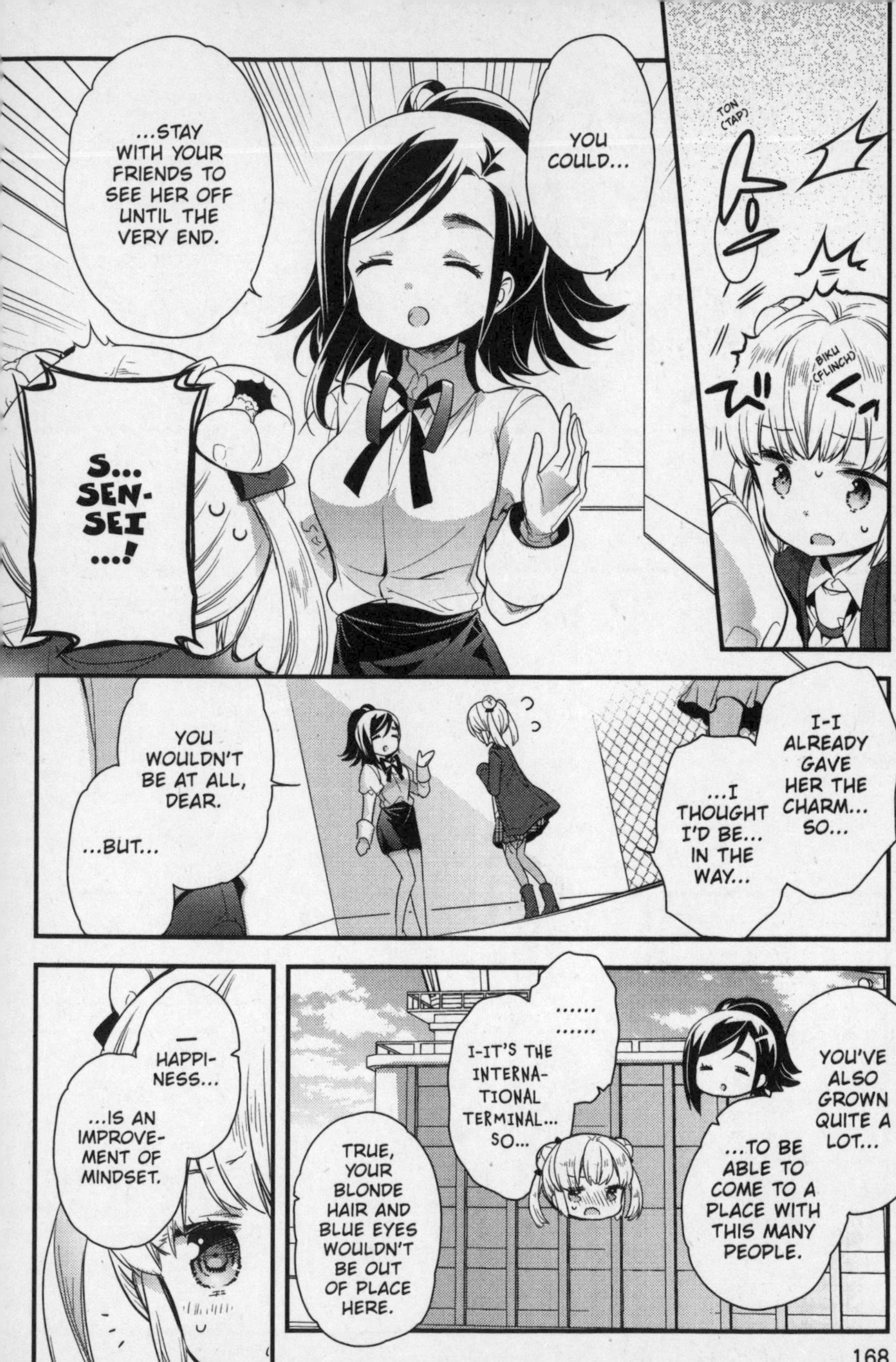
TON (TAP)
BIKU (FLINCH)
YOU COULD...
...STAY WITH YOUR FRIENDS TO SEE HER OFF UNTIL THE VERY END.
S... SEN-SEI ...!
I-I ALREADY GAVE HER THE CHARM... SO...
...I THOUGHT I'D BE... IN THE WAY...
YOU WOULDN'T BE AT ALL, DEAR.
...BUT...
YOU'VE ALSO GROWN QUITE A LOT...
...TO BE ABLE TO COME TO A PLACE WITH THIS MANY PEOPLE.
....
I-IT'S THE INTERNATIONAL TERMINAL... SO...
TRUE, YOUR BLONDE HAIR AND BLUE EYES WOULDN'T BE OUT OF PLACE HERE.
—HAPPINESS...
...IS AN IMPROVEMENT OF MINDSET.

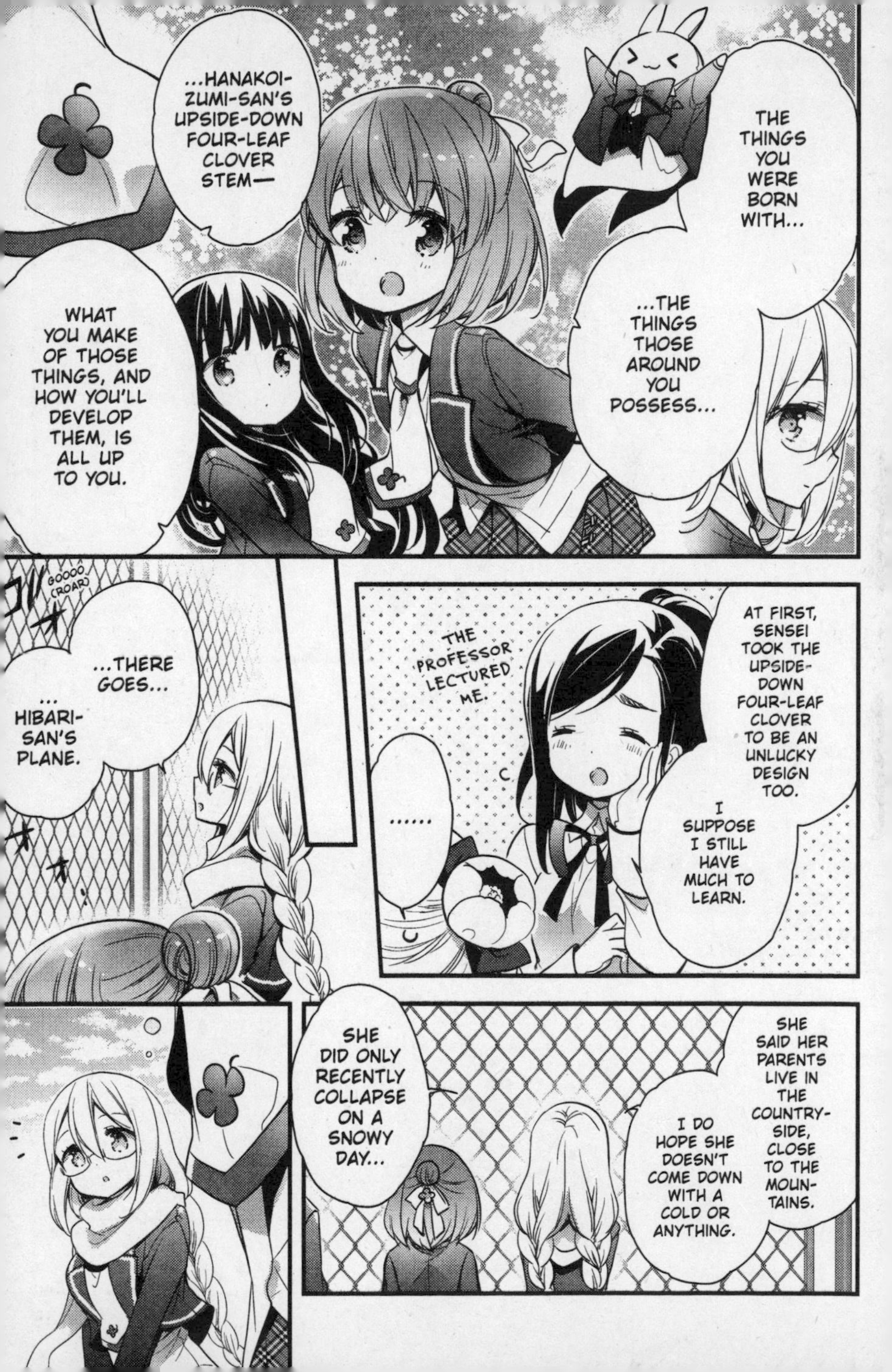
THE THINGS YOU WERE BORN WITH...
...THE THINGS THOSE AROUND YOU POSSESS...
...HANAKOIZUMI-SAN'S UPSIDE-DOWN FOUR-LEAF CLOVER STEM—
WHAT YOU MAKE OF THOSE THINGS, AND HOW YOU'LL DEVELOP THEM, IS ALL UP TO YOU.
AT FIRST, SENSEI TOOK THE UPSIDE-DOWN FOUR-LEAF CLOVER TO BE AN UNLUCKY DESIGN TOO.
I SUPPOSE I STILL HAVE MUCH TO LEARN.
THE PROFESSOR LECTURED ME.
......
GOOOO (ROAR)
...THERE GOES...
...HIBARI-SAN'S PLANE.
SHE SAID HER PARENTS LIVE IN THE COUNTRYSIDE, CLOSE TO THE MOUNTAINS.
I DO HOPE SHE DOESN'T COME DOWN WITH A COLD OR ANYTHING.
SHE DID ONLY RECENTLY COLLAPSE ON A SNOWY DAY...

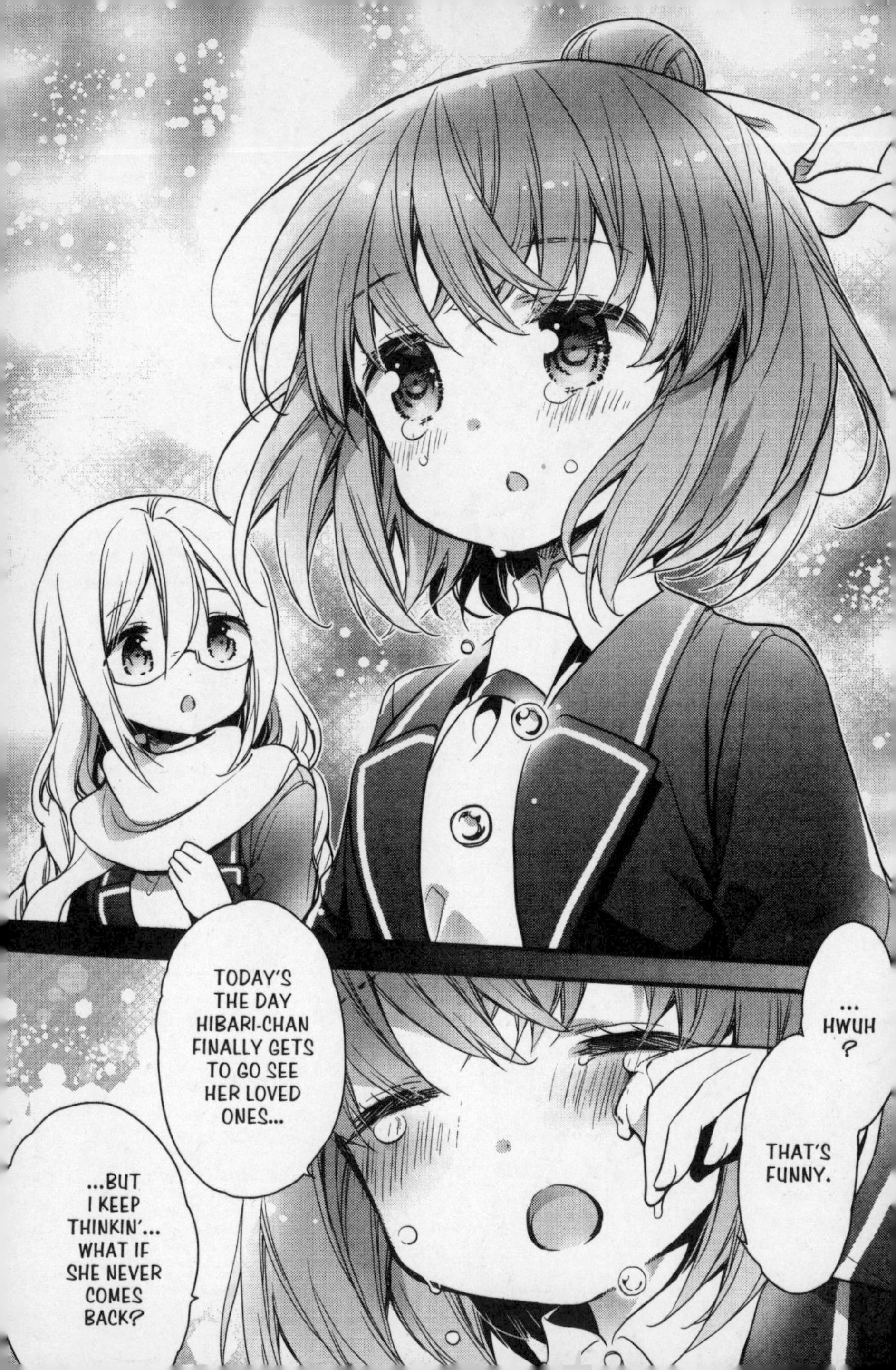
...HWUH?
THAT'S FUNNY.
TODAY'S THE DAY HIBARI-CHAN FINALLY GETS TO GO SEE HER LOVED ONES...
...BUT I KEEP THINKIN'... WHAT IF SHE NEVER COMES BACK?

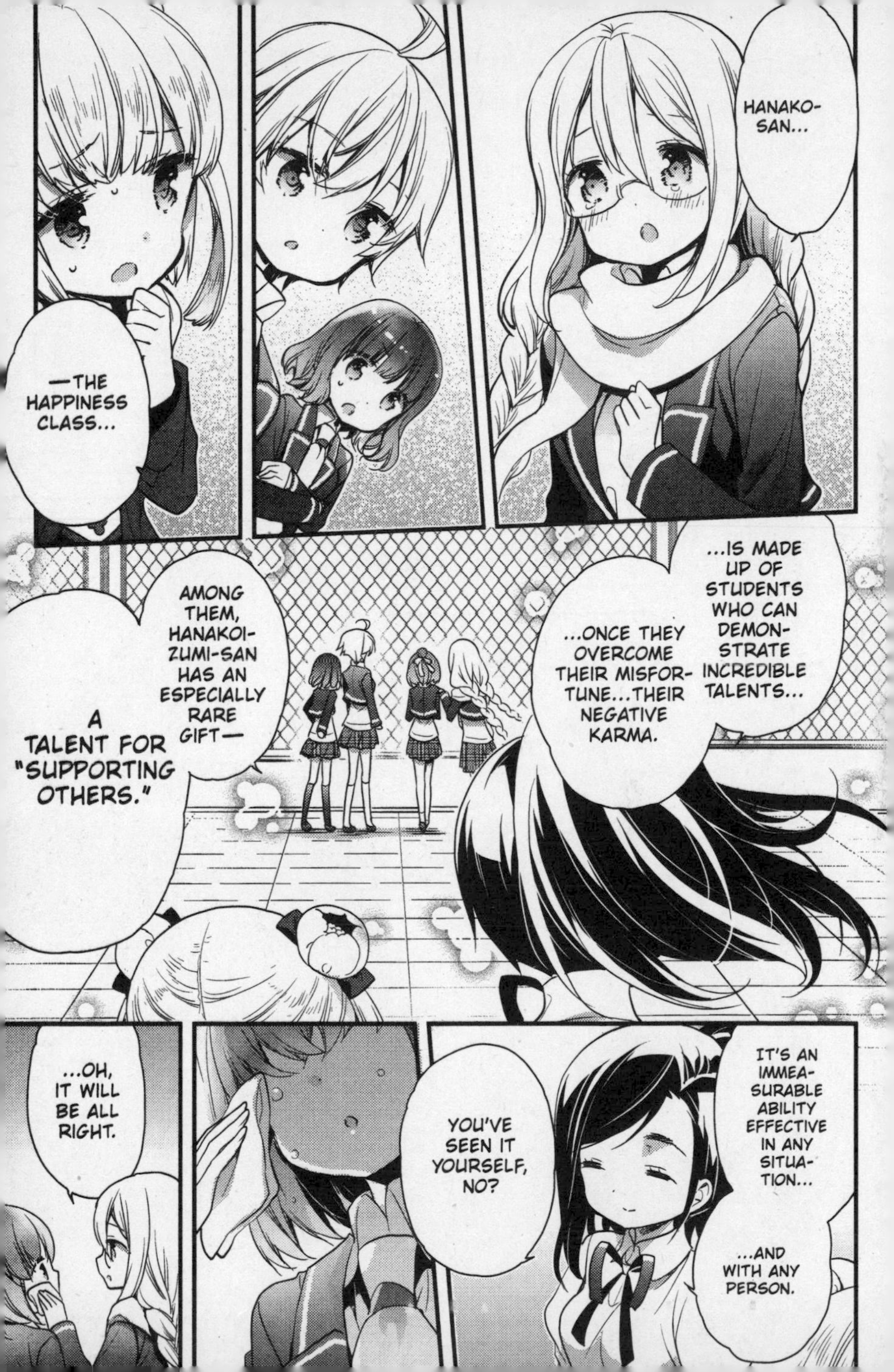
HANAKO-SAN...
—THE HAPPINESS CLASS...
...IS MADE UP OF STUDENTS WHO CAN DEMONSTRATE INCREDIBLE TALENTS...
...ONCE THEY OVERCOME THEIR MISFORTUNE...THEIR NEGATIVE KARMA.
AMONG THEM, HANAKOIZUMI-SAN HAS AN ESPECIALLY RARE GIFT—
A TALENT FOR "SUPPORTING OTHERS."
IT'S AN IMMEASURABLE ABILITY EFFECTIVE IN ANY SITUATION...
...AND WITH ANY PERSON.
YOU'VE SEEN IT YOURSELF, NO?
...OH, IT WILL BE ALL RIGHT.

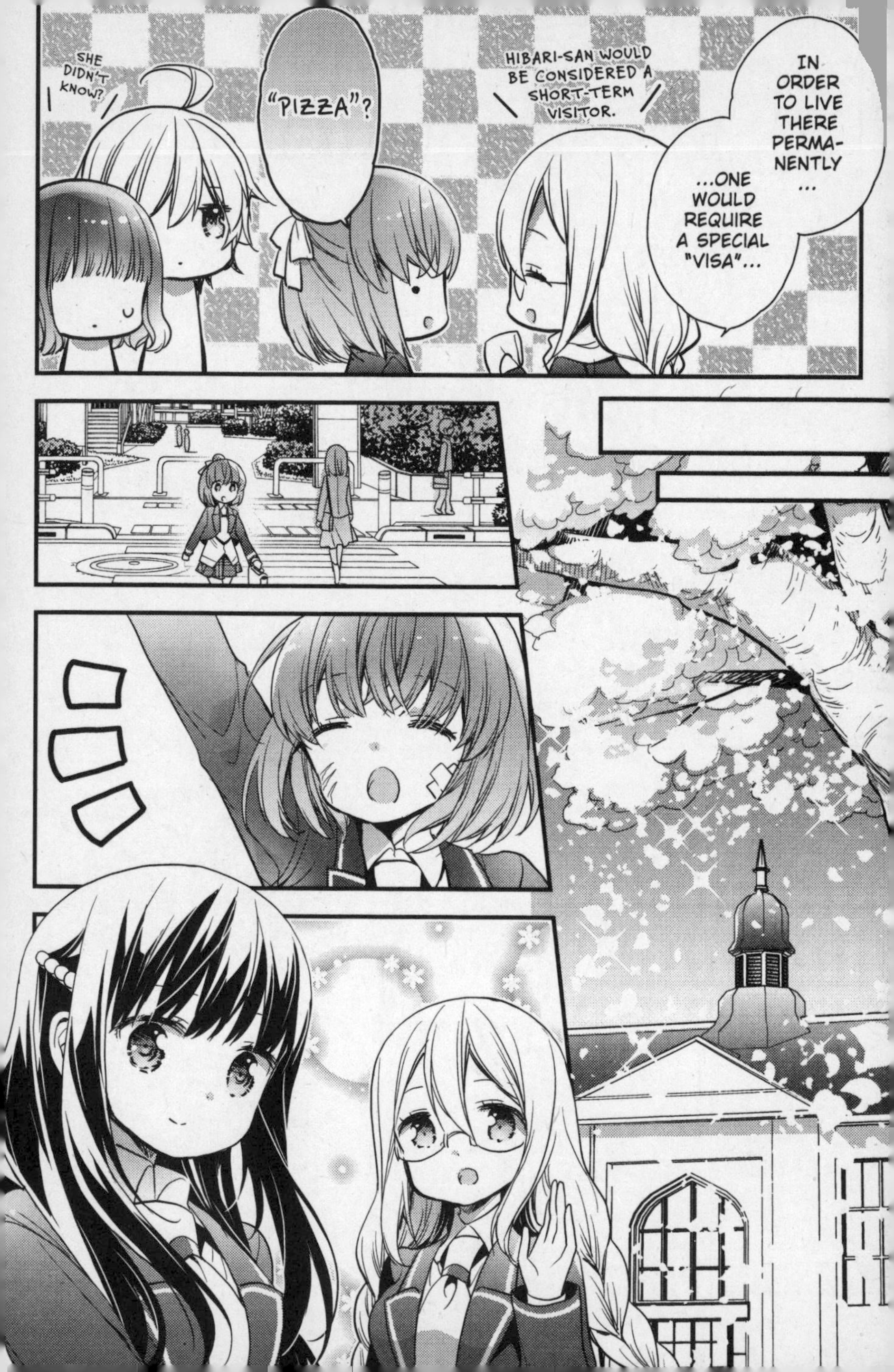
HIBARI-SAN WOULD BE CONSIDERED A SHORT-TERM VISITOR.
IN ORDER TO LIVE THERE PERMANENTLY...
...ONE WOULD REQUIRE A SPECIAL "VISA"...
"PIZZA"?
SHE DIDN'T KNOW?

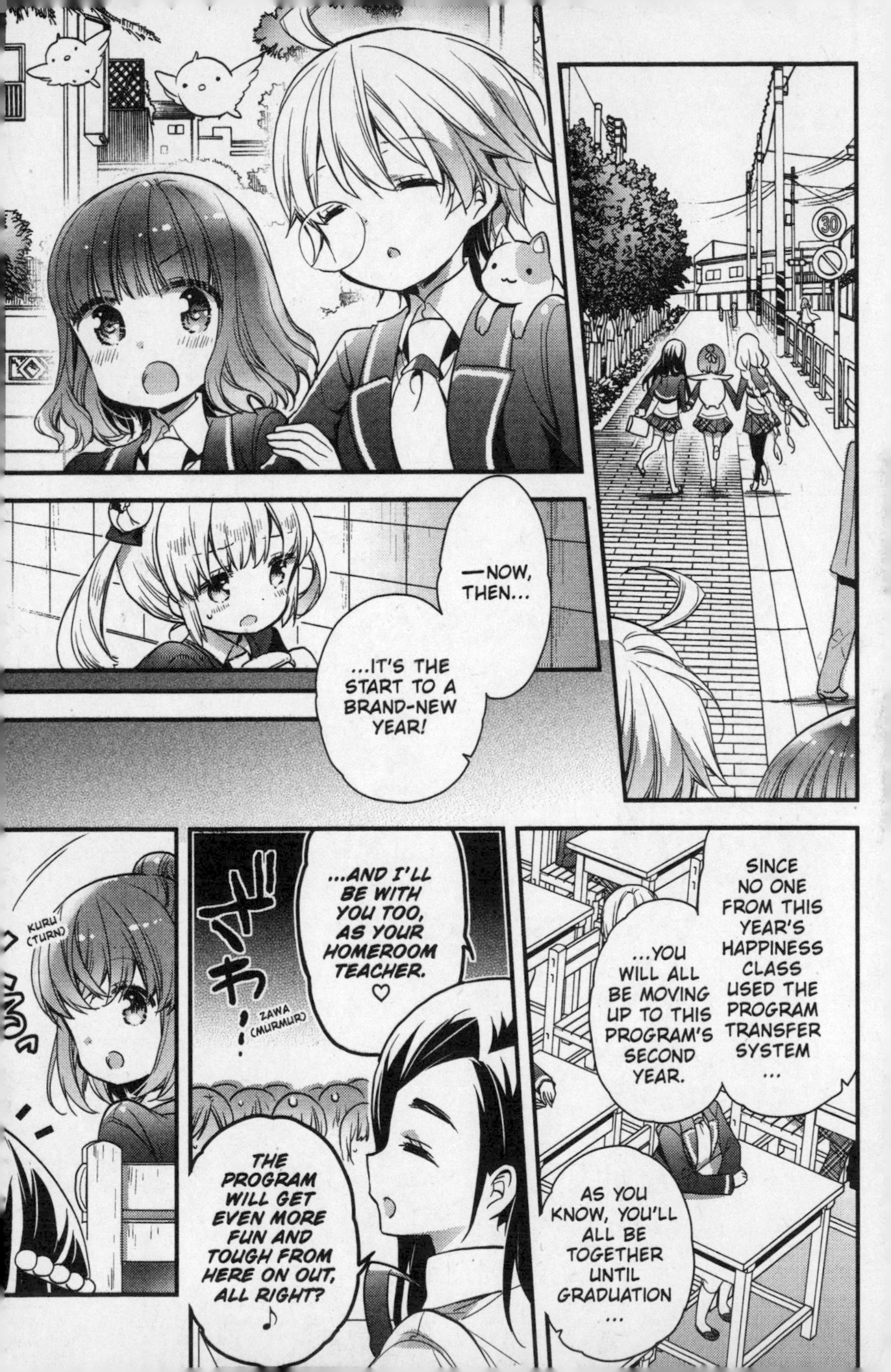
—NOW, THEN...
...IT'S THE START TO A BRAND-NEW YEAR!
SINCE NO ONE FROM THIS YEAR'S HAPPINESS CLASS USED THE PROGRAM TRANSFER SYSTEM ...
...YOU WILL ALL BE MOVING UP TO THIS PROGRAM'S SECOND YEAR.
AS YOU KNOW, YOU'LL ALL BE TOGETHER UNTIL GRADUATION ...
...AND I'LL BE WITH YOU TOO, AS YOUR HOMEROOM TEACHER. ♡
ZAWA (MURMUR)
THE PROGRAM WILL GET EVEN MORE FUN AND TOUGH FROM HERE ON OUT, ALL RIGHT? ♪
KURU (TURN)

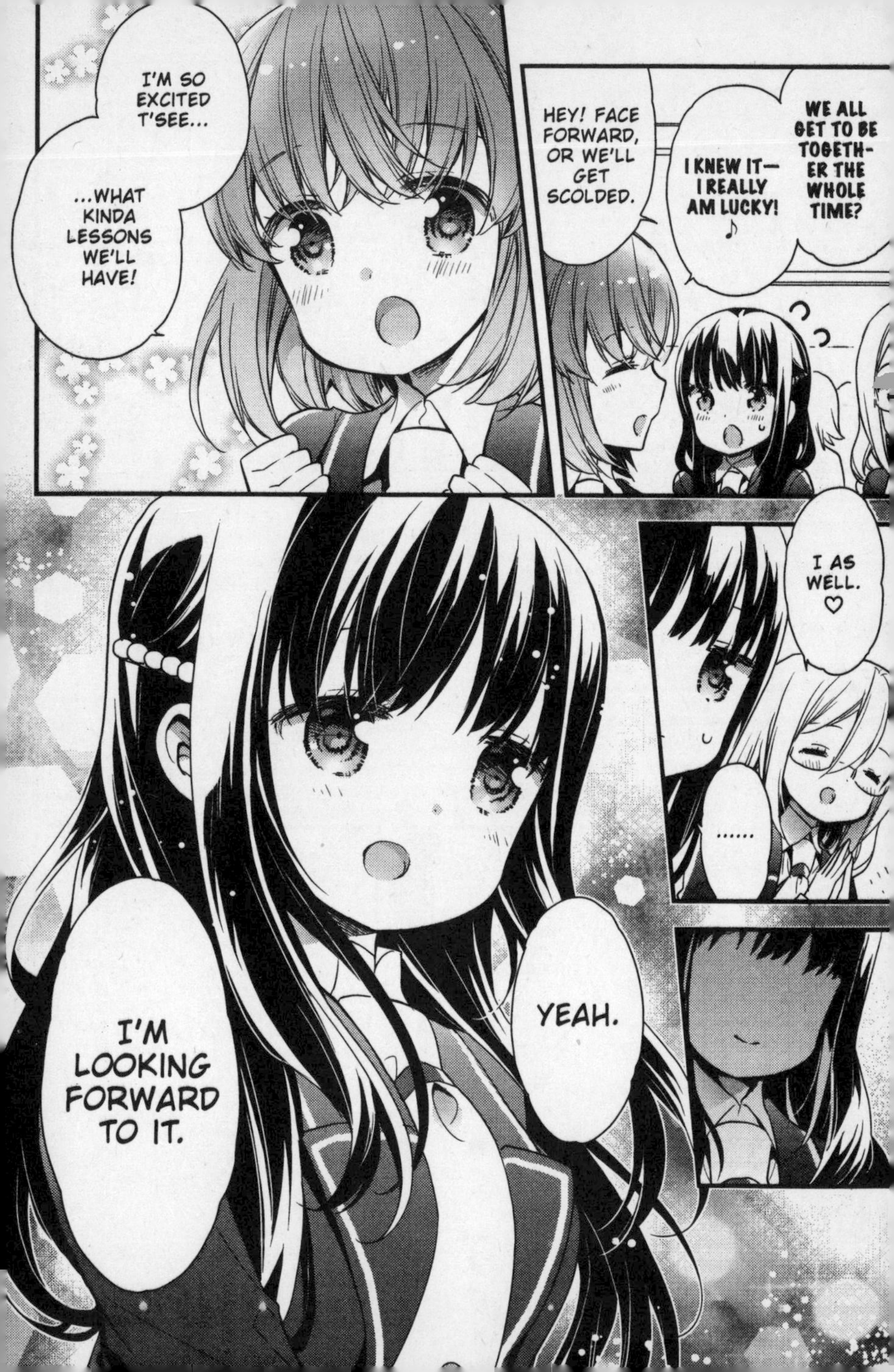
WE ALL GET TO BE TOGETH- ER THE WHOLE TIME?
I KNEW IT— I REALLY AM LUCKY! ♪
HEY! FACE FORWARD, OR WE'LL GET SCOLDED.
I'M SO EXCITED T'SEE...
...WHAT KINDA LESSONS WE'LL HAVE!
I AS WELL. ♡
......
YEAH.
I'M LOOKING FORWARD TO IT.

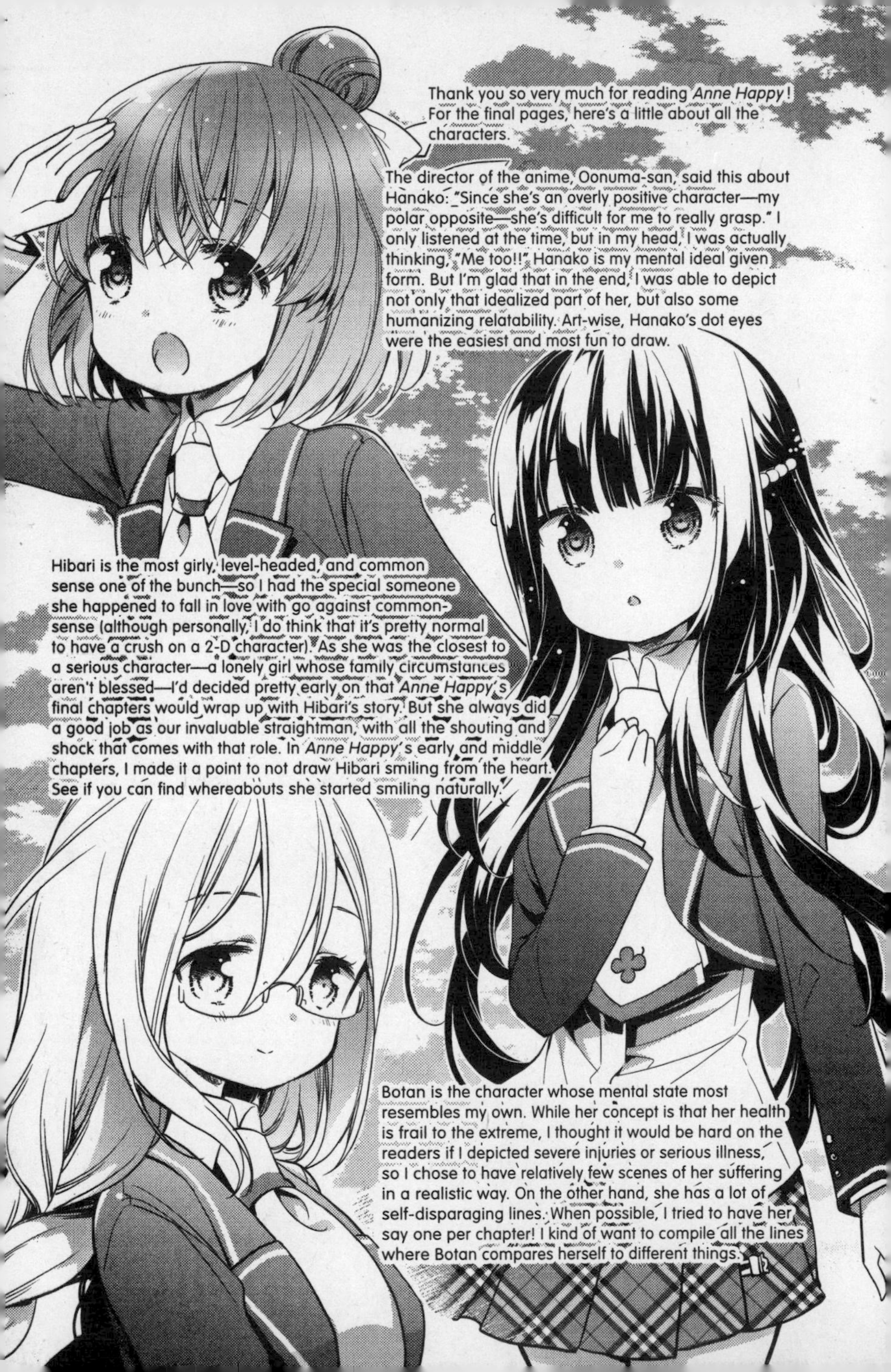

Thank you so very much for reading *Anne Happy*! For the final pages, here's a little about all the characters.

The director of the anime, Oonuma-san, said this about Hanako: "Since she's an overly positive character—my polar opposite—she's difficult for me to really grasp." I only listened at the time, but in my head, I was actually thinking, "Me too!!" Hanako is my mental ideal given form. But I'm glad that in the end, I was able to depict not only that idealized part of her, but also some humanizing relatability. Art-wise, Hanako's dot eyes were the easiest and most fun to draw.

Hibari is the most girly, level-headed, and common sense one of the bunch—so I had the special someone she happened to fall in love with go against common-sense (although personally, I do think that it's pretty normal to have a crush on a 2-D character). As she was the closest to a serious character—a lonely girl whose family circumstances aren't blessed—I'd decided pretty early on that *Anne Happy*'s final chapters would wrap up with Hibari's story. But she always did a good job as our invaluable straightman, with all the shouting and shock that comes with that role. In *Anne Happy*'s early and middle chapters, I made it a point to not draw Hibari smiling from the heart. See if you can find whereabouts she started smiling naturally.

Botan is the character whose mental state most resembles my own. While her concept is that her health is frail to the extreme, I thought it would be hard on the readers if I depicted severe injuries or serious illness, so I chose to have relatively few scenes of her suffering in a realistic way. On the other hand, she has a lot of self-disparaging lines. When possible, I tried to have her say one per chapter! I kind of want to compile all the lines where Botan compares herself to different things.

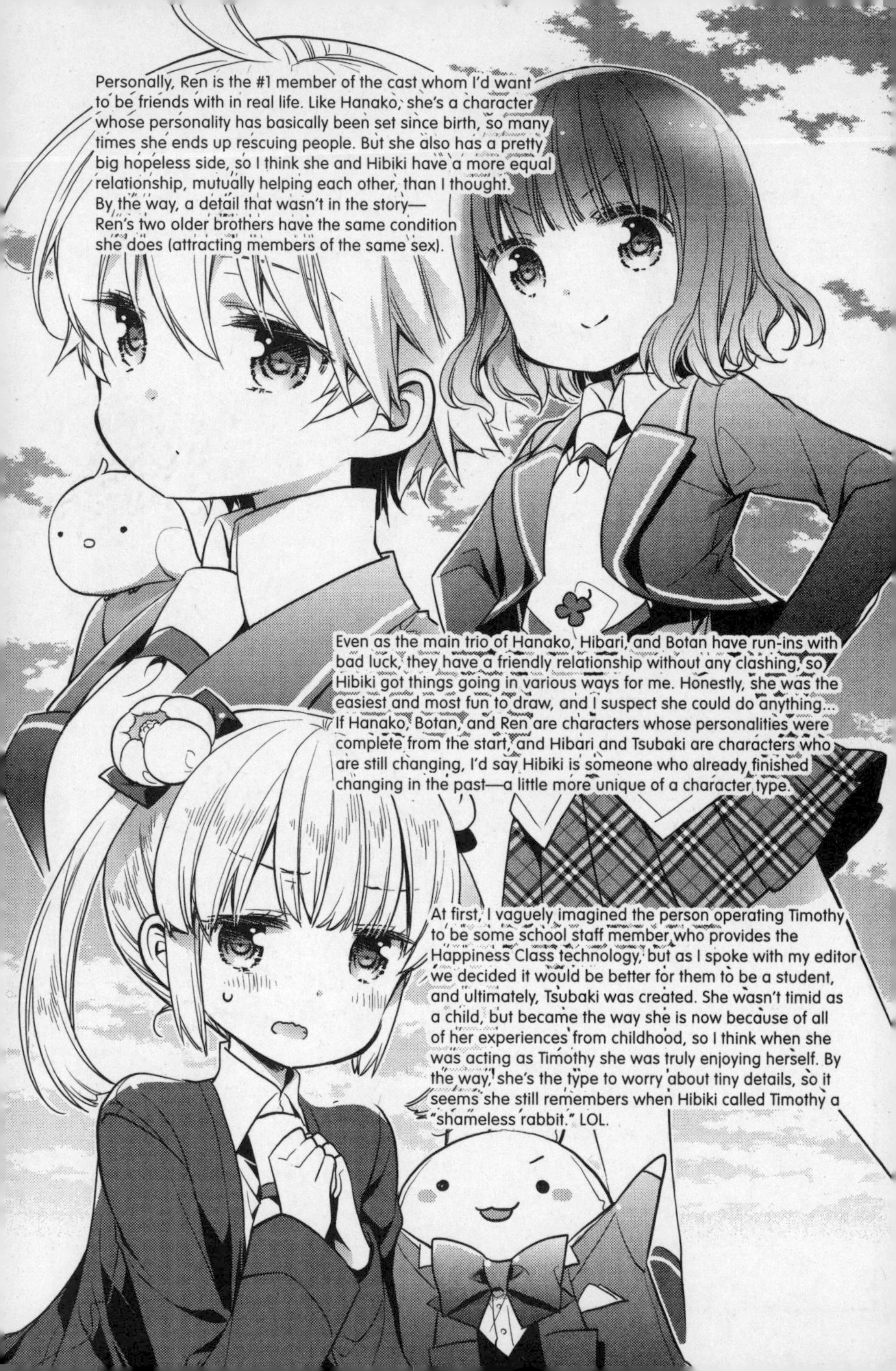

Personally, Ren is the #1 member of the cast whom I'd want to be friends with in real life. Like Hanako, she's a character whose personality has basically been set since birth, so many times she ends up rescuing people. But she also has a pretty big hopeless side, so I think she and Hibiki have a more equal relationship, mutually helping each other, than I thought. By the way, a detail that wasn't in the story— Ren's two older brothers have the same condition she does (attracting members of the same sex).

Even as the main trio of Hanako, Hibari, and Botan have run-ins with bad luck, they have a friendly relationship without any clashing, so Hibiki got things going in various ways for me. Honestly, she was the easiest and most fun to draw, and I suspect she could do anything... If Hanako, Botan, and Ren are characters whose personalities were complete from the start, and Hibari and Tsubaki are characters who are still changing, I'd say Hibiki is someone who already finished changing in the past—a little more unique of a character type.

At first, I vaguely imagined the person operating Timothy to be some school staff member who provides the Happiness Class technology, but as I spoke with my editor we decided it would be better for them to be a student, and ultimately, Tsubaki was created. She wasn't timid as a child, but became the way she is now because of all of her experiences from childhood, so I think when she was acting as Timothy she was truly enjoying herself. By the way, she's the type to worry about tiny details, so it seems she still remembers when Hibiki called Timothy a "shameless rabbit." LOL.

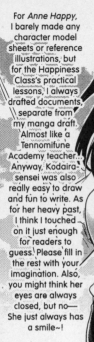

For *Anne Happy*, I barely made any character model sheets or reference illustrations, but for the Happiness Class's practical lessons, I always drafted documents, separate from my manga draft. Almost like a Tennomifune Academy teacher... Anyway, Kodaira-sensei was also really easy to draw and fun to write. As for her heavy past, I think I touched on it just enough for readers to guess. Please fill in the rest with your imagination. Also, you might think her eyes are always closed, but no— She just always has a smile~!

Saginomiya-sensei served the role of offering a dose of reality and doubt—to the Happiness Class environment, which is easy on its students at the end of the day, and to Kodaira-sensei too. I hope I got across the feeling that she's a teacher who is more than just strict—she praises students who show effort, and is at the end of the day a softie herself after all. She's actually in the final chapter in a small way, but she might be too small to tell it's her...Try finding her if you'd like.

As I happily and desperately drew Hanako and the girls' cheerful and hectic everyday lives, I had so many milestone experiences, such as my first series to hit ten volumes and my first anime adaptation, and the days flew by before I knew it. Thanks to *Anne Happy*, in these last six years, I think I've done a lifetime's worth of thinking about the question, "What is happiness?" If this manga was helpful, if it gave you any little bit of fun, or happiness, or some answers, that would make me extremely happy.

To everyone who was involved in the *Anne Happy* manga, anime, and more, and to all the readers: thank you so, so, so much...!

Cotoji

COTOJI

TRANSLATION: AMANDA HALEY
LETTERING: ROCHELLE GANCIO

ANNE HAPPY ♪ VOL. 10
© 2019 CotoJi. ALL RIGHTS RESERVED. FIRST PUBLISHED IN JAPAN IN 2019 BY HOUBUNSHA CO., LTD., TOKYO. ENGLISH TRANSLATION RIGHTS IN UNITED STATES, CANADA, AND UNITED KINGDOM ARRANGED WITH HOUBUNSHA CO., LTD. THROUGH TUTTLE-MORI AGENCY, INC., TOKYO.

ENGLISH TRANSLATION © 2019 BY YEN PRESS, LLC

YEN PRESS
150 WEST 30TH STREET, 19TH FLOOR
NEW YORK, NY 10001

VISIT US AT YENPRESS.COM
FACEBOOK.COM/YENPRESS
TWITTER.COM/YENPRESS
YENPRESS.TUMBLR.COM
INSTAGRAM.COM/YENPRESS

FIRST YEN PRESS EDITION: OCTOBER 2019

YEN PRESS IS AN IMPRINT OF YEN PRESS, LLC.
THE YEN PRESS NAME AND LOGO ARE TRADEMARKS OF YEN PRESS, LLC.

THE PUBLISHER IS NOT RESPONSIBLE FOR WEBSITES (OR THEIR CONTENT) THAT ARE NOT OWNED BY THE PUBLISHER.

LIBRARY OF CONGRESS CONTROL NUMBER: 2016931012

ISBNS: 978-1-9753-5854-9 (PAPERBACK)
       978-1-9753-0638-0 (EBOOK)

10 9 8 7 6 5 4 3 2 1

WOR

PRINTED IN THE UNITED STATES OF AMERICA

P9-CEM-747

US: $13.00   CAN: $17.00

ISBN 978-1-9753-5854-9

51300 >

9 781975 358549

TEEN
T
L

Yen
Press

Follow us on

or at yenpress.com

After months of self-discovery and the craziest tests imaginable, the H̶a̶p̶p̶i̶n̶e̶s̶s̶ Class has, at long last, ̶f̶i̶n̶i̶s̶h̶e̶d̶ ̶t̶h̶e̶i̶r̶ ̶f̶i̶r̶st year at Tennomifune ̶a̶c̶a̶d̶e̶m̶y̶.̶ ̶W̶h̶e̶t̶h̶e̶r̶ ̶t̶h̶e̶y̶ ̶r̶ealize it or not, Hibari, ̶A̶n̶n̶e̶,̶ ̶B̶o̶t̶a̶n̶,̶ Hibiki, Ren, and Tsubaki have ̶l̶earned to chase their dreams and overcome the odds—but do they truly know what it means to be happy? Keep your fingers crossed for these luckless girls in this final volume of *Anne Happy*!